Museums:

In Search of a Usable Future

Museums:

In Search of a Usable Future

Alma S. Wittlin

The MIT Press

Cambridge, Massachusetts,

and London, England

"The need is to upset conventions in order to close the gap between what museums are doing and what the world expects of them."
What F. P. Keppel, president of the Carnegie Corporation, wrote in his Annual Report of 1937 has to this day retained full validity in many museums, and some validity in all. Even more so if one metamorphoses the end of the statement into "what the world ought to expect from them." What, then, is it that the contemporary world ought to expect from its museums?

"Certainly our Nation's more than 5,000 museums constitute a cultural resource of profound significance, and yet it is clear that many of these museums face difficult problems. . . ."
Senator Claiborne Pell in his opening statement of the Congressional Hearings preliminary to the passing of the National Museum Act of 1966.

"Museums receive dangerously automatic acceptance. . . . museum men too rarely encourage dissent. . . . They say 'don't rock the boat,' forgetting that one of the characteristics of a moving boat is that it rocks occasionally."
Richard Grove, "Some Problems in Museum Education," in *Museums and Education*, edited by Eric Larrabee (Washington, D.C.: The Smithsonian Press, 1968).

List of Illustrations

Foreword

I am glad this book is called *Museums*, and that this word continues
to be used. Although it is very difficult to define a museum, and although the word has connotations of dullness or death, it is a word
that is here to stay, and it is far better to face up to it. This is more
than a revised edition of Alma Wittlin's previous book, for it is brought
up to date, and the past few years have shown museums expanding
all over the globe, as well as exploding into people's consciousness.
In addition Miss Wittlin has posed her own questions about the future
of museums in a fresh and useful manner at the end.

Museums are becoming more and more important. For one thing,
as Dr. Wittlin points out, museums provide immediate encounters
with authenticity, or a reasonable simulacrum of it. They provide
new ways of teaching and learning, and an introduction to processes
of lifelong education, now a priority for everyone. Museums are flexible in contrast to schools. They provide questions, and not all the
answers. They exhibit truths in the form of objects. A museum has
been called a social planetarium, and this is true, for not only does it
serve as a collecting and retrieval point for stages in man's evolution through the past but also it can and should reflect the present,
thus acting as a reflection on our age, a social aid in the service of
man. Beyond all this there is no reason in the world why a museum
may not, like a planetarium, focus its materials in context, so as to
project the future.

The very nature of a museum, its unstructured quality, holds out
promise for the future of education. Perhaps universities of the future will have to design themselves to be a little more like museums,
a theater of interrogation, based on a substructure of relevance, the
roots naked and exposed to view.

Out of the welter of ignorance which surrounds us, it is difficult to
gainsay the fact that only objects possess truth in themselves. I am
constantly surprised (because of my university training I suppose)
by the difficulty of obtaining truth from the printed word, or the television screen. It is as difficult to obtain the facts from a newspaper
story as it is to learn history from reading books. As someone has
said rather indignantly recently, we seem to be trapped, from the
earliest stages of textbook learning, in a morass of legitimized social
stupidity. Whether or not this is deliberate, an Establishment plan,
as the author dourly suggests, is another matter. If, however, children all over the world are to be brought up in the presence of school
curricula which include bland textbooks about myth figures like
"Dick and Jane," then presumably most people everywhere will con-

tinue to be educated for stupidity, and will continue to be insensitive to developing trends which produce war, better bombs, technological imbalances, development for development's sake, environmental pollution, and the cultivation of smugness and self-assurance.

By what winnowing process a few people manage to maintain some degree of objectivity in this educational crucible is never explained. Is it by what used to be known as personal revelation, by psychotherapy, by a mysterious combination of gene interaction and environmental conditioning, or by some other alchemy, some nostrum affecting the neural pathways? In this brave new world of ours, perhaps only objects which inherently possess truth can teach truth. An object to be touched, seen, felt, smelled is true. It is furthermore a source of data, part of the only data bank we possess; what it was like before. I suppose I am in love with the past, but without being so there is no living with the present, nor indeed is there any resolution for the future.

Miss Wittlin talks of the present interest in environmental biology in her summing up of museums of the present and future, and speaks of it, colloquially, as the "hottest" subject for exposition and display in the science and natural history fields of the museum world. I am not sure exactly in which sense she means this? Does she mean the "coolest"? Perhaps she really means the hottest, in that the subject is the dirtiest, most unformed, unfathomable, least understood of all branches of biology, a subject which most ecologists, by the very training process to which they have been subjected, are skirting gingerly, gathering small mustard grains of information, still devoid of an overall set of compelling theorums or formulas.

Today we must know more in order to be able to survive. Everyone must somehow know a bit more of everything in order to be able to formulate some personal synthesis, some approach to life itself. Miss Wittlin quotes John Adams in the beginnings of our republic in 1780. Writing to his wife, he said; "I must study politics and war, that my sons may have liberty to study mathematics and philosophy. My sons ought to study mathematics and philosophy, natural history and naval architecture, navigation, commerce and agriculture, in order to give their children a right to study painting, poetry, music, architecture, statuary, tapestry, and porcelain." This has been an age-old dream from the days of Greece; let us labor at war or commerce so that our children can reflect our basic urge to culture by indulging in the pleasures of cultivated tasks at leisure, supported by the wealth or security we have created for them. Today in the re-

finements of the technological world which is upon us, I submit that
none of this is true. Narrow specializations are not appropriate to the scene. To survive one must be skilled not only in "politics and war," but also in poetry, music, and mathematics, lest the urgent clangor of our environment deafen us to the very meaning of life itself. We risk being dehumanized in a single generation, so that every generation must be all things to itself. There is no waiting, no putting off. In order to preserve anything at all we must seek total personal integration. The perfect vantage point for this integrative point of view is the museum of the future.

Dillon Ripley
Secretary of the Smithsonian Institution

Preface and Acknowledgments

It has been said of fiction writers that each has but one story to tell and that he tells it in a variety of ways in a number of books. In this sense this is a new book, although I have reflected on museums and written about them for many years. The direct predecessor of this volume, *The Museum, Its History and Its Tasks in Education* (London, Routledge & Kegan Paul: 1949), which is out of print, was a prelude to the now presented volume. Even the historical chapters were expanded, and pertinent material from the United States and the British colonies in America was added to them. In later chapters emphasis was laid on Early American collections and museums which in the previous book had been omitted. Twenty years ago I was a European addressing mainly my fellow Europeans, although experience revealed that Americans were more responsive to my message than others; now I am writing as an American, mainly but not exclusively for my fellow Americans. The previous volume ended with the outbreak of the Second World War; this time I undertook to give an account of the tremendous museum developments in all parts of the globe between 1945 and the present. An account of my experimental work concerning communication by exhibits will be published in a separate volume. In this book references to communication are kept brief.

My special thanks are due to two experts in Early American History, Professor H. C. Kirker of the University of California in Santa Barbara and Professor R. B. Morris of Columbia University, who read the pages on early collections and museums in the United States and commented on them. Dr. Frank A. Taylor, director of museums of The Smithsonian Institution, read the brief account of the establishment of the United States National Museum. Their criticisms of some points, their suggestions of additional literature, and their encouraging general acceptance of my interpretation, all represented most valuable assistance.

A questionnaire sent out to museums and other pertinent agencies in all parts of the globe elicited such willing cooperation and plentiful information about current events in museums and about plans for the future that my original intention of listing corresponding institutions was brought to nought. Pages would be needed to list them, and I trust that all my new and old friends will accept the expression of my deep appreciation in this abbreviated form. Thanks are due to Mrs. Kay Allen Rector for her help in proofreading.

My first experience in the use of museum materials as nonverbal records occurred during my college years at the University of Vienna, where lecture-demonstrations often took place in front of an open museum case. Formal training in Museology followed at the State Museums in Berlin, which were rightly famed for their instruction in aspects of identification, preservation, and cataloguing, and where I first became aware of the need for a study of communication which remained, and still mostly remains, disregarded.

During the preparation of my book on museums published in Great Britain several distinguished scholars stood by me with their counsel and provided inspiration: Sir Frederic Bartlett, director of the Institute of Experimental Psychology of the University of Cambridge, guided me toward the realization that museum work implies to a considerable extent problems of visual perception, which it shares with numerous psychologists working in laboratories; the sociologist Karl Mannheim enriched my awareness of the museum's function as a public institution; Sir Herbert Read, poet, humanist, and sage, never vacillated in his faith in the environmental and aesthetic education museums and galleries can offer to human beings bemused by a surplus of verbal ambiguity. Sir Frederic G. Kenyon and Madame Aulanier of the Louvre Museum checked on historical data related to English and French museums. A fellowship of the International Federation of University Women financed a part of that earlier work.

It has been my good fortune, and at times a source of considerable frustration, to consider museums from both inside and outside their walls, as a museum worker and as a student of learning, as a practitioner and as an experimenter. By commissioning a Report on Post-War Museum Reconstruction, the British Association for the Advancement of Science prevented my thinking from getting rusty. A call from Toynbee Hall, a Settlement House and Community Center in the East End of London, introduced me to compensatory education before the formal beginning of the war against poverty; I obtained an opportunity to observe the eager response of culturally unprivileged children in the slums of London to the multisensory stimuli of objects. When the Ministry of Education set up their research branch as Foundation for Educational Research, I left the University Museum of Archaeology and Anthropology in Cambridge to explore under the aegis of the Foundation the use of museum resources in education below college level.

On the occasion of a conference of ICOM (International Council of Museums) in Paris in 1949, at which I represented the Ministry, I became acquainted with American museum leaders. In due course I received an invitation from the education department of the American Museum of Natural History in New York to visit the United

States; after a three-month tour to forty-four museums I spent a brief period of time at the Royal Ontario Museum in Toronto, Canada. In 1952 I returned to this country, became a resident and later a citizen. New Mexico captured my imagination; I organized and conducted for over eight years a traveling museum of science and anthropology, with headquarters in Santa Fe and Albuquerque, from which communication lines extended to small villages and dead mining towns in northern New Mexico. The intercultural public, Anglo, Spanish, and Indian, provided an uncommon challenge.

In 1961 I felt ready for a period of contemplation which the newly founded Radcliffe Institute in Cambridge, Massachusetts, offered. What we had endeavored to do in New Mexico with the small means of the nonprofit organization "Science Comes To You, Inc." had by now acquired national status: the appearance of Sputnik turned the attention of people toward learning by firsthand experience and with the aid of objects, laboratory-style.

The last few years were conducive to asking questions rather than to finding answers. During the period between the two world wars the United States was front-runner in matters of museums. It does not appear to be so now, but the causes of the condition can hardly be sought within museums, which are but a small part of the enterprise of learning and of recreation, which in its turn hinges on the general philosophy of life. As an ex-European of fairly recent date I am, however, acutely aware of the ultimate power of what Gunnar Myrdal, a Swede who knows the United States and who loves it, calls the American Conscience.

A.S.W.

The word Museum echoes a multiplicity of meanings rooted in history. A list of its synonyms and notes on their etymology follow in the Appendix; each lights up another facet of our term. The following qualities are inherent in them: inspirational values; an encyclopedic approach to learning and inquiry; privacy and secrecy; rarity and costliness; features related to the storage and hiding of things. Which of these qualities have retained validity in the contemporary public institution known as Museum? What order of priority are we to assign to each of them?

Museums provide information and stimulation by means of objects, in distinction from libraries or classrooms, where experiences are generated by symbols, by the written or spoken word. Live animals can be found in a small number of museums, but they are not the stock-in-trade as in zoos or in aquaria; a planetarium and a museum are sometimes under the same top administration or are located in adjacent buildings, but a planetarium is not necessarily an integral part of every institution dealing with science or natural history.

It is generally considered that museums fulfill three main functions. They serve as *depositories* devoted to the preservation and conservation of objects of particular value—treasured for their association with events and personalities of history, for their significance in representing human excellence in terms of scientific ingeniousness or of artistic achievement, and for providing samples of the natural environment or objects related to human ways of living at different times and in different societies. They are *centers of research* and *educational agencies.* Some institutions are mainly or exclusively devoted to a single function; others endeavor to serve two of them or all three.

In recent years numerous peripheral functions have been added to museums, especially in the United States, which are summed up under the name of a cultural center. The merits and pitfalls of the extension—including ballet and garden club meetings, career days and concerts, and in one institution a choice between a summer course in astronomy and another in feminine charm—depend on too many factors to be either summarily accepted or condemned. Peripheral features may enrich an institution or lead to a draining of energies and to a dimming of focus. The character of a community has to be considered, its overall facilities in relation to the composition of its population. What may suit a museum in the United States, where pluralism is a built-in feature, may not be desirable elsewhere. Fundamentally, most peripheral features can be listed under education; the serendipity of some may open up insights into new ways of teaching and learning at a time when continuous, life-long education is becoming a necessity.

A characteristic of museums, of whatever content or scope, is their flexibility; they allow a wide gamut of differences in the use people make of them. If compared with schools set up to serve specific age groups and directed by law to offer prescribed curricula, museums as a rule open their doors to adults of all ages as well as to children; most visitors come voluntarily; they come singly or in groups; they may choose to join a conducted tour or gather impressions by wandering through exhibit halls. They may come at all seasons of the year and stay as long or as briefly as they wish. The viewing of a particular hall is not needed as a prerequisite for entering other halls; no certificate or license is granted to learners, good or poor, or is sought by them. Many, if not most, visitors to a museum hardly distinguish between learning and recreation. The people who engage in research in museums, in many fields of study and on differing levels of attainment, may be college students preparing for a degree, proven scholars, or amateurs.

As every other environment of research, learning, or recreation, museums have their congenital strengths and limitations. Their prime assets are the direct appeal to the eye and to the sense of touch, and the potential capacity to present a number of facts simultaneously and in palpable context. They are unique in offering to people immediate encounters with authenticity, be it in the form of a painting by Rembrandt or by Picasso, or of dinosaur skeletons. Many round-the-globe trips would be required to gain access to the study collections made available on the shelves of some museums, or to get glimpses into the kaleidoscope of life on earth that can be offered in a few exhibit halls.

The traditional triple function of museums retains its validity, but each function awaits continuous re-examination by every individual institution at a time of extending frontiers of knowledge, of rising standards of general education, and of access to new techniques based on scientific advances, which lend themselves to the identification of objects, to their recording, and to their conservation. The asset of the wide compass of a museum harbors the hazard of ineffectiveness unless goals are and remain defined, and unless constant check is kept on the achieved approximation to expectations.

In the sense of this essay, *museums are not ends in themselves;* they are means in the service of man and of his cultural evolution. To accomplish their mission they have to excite people as well as to inform them.

"The only use of a knowledge of the past is to equip us for the present." – Whitehead*

In their current meaning public museums are institutions of relatively recent origin, the earliest ones having been founded in the last quarter of the eighteenth century, in both the Old and the New World.[1] The collections that preceded them were connected with places of worship, belonged to groups of people who shared a common interest or, in their majority, to private individuals.

The human desire to collect specimens of no direct utilitarian value, in the sense of food, clothing, or materials for building a shelter, has been recorded throughout the millennia. Some motivations to collecting appear to be perennial. Others change: they lose priority within a shifting framework of values, religious, aesthetic, or intellectual; they cease to be socially acceptable and are no longer overtly expressed, or fade out altogether.[2]

In selecting illustrative collections, I avoided repetitiveness and no doubt omitted important ones; to reflect on human ambiguity and the change of attitudes at different periods of history, I referred to the same collection more than once. A collector may follow several motivations which seem difficult to reconcile, and the same objects may repel one generation and captivate another. The oscillation between the destruction of ancient classic remains, for fear of them, in the Middle Ages moved full cycle to the opposite pole during the Renaissance, when every relic of the early Mediterranean culture was venerated.

Collections, like other products of human endeavor, require criteria of surveying and assessment which are germane to them and which differ from those of products of nature. It is one thing to list plants and another to list collections. A register of the physical properties of a mineral can hardly serve as model for recording a prehistoric tool, an ancient dance mask, or a modern work of art; it does not exhaust the issue. There still remains the need to tell, or to speculate, what role the thing played in human lives, in actual practice or in fantasy; whether it represented a link between the living and the deceased, or served as an aid in facing a veiled future. The relationship between human beings and objects, be they of everyday use or collectors' items, is not a simple one-track process. People concurrently live in three environments, the one that is, or could be, accessible to their senses, another in their memory, which houses their individual past and inherited traditions, and another still in the imagination. Both memory and imagination may endow objects with a spellbinding force with which actual experiences cannot always compete.

An account of collections preceding public museums could be presented in historical order or in accordance with geographical areas, but either approach would hardly offer more than the bare bones of the matter. Since collections both reflect and affect human ways of life, a listing of their functions offers greater promise of insight, and it is the *function* that serves as categorizing criterion in the following description of *ante museum* collections. It was chosen in the hope that it may best help us in identifying the potential of museums in our era, in alerting us with regard to motivations which officially are considered as obsolete but which on occasion constitute the hidden driving forces in the choice of an unsuitable but impressive architectural style for a new museum building, in a casual disregard for the bad fit between projects and the public to be served, or in numbing our responsiveness to entirely new calls on the museum enterprise.

The following list could no doubt be both varied and enlarged. Whatever the choice of categories, however, they cut across the less orderly patterns of life.

Economic Hoard Collections

Social Prestige Collections

Magic Collections

Collections as Expressions of Group Loyalty

Collections as Means of Stimulating Curiosity and Inquiry

Collections as Means of Emotional Experience

Economic Hoard Collections

An ancient hoard collection has been preserved in Homer's description of Priam, King of Troy, who gathered in his treasure chamber offerings that would redeem the body of his son Hector, slain by Odysseus, from the besieging Greeks. The pertinent passage in the *Iliad* runs:

He spake, and opened the goodly lids of chests, wherefrom he took twelve beauteous robes and twelve cloaks of single fold, and as many coverlets and as many white mantles, and therewithal as many tunics. And of gold he weighed out and bare forth talents, ten in all, and two gleaming tripods, and four cauldrons, and a cup exceeding fair, that the men of Thrace had given him when he went thither on an embassage, a great treasure; not even this did the old man spare in his halls, for he was exceedingly fain to ransom his dear son.[1]

Similar hoards were ascribed by Homer to Odysseus himself, and to Menelaus of Sparta. The excavations at Hissarlik,[2] which Dr. Schliemann claimed to be ancient Troy, and at Mycenae[3] made the hoard collections of the ancient Euro-Asiatic world tangible. These treasure chambers feature the economic conditions of a period when production aimed mainly at satisfying the needs of the producer himself, when exchange of goods by trade was very limited and currency in the form of standardized money, as we know it, hardly existed. The few who possessed more than required for the satisfaction of their immediate needs stored their surplus: foodstuffs if not too quickly perishable; garments woven in the household; and better still, metal, whether in the form of ingots or of finished articles, be it for future use or for the purpose of exchange in barter trade.[4] Durability and divisibility without loss of value make metal superior to almost any other material, and once the process of smelting is discovered, a greater variety of objects can be fashioned in metal than in any other material. The possession of precious metals in ancient times represented condensed wealth as nothing else could, and it decided the fate of nations. The silver of the Attic mines gave Athens the power to master other Greek cities, and the silver mines of Spain enabled first Carthage, then Greece, and later Rome to pay mercenary armies in their bid for world domination.[5]

When threatened by Persian invasion in the early fifth century B.C. the Athenians used the silver accumulated in the form of bullion and of votive offerings in the temples serving as public treasuries for the purpose of building ships of war which helped to win the battle of Salamis. At the beginning of the Peloponnesian war another crisis arose which sent to the mint the anathemata, those ". . . monuments of the piety of individuals, and of the glory of the people, its colonies, Council, priests of private citizens."[6] At that time the temple of Athene on the Acropolis of Athens contained uncoined silver and gold in the form of votive offerings and of vessels used in the processions and games, worth altogether not less than 6500 talents. These treasures were declared available for the prosecution of the war by Pericles, who announced to the people: " . . . if . . . absolutely cut off from all other resources they might use even the gold plates with which the statue of the goddess herself was overlaid. This treasure they might use for self-preservation, but they must replace as much as they took."[7]

The functions fulfilled by the Greek Temple collections were manifold. Their statues and votive offerings enshrined national customs, ideas, and memories, featured beauty, and conspicuously demonstrated communal purchasing power to the satisfaction of every visitor to the temple. In an attractive guise the temple collections performed the role of a bank and of a public treasury. This was one of their functions, and at times it may have been the primary one. When the financial needs of the community became pressing the number of ex-votos in the temples dwindled. Then once again the offerings appeared in the *cellae* and the growing hoard indicated both the increasing well-being of the community and the stability of peace.

In Rome the communal hoard collection of the temple appeared not as a gradual accumulation of individual offerings but as a sudden acquisition of booty from the victories that transformed a small community into a world Empire. Marcellus, the first Roman General to conquer a Greek city, kept for himself of the spoils reaped at Syracuse nothing but a globe and dedicated everything to the deities Honor and Virtus in a temple he erected to them in front of the gate leading out of Rome in the direction of Sicily. The influx of wealth to Rome from the conquered territories was prodigious[8] and hoarding continued, but soon the hoard collection of the individual replaced that of the community, and a variety of valuables joined the specimens of precious metal. The administration of the community, so immensely increased in area and in the number of its inhabitants, did not keep pace with the military achievements that had created the grandeur. The war indemnities and the booty from conquered lands, together with the taxes drawn from them, were not long directed to the common treasury, but remained in the grasping hands of individuals.[9]

Sulla, notorious also for his hoarding, was among the generals who had fought the victorious battles abroad and succeeded in establishing themselves for a period as dictatorial rulers at home. It fell to his lot to plunder Athens and Delphi. When the property of persons he had sent into exile was auctioned, he saw to it that estates, houses, and works of art fell to his partisans. Whatever the character of things so won, he called it "booty" (*praeda*). General Mummius brought from his campaigns paintings and marble statues, others chose bronzes and tapestries. Quantity seemed to be valued as much as quality, and Scaurus, Sulla's son-in-law, had in his private theater more than 3000 statues.

In one of the rhetorical accusations in which he excelled, Cicero gave a description of the hoard of Chrysogonus, one of Sulla's lieutenants. He described his house "crammed with Delian and Corinthian vessels," his silversmith work, tapestry, paintings, statues, and marbles, and everything in large quantities. "As much, of course, as could be heaped up in a single house, taken from many illustrious families during times of disturbance and rapine."[10] In his indictment against Verres, the corrupt Governor of Sicily and perhaps the most famous of Roman collectors, Cicero, the lawyer, asserted that in all Sicily, there was no object of gold or jewel, no marble or ivory statue, or embroidery, not a single silver vase or a bronze figure from Corinth which Verres did not seek, did not examine, and did not take away if he liked the object.[11] Some years later Cicero himself owned eighteen villas filled with works of art. He, too, succumbed to a mania of collecting. Like Verres, Cicero appears to have been driven as much by a lust for hoarding as by an infatuation with art. The letters he wrote to Atticus, his trusted agent in Greece, are entreaties rather than commissions. "Those figures of Hermes in Pentelic marble with bronze heads . . . I have already fallen in love with: so please send them . . . the more the merrier and the sooner the better . . . my appreciation of art treasures is so great that I am afraid most people will laugh at me. . . . My purse is long enough. . . ."[12]

Cicero was in his early forties, and after years of political strife he may have looked forward to a period of repose in his villa in Tusculum near Rome, where he was setting up a library and was using Greek statuary for the decoration of his rooms, his gymnasium, and his palaestra.

Even if not transmutable into coins in the direct manner of the Greek votive offerings sent to the mint, the contents of the Roman collections represented considerable condensed wealth. Objects of gold, silver and precious stones were much sought after, and prices were fanciful. Objects often changed hands not only through the vagaries of politics but by way of sale and purchase. Auctions were held regularly, and shops were opened in the vicinity of the Via Sacra and the Via Septa.

In the period following upon the disintegration of the Roman Empire, wealth in dynamic form, as organized production and trading, disappeared from the West, the population of Western Europe decreased in numbers and reverted to the primitive economy of small, self-providing areas.[13] In this process of reorganization the possession of an economic hoard was a matter of growing importance to those who strove for power. Among the nomadic peoples the leading families sought to lay up a store of gold. In 568, Leuvigild, King of the Visigoths, exhibited his treasure as he sat on his throne in royal robes. From his day onward, the bulwarks of kingly power were "realm, people and treasure."[14] For many centuries the treasure chamber was a feature of princely residences, and traces of it can be seen in almost every European capital, even if in later days the emphasis to a considerable degree shifted from the purely material value of its contents to symbolic ones, to the association of objects with national events and outstanding personages.

The Princes of Moscow had their Treasury in the Kremlin. In the

"Green Vaults," the famous collection of the Princes of Saxony, a trapdoor led down to a secret hoard (*geheime Verwahrung*). In the Imperial *Schatzkammer* in the castle of Vienna, which had been the home of the Hapsburg dynasty, crown jewels and other valuables were exhibited till 1938, if not later, and enshrined traditions going back to the medieval treasure chamber of the Dukes of Burgundy, to whom the Hapsburgs were related by marriage (Fig. 1). The Dukes of Burgundy held a place of pride among the collectors of the early fifteenth century, but after the battle of Agincourt, in 1415, in which Burgundy lost its short-lived glory of predominance in French and European affairs, part of the famous goldsmith work of Jean de Berry, Duke of Burgundy, was sent from his castle Mehun-sur-Vevre to the mint, to provide badly wanted funds for state expenses.[15] The inventory of the collection became a useful guide to objects which escaped destruction and appeared later in the treasure chambers of the Hapsburgs in Vienna and in Madrid.[16]

In the magnificence of their treasuries some of the medieval churches could vie with secular princes. Abbot Suger listed objects contained in the Abbey of St. Denis in France in the twelfth century.[17] Sacred relics and other valuables gathered from numerous churches in Western Europe came to be deposited in the Treasury of San Marco in Venice, as collaterals for a passage of Crusaders' armies on Venetian ships.[18] On several occasions French sovereigns drained ecclesiastical treasuries and sent religious pieces of goldsmith work to the foundry. It happened after the Hundred Years' War and as a tax imposed on churches with papal permission in the course of Charles IX's fight against the Huguenots.

Gradually the hoarding of precious metals in the form of bullion was replaced in Europe by the hoarding of coined money. The change began in the thirteenth century, but a tendency toward more primitive forms of investment reappeared at various periods of history and was an indication of political insecurity and of retrogression in economic conditions. In times of war and civil strife people came to regard a weight of sheer gold or silver or precious stones as the best means of making provision for the future. Precious metals were internationally negotiable, were durable, divisible without loss of value, and within certain limits, portable. In sixteenth-century Sweden, at the time of the warrior-king Gustavus Adolphus, the peasants liked to invest their savings in spoons of heavy silver. At the time of Law's experiments in currency in eighteenth-century France, articles of everyday use were fashioned in gold and silver. Old hoarding instincts were reawakened during both world wars of

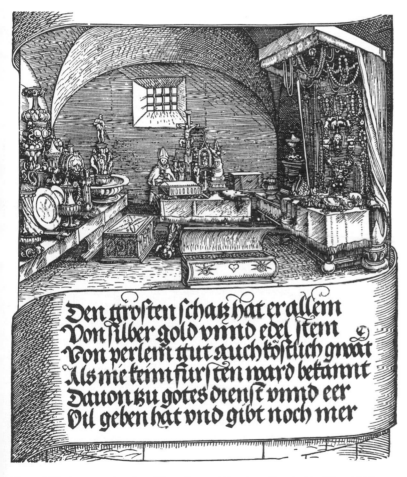

Den grösten schatz hat er allem
Von silber gold vnnd edel stein
Von perlein gut auch köstlich gwat
Als nie keinm fürsten ward bekannt
Dauon tzu gotes dienst vnnd eer
Vil geben hat vnd gibt noch mer

Figure 1. The treasure chamber of the princes of Hapsburg. Woodcut by Albrecht Alt-
dorfer, of 1515, from a series of illustrations known as *Die Ehrenpforte* (Arch of Honor),
in which homage was paid to the reigning emperor Maximilian I of Austria. According to
this picture the contents of the treasure chamber were set up in three groups: plate,
reliquaries and vessels for church service, and imperial insignia. In the foreground
stands a chest with coined money. In reality Maximilian was often short of coin.

our century and gave to people a sense of reassurance in a period of unprecedented economic complexity.

In periods of war and inflation confidence is revived to this day in the tangible bar of gold, jewels, or works of art of established reputation. People go about their hoarding in silence, keeping it secret from their neighbors, their minds uneasy through fear of theft. Soon the old legend of the Thesaurus reappears, of the treasure left behind by refugees on their flight, buried in a field or bricked in the wall of a cellar, forgotten, and waiting to become the property of a lucky finder. The legend stirs human imagination and in some cases proves to be sober reality.

Sometimes hoards appear in disguise. Their contents may not be marketable, but they possess a luster of their own which they derive from the quantity of the accumulated objects and their variety. Philip IV of Spain was a noted connoisseur with an acute sense for quality, but no single work of art and no collection he owned gave him final satisfaction. His desire to outshine all other collectors shows in a dialogue, more likely imagined than genuine, but probably containing a grain of truth, between the King and Velazquez, his court painter. In this conversation the King spoke of his desire to add further paintings to his gallery. Velazquez answered: "His Majesty ought to possess better paintings than any other man." The king: "How could this be brought about?" Velazquez: "With your permission, Sir, I would venture to go to Rome and to find the best pictures ever painted by Titian, Veronese, Bassano, Raphael, and other artists of similar quality. . . . I'll seek these works with great zeal and return with a great number of pictures . . . and with ancient statues and casts as well. . . ."[19]

Philip IV as collector had for his field all Spain, Italy, and the Low Countries. Italian churches were ransacked; the owners of private Spanish collections were forced to open their doors to royal envoys requiring certain objects of art as "presents" for the King. To escape the menace of being either robbed of their treasures or punished for lack of loyalty, people decorated their walls with copies of the pictures whose originals they had contrived to hide. To add to Philip's collection an army of men was set in motion; they traveled, created masterpieces, bargained, cheated, were decorated, made fortunes, were sent into exile and to prison. Hardly had he obtained the urgently sought objects for one of his palaces than he turned his attention to another place or another hunting box as an excuse for more collecting and as a shell to be filled with further hoards. It was his fate to be the sovereign of a country of great traditions on the verge of ruin, and to be mocked by the travesty of almost divine honors paid to him in his immediate environment. His courtiers called him *"Rey Planeta"*; was any collection exquisite enough and large enough for a Planet King? He created a substitute world for himself, a continuous series of festivals, games, theatrical plays, and collections never to be completed.[20]

Other varieties of the hoarder are the bargain hunter and the *marchand-amateur*. To them the prospect of financial gain has priority, and they are fascinated by the possible stupendous changes in the prices of works of art and of some curios.[21] The businessman, the gambler, and the aesthetic connoisseur are embodied in the *marchand-amateur*; he illustrates human variableness and instability.

In more recent years some American collectors combined in varying proportions true connoisseurship with delight in quantities.

The Walters of Baltimore, father William Thompson and son Henry, appreciated excellence.[22] They accumulated some 22,000 works of art from the great periods of European creativity to the legacies of Egypt and of areas of Islam. Their combined lifetimes spanned more than a century, from 1820 to 1931. While Henry was a serious student of art, to his father collecting was an avocation which he pursued under auspicious circumstances. A sympathizer with the South, he left the United States during the Civil War and received in Europe exposure to art and artists, especially to contemporary French painting. His funds, derived to a considerable part from "Ribbons of Rust" — from the consolidation of numerous financially unstable railway lines — were exchanged for works of art, and the buying continued on the occasion of visits to the great Expositions in Paris, in 1867, 1878, and 1889, as well as in Vienna in 1873.

Henry dedicated three months of the year to collecting and once chartered a transatlantic vessel to ship a collection of Italian pictures to America. He added a large third gallery to the two smaller ones his father had built in his home, but the collections kept on outgrowing all available space. After his death 243 packing cases were found in the basement, still unopened.

William Randolph Hearst's loot from all parts of the world dwarfed even his huge palace, San Simeon, in California, including a two-acre storeroom under the Casa Grande.[23] Dormant in their wrappings lay thousands of objects in the Hearst warehouses in New York, where they occupied a city block at 143rd Street near Southern Boulevard. A dismantled Spanish castle was one of the items, each of its parts numbered or lettered. Hearst specialized in collecting entire buildings—churches, monasteries, and palaces. His tastes were all-embracing; from armor to choir stalls, from mummies to Cardinal Richelieu's bed, from wall hangings to tiny scarabs.

The economic pressures of the thirties affected even one of the richest men of the world. He had to part with some of his holdings, but auction sales were unable to cope with the gigantic Hearstian dimensions. True to character the owner availed himself of an un-traditional manner of disposal which resembled his flamboyant editorial style. His art treasures were sold in stores which stocked ordinary goods, from the fashionable setting of Saks on Fifth Avenue to the more homely milieu of Gimbels, with prices ranging from hundreds of thousands of dollars to thirty-five cents for an item or a set of objects. Not unlike the presentation of new theatrical productions, sales in Chicago, St. Louis, and Seattle preceded the happenings in New York in 1941.

Drama was added by dissonances worthy of a great showman. In New York, high society, represented by foreign ambassadors, members of patriotic organizations, habitués of gala performances, and persons distinguished by having a charge account in the store, received engraved invitations to formal evening previews. On one occasion they came to face *objets d'art* covering a floor space of more than one hundred thousand square feet, where in more sober moments clothing for children and infants bore the price tags. Some thirty thousand people who had never before purchased a collector's item supposedly succumbed to the seductive offerings in the familiar setting of shops. Large crowds viewed the Hearst collections put on sale, and individuals who never entered an art gallery or a museum may have felt the impact of an artistic message for the first time in their lives.[24]

Social Prestige Collections

Throughout millennia ruling dynasties, communities, and commoners have practiced image-making in this form. Among them were men and women of sophistication and illiterates who went half-naked about their daily business. Indeed, under primitive conditions, the motivation to such manner of collecting can be more readily identified than in complex settings where even the owner of a collection may not always be able to disentangle one of his urges from other appetencies. Describing customs of natives in the western Pacific, the anthropologist Malinowski wrote: "the accumulation of food is not only the result of economic foresight, but also prompted by the desire of display and enhancement of social prestige through possession of wealth . . . food is allowed to rot . . . yet the natives want always more, to serve in its character of wealth."[1]

A Greek description of a festive procession held in Hellenistic Alexandria in the third century B.C. has come down to us and has given permanence to what once was a mobile collection.[2] King Ptolemy Philadelphus ordered the arrangement: thousands of slaves, prisoners of war, and natives walked in procession carrying vessels of gold and silver, golden crowns and shields, gilded images and figures symbolizing myths, the total value amounting to thousands of talents. Apart from their sheer number, the size of some of the items was impressive, of torches, braziers, and figures standing as high as thirty feet, and of a phallus of a similar length. Rows of sacrificial oxen followed and a display of elephant tusks, of hides and tapestries. Music and showers of flowers accompanied the procession.

Notwithstanding the costliness of the objects displayed in the procession, their effect on people is likely to have outweighed their market value. It was the concerted performance that mattered most. In overwhelming numbers, the single vessel or figure became priceless and attained extraordinary standards when presented against a background of youth, of conquered enemies, of animals of perfect breed, and of the radiance of flowers and of music. Inevitably such display contributed to the aggrandizement of the monarchs, not merely among the people who viewed the procession but among those, much more numerous, who shared secondhand in the performance through tales and rumors.

Ostentatious display seems to have been the main concern of some Roman collectors. Freedmen were apt to hide their humble origin in houses built on pillars of alabaster and tortoiseshell, and equipped with water pipes made of silver.[3] To a certain extent any of the Roman collections described in the chapter on Economic Hoards could be quoted again under the heading of Social Prestige.

The Medici of Florence had the entire inner walls of a rotunda of a diameter of ninety feet covered with a mosaic of precious stones. Collections of vessels of precious metal and decorated with gems were a familiar feature of later princely courts. After his visit to Hampton Court in 1520, the Venetian ambassador wrote: "The whole banqueting hall being decorated with huge vases of gold and silver, that I fancied myself in the Tower of Chosroes, where that monarch caused divine honours to be paid to him." Another envoy of Venice reported having seen gold and silver plate to a value of 300,000 ducats (presumably $3 million).[4] The French king Francis I's residence could boast of a great number of vessels of semiprecious stones, agate, chalcedony, and jasper, and later French monarchs took pride in the possession of candlesticks and other objects designed by artists and executed in gold of heavy weight.[5] In his description of the "main cabinets" of collectors in seventeenth-century Paris, Abbé de Marolles described two collections — those of the Duchess d'Aiguillon and of Mme. de Chavigni — as follows: "These cabinets are second to hardly any other in the splendor of their crystals, agates . . . chalcedonies, corals, amethysts . . . garnets, sapphires, pearls and other stones of great value which are set in silver and in gold in the shape of vases, statues, fans, mirrors, globes, candleholders . . . and other similar objects."[6]

No country equaled Spain in the accumulation of household articles.[7] It required six weeks to weigh and list the vessels of gold and silver in the house of the Duke of Albuquerque at the time of his death. In spite of the recurrent Sumptuary Laws issued by the King, forbidding the exaggerated use of precious metals for furniture, the sister of Philip II had round her bed a balustrade of silver weighing 121 pounds. The King's secretary, Antonio Perez, kept many *plateros* busy, and owned beds, chairs, and tables made of silver. One of his silver braziers cost 60,000 ducats. Conde de Villalonga, court justicier in the early seventeenth century, had twenty-four fountains of silver studded with precious stones, 4000 plates, and an entire kitchen equipment of silver. The Countess' desk was of gold.

The tendency to amass household articles of precious metal was symptomatic of the state of economy and of the trend of mind in Spain in the later sixteenth and the seventeenth centuries. The Peninsula was living a Don Quixote existence. In the centuries of fight against the Moors in the south of the country, the Spaniards had become alienated from the arts of peace and had developed standards of value according to which work on the land, in industry and commerce were inferior occupations. While the silver and gold of the American mines was shipped to Europe under the Spanish flag, Spaniards found anachronistic delight in the possession of static hoards, cherished mainly for their prestige value; they did not use their enormous capital to generate production and commerce. During the centuries of religious warfare in Spain a new type of man emerged, that of the gentleman who, without the drudgery of professional occupation, had command over riches, his heritage marking his descent from noble conquerors. In their desire to manifest the excellence of their family tree, Spaniards developed many conspicuous habits and regarded household articles of silver and gold as an excellent means of displaying wealth, genuine or faked. An ordinance of Philip III, of the year 1600, which requisitioned all vessels of gold and silver in the country in order to have them melted and coined for the benefit of the Exchequer, met with little success. In fact, the fashion spread over the frontiers of Spain and finally degenerated into a nineteenth-century European middle-class fashion of desks and cupboards covered with inexpensive shining gold paint.

Another variety of the boast-collection may be illustrated by a further Spanish example. Philip IV ordered Rubens to decorate one of his reception rooms in the royal palace El Retiro near Madrid with wall paintings representing twelve Spanish victories in war. At the same period, at the much frequented theater of Madrid, a play was performed which was entitled *Las Victorias del Año 1638*. Both the paintings and the play performed a propaganda function and aimed at the denial of commonly known facts – the decadence and the ruin of a country of fallow fields, dead industry, and destitute population.

The art collection assembled in the Musée Napoléon in the Louvre illustrated a desire for prestige on a scale of megalomania (Fig. 2). From the territories conquered by the *Grande Armée*, famous works of art were sent to Paris. As a collector, as in all else, Bonaparte desired to be superior to others; indeed, the Musée Napoléon became unique in regard to the quality, the variety, and the quantity of its specimens. The number of ancient statues and paintings by famous masters ran into thousands. Yet the collection was, like its creator's career, of brief duration. The Congress of Vienna, which had the task of reordering the affairs of Europe unsettled by Bonaparte, decreed that the objects carried away from the invaded countries should be restored to their previous owners, so far as ownership could be established, and the Musée Napoléon, unique both as a collection of masterpieces of art and as a device of domestic and foreign propaganda, disintegrated.[8]

In the later nineteenth century social prestige collections received renewed emphasis on American soil, in an atmosphere charged with power in two forms: of advancing technology coupled with human ingeniousness. The change from a largely agrarian society to an industrial one blended with the political unification following the Civil War and fostered condensation of wealth in the hands of a small minority.

A desire for conspicuous consumption characterized many of the men who unleashed the forces inherent in the application of inventions to a large-scale production of goods, to the building of railroads, and to the exploitation of mines and oilfields. Some of the

Figure 2. Triumphal entry into Paris of works of art plundered by Napoleon Bonaparte's armies in occupied countries. Before being delivered to the Musée Napoléon in the Louvre, the masterpieces from all parts of Europe were paraded on the Champs de Mars. The citizens were to see what Napoleon had done for them. The grandiose display took place in 1798, the sixth year of the Republic.

tremendous surplus wealth was lavished on mansions, on extravagant parties, on servants, fine horses, and carriages — and on collections which expressed a pecuniary philosophy of life of a new breed of Americans. Each business boom propelled new multimillionaires to the markets of art and antiques, genuine or faked. Since the palace of Versailles could not be purchased, one of the members of the new elite, Bradley Martin of New York, had the interior of the Waldorf Astoria Hotel transformed into a copy of the historical home of French royalty. Another conquistador had a dozen portraits of himself painted.[9]

John Pierpont Morgan acquired eminence among his peers not only as a businessman but as a collector.[10] Whether the sum of money he supposedly spent on collecting reached $60 million would seem to matter less than the excellence of most of his acquisitions. Prices on art markets zoomed under the impact of his competitive spirit, but the conqueror was a genuine lover of art, or came to be one in the intimacy with masterworks, and was concerned with his country's need for nonmaterialistic endowment.

The Americans who became intoxicated by big money outranked their predecessors in England owing to the accelerating pace of industrialization, the dimensions of the United States, and its wealth of natural resources. Both their achievements and their defaults, as businessmen and as collectors, were conspicuous, especially as contrasts to the immediate past of the country. Jefferson had dreamed of a new aristocracy of talent and virtue, but talent far outweighed virtue among the early entrepreneurs; the principle of human rights so devotedly pronounced in the Declaration of Independence was mocked by the deprivations endured by factory workers in the process of capital accumulation needed for the development of a large-scale economy.

Magic Collections

A catalogue of an imaginary collection of objects, such as would have delighted many of our forebears throughout the centuries of ancient and medieval times and later still, is contained in that early encyclopedia which is Pliny's *Natural History*. There is, for instance, the horn of a stag, to which was ascribed the power of dispelling serpents by its odor when burning, in accordance with the assumed traditional enmity between stags and snakes; there are the fishes' teeth, an amulet containing a piece of a frog's carcass wrapped in a piece of russet-colored cloth, both valued for their medicinal properties, and there is a variety of stones to which magic powers were attributed.[1] Inventories of once actually existing collections of the fifteenth and sixteenth centuries read like versions of Pliny. An ample provision of magic stones was owned by the prodigious collector Jean de Berry, Duke of Burgundy; and Emperor Charles V kept stones as preventives of disease and cures from sickness. His four Bezuar stones set in gold were regarded as charms that could defeat both plague and poison; in case of gout he took recourse to other stones.[2] In Spain's Golden Age of medicine, Dr. Nicholas Monardes held that precious stones, especially pearls, were an antidote to any kind of poison, and also helped as medicine in cases of heart disease, fever, plague, and last but not least, in treatments for rejuvenation. De Boodt, court physician to the Emperor Rudolph II of Austria, in his "*Gemarum et lapidum historia*," 1609, put forward a suggestion for a new crown for his master; he believed in the supreme beauty of jewels, which in his view were an expression of the divine powers enshrined in them.

Less illustrious persons of the past, of whose passions and collections no record has been preserved, may have been equally anxious to possess objects that would endow them with extraordinary powers. Alexander Neckam (1157 – 1217) in his book *De Naturis Rerum* is likely to have voiced thoughts current among medieval men when he wrote of the Egyptian fig which makes the wrinkles of old age vanish and tames the fiercest bulls, and of the stone which provokes confidences of marital infidelity when placed on the head of a sleeping wife, or brings victory in war to the man who carries it in his mouth.[3]

Unicorn horns[4] and mummies were collectors' items which fetched thousands of ducats between the fifteenth and the seventeenth century.[5] They were credited with having power not merely over disease but over evil forces of any kind. Grand Inquisitor Torquemada was among the public figures who carried on his body a piece of unicorn horn as a talisman against assassination. Maximilian I pawned a sword with a hilt made of the horn at a time of financial need in 1491; two centuries later descendants of the moneylenders offered the sword for sale, and among the potential buyers were the Signoria of Venice and an Indian Rajah, but eventually the abbot of the monastery of Fulda signed the deal in return for a mere 6000 thalers, though originally a sum of 20,000 had been demanded. The abbot's purpose in purchasing the sword was to return it to the imperial family. Another similar sword in the possession of the Hapsburgs was regarded with even greater respect, for it was believed to be part of the horn of the lengendary "moniceros," which according to Physiologus was a symbol of Christ and endowed with supernatural powers. A mummy was believed to be vested with such faculties "that it pierceth all parts, restores wasted limbs, cures consumption, heckticks, and all ulcers and corruptions."[6]

Groping for insights into causes and effects of natural events, men sought comfort from supernatural agents. Sanctuaries of different faiths contain votive donations which give evidence of the fervent human desire to engage the sympathy and assistance of superior powers. The *anathemata* in Greek temples embodied a variety of human thoughts and feelings, fear, hope, gratitude, appeal, and vow.[7] The occasions for the offerings were as numerous as the situations in which the men of those days felt acutely conscious of their inadequacy in dealing with problems: with elemental forces, disease, floods, or drought menacing their existence, or that of their animals or crops; when entering on a new task in peace or war, or after its performance. Any object could serve as a votive offering, whether of precious or unassuming material, of lesser or greater artistic quality. Sometimes an object remarkable for its odd appearance, for its rarity or its age, was found worthy of sacrifice to the gods. In some cases the donation was symbolic of its special message, and took the form of a statue representing the god to whom the donor addressed himself or of a figure referring to the event with which the act of donation was connected.

The temple of Apollo at Delphi contained a collection of statues. It was an assembly of victorious generals, of infantry and horsemen distinguished in battle, of captive enemy women, and of slain enemy bodies. Shields and figureheads of ships captured in war formed part of the collection, and there were also figures of oxen in memory of the freedom to till the ground which had been won by the victory of Greek tribes over Barbarians. Another tribe, the Sicyonians, had sent images of the god Apollo himself, for he had assisted them by flooding, and thus reopening, their blocked gold mines. All these votive gifts, whatever their form, enshrined the same spiritual meaning. They all, in a chorus, voiced people's gratitude for success meted out to them. In an Arcadian temple the hide of a Calydonian boar was shown, valued maybe on account of its rarity, if not as another token of gratitude to the powers which had enabled man to obtain mastery over brute force.

In temples throughout the isles objects were kept which enshrined associations with Greek history, more often legendary than actual. There were the spears of Achilles and of Agesilaus, the sword of Pelops, the writing tablet and stilet of Euripides, the corselet of Masistius, who had commanded the cavalry at Platea. Such objects may

be approached in different frames of mind, and may arouse different thoughts and feelings — nationalistic pride, enthusiasm for extraordinary human achievement or the inquiring mood of a student.
The dedication to the gods implies the humble admission that gods
have the right to own the best of human possessions, and that outstanding deeds are in fact ordained by a higher will and therefore to
the credit of the gods rather than of the men who have carried out
the tasks. A scepter kept in Chaeronea was supposed to have been
produced by the god Hephaistos and to have been wielded by Agamemnon, and daily sacrifices were offered to it by a priest, while a
table covered with meat and cake stood beside it.

  The outer frieze of the temple at Olympia was decorated with
twenty gilded shields dedicated by the Roman general Mummius,
who had conquered the Acheans, taken Corinth, and expelled the
Dorian inhabitants. In the usual human manner the general felt confidence in the righteousness of his cause and in the deserved mishap
of his adversaries, and he did not hesitate to honor the gods by offering them, on Greek soil, in a temple bearing witness to Greek piety
and splendor, war trophies he had won in conquering the Greeks.

  Objects of magic character reappeared in the Christian Church,
and illustrated the scope of human credulity.[8] In his *Dictionnaire
Critique des Reliques et Images Miraculeuses*, written for the purpose of combating the superstitious veneration of skeletons, Collin
de Plancy recorded that nineteen churches claimed to possess the
jawbone of John the Baptist, and that the Benedictine monastery at
Vendôme in France prided itself on owning a tear wept by Jesus on
the death of Lazarus and preserved in a phial in their church. The
Cathedral of Chartres, the church of the royal residence Escorial
near Madrid, and the church of St. Cecily in Rome claimed the privilege of possessing a hair of Jesus'.[9] True to the dictum of the Council of Trent, 1545 – 1563, the relics of saints and martyrs were wor-
shiped by the believers. Gregor of Nyssa wrote that it was a great
privilege to touch the relic of a saint. He described how people rev-
erently embraced and kissed the holy remains, how they avidly
viewed them, how they pressed them against their eyes and ears
and communicated with them through their senses and begged
them to be their spokesmen and patrons before God.

  The great impecunious masses of the Middle Ages had to be satisfied with a fragmentary piece of a skeleton in their local church or
with the occasional experience offered by a peddler who brought a
relic to the village and in return for a small contribution allowed

people to view and to touch it. Even the prosperous were limited in their opportunity to maintain large collections of any kind. The lack of facilities for the transport of goods compelled wealthy people to divide their year among several residences, if they wished to utilize provisions available in different localities,[10] and the migratory style of life discouraged the accumulation of things. An object coveted above all by these luxurious nomads was the reliquary, which was known as the most precious ornament in the Lady's chamber, in the Knight's armor, in the King's hall of state.[11] They would display relics on the ramparts of besieged fortresses, and the traveler would hold them aloft when the skies threatened him with thunderstorm.

Unsurpassed by any other collection of relics was that amassed by Philip II, who reigned from 1556 to 1598. The Defender of the Faith, though engaged in ruling two hemispheres, did not deem it too small a task to dispatch a special envoy, Ambrosio de Morales, to various parts of the Peninsula to collect relics of saints and martyrs.[12] Graves closed for centuries and jealously guarded under threat of excommunication opened up to the royal messenger to give up a few bones, some "still of sweet smell." Another mission was sent by Philip to the Low Countries and to Germany, to rescue holy remains from damage and neglect at the hands of the Protestants. By such efforts Philip succeeded in assembling at his residence near Madrid a collection containing eleven complete skeletons, thousands of skulls, leg, arm, and finger bones, apart from a number of miscellaneous pieces. On occasions of royal illness, up to the death of Charles II in 1700, processions with holy images and the application of relics to the patient's body were part of the attempted cure.

In spite of numerous attempts by reformers, including Calvin in his treatise against the veneration of relics, the worship of skeletons went on in Europe. In the nineteenth century, churches in Italy and in Spain still listed relics for legitimate worship, and to this day men and women seeking liberation from disease, infertility, or some other calamity, go on pilgrimage and offer ex-votos.

In Spain, more than anywhere else, images wielded power over men, and there were people on the Peninsula who believed that they had seen a figure in stone or wood give an order by moving head or hand. When in the sixteenth century the sculptor Becerra was at work on a new figure of the Virgin in the Convent de las Descalzas at Madrid, he had to attempt no less than three times to carve the head of the figure. The two first heads were not satisfactory, but the third was, owing to the aid of the Madonna herself. In his dream the artist heard her voice ordering him to take from his fireplace one of the logs of oak and shape her countenance.

It was the association between all things pagan and the forces of evil which for centuries made men avoid contact with remains of the classic world, even though a guidebook for medieval pilgrims, *Mirabilia Urbis Romae*, referred to both churches and ancient monuments. St. Augustine had come to condemn pagan gods as demons, and pagan statues appeared to be demons in stone. The medieval farmer who by chance dug up a fragment of a Roman statue would hurry to rid himself of the token of accursed paganism and deliver it to the priest, who might, as he occasionally did, render it harmless by having it bricked into the masonry of the church wall. In the fourteenth century the ancient pagan relic was still occasionally accused of harboring evil powers. When Siena suffered a setback in a feud with Florence, some citizens accused Lysippus' statue of Venus, which not long before had been set up with general acclamation in a public square, of casting an evil spell, and the statue — the *cosa disonesta* — was broken up in pieces and buried in the soil of Florence.[13] In the late fifteenth century the dread of paganism discouraged Pope Innocent VIII from interesting himself in the classic collections of the Vatican which had been assembled by some of his predecessors.

Collections as Expressions of Group Loyalty

To contend with his environment and to rise above the raw struggle of life man has invented a variety of tools and has, even if as yet rather imperfectly, devised methods of uniting individuals into groups whose capacities in many ways surpass the sheer sum of the members' individual powers. A partnership may be based on a shared practical activity, be it an agricultural cooperative or a military unit, or it may be a commonwealth anchored in the human imagination. If collections are considered as records of human attitudes, Western man appears as a member of several realms which profoundly affected his thoughts and his emotions and which contributed to the shaping of his superego.

Kinship with a Golden-Age Ancestry. The creation of the first man is one of the great questions obsessing people's minds. According to one interpretation, celestial beings begot a race of heroes who, in their turn, procreated the first humans.[1]

Greek temples contained objects connected with a past when humans still enjoyed the immediate cooperation of the gods.[2] In the Pallas temple at Metapontum, smiths' tools were venerated as the implements with which the Trojan horse had been constructed. Paintings represented the giant race that once had dwelt in the land. Skeletons of colossal proportions were believed to be the remains of giant ancestors and were honored as relics of a Golden Age ancestry; of a legendary human race that once had held sway and that continued to wield power by blessing or by curse. Pliny wrote of bones of men of unusual size which were kept in the gardens of the Sallust family and in their "conditorio,"[3] and Suetonius mentioned bones of wild beasts known as the "bones of the giants" in the villa of the Emperor Augustus.[4]

The common characteristic of those tokens was their connection with a legendary past, as distinct from a dated and otherwise recorded historical fact. They were, in their own way, a cultural force contributing to the unity and the vigor of the community: the identification with ancestors of superhuman powers enhanced self-confidence and encouraged ambition. A collection of tokens of superhuman ancestry was almost tantamount to a charter conferring privileges on a people; such tokens may not have withstood intellectual inquiry, but did engage the emotions of people.

Interest in a legendary ancestry survived the pagan period of Europe, and numerous churches treasured relics of a mythical past. St. Stephen's in Vienna was one among many churches owning skeletons of gigantic proportions. Since St. Augustine had indicated the possibility of giants being the offspring of a union between angels and mortal women, the suggestion of the descent of men from giants was not altogether out of place in a church.

The mementos of a Golden Age ancestry were not necessarily remains of outsize bodies. What mattered was the bond between the living and superior men of a legendary, distant past who were credited with such feats as the invention of agriculture and astronomy, of the calendar, or of music and dance. The English traveler Addison wrote after his tour through Italy, in 1701, "The cathedral of Milan is very rich in relics which run up as high as Daniel, Jonas and Abraham."[5] In Rome at St. Jacob's a marble table was regarded as the altar upon which Abraham had prepared to sacrifice Isaac. The Abbey of St. Denis in France possessed a curious goblet of rock crystal which was formerly in Solomon's temple.[6]

Some types of Roman collections stretched the idea of an ancestral gallery into the realm of legendary forebears. A procession of men wearing ancestors' masks would march in the funeral ceremony of eminent Romans, and the number of images in the mobile gallery would enhance the distinction of the family. Ancestors' images

Figures 3a and 3b. Ancient ruins in Rome and the display of a private Roman collection of antiquities in the courtyard of the Casa Sassi. The two drawings, by Marten van Heemskerck, of the mid-sixteenth century, are preserved in engravings owned by the Kupferstichkabinet in Berlin.

Hieronymus Cock engraved the picture of the ruins, and Dirks van Coornhaert the picture of the patio.

in the form of statues and reliefs in private homes decorated the walls of the arcaded courtyard, the atrium, the scene of the daily life of the family. The association of the shieldlike shape of many of these reliefs with militancy seems to have emphasized heroic qualities.[7]

Patriotism. The men and women who went about their business in the streets of ancient Greece, in Athens, Delphi, Corinth, and other towns, were given an opportunity of keeping in touch with a community much larger and more august than that of their contemporaries. The past of their community was kept alive for them: "At Delphi the road which wound up the steep slope to the temple of Apollo was lined on both sides with an unbroken succession of monuments which illustrated some of the brightest triumphs and darkest tragedies in Greek history."[8] In the famous Painted Colonnade near the marketplace of Athens were shown scenes of the battles of Marathon and Mantinea, and the conquest of Ilium; there one could see and touch bronze shields taken from the Sicyonians.

"The great sanctuaries of Olympia and Delphi served in a manner as the national museums and record-offices of Greece. In them the various Greek cities . . . set up the trophies of their victories and deposited copies of treaties . . . . They offered a neutral ground . . . where they could survey, with hearts that swelled with various emotions, the records of their country's triumphs and defeats."[9]

In feudal times it was difficult to draw a definite line between ancestral and patriotic or nationalistic collections. A series of images of sovereigns representing a dynasty was charged with an intense nationalistic message. The sequence of rulers by inheritance was considered god-willed and vested each individual with authority over people inhabiting a certain territory; in their turn, people and territory felt represented in the sovereign's image.[10] Where rulers could not claim to be related by blood, the soil could become a symbol claiming loyalty. When ancient Rome surfaced in the consciousness of the inhabitants of Italy after centuries of submersion during the Middle Ages, Dante wrote that the very walls of Rome deserved reverence. A century before him, in 1162, an edict of the Roman Senate decreed that the Column of Trajan must never be destroyed or mutilated.

The ancient remains made the "Gloria" of the past near and tangible to generations of Italians striving for a reorganization of their national existence[11] (Figs. 3, a, b). Since the breakdown of the Roman Empire Italy had not found its balance. Though the Vatican represented a center of gravity of a worldwide Catholic Empire, Italy

itself was a noncoordinated bundle of independent small sovereign-
ties. The Pope's migration to Avignon in 1309, with the implicit loss
of influence of the Church, was an event likely to foster Italian patriotism and to encourage the creation of collections of patriotic substance even if later the return of the Popes to Rome and the revival
of papal power, in their turn, engendered enthusiasm for the legacy
of antiquity. To indulge in his antiquarian interests Pius II had himself borne in a litter through Italy. Later Popes chose the carnival as
an occasion for magnificent processions representing the "Triumphs
of Roman Imperators," which were in fact mobile galleries.

During the Middle Ages Rome had been allowed to fall into ruins.
In the early fifteenth century Poggio Bracciolini in his book *Vicissitudes of Fortune* complained that of the once famous wealth in statuary in Rome there remained only six statues, five of marble and
one of bronze. In the same period Blondo Forli suggested in his
Roma Instaurata that the relics of saints should be regarded as a
consolation for the ruin of the ancient city.[12] When Brunelleschi and
Donatello visited Rome and measured the ruins of ancient architecture, they found the roads leading to the town littered with broken
statues.

Individual efforts at collecting ancient remains went back to the
eleventh century, when Nicholas Crescentius built in Rome his
house containing remains of ancient buildings. The oldest actual
collection of which a record has been preserved existed about 1335
at Treviso, where a wealthy citizen, Oliviero Forza, collected ancient
medals, coins, marbles, and manuscripts. Of this, only a list survived in which the collector named things he wished to purchase
and where he referred to contemporary collections in Venice similar to his own. Another early Renaissance collector known by name
was the author Poggio, who took special interest in inscriptions and
who decorated his house at Terranuova near Florence with *confrac-
tis marmorum reliquiis*. In the early sixteenth century palaces of
wealthy merchants, princes, and clerics in Rome, Tuscany, and
Venice were filled with relics of the Roman past, with medals, coins,
statues, and inscriptions. At Florence the Medici declared the importance of a collection to be equal to that of a library.

The Florentine collector Niccolo Niccoli was probably one among
others who used ancient objects in his everyday life, and the contemporary author Vespasiano Fiorentino wrote of him: "At table he
ate from beautiful ancient vessels. It was lovely indeed to watch him
in that ancient style of manner which he adopted."[13] Artists — Ghiberti, Squarcione, Mantegna, Lombardi, and others — assembled

Figure 4. A great social event at Napoleon's Court: the sculpture group of the *Laocoön* has arrived. Napoleon and his new Empress, Maria Louisa of Hapsburg, lead a procession of illustrious visitors to admire the famous work of art. Pen drawing by Benjamin Zix. (By Courtesy of the Louvre Museum.)

ancient statues in their studios, inspired by the idea of being descendants of the creators of the works in their collections and inspiring others to interest themselves in relics of antiquity.[14] Raphael, when commissioned by Pope Leo X to undertake the reconstruction of ancient Rome, wrote in a letter that one must rescue the divine soul of antiquity, a source of inspiration for all those who are capable of high things.

The appeal of tokens of the past could attain such power that a newly dug-out ancient statue was carried about in the streets amidst the jubilation of the people. When, in January 1506, a sculptured group, known as *Laocoön*, was unearthed near San Pietro in Vincoli, the people of Rome came out streaming to see "the greatest masterpiece ever seen" while it was still standing in a hole in the ground, and Pope Julius II had it guarded by night. When it was removed to the Vatican, church bells rang and cannons boomed[15] (Fig. 4).

In 1534 the Pope banned the export of works of art from Italy.[16] The ban, which in practice had only limited effect, emphasized the fact that the *Rinascimento* was not only the expression of local Italian loyalty, but that it was a European event: one of the few great Western experiences of unity and continuity.

Scions of the Mediterranean World. Efforts toward a homogeneous Occidental culture, as distinct frm an Oriental one, preceded the Italian Renaissance. The Hellenistic rulers of Pergamos and Alexandria were anxious to collect Greek manuscripts, inscriptions, statues, casts, and gems.[17] In Imperial Rome the ancient cultures both of Rome and Greece were venerated as a priceless legacy, and the fascination with the Mediterranean past inspired the men of the Empire in their efforts after a New Order and a *Novum Saeculum*.[18] The Romans desired not merely to appropriate the material possessions of vanquished Greece but also to absorb the Greek spirit. Young Romans were taught the thoughts of Greek philosophers, Roman architecture was clothed with Greek ornaments, and almost any object originating from Greece, even if without special beauty or interest, was treasured as *Res Fatalis* and as a token of future success.[19]

Few Romans could afford the possession of a collection of Greek tokens, but many could undertake a journey to Greece. Pausanias, who wrote his *Description of Greece* in the second century A.D., was preceded by numerous *Cicerones* or *Periegetes* who had described and interpreted to their Roman contemporaries the ancient Greek remains.[20] There had been Polemo of Illium, in the first century B.C., Heliodorus of Athens, who is supposed to have been one of

Pliny's sources in matters of art, and other authors, in addition to the much more numerous guides who did not commit their information to writing but served tourists by word of mouth. It was to these that Cicero referred when he wrote: ". . . *qui hospites ad ea quae visenda sunt solent ducere et unum quidque ostendere, quos illi mystagogos vocant. . . .*"[21] Plutarch was amused by the routine manner in which the guides entertained their public, who apparently wished to listen to stories, true or invented, of heroes whom they claimed as their ancestors. Atticus wrote in a letter to Cicero: "My darling Athens attracts me, not so much for her Greek buildings and monuments of ancient art, as for her great men, where they dwelled and sat, talked and lie buried."[22]

The image of the Roman Empire survived its political disintegration and Byzantium's ascent to power and a center of culture. The course of events in which the Teutonic tribes migrated to the West, were christianized and assimilated to the Latin and previously latinized groups led to another effort toward a homogeneous Occidental culture. The Frankish king Charlemagne adopted the imperial title and sent monks to Italy to purchase early Christian works of art in which classic and Christian traditions blended.

With an upturn in trade and prosperity in the later Middle Ages interest quickened in matters of the mind.[23] The imaginary integration of Greek and Roman legacies which had begun in Imperial Rome was revived over widening areas: eventually all Western countries laid claim to them and sought them far beyond the boundaries of Greece and of Italy. The humanist Ciriaco of Ancona, who acted as Emperor Sigismund's cicerone in Rome, traveled to parts of Asia and Africa as far as the ancient Mediterranean genius had extended. The Florentine savant Poggio Bracciolini corresponded with educated Greeks in Byzantium and advocated the restoration of Greek statuary. In founding the Platonic Academy in Florence, Cosimo de' Medici may have had a vision of a regeneration of Italy by the spirit of ancient Greece rather than by a consciousness of a chthonic relationship with ancient Rome.

The idea of the Imperator as a symbol of peace and order lived on in the imagination of the West. The title survived and added prestige first to Germanic kings and later to the Hapsburg dynasty. Medals and coins bearing portraits of Roman emperors attracted much interest. When the Italian poet Petrarch met the Emperor Charles IV in Mantua in 1354, he presented the sovereign of German extraction with a collection of Roman coins and urged the ruler to follow the example of his ancient predecessors.[24] In the sixteenth century hundreds of collections of Roman coins existed in Western Europe.[25]

Next to coins bearing portraits of Roman emperors, their busts and paintings commemorating their deeds were much sought by collectors. "As the comfort and security of life increased . . . walls had to be covered with something more inviting than the lives of the Saints. . . . The story of Cæsar was a favourite decoration." Philip II of Spain was presented with a series of busts of Roman emperors, and in England Cardinal Wolsey had portraits of emperors in the form of terra-cotta medallions affixed to the gateway turrets of Hampton Court. Cardinal Mazarin called one room of his collection (in the later Palais Royal) "Serie de Cæsari" and Napoleon Bonaparte had a "Hall of Emperors" in his museum in the Louvre (Fig. 5).

At his palace at Fontainebleau, Francis I of France assembled not only works of contemporary Italian masters, of Cellini and Leonardo da Vinci, of which French troops occupying Milan were the conveyors, but ancient works of art as well. He engaged artists for their purchase; Andrea del Sarto spent the funds entrusted to him for his own purposes, but Primaticcio returned with 124 ancient statues and numerous casts. In 1648 Velazquez was sent by his king, Philip IV, to Rome with an extraordinary embassy to Pope Innocent X for the purpose of purchasing original paintings and antique statues and of having casts made from some of the best. He brought back to Spain 32 casts of full-length Roman statues and busts.[26]

Both individuals and groups of people were seized by the desire for a spiritual return to the classic era. The French town Lyons may serve as an example. Becoming conscious of their ancient past, the community began to collect Roman remains in their area.[27]

In England the beginning of classic collections is associated with the name of Thomas Howard, Earl of Arundel, with whom the slogan "Transplant Old Greece to England" was connected[28] (Fig. 6). He was the first to bring inscribed Greek marbles to his country. In the year 1613 the Earl of Arundel, in company with Inigo Jones, visited Italy and made Siena his headquarters for the winter. A special permit of King James enabled the earl to visit Rome, a place generally forbidden to citizens of the islands of the Reformed Church, and to make excavations which resulted in the unearthing of many Roman statues. Of the Arundel collection near the Strand in London, the German artist Joachim von Sandrart, who visited England in 1627, gave the following account: "Foremost among the objects worthy to be seen, stood the beautiful garden of that most famous lover of art, the Earl of Arundel, resplendent with the finest ancient statues of marble, of Greek and Roman workmanship. . . . Some

Figure 5. The Hall of Roman Emperors in Napoleon Bonaparte's Louvre Museum had two connotations: it reinforced the popular current mythology of the benefits derived by France from being ruled by Emperor Napoleon, and it was part of a general European ideology in which the Roman empire was a Golden Past. Engraving by Hibon after a painting by Cibeton. (By courtesy of the Louvre Museum.)

Figure 6. "Transplant Old Greece to England" was the call of Thomas Howard, Earl of
Arundel, which expressed his loyalty to the ancient Mediterranean world, a loyalty he
shared with many men of the fifteenth to the eighteenth century, in Europe and in the
young United States as well as in the British colonies that preceded it. Arundel House in
London was demolished in 1678. The picture shows the Earl in his sculpture gallery at
Arundel House. (By courtesy of the Duke of Norfolk and of Sir Robert Witt, London.)

full-lengths, some busts only, with an almost innumerable quantity of heads and reliefs all in marble and very rare."[29] Other collections of kindred character in London in the late seventeenth century belonged to C. Townley and to J. Kemp. In his *Diary*, R. Thoresby gave the following description of Kemp's collection: "I . . . visited Mr. Kempe who showed me his noble collection of Greek and Roman medals . . . he had two entire mummies . . . what I was most surprised with was his closet of the ancient deities, lares, lamps and other Roman vases. . . ." (January 26, 1709).[30]

In the century following Arundel, the ancient Mediterranean world came to be the cultural background and spiritual homeland of numerous Englishmen. The young gentlemen who made their Grand Tour on the Continent, an important feature of their education, interested themselves in the Mediterranean legacy. England was enjoying an era of political consolidation and of commercial progress, and ancient Mediterranean culture became associated with social status in the modern world. The eighteenth century saw the rebuilding of many country houses in the simple and dignified style of the Renaissance architect Palladio. Separate galleries were provided for the housing of ancient marbles, or at least niches for statues. In 1734 the Society of the Dilettanti was founded in London, an association of men who had traveled in Italy and who regarded classic culture as the proper background for their prosperity.[31] At the first meetings of the Society of the Dilettanti the president appeared in a scarlet Roman toga, and the box in which the books of the society were kept was called "Bacchus' tomb." In spite of this lighthearted approach, the activities of the Dilettanti deserve commendation for the part they played in initiating and supporting undertakings by which the remains in Greece and the Levant were explored for the benefit of the world. Whereas excavations in Italy had been carried on since the Renaissance, the soil of Greece and of the Near East under Turkish rule had remained closed to antiquarians, even if casual spoils reached the West through Venice.[32]

In the eighteenth century loyalty to classic Mediterranean culture came to be shared by men of different nationalities, and it extended across the Atlantic to America. In Rome and Venice students of classicism would meet, Germans, Frenchmen, Englishmen, and Danes, artists, writers, and diplomats (Fig. 7). Among them was the Yorkshire architect Thomas Harrison, on whose advice the Earl of Elgin embarked on collecting antiquities which were to include the famous Elgin marbles.[33] In his *Italian Journey* Goethe expressed his wish to be conducted through Italy by an Englishman with knowl-

Figure 7. A gathering of *cognoscenti* in the Tribuna in the Medici Gallery, Florence,
painted by J. Zoffany between 1770 and 1780, when the collection was owned by the
princes of Lorraine. Visitors had to obtain the permission of the owner to view the famous
paintings and statues kept in this select part of the gallery. Well-known collectors were
apparently permitted to come close to the exhibits and to handle them, maybe in order
to see them in different illuminations.

Zoffany's painting currently belongs to the Queen of England and is at Windsor Castle.
A catalogue of the royal collections, of 1937, lists some of the persons portrayed in the
picture. The keeper of the gallery, M. Bianchi, in the foreground to the right, holds up
Titian's *Venus*, while Zoffany, to the back at the left, lifts up a picture of Raphael for close
inspection by a group of connoisseurs.

All represented persons happen to have been Englishmen, but they could have been of
different nationalities. The connoisseurs of the period were an international league. (By
courtesy of the Surveyor of the Queen's Pictures. Copyright reserved.)

edge and understanding of art. Englishmen were most active in the lively trade in marbles—Sir William Hamilton in Naples and others in Rome; Joseph Nollekens specialized in the reconstruction of statues from small fragments.[34]

Around the middle of the eighteenth century the interest in classic ancient art seemed to flag, but the discoveries at Herculaneum and Pompeii renewed the enthusiasm. Generations of Europeans were imbued with the teaching that ancient art marked the highest standard attainable. The famous German archaeologist Johann Winckelmann wrote: "The only way for us to become great, nay inimitable, if that be possible, is to imitate Antiquity." Diderot declared that to perceive nature it was necessary to study ancient art. Similarly, Sir Joshua Reynolds preached to his students that they should study the works of the ancients in order to attain to the real simplicity of nature. Winckelmann declared the connoisseurship of anybody who had not formed his taste upon antiquity to be a parcel of whimseys. Such dogmas triggered a production of fake antiquities and a tolerance for emasculated imitations of classic architecture. Toward the end of the eighteenth century Greek and Roman styles which had inspired men with an awareness of excellence began to deteriorate to mediocrity and to a fetish of social responsibility.

The Fellowship of Christian Gentry. The ancient Graeco-Roman world was an essential part but not the whole of the imaginary collective ancestry of the Occident in the centuries following the Middle Ages.

By surrounding themselves with paintings and sculpture commemorating the lives of saints and martyrs, people remained aware of their membership in that great fellowship of the *Res Publica Christiana*, a segregation of the righteous from the wicked. Whatever a man's citizenship or tongue may have been he could join the community. In all Catholic countries in Europe artists were featuring the heroes and heroines of Christendom in paint, stone, wood, and metal. Some of their work was art, but most of their industrious production was craftsmanship. Bands of artists of mediocre talent were engaged in Spain and in Italy in copying famous images of saints and biblical scenes as outward-bound cargo for Spanish ships which went out to fetch gold and silver from the mines in Spain's colonies in America.[35]

Another feature of the European mind which expressed itself in collections of the sixteenth and seventeenth centuries concerned a new approach to leisure. Inventions and discoveries, and a more settled life, had brought command over objects which had been beyond the reach of men of medieval times. In his *Perspectiva*, Alberti had written of *letitia* as a means of enriching life by study and enjoyment. A collection offered an ideal opportunity of experiencing so many things newly won or discovered and of spending hours of leisure in a distinguished manner.

Portraits became sought for collectors' items. Margaret of Austria, a daughter of Emperor Maximilian and herself the much respected Governess of the Netherlands, owned numerous portraits of excellent quality. Another Hapsburg, Archduke Ferdinand, accumulated more than a thousand painted and engraved effigies, mainly of princes and other titled persons, at his Tyrolean castle Ambras near Innsbruck.[36] With rising economic prosperity and a new emphasis on the individual, Europeans of the Renaissance period were changing the collective image of their ancestry; saints and martyrs were joined by successful men of secular pursuits, by soldiers, doctors, explorers, scholars, and artists. The memory of this "honest company," as they were referred to in castle Ambras, was kept alive by their portraits and by biographies. *Viri Illustres* was the summary title of Paolo Govio's sixteenth-century collection of pictures in Como which he described in his *Musaei Imagines*. In his book *De Viribus Illustribus* the fifteenth-century author Bartholomeo Facio proclaimed the collecting of pictures and other objects to be an activity worthy of a great man.

Judging by the scope of interests illustrated by the contents of the Ambras collection, the mental horizon of the "Complete Man" of the Renaissance was remarkable in its width. He interested himself in nature and in man; the veneration of a Mediterranean ancestry was combined with awareness of contemporary events and of manners of life in distant countries, including the newly discovered Americas; there was appreciation of both artistic creation and mechanical skill — represented by newly devised instruments, musical, astronomical, optical and mathematical, by watches and clocks.

In spite of the Thirty Years' War the European mind went on struggling for a widening of the frontiers of knowledge. If compared with a gentleman's collection of a few generations before, and even with such an outstanding one as that of the Duke of Berry, the emphasis was shifting from objects valued mainly for their rare or precious material, or their supposed magic properties, to objects illustrating man's natural environment and human ingenuity, including artistic skill. In Spain collecting of this kind was known as "*virtuoso divertimiento.*" The possession of a heterogeneous variety of things added dimension to life without requiring commitment to special effort;

it was a pastime. The pages from descriptions of collections by travelers in the sixteenth, seventeenth, and eighteenth century, which are reprinted in the Appendix of this book (pp. 241–250), confirm this impression.

The scope of interest of seventeenth-century collectors of *varia* may be further illustrated by Spanish aficionados whose activities were described by contemporary authors.[37] At their regular meetings held in private houses they exhibited the latest purchases and objects they wished to exchange. On one such occasion attended by distinguished gentlemen, artists, and scholars who "showed refined taste and thorough knowledge," the following articles were handled and discussed: paintings by great masters, armor, weapons, sculpture, furniture, ivory carvings and goldsmith work, costly prints, musical and arithmetical instruments, chess and other games, precious stones, furs, and fragrant spices.

The mighty and rich of Western Europe were not alone in their desire for the possession of beautiful and interesting objects; gradually they were joined by people of the middle classes.[38]

Loyalty to the Future. To early American collectors history consisted to a considerable extent of contemporary events and of events in process. As Henry Steele Commager wrote, confidence in their future combined with the idea of Manifest Destiny formed the habit of looking forward instead of backward.[39] They considered themselves as the ancestors of coming generations throughout a boundless future for whom they wished to preserve records of the beginnings of American greatness.

Pierre Eugène du Simitière of Philadelphia collected documents related to important contemporary events, portraits of leading citizens, and military relics, and encouraged others to do so. He died in 1784, soon after the beginning of his project. John Pintard, whose collection in New York was known at the time as American Museum, wrote in 1790 to Secretary of State Jefferson and requested that any supernumerary papers, gazettes, and so on, be sent to him for the patriotic purpose of contributing to a memorial of national events. Mr. Pintard's enthusiasm was shared by the Reverend Jeremy Belknap of Boston and his associates, who founded the Massachusetts Historical Society, the first of its kind in the country. Apart from written records they planned to assemble antiquities as means of rescuing true history "from the ravages of time and the effects of ignorance and neglect."[40]

One of the numerous and short-lived private collections known as a museum and open to the public was Mr. Browere's Gallery of

Busts and Statues. Originally a sign painter, he advanced to the position of an artist who portrayed noted personalities. By good judgment or good luck he exhibited also work of the great French sculptor Houdon — busts of Washington, Franklin, and Jefferson.[41]

Collections as Means of Stimulating Curiosity and Inquiry

Pliny described human nature as "migratory and curious." In his era, circumstances in the Roman Empire encouraged curiosity and travel; the worldwide empire was knit together by roads, and during a prolonged period of peace, standards of security and comfort had been increasing. People made sea voyages and endured long journeys for some remote sight; they were anxious to view things for the sake of their rarity or strangeness, for their fame or literary notoriety.

"First of all travelers bent their steps to the temples, as best satisfying their craving for sights and information. . . . The precincts of temples often enclosed . . . parks and preserves of sacred animals and birds. . . . Temples also abounded in dedicatory gifts and rarities. . . ."[1] Among the exhibits in the temple of the Syrian goddess at Hierapolis were barbaric garments, Indian jewels, tusks of elephants, and the jaw of a snake. In the temple of Hercules at Rome was a display of hides of animals which killed people by merely looking at them; such was their record, maintained by tradition since the Jugurthine war, when Roman soldiers had supposedly encountered the beasts in Africa. In the temple of Juno Astharte at Carthage skins of hairy savage women could be seen. The "Curiosa Naturalia et Artificialia" included skeletons of human and animal monstrosities, rare plants, and strange instruments such as a forceps for pulling teeth, an obsolete flute, and foreign weapons.

Objects received from the provinces were exhibited within and around temples on the occasion of games and processions.[2] In his *Description of Greece*, Pausanias wrote of tritons, of Ethiopic bulls (which they called rhinoceroses) and Indian camels he had viewed.[3] The existence of such a fabulous creature as a triton was apparently accepted without questioning. The transformation of a feeling of awe to a spirit of inquiry is a slow process, and as yet an imperfect one.

Interest may be expressed in a manner of curiosity or of inquiry. Whereas the *curieux*' mind jumps from one item to another, the inquirer charts his path of thought according to some plan and steadily travels along it. Whereas the inquirer's response is based primarily on reason, the *curieux* gives vent mainly to emotions.[4] The evolution of a spirit of inquiry was a mark of the ancient Mediterranean civilization. In their midst arose Greek thinkers and Roman lawgivers, and the Hellenistic period saw the rise of the large-scale research institute known as the Museum of Alexandria.

In the small self-contained communities of agricultural and pastoral character to which Western Europe largely reverted after the downfall of the Roman Empire, human endeavor was directed to the solution of everyday tasks rather than to philosophical contemplation. Final answers to all questions were offered by theologians equipped with readjusted Aristotelian learning, and all faithful of the Catholic Church were expected to put their trust in them. Papal dictates warned men to "be content with the landmarks of science fixed by their fathers, to have due fear of the curse pronounced against him who removeth his neighbour's landmark, and not to incur the blame of innovation and presumption."[5]

In this atmosphere of apocalyptic fear the potentialities of the European mind to develop independent thought revealed themselves in Bacon's *De Scientia Experimentali*, a signal event, even if its immediate influence on progress through inquiry was deferred by the newly founded Dominican and Franciscan orders. They could delay but not defeat the soaring of the human spirit. Early in the seventeenth century men worked on such inventions as a "telegraphy with cannons," an "unsinkable ship," "a floating fort," "a flying machine," and "a calculating machine."[6]

Some collections of the sixteenth and the seventeenth century illustrated the watershed between medievalism and humanism. They represented a spirit akin to that of the Cosmographies in which the world was described by authors with minds half turned toward sound observation and half immersed in a mist of fables. What was unknown and unfamiliar, and not taught by the Scriptures, was regarded as abnormal, as terrible, and yet as thrilling: thus a *Mundus Mirabilis* was constructed by the authors of the *Specula Historialia* and the *Bestiaria*. The information could either deepen religious loyalty or stimulate curiosity.[7]

The new curios of Jean de Berry, Duke of Burgundy, were kept together with specimens generally credited with magic powers. Such things as mechanical instruments and telescopes illustrated nascent judicious reasoning and the desire to advance human knowledge; the jawbone of a serpent or the gospel of St. John written in microscopic letters on a piece of parchment the size of a silver coin could be valued either as samples of nature and human skill or as charms against evil forces.

Fanciful belief in miracles and thirst for sober information combined in the mind of Emperor Rudolph II in Prague.[8] In the company of astrologers and alchemists, and in the microcosm of his museum, he sought to overcome his melancholic temperament and to seek refuge from the problems of his empire. In addition to hundreds of paintings by European masters, bronzes, and other objects of art, he had idols and utensils from Egypt and India, globes, periscopes, tools, games, and musical instruments. Rudolph was one of the numerous intellectual adventurers of the sixteenth century. He hoped that a new invention would enable men to transform any metal into gold, thus offering a solution to all problems of state finance, and had a "chemical kitchen" installed in his palace; he regarded horoscopes as reliable records of human character and human fate, and he believed in the intercourse between the living and the dead. Yet fettered as his mind may have been by medieval superstitions, his intellectual restlessness held something of the spirit of inquiry characteristic of generations to follow. By his manner of collecting, Rudolph expressed the spirit of the sixteenth and seventeenth centuries when workmen and princes rivaled in inventing. The Faust-Spirit that declared all invention of new devices a Black Art and a fruit of intimacy with the devil was declining, yet Agricola, the sixteenth-century author of *De Re Metallica*, combined scholarship with belief in demons as important agents in mining.[9]

The revived tendency toward searching investigation began with the study of pagan classic literature in Italy. Poets were among the first to honor the classics, and they were joined by wealthy citizens of the independent Italian towns. In 1360 a chair of Greek literature was established in Florence. Interest in Greek traditions, for centuries stifled in the West, was stimulated when Greek scholars sought refuge in Italy after the capture of Byzantium by the Turks in 1493. The search of collectors for Greek manuscripts was on; it extended to stones with Greek inscriptions and to statuary.

The opposition to scholasticism documented by classical study developed into a general spirit of inquiry and of invention. In the sphere of religion it expressed itself in the Reformation, and it acquired prominence in investigations of the natural environment, in the sciences. The common driving force sprang from a changing mental climate in which men "no longer thought of the world either as settled or as well taken care of. They saw the world as man-made and ordered by man. . . ."[10] The great questioning minds of Kepler, Descartes, Bacon, Newton, and Leibnitz were reflected both in the "Academies"[11] and in the "Cabinets" or "Museums" which came into existence in the later sixteenth and in the seventeenth centuries. The *curiosi*, *otiosi*, and *virtuosi*, as the academicians and the collectors were called, stood for Francis Bacon's interpretation of knowledge as power, as a means of increasing human control over nature and of fostering innate human ingenuity. The scope of their interests was encyclopedic and embraced under the title of Experimental Philosophy the moral and natural sciences, archaeology and ethnology, history and literature.

The new emphasis on study by observation encouraged the formation of new collections which at times were connected with laboratories. The new collectors were dedicated to the pursuit of knowledge; they did not cultivate elegant pastimes as many of their predecessors had done. Their systematic style led to a more careful recording of specimens in catalogues they wrote themselves or had written by others. The catalogues which have been preserved are documents of intellectual history (Fig. 8).

When the first Society of Antiquaries was founded in London, in 1572, its purpose was "to separate falsehood from truth and tradition from evidence," and to sift history by the "sagacity of modern criticism," "in an age wherein every part of science is advancing to perfection, and in a nation not afraid of penetrating into the remotest periods of their origin, or of deducting from it anything that may reflect dishonour on them." The antiquarian collection was recommended as supplying the materials for research in history and as an aid in the preservation of remains.[12]

The physician Ulisse Aldrovandi of Bologna, Italy, set himself the lofty task of gathering specimens that would represent all external nature. For over thirty years he employed an artist at an annual salary of 200 crowns for the purpose of illustrating an encyclopedia of natural history; he saw it completed but died a poor man. In addition to his interest in nature, Aldrovandi was an antiquarian who had studied the remains of ancient Rome and had collected antiquities mainly for their ethnographical interest, for instance idols as illustrations of mythology. His collections were acquired and enlarged by Cospi, an amateur physicist and mechanic known in Bologna as the *nobile mechanico*.[13]

Seventeenth-century Italy produced a wealth of inquisitive minds. In Verona, a certain Calceolari started a collection of natural history which changed its character when it came to belong to Moscardi, a nobleman of predominantly antiquarian interests.[14] In Rome, the Jesuit Father Athanasius Kirchner, a native of Germany, set up a remarkable collection which he bequeathed together with his laboratory to the Jesuit College. His writings ranged over optics, physics, physiology, fossils, music, languages, art, the *perpetuum mobile*, and the Kabbala. His museum was no less colorful.[15] The Milan physician and *virtuoso* Settala and his son established in their house a museum containing medals, cameos, philosophical instruments, articles of glass and metal, and chemical preparations.

Physicians were numerous among seventeenth- and eighteenth-century collectors. The Dane Olaf Worm combined natural history with archaeology and composed a museum catalogue which became a popular textbook[16] (Fig. 9). The learned Dutch physician Paludanus, a great traveler, in 1651 sold one of his collections to the German prince of Gottorf, and the *Gottorfsche Kunstkammer* became one of the sights of Europe[17] (Fig. 10). Another man of science, the mineralogist Agricola, preceded the two doctors by inspiring a prominent layman to form a private museum. Under the influence of Agricola's writings, the German Elector Augustus of Saxony built up a *Kunst und Naturalienkammer*. Doctor Valentini, court physician to the Duke of Hesse and professor of medicine and experimental sciences at Giessen, owned a repositorium of natural and artificial curiosities. Dr. Richard Mead's house in London was a museum of encyclopedic dimensions befitting his erudition; he had studied classical archaeology at Utrecht and botany at Leyden. The collection that was to become the nucleus of one of the great public museums of the world, the British Museum in London, belonged to Sir Hans Sloane (1666 – 1753), famous London physician, and president of the College of Physicians and of the Royal Society. On a trip to Jamaica he began to collect plants of interest to a medical man. By 1725 he had amassed thousands of specimens of natural history; by 1733 the collection numbered 69,352 items — books printed, handwritten, and illuminated, things related to the customs of ancient times, instruments, urns, pictures (only partly referring to natural history), mathematical instruments, vessels made of agates, jaspers, and crystal, cameos and seals, coins and medals.

In Holland the Anatomy Hall at Leyden developed into a museum where objects of archaeology and ethnology were added to anatomical specimens. The collection illustrated a newly awakening interest in distant countries. In antiquity such interest had dawned in Greece, and Herodotus had been followed by the geographers of Alexandria under the Ptolemies. Relations between West and East waned during the Middle Ages, and it was only in the Renaissance that Europe regained a clearer awareness of Asia. Portuguese navigators brought exotic objects from the Orient, which enjoyed popu-

Figure 8. The private museum of Ferrante Imperato (1550–1630) of Naples, an ardent
student of nature, founder of botanical gardens and of a famous collection; the study-
style presentation suits the needs of a scholar and of his visiting peers, who focus their
attention on single specimens that are of relevance to them. They require neither context
in display nor an interpretating guide. They exchange knowledge that they carry in their
minds and add to it in the course of the visit to the museum. Frontispiece of Imperato's
Dell' Historia Naturale, Libri XXVIII, Naples, 1599.

Figure 9. The newly reawakened spirit of curiosity knew no national boundaries. Frontispiece of the catalogue of Olaf Worm's collection, of 1655, which served as a textbook of
natural history. Worm was a Dane who entertained connections with the Netherlands.

Figure 10. The Kunstkammer of the princes of Gottorf. Frontispiece of the catalogue of
the collection, of 1674, by its keeper, Olearius.

larity in seventeenth-century England when Charles II married a Portuguese princess, Catherine of Braganza. As explorers set foot on American soil, European collectors began to interest themselves in articles produced by the natives of the far-off continent, and in its beasts and birds. In his *Reisebriefe* of June 6 and 7, 1521, the German painter Dürer referred to the Treasure of the Mexican emperor Montezuma he had seen in the cabinet of Margaret of Austria at her residence in Malines in the Netherlands. The great French essayist Montaigne had American Indian artifacts. The English Court sent John Tradescant, a supervisor of the royal gardens, to the Colonies in America to collect anything rare and curious. Tradescant's private collection, known as "The Ark of Lambeth," eventually became the Ashmolean Museum in Oxford, and a catalogue of 1656 presents the contents of the collection at that time.[18]

Eighteenth-century Holland was noted for its collections specializing in natural history, and often in a specific chapter of biology. The Amsterdam apothecary Albert Seba and George Clifford, the director of the Dutch East India Company, collected zoological specimens and obtained tropical butterflies and beetles from Dutch colonies abroad. Clifford's superintendent of his cabinet at De Hartenkamp near Haarlem was the young Swede Linnaeus, who sought and found better chances for his talents in Holland, where extensive commerce with countries overseas had created wealth. He published several works based on private cabinets and in this manner exercised influence on their systematic arrangement. Becoming classified, a natural history collection had no longer room for miscellaneous curios and objects of virtu. Since Linnaeus combined logic with a vivid presentation—as in discussing the "loves of plants" and the "spurious polygamy" of the daisies which accommodated the beds of the married in the disks of their flowers and the harlots in their circumference—botany attracted lay readers in sufficient numbers to make the publication of scientific books with colored illustrations a practical proposition[19] (Compare Fig. 11).

The establishment of collections revealed the same spirit of inquiry as the foundation of academies in the seventeenth century. At the opening of the Academy in Valladolid, one of the new centers of learning at a time of discontent with the contemporary universities, the Conde de Lemos, one of its main protagonists, declared: "The purpose of this Academy is to bring together men of different interests. . . . Laziness is a pestilence and the worst pestilence is ignorance. . . . In these meetings each of us shall be both a teacher and a student."[20]

Another somewhat later Academy, in St. Petersburg in Russia, was mainly devoted to science and became a cradle of scientific research. Czar Peter the Great (1672–1725) was a man of an inquisitive turn of mind and believed that the elevation of Russia to the status of a great power could only be accomplished by an increase in knowledge. He invited technicians and army experts from Central and Western Europe to train some of his subjects, and twice visited Europe; he studied anatomy in England, gunnery in Germany, and shipbuilding in the Netherlands. Ships and guns loomed large in his plans to obtain an ice-free port on the Baltic Sea by making war on mighty Sweden. The first paintings that aroused his interest were marine pieces. In the course of his first sojourn in the West, in 1697–1698, Peter the Great dined at the table of the anatomist Ruysch in Amsterdam and spent whole days in his Cabinet, which he later purchased for 30,000 florins (Fig. 12). Two other famous Dutch collections were sold to Peter: that of the naturalist Seba of the Dutch East India Company and Schynvoet's cabinet of coins. In 1728 the Imperial Russian *Kunstkammer* was transferred to the Academy of Sciences, where it was combined with a library and an observatory. Expeditions of the Academy, during the time of Peter the Great and later, brought home ethnological articles from Siberia, from Pacific Areas, and from North America. An important accession, in 1779, was the collection of the famous English navigator James Cook.[21]

Rational thinking by no means advanced in a straight line; superstitions continued to grip human minds; two prominent "museologists" of the eighteenth century made revealing statements. In the catalogue of the Gottorf Museum, its curator Olearius described the jaw of a whale which measured 62 feet in length and 17 feet in height, so that a tall man could stand within. The whale was credited with magic forces when a year after its appearance on the beach of Westerhafen, a peace treaty was signed between Germany and Sweden. In the catalogue to his own famous collection, Neickelius described a corpse of an Indian whose life spirits had been extinguished by the winds in the mountains of Chile. He held the view that all mummies resulted from conditions in the African desert and that human souls sought a new embodiment once in 7000 years and retired finally after an activity of 40,000 years. In 1727 Neickelius published a book entitled *Museographia* which may be the earliest essay dealing strictly with arrangements in museums[22] (Fig. 13). His philosophy of life was based on the maxim "idleness creates wickedness." He compared the human mind with a *perpet-*

Figure 11. The Dutch merchant Levin Vincent's Gazophylacium or Theatrum Naturae, which he displayed in various Dutch towns. From the description of the collections, in Latin and French, by R. de Hooge, Haarlem, 1719.

Figure 12. One of the cabinets of Fredrik Ruysch (1638–1731), professor of anatomy and botany in Amsterdam, who set up several cabinets and sold them for high prices to royalty. Frontispiece of Ruysch's *Opera Omnia*, Amsterdam, 1722–1737.

Figure 13. Eighteenth-century blueprint for a gentleman's "museum." From Neickelius'
Museographia, Leipzig, 1727.

uum mobile and recommended collecting as a preventive of laziness.

The extending intellectual horizons, encompassing a growing spirit of inquiry and a surviving shallow curiosity in the strange and the rare (and possibly endowed with magic forces) acquired palpable form in the exhibits presented in coffeehouses in London and in barbershops and whaling inns in the United States.[23] Don Saltero, the owner of a well-known coffeehouse in Chelsea in London, had a vivid imagination when it came to presenting and interpreting the specimens that adorned his locale. Interest in the bizarre persisted into the nineteenth century as could be seen from attendance figures at Mr. Bullock's famous Egyptian Hall on Piccadilly in London where hundreds of people in 1822 came to view a mermaid — the product of an ingenious Japanese craftsman who had manufactured her by combining the body of a fish with the head and shoulders of a monkey.[23]

The international spirit of seventeenth-century scholars encouraged learned men in England, including Robert Boyle, the famous chemist and physicist of Irish descent, to plan the establishment of a society for the promotion of knowledge in the colony of Connecticut. Charles II prevented the realization of the project by taking the scholars under his protection — no doubt in fear of both brain drain in England and of unrest stirred up by an increase in knowledge among the colonists. It was left to Benjamin Franklin to issue in 1743 a circular urging that a society be formed of *virtuosi* and ingenious men for promoting useful knowledge among the British plantations in America, which eventually became The American Philosophical Society in Philadelphia, with Franklin as its first president. Boston followed the example, with the establishment of the American Academy of Arts and Sciences, which to a large extent was instigated by John Adams. The encouragement he gave to the formation of scientific institutions may be better known than the enjoyment he derived from viewing in 1774 a collection of American birds and insects belonging to a Mr. Arnold at Norwalk in Connecticut, as well as collections in France, including the royal cabinet. In a memorandum written in 1809 he referred to these experiences and to his wish "that nature might be examined and studied in my country."[24] In a conversation John Adams conducted in 1779 with the Reverend Samuel Cooper of Boston, he made reference to the collection of Mr. Arnold, as well as to other cabinets. The proposal for a learned academy in Boston was discussed in the course of the same meeting.

Numerous individuals appear to have shared John Adams' interest in the sciences, judging by the crop of collections that sprang up one after another in America, some even before the achievement of political independence, and of visitors to such private museums, which were mostly of short duration. The economic circumstances of the country forced them to close down or to turn into commercial ventures which bore profit for a brief period and flickered out. An outstanding *curioso* of the period was the artist Charles Willson Peale, another early paleontologist, who with the cooperation of his sons, Rembrandt and Rubens, conducted experiments in chemistry and physics before audiences.[25] Of them more will be said in the context of early American museums.

An epitome of the questioning minds that began to reshape Western civilization in the seventeenth and eighteenth centuries was Thomas Jefferson. One could consider him a naturalist and an inventor who was handicapped by his political career, had he not been one of the leading intellectual patriots of the American Revolution — one of a complex breed of men.

His library of the classics was well known, and he had his share in inventing mechanical contrivances, from a plow for which he received a prize from France to a music stand. As an architect he was both humanist and engineer. Confirming the receipt of a letter from a friend, he wrote: "Your first letter gives me information in the line of natural history and the second promises political news; the first is my passion, the last is my duty, and therefore both desirable." There is in a single sentence the dialogue between social conscience and a yearning for unshackled freedom which characterized the period in which the political independence of the United States was shaped. There was a religious element in that morality, and it existed side by side with a fascination for extinct prehistoric animals, which contradicted the teaching of the Bible, according to which everything on earth was created together and forever. When Jefferson came to Philadelphia in 1797 to be inaugurated Vice President, he carried in his baggage a collection of fossilized animal bones and presented a paper on the topic before the American Philosophical Society.[26] At the time of the much criticized Embargo Act of 1808, introduced by President Jefferson to avoid an entanglement of the United States in the war between England and France, which inflicted economic losses on American citizens, three hundred fossil bones were spread out in a large room of the White House. Their arrival followed years of expectation with regard to the yield of Big

Bone Lick in Kentucky, where William Clark, of the Lewis and Clark expedition, had been exploring at the expense of Jefferson, a patron of modest financial means.[27]

In sending one third of this early paleontological collection to France, Jefferson was both scientist and patriot. He was providing "ocular" evidence of the physical equality of American animals with specimens of their kind in Europe and was rebutting a thesis promoted by the noted French zoologist Buffon and Abbé Raynal, according to which animal species occurring on both continents degenerated in America to a smaller size. Even members of the Caucasian race presumably deteriorated in body and mind when transferred across the Atlantic, supposedly owing to the cold and moist climate in America. When confronted first with a moose and with the horns of several animals, a caribou, an elk, and a deer, and later with the fossil bones, Buffon made comparative measurements and withdrew his accusation.[28]

Among the objects Jefferson collected were Indian artifacts which at one time were exhibited at his home at Monticello. When the purchase of Louisiana from France in 1803 became an added incentive to an exploration of the Northwest, Jefferson was not only instrumental in its organization, supported by a congressional appropriation of $2500, but gave detailed instructions as to matters to be studied and documented by the Lewis and Clark party, in the form of notes, maps, and specimens. They were to observe mineral deposits, plant and animal life of the hitherto undescribed area, as well as the tribal customs and activities of the natives.

The collections they brought home were the beginning of a large stock of specimens gathered in the course of several following expeditions made by explorers under the aegis of the government. The diversity of the objects may be gleaned from the following samples to which reference is made in different parts of the journals kept by the Lewis and Clark company. There were antelopes, male and female, stuffed and with complete skeletons — the horns of a mountain ram, or Bighorn, a pair of large elk horns, a variety of skins, such as those of the red fox, white hare, marten, and yellow bear, obtained from the Sioux — also a number of articles of Indian dress, among which was a buffalo robe representing a battle fought between the Sioux and Ricaras against the Mandans and Minnetarees, in which the combatants are represented on horseback — boxes of plants and of insects — and three cases containing a burrowing squirrel, a prairie hen, and four magpies, all alive.

Collections as Means of Emotional Experience

In a scene in the *Mimes*, by Herodas, two women, Kynno and Kok-kale, in ancient Greece come to the temple to sacrifice to Asklepios. After having deposited their votive table they conduct a conversation about the statues and paintings in the temple. Kokkale: ". . . why one would say the sculpture would talk . . . in time men will be able even to put life into stones . . . Only look, dear Kynno, what works are those there! . . . Look this naked boy, he will bleed, will he not, Kynno, if I scratch him . . . for the flesh seems to pulse warmly as it lies on him in the picture . . . have they not all of them the look of light and life?"[1]

The women felt exhilarated by the rhythm, the harmony, and the colors of the works of art, and their joy in being alive was enhanced by the vitality of images in stone and paint. To shake the earth from winter sleep the Greeks danced their emotion-charged, leaping dance, their "dithyramb," assumedly the origin of the drama, and from their own performance they drew encouragement and confidence in the continuity of life.[2] Static images may have equal dynamic powers as the dance, the more dramatic perhaps since experienced in a few brief moments. The lifting inchoate life-force may appear under the cloak of different symbols—of religion, of patriotism, of the drive for success in any enterprise, or of eros. Pausanias described the statue of Zeus in the Council House in Olympia as "of all the images of Zeus the best calculated to strike terror into wicked men."[3] Referring to Parrhasios' allegoric painting of the "demon Atheniensium"—of the People of Athens—Pliny wrote that he had displayed them as "fickle, choleric, unjust and variable, but also placable and merciful, compassionate, boastful, lofty and humble, fierce and timid—and all these at the same time."[4]

The statues representing women and children evacuated from Athens at the time of the pending Persian invasion recorded an episode in a great war and were a means of conveying information. Their role, however, was of larger scope than that of a bare statement of facts: the figures enshrined a variety of emotions and suggested ethical principles. Through its artistic form the information could grow into a message and widen to a legend. An image may arrest the attention of indifferent passersby, provoking thoughtfulness even in the less contemplative and stir the imagination of the dull. The representation of an episode may open up vistas into a panorama of history of which the particular incident was a part, and turn a distant event into a perennial human theme. What G. Scott wrote with regard to architecture may be said about painting and sculpture—that they convey refinement of meaning and awaken trains of association of which mere unassisted syntax is incapable.[5]

More recently the philosopher Susanne Langer advanced the hypothesis that in its elemental form mind is feeling rather than knowing. This may shock those among us who are steeped in a think-oriented tradition, but it gives high status to aesthetics; to a recognition of art as an essence of meanings which address themselves to us with a shortcut.[6]

Different individuals or members of different cultures and traditions may respond to works of art of specific contents or styles and remain impassive with regard to other themes or other compositions. The Italian sixteenth-century author Armenini extolled Titian, Corregio, Giulio Romano, and other Italian artists; he wrote that their stories of Christ and Mary were so full of life that they brought tears to the eyes of people who saw these pictures. His contemporary, the artist Francisco de Holanda, did not share his enthusiasm. He wrote in his "Dialogos de la Pintura":

> The Flemish manner of painting will satisfy almost every believer better than any Italian picture which will cause nobody to shed a single tear, whereas the Flemish ones make men weep. Paintings make sad people feel joy and let the contented discover the existence of misery, they make the obstinate feel guilty, the worldly penitent, the heathen fearful and ashamed of himself. Paintings give us the experience of the torments awaiting us in hell, and the glory and peace in store for the men of good deeds . . . they make us realize the modesty of the Saints and the constancy of the martyrs, they make us experience love . . . pity.[7]

The popularity of mythological scenes in the sixteenth and seventeenth centuries was connected with the satisfaction many patrons derived from an association with ancient Mediterranean culture. In addition, these themes offered an opportunity for depicting nudes of greater appeal than the skeletonlike forms introduced sometimes into the respectability of medieval religious histories. When Philip II beset Titian with orders for paintings illustrating Ovid's Fables, and decorated an entire room with a series of them (The Bathing Diana, Diana and the Swan, Adonis), he succumbed to a human weakness which on other occasions he tried to suppress or to hide behind rigid austerity.[8] Rudolph II was another royal erotic. Their contemporary Federigo Gonzaga of Mantua wrote in a letter of 1524 to an agent who conveyed his orders to the painter Sebastiano del Piombo: "I do not wish stories of Saints, but some pictures of more general character and beautiful to the eye."[9] The demand for pictures of nudes was confirmed by various writers. The author known as "The Anonimo," who seems to have been intimately familiar with

Italian sixteenth-century collections, noted that pictures of nudes decorated bedrooms, and a similar statement was made by Volkmann, the eighteenth-century German traveler and author. In his usual grave manner he described paintings in the Palazzo Borghese in Rome which were likely to encourage sensuous thoughts.[10]

Pictures challenging courage and bravery were recommended in 1600 by G. Gutierrez de los Rios. In his opinion the paintings and tapestries of the royal collection which represented scenes of war were to be used to inspire others to emulation and to striving for fame.[11] During the Napoleonic war a portrait of the ruling king Fernando VII was exhibited from the balcony of the town hall of Madrid and proved to be a successful appeal to men to join the army.

In the absence of pictorial mass media, the environment of people was limited to what their senses could reach and to what artists could show them of a larger world, of fact or fancy. In his *Museo Pictorico* (1715) the Spanish painter and author Palomino listed artists according to their subject matter, as painters of battle scenes, fruit, or portraits. The Bohemian engraver W. Hollar was internationally known as an illustrator of scenery, towns, types of men in different countries, and of the clothes they wore. Similarly, Vasari wrote in 1547 in a letter to a friend that German paintings enjoyed great popularity in Italy because they represented landscapes (while the Southern artists preferred portraying the human figure).[12] The French eighteenth-century collector Abbé de Marolles succeeded in accumulating 500 volumes of engravings, a truly encyclopedic body of "pleasurable information on all things imaginable."

In times lacking the device of photography, portraits by artists were in demand by people who could afford to pay the required fees. Portraits, mostly in the form of statues and busts or in relief were common in ancient Rome. Over the centuries princes saw the countenances of their potential brides first in portraits painted for the occasion. Emperor Charles V engaged two artists, one for portraits and another for "historias" of the Bible.[13] The portrait painter was a certain Rolan Mois, a "wonderful Flemish artist" ("*Flamenco maravilloso retratador*"), whose first task in Spain was to paint the images of sovereigns of the past. He had to draw his inspiration from existing pictures of poor quality, "dry and stiff," but the result was excellent and brought him many new and well-paid orders. Master Mois was succeeded in later years by the creator of the portrait of Charles V known as *Gloria*, in which Titian's subtle brush contrived to indicate something of the complexity and contrariety of the man Charles and of the contemporary affairs of Europe. There is the Imperator Triumphans, an embodiment of stability, who in the battle at Mühlberg in 1547 had defeated the Protestants menacing the established order of things, but there is also the shadow of resignation, a foreboding of tragedy. In reality Charles V seems to have soon comprehended that the Protestants vanquished in battle remained undefeated in spirit, and his abdication from the throne and retirement to the solitude of Yuste, in 1556, were contradictory to the ebullient activity of his former years. It must have required the second sight of a great artist to look behind the defenses in the mind of the sitter for the portrait, if indeed the robust Charles was at all conscious himself at that time of what may have occasionally clouded his horizon.

El Greco's picture *The Dream of Philip II*, which showed the king as a kneeling sinner at the gates of the Beyond, may not have satisfied the expectations of Philip himself, but it nevertheless enshrined a unique assortment of associations between the earthly and the heavenly spheres; it amalgamated features which might seem inconsistent on the plane of reason and if expressed by means of the articulate word: a description proceeds from one item to another, but a painting or sculpture presents numerous features simultaneously, and the impact carries a new meaning.

Royal personages were not the only patrons of portrait painters. When professional Corporations took over the place of authority in the Netherlands, held before by feudal families, group portraits of men began to appear in the latter part of the sixteenth century. The democratized version of power was depicted against a lavish background. The portraits advertised the status and wealth of the towns, which were centers of political and social forces, as well as of specific corporations, and no doubt added to their promotion.

In his *Mémoires* the Duc de Brienne gave an account of the sad moments in which Cardinal Mazarin took leave from his treasures shortly before his death, in 1661.[14] He was apparently thinking aloud being unaware of a witness. "I must leave all that," he said with great feeling, "And this too. . . . What effort it was to acquire these things. How could I abandon them without regret? . . . I shall not see them anymore where I am going." He refused to discuss affairs of the state when he noticed de Brienne's presence and pointed to some of his paintings. "Look at this fine picture of Correggio. . . at that Venus of Titian. . . at Carrachi's incomparable 'Deluge'. . . . Goodbye dear pictures that I have loved so much and which have cost me so much" (Fig. 14).

For many years Mazarin had been the power behind the throne of

Figure 14. Cardinal Mazarin in his gallery. Engraving by Nanteuil and Van Schuppen, seventeenth century. When the Cardinal felt in 1661 that his death was approaching, he lamented the separation from his art treasures, which were later acquired for the Louvre.

Louis XIV, and he may have craved power even at the cost of extreme loneliness. His relationship to his treasures of art provides a glimpse of the complexity of human nature.

"I would give away all my collections if I could achieve one good picture" was the thought that haunted a French collector of the nineteenth century, M. Dutuit of Rouen.[15] The wealthy independent man became the *rapin*, the servant-friend of the painter Couture, who had found Dutuit's artistic talent inadequate for a student in his studio.

M. Dutuit may have expressed the thoughts and feelings of numerous other art collectors throughout the ages who sought and seek substitutes for their inability to project their visions on canvas or to mold and hammer them in tangible materials: they crave the sight of works of art in their daily environment, they pour their energies into the establishment of art museums, and they are willing to pay prices within and beyond their means. An early American art collector, the businessman Robert Gilmor, Jr., confessed in his *Diary* that "the compulsion he felt to seek enjoyment in the contemplation of works of art might push him beyond the bounds of prudence." He wrote: "But as long as I can restrain it . . . I am convinced . . . (it) will prove one of the greatest sources of pleasure, amusement and relaxation from the serious concerns of life."[16]

In his *Confessions*, St. Augustine considered aesthetic consciousness antagonistic to the beauty of righteousness, and Thomas Aquinas in his *Summa Theologica* allowed little play to aesthetic emotions; their attitude received renewed emphasis among the people who constituted a strong section among the European emigrants who created the United States. In the late 1830s an English visitor to America reported having seen a plaster cast of the nude Apollo of Belvedere completely draped in cloth.[17] Visitors to the Columbianum, the American Academy of Painting, Sculpture, and Architecture, established in Philadelphia in 1795, had to divide into two groups to view the cast of the Venus of Medici; ladies were admitted separately from gentlemen. Yet in spite of this cautious measure, the Academy was of brief duration. For obvious reasons collections of natural history specimens and of mechanics had priority in the early decades of the republic. In 1780 John Adams wrote in a letter to his wife: "I must study politics and war, that my sons may have liberty to study mathematics and philosophy. My sons ought to study mathematics and philosophy, geography, natural history and naval architecture, navigation, commerce and agriculture, in order to give their children a right to study painting, poetry, music, archi-

tecture, statuary, tapestry, and porcelain."[18] The prognostication
proved correct.

The Presentation of Objects in Collections

Two main aspects characterize a collection: the selection of its
items and their combined presentation. The manner of presentation may shift the emphasis in the character of an exhibit to the
degree of metamorphosing an art collection into a hoard, or a collection of natural history specimens into a decorative environment.
Incongruities between objects and their presentation are among
the major problems besetting contemporary museums: We are almost at the gates to the third millennium A.D., but our exhibit halls
often still display legacies of our museological ancestry — of royal
courts, of cabinets of amateur scholars, of temple treasuries — and
sometimes combinations of several of them, which multiply incon-
sistencies and conflicts in appearance and in meaning.

However numerous, legacies can nevertheless be classified. As
any man-made grid that is to facilitate the perception of heterogeneous phenomena, the following grouping claims merely substantial evidence but no finality. The pattern I perceive rests on two
main categories which in this context are antipodes, and it contains
a number of subgroups. The two antipodal categories are collections representing monologues of collectors, and others which stand
for dialogues between someone who planned the arrangement of
the objects and those who view them, who are supposed to receive
an intended communication, and to react to it, overtly or in the silence of their minds, immediately or with some delay. In the case
of numerous viewers, the dialogue turns into a discussion, even
though the participants may appear at different times.

Presentations in the Form of Monologues: Collectors who used the
Storeroom-Style of Presentation as a rule conducted monologues
from a distance and not in direct confrontation with their collections. When a titled personage wished a few of his treasures brought
from their storage place to the living quarters for a period of time,
he issued an order which eventually percolated to the people who
performed the menial task. The efficient execution of the job depended on the visibility and accessibility of each item in storage.

An inventory of Emperor Charles V's collection in Spain stated that
five pictures, three portraits of the empress and two representing
the Last Judgment, were contained in a bag of mulberry-colored
silk, and that other pictures were kept in a similar silk bag, whereas
a black leather box lined with scarlet velvet housed four Bezoar
stones regarded as agents counteracting poison, a reliquary with a

fragment of Christ's cross, a silver scent-sprinkler, two gold arm-
bands and rings as a cure against hemorrhoids, and a blue stone as
a medicine against gout. In another casket were kept a crucifix, two
scourges for self-flagellation, a number of golden toothpicks and
spectacles, and some mathematical instruments.[1] It required little
knowledge to distinguish bags by their color, or bags and boxes by
their shape; in fact, those who moved the packages were hardly interested in viewing the contents for their own sake. Since most of
the collections kept in treasure chambers or *Guardaropas* consisted
of a multitude of objects, economy in the use of space mattered,
and a principle of order was helpful, whether based on the function
of the objects, the raw materials from which they were made, or
otherwise. Inventories of the Medici tell of the wealth of objects
accumulated by three generations of collectors; carpets were piled
up in cases, and precious vessels were packed under beds.[2]

   When the objects came to be viewed, each was seen in isolation
from the storeroom crowd of things and in a suitable context, which
added to the impression it made on a beholder who was well condi-
tioned to react to it: to feel reassured in his religious faith or in his
self-confidence that sprang from a consciousness of power and
wealth; to feel animated by the colors and rhythm of a work of art;
or to experience several such sensations combined.
   The Dutch artist Teniers portrayed the famous seventeenth-
century art collector Archduke Leopold Wilhelm of Hapsburg in the
storeroom of his paintings (Fig. 15). The picture shows the archduke
in the company of several other persons, in discussion with one of the
men, while the others stand around or near a table on which large
sheets of paper are spread, apparently sketches for paintings to be
added to the collection. In the style of presentation the manner of a
storeroom prevails, with paintings not only covering the walls without an inch of space between them but also deposited on the floor.
Indeed, it was a storeroom even if it served the additional purpose
as a meeting place of the collector with his artists who presented
sketches for evaluation. The indifferent manner of presentation
hardly prevented a flow of communication between the pictures
and their beholders. The owner, his courtiers, and artists who were
intimately familiar with each picture and were connoisseurs of art
in general had no trouble in focusing on a single painting, and they
benefited from the opportunity of a close comparison between several works of art. Each man conducted first of all a monologue and
shared it to some extent with others; what they saw was highly meaningful to them.[3] "There was little impedance to the flow of commun-

Figure 15. Archduke Leopold Wilhelm of Hapsburg in his gallery in Brussels. Painting by
D. Teniers, Jr. (By courtesy of the Kunsthistorisches Museum, Vienna.)

The presentation in the manner of a storeroom was a suitable setting for a connoisseur
of art and his equally well informed visitors — other collectors or artists presenting
sketches for commissions. Each of them could conduct a monologue in confrontation
with works of art that were relevant to them by their topics and their style. Yet if we adopt
features of this gallery for use in a public institution of our era, breakdowns in communication are bound to occur.

Figure 16. A private collector explores his works of art by touch as well as by sight. Andrea Odoni's portrait by Lorenzo Lotto was recorded as being in his home in 1532. It later came into the possession of the Netherlands, which gave the picture as a present to Charles II of England in 1653. It is now at Hampton Court in London. (By the courtesy of the Surveyor of the Queen's Pictures. Copyright reserved.)

The *Notes on Pictures of Art in Italy* by The Anonimo (Morelli) included a description of Odoni's sixteenth-century house and collection. The *Notes* were published in London in 1903, translated by P. Mussi, and edited by G. C. Williams.

ication between display and viewers, and among the viewers. The pictures represented topics familiar and important to them—portraits of . . . celebrities, scenes from the Bible, from history and mythology, with each painting contributing an informational detail or an emotional tone to the store of similar images in the viewers' minds. . . . The margin of possible misunderstandings was small and the experience was likely to strengthen the feeling of identity and of stability of each individual and of the group. It reinforced directives toward an established pattern of life."[4] Each of these viewers would carry on his monologue when facing one of the paintings in solitude and in his private, familiar environment, the artist in his studio and the collector in an apartment in his palace.

In the *Study-Style Presentation* of a private scholar's or connoisseur's collection, objects often stood in closed ranks on shelves, not unlike books in a library, but the familiarity of the beholder with all objects brought each item easily into the focus of his attention, the rest being shuttered off by his thoughts, which at this particular moment were concentrating on a single thing. The owner-collector could lift a specimen out of the mass and hold it in his hands to examine it closely, the tactile sensations enriching the message that reached the eye, and his few selected visitors often enjoyed the same privilege (Fig. 16).

Emperor Rudolph II's collection in his castle in Prague may have offered answers to some of the numerous questions that agitated his mind and stimulated further ones, but to an outside observer its overall appearance was that of a hoard. Four vaulted rooms contained natural and mechanical products, curios, jewels, and works of art. Large objects were placed on tables and small ones in the drawers and on the shelves of thirty-seven cupboards. Paintings decorated the walls of all the apartments of the royal residence and were placed in stacks on the floors leaning against the walls where no space was available to hang them.

To facilitate the finding of specific objects, the owners of miscellaneous collections used various manners of grouping, on the basis of raw materials, as Pliny had recommended for classification in his *Natural History,* or according to a common function. The Dane Ole Worm set out his specimens as "earths, salts, clays . . . stone objects . . . metal, glass, wood," irrespective of their being works of nature or of man, and so did the Italian Aldrovandi, who qualified whether the material was in its "natural" or in a "manufactured" state and who classified his *cose artifiziose* as tools, weapons, vases, and so on. The elector Augustus of Saxony, who founded the famous collection in the Green Vaults in Dresden, gave precedence to the function of objects and followed it up with a classification according to raw materials, a procedure which obviously led to repetition.[5] He presented in seven rooms mechanical tools, precious vessels, pictures and treasure chests, mathematical instruments, mirrors, objects of nature, pictures of stone and metal, and other materials. The specimens were set out on tables, valuable in themselves, on brackets, and on boards placed across mirrors. In his *Museographia* of 1727, a kind of blueprint for a scholarly collection, Neickelius recommended that six shelves should be placed along the walls and should contain on one side Naturalia and on the other Artificialia (Fig. 13). The Naturalia should begin with human anatomy — that is, skeletons and mummies — on the top shelf, and go on to quadrupeds, fishes, and minerals. Among the Artificialia, ancient and modern things should be separated, and both the meaning and the form of a specimen should be taken into account when placing them. At the narrow short end of the room opposite the entrance, and lit by three windows, the cabinet for coins should be placed. The space available over the shelves should accommodate portraits of famous men. While Neickelius wished to bring clarity into his arrangement, he nevertheless remained anxious to utilize all space available, as if the exhibition room had been a storage chamber.

Numerous collectors of the seventeenth century who ambitiously sought to make their cabinets small encyclopedias of knowledge followed the sequence of "man — animals — plants — rocks," with man and his works occupying the top shelves. The size of objects was sometimes decisive with regard to their location, such items as large skeletons and stuffed animals being kept out of the way by being fastened to the ceiling. Objects of art were allotted a modest place by many collectors of Artificialia, or works of man. They were named last, as in the catalogue of the Museo Calceolari, or were appreciated for their informative value, as by Cospi, who took interest in ancient art mainly as an illustration of mythology. Neickelius, too, seemed to value paintings and sculpture as means of picturing events or ideas, if not as decorative accessories to specimens of natural history and to curios. Individual collectors expressed their preferences by the sequence of their specimens. Cospi, for example, put instruments of mathematics before those of war, with musical instruments between them, whereas Father Kircher, a man of the church, put idols long before mathematics, without however adhering to any strict order whatever. He was as insatiable as a collector as he was as the author of the book *De Omnibus Rerum et de quibusdam aliis*.[6]

Some systems of classification were more sophisticated than others. Charles Townley, the great collector of Greek and Roman antiquities, explained in a memorandum that the "symbolical values" and "the mystic system of emanations" of ancient works were to be the guiding principles in their arrangement. Statues of the supreme triad Jupiter, Pluto, and Neptune, representing the powers of "generation," "preservation," and "destruction," were to be the central points of the presentation. In his book *Suggestions for Travelling Students*, of 1762, J. D. Koehler advised collectors to be "systematic" and to subdivide statues into "upright standing" and "seated" ones, into "nudes" and "clothed." In a critical essay on arrangements in seventeenth-century collections, the contemporary writer D. B. Major took issue with the presentation of incongruous objects according to their sizes. In the same period Scamozzi in his book on architecture described the manner in which Andrea Vendramin of Venice attempted to put some order into his art collections. He wrote: ". . . in two rooms there stood three rows of statues, reliefs, medals . . . and a hundred and forty large and small paintings of fine quality."[7] In the Galleria Palatina in Rome all pictures were put into uniform frames and were hung according to the rules of symmetry; a similar presentation could be found in other galleries of the *seicento*.

Sir Hans Sloane, whose private collection later became the nucleus of the British Museum in London, kept his hoard under strict control.[8] Most specimens were kept in cases and drawers and put on view temporarily only, when required for study and inspection. A visitor would be shown a set of objects at a time. (See the description of a visit in 1748, Appendix p. 248.) In contrast, Herr von Reider of Bamberg enjoyed the hoard in his private residence even when the mounting number of outstanding articles of German arts and crafts came to cover his own bedstead, from which they had to be removed every day at bedtime. The collection was later incorporated in the Bavarian National Museum in Munich.[9]

In his *Museographia*, Neickelius combined objects and books in a one-room collection. In the imperial residence of the Hapsburgs in Vienna emphasis was laid on the library, with objects as additional founts of information (Fig. 17). The memory of Philip II's installation in the Golden Tower of the royal residence in Madrid has been preserved in Gil Gonzalez Davila's *Teatro de las Grandezas de Madrid* and in the accounts of other writers. A fire in the eighteenth century

Figure 17. Another combination of library and museum (compare Figure 13). Emperor
Leopold I (1640 – 1705) visits the imperial library and chamber of rarities in Vienna.
Engraving from the German translation of E. Brown's *Travels*, Nuremberg, 1711. (By
courtesy of the Kunsthistorisches Museum, Vienna.)

destroyed the grandiose arrangement, in which the architecture both articulated the purpose of each part and orchestrated all parts into an organic whole. A semicircular room on the ground floor was lined with cupboards for architectural sketches and copperplate engravings illustrating the excavated remains of classical Rome. Here the King saw his artists, whose studios were in the old treasure chamber of the palace and were connected with the tower by a special corridor. Above this room was the library with books in Spanish, Italian, and French on painting, architecture, archaeology, geography, and astronomy. On the top floor was the gallery containing a series of Titian's pictures illustrating Ovid's *Metamorphoses.* Another room was reserved for Bosch's paintings. The juxtaposition of Titian and Bosch, masters representing the different tempers of the South and the North, was apt to reveal more of each; pictures in the process of being painted could be compared with contemporary and ancient work; there was a cross-fertilization between visual messages and knowledge gained from books; and there was the process of continuous contact between patron and artists.

The gallery in the Golden Tower contained only a small part of Philip's art treasures. Many were stored in the *Guardajoyas*, the Treasure Chamber of the palace, together with jewelry and vessels valued for their precious metal, and were for periods of time transferred to the royal living quarters. In numerous instances a "gallery" was the favored term used for the elongated hall in which a collector kept his works of art, which were to be lit from above and indirectly. Rembrandt, whose passion for collecting ended in bankruptcy, combined in himself patron and artist.[10] Some of the things in his *Kunstkammer* and the adjoining rooms appeared in his paintings — musical instruments, weapons and armor. For all their differences, the Spanish monarch and the Dutch artist had something in common as collectors: completed works of art in their cabinets retained intimacy with the creation of art, even though Philip experienced the latter only secondhand.

It was the relationship between an individual, the owner, and his collections that mattered primarily in all quoted instances. He selected the objects, he chose the manner of their presentation, and he was their main explorer. The few visitors who were admitted came as invited guests and as a rule possessed a good deal of knowledge about the objects they came to view, or about similar ones. Misinterpretations or breakdowns in communication were not likely to occur, and where a void existed, it would narrow down or disappear in a dialogue between host and visitor, to the benefit of both people involved, or in a discussion among a few consonant minds.

In 1681 the royal French collection of paintings was transferred from Fontainebleau to the Louvre and *Le Mercure Galant* reported:

On Friday, 5th December, His Majesty came to Paris to visit his cabinet of paintings. Some of the rooms are more than fifty feet long. Those with the highest ceilings are adorned till the space above the cornices and the shutters are on both sides covered (with pictures). In eleven rooms there are sixteen Raphaels, ten Leonardos, twenty-three Titians. . . . The most precious ones are enshrined in painted cases and one may say that one painting covers another. . . .

To an observer using hindsight the notice contains forebodings of unfortunate developments. On this occasion Louis XIV did not appear as a sensitive connoisseur but as the boastful possessor of treasures, and as a political figure who may have traded a gesture of deference to a demand of a court clique for the pictures to be kept in Paris in return for their cooperation in other matters. If he knew the desire for a monologue with a work of art under more favorable conditions, he could hardly achieve a rapport when confronted with a phantasmagoria of lines, shapes, and colors, and with stacks of goods rather than with message and meaning. Should members of the monarch's company have felt affinity to a work of art, they could not hope to find an interpreter or a passionate peer in their host. The visit was a matter of protocol, with etiquette stifling inspiration.

The mercantilist spirit of the period, represented in France by Colbert, the minister of finance, had its day: works of art were regarded as capital investment. They also served as domestic propaganda which would enhance the power of the royal court. Louis XIV's Cabinet of 1681 was neither a storeroom nor a display gallery; it was a hybrid of the two, and was barren as a means of either communication or communion.

Presentations in the Form of Dialogues and Discussions: These displays were set up to convey messages to individuals and to groups of people who had no influence on the selection of objects and on the planning of exhibits.

At the Olympic Festivals in ancient Greece games were the central events, but collections presented in this *Environmental Setting* grew in power to instill people with lofty thoughts and to arouse their feelings. Excellence of body and mind was cast in the form of outdoor statues of athletes and rhetors. The reliefs on the gables of the Temple of Zeus illustrated the struggle between men and centaurs, in which the humans subdued the unsightly, violent creatures with the features of men and the hoofs of beasts: a symbol of human progress and of the eternal contention between the forces of light and darkness in man. Entering the temple visitors faced the statue of King Iphitos of Elis being crowned with laurels by the Goddess of Peace, another memorial of progress from violence to reasoning argument. Works of art were important releasers of catharsis during the events at Olympia, spaced by four years of waiting and offering opportunities for relief from human frailty and for a renewed apperception of positive aspects of life.

Here they used of old to meet and talk over both mythological and more serious subjects, wrote Pausanias in describing a "place for talk" (lesche) in Delphi, with mural paintings by Polygnotus forming the background — pictures of Greeks setting sail for Ilium and the capture of the town, and other great events of the past. Outdoor statuary and paintings on the outside walls of buildings existed in many Greek cities; they contributed to the widening of the horizons of citizens beyond their immediate community and to perceiving the brevity of an individual lifetime. The statues and paintings of philosophers, statesmen, and heroes provided a company far more illustrious than that of immediate associates of flesh and blood. The dominant figures set up high standards and held up ethical principles and their themes were carried on in a more dramatic and fanciful pitch by figures of the celestial hierarchy, of gods and goddesses.

A different mood was called up by the collection of statues in an enclosure, about four furlongs in length and width, next to the sanctuary of Zeus in Athens. It was crowded with portrait statues all representing Emperor Hadrian, who had dedicated the temple. Almost every Greek city had set up a statue, and the two biggest, made of ivory and gold, had been donated by Athens.[11] Obviously, the cities had vied with each other in the donations, and Athens had secured the privilege of having presented the two biggest and most precious statues. In this case size was a legitimate principle in ordering the presentation. It kept citizens of the different city-states aware of their position; it fostered fear of Athens, but at the same time proclaimed unity.

The public baths which served as social clubs in Rome offered collections of statuary as well as recitals and books. The famous Laocoön group was excavated in the Baths of Titus.

The identification of viewers with works of art closely connected with their historical past and their ideology endowed each statue or

picture with the role of a significant messenger, and the comprehension of familiar contents may have led to an appreciation of
purely visual qualities of art against a dimming background of story-
telling.

In the later seventeenth century, if not before, the number of visitors to private collections in Europe appears to have risen, and se-
lectivity with regard to admission seems to have lost severity. The
consequences were somehow unexpected: the situation proved to
be a disappointment to many owners of collections and probably to
much more numerous visitors. The collectors felt that they received
ingratitude in return for their favors, and many visitors were frus-
trated and angered. They had endured humiliating interrogations to
obtain admission to a place described to them as a land of wonders,
and they discovered that they were aliens in it. Some people found
an outlet in inappropriate and rambunctious behavior. Without
clues to the many strange things around them either in their own
minds or in such explanations as were offered in private cabinets
and galleries, people would rush around from one thing to another
and hunt for meaning. They lacked in most cases not only a background of specific knowledge into which the new experiences could
be fitted but all general education of a literate kind.

D. B. Major, one of the few known early writers about display, was
anxious to remedy the situation. He wrote: ". . . at the entrance of
the collection the visitor's eye should be caught by a few conspicuous specimens, such as a crocodile, a stuffed bear, tiger or lion, a
dried whale, or some other objects that would impress people by
their 'splendor,' 'venerable character' or 'ferocious looks.' "[12]

Even an informed man like the German eighteenth-century traveler
Volkmann described in ill humor the Palazzo Giustianini in Rome.
He referred to it as a place where statues are accumulated indis-
criminately and rather in the manner of herring tightly packed. He
overlooked the fact that the presentation had not been planned for
him or other outsiders and that the statues would remain incom-
municado to anybody who did not arrive with a suitable *milieu intér
ieur* in his mind.

A perfect environmental setting for the presentation of a variety of
works of art was, and is, a church, in which architecture combines
with statuary and pictures, in paint or made of stained glass, with
goldsmith work and vestments worn by the clergy. Organ music and
incense add to the visual experience. The distribution of light, from
its flow over the altar to an overall dimness, shelters both clergy and

parishioners from the fracas outside the building and veils some of the pedestrian concerns within them; they are alerted to the reception of a message.

The Performance as a Framework or Background of Presentation.
When the attenders of the church service stand up to participate in the singing of hymns, or when they make responses to words spoken by priests at the altar, the setting changes from a static environment to a dynamic performance. Yet it remains in a low key inside the church if compared with the behavior of people who occasionally viewed in the streets displays of objects from church treasuries. At medieval church festivals objects of art and curios were taken out and were solemnly shown to people gathering outside, apparently in crowds.[13] Paintings and statues in the medieval Church formed the background of plays staged at Christmas and Easter in celebration of the Lord's birth and resurrection. Descriptions have been preserved which amount to brief catalogues. These presentations of church treasures were known as *Heiligtümer* ("sacred things") and as a rule took place once in seven years. There were relics of saints and martyrs, partly enshrined in statues and busts and partly in coffins, garments of former kings, goldsmith work, and curios of great variety. The specimens were presented in relays (in *Gängen*). The appeal of these exhibitions to spectators must have been considerable, judging by the admonitions requesting visitors to behave in a restrained manner, lest those who pushed their way too near the exhibits might find themselves ejected.

Objects of art, statues, and paintings were closely related to a festival held once in four years in honor of the Goddess Athene in the temple of the Parthenon. Magistrates, musicians, and sacrificial animals joined in the procession, and a deputation of the women of Athens carried a garment they had woven for the Goddess, who symbolized the divine qualities of the people of Athens — beauty and decency, discipline and liberty. Reliefs on the frieze around the temple commemorated the procession and kept its memory alive during the years between the festivals.

Some of the Popes staged feasts in the attractive environment of the Belvedere in the Vatican, where one of the courtyards housed beautiful ancient statues. On a much smaller scale but not less characteristic was the arrangement in some sixteenth-century collections in Northern Italy, where the room containing musical instruments would at times be turned into a concert room and the room in which armor was kept would occasionally serve as a fencing ground.[14]

Paintings in a newly opened gallery at the Louvre added glamour
to the wedding procession of Napoleon Bonaparte.

On some occasions works of art played an even more active role in
a performance. There were the ancestral masks worn by mourners
in the funeral processions of distinguished men in ancient Rome;
the statues representing mythological figures in the processions
staged by the Hellenistic rulers and in the displays at royal courts in
the seventeenth century; and the statues that were, and still are,
carried in the processions of the Roman Catholic Church.

Spain appears to have been an especially fertile ground for this
type of presentation. When Charles I, as Prince of Wales, visited
Spain in the spring of 1623, sculpture groups carried in processions
formed part of the festivals staged in the guest's honor, together
with theatrical plays, bullfights and *Autos Sacramentales* ("tragedies upon sacred subjects").[15] It began with a procession through
the streets which stopped at certain places where the *Autos* were
staged on movable cars. By the emotional tension of their facial
expression and their gestures, the statues could attain extraordinary dramatic effect. Their coloring and the realism of their garments, which often were of cloth, enhanced the immediacy of their
presence, and the play of light and sun, as well as the motion of
marching, intensified the impression. Collections of such statues
were stored in the repositories of churches and monasteries, await-
ing the day when they would be required to play their part.

Different in their content, yet in their dramatic character similar to
the religious statues, were the allegorical figures in contemporary
performances staged at all courts of Europe and much favored in
Spain. A festival at the royal palace of Madrid in June 1606 illustrates the synchronization of statuary and live actors on such occasions. A "Temple of Good Fortune" (Templo de Felicidad), made of
imitation porphyry and alabaster, enshrined a figure of "Fama" with
all the pertinent trophies, and four young ladies in waiting (*meni-
nas*) personified the virtues of the ruling King Philip IV, his justice,
generosity, constancy, and prudence. There was a dance of "Roman
Heroes," a miniature triumphal car in which the five-year-old Infanta Anna sat in the midst of fruits from the American Indies and
feathers from Africa, and at dinner dishes were served in the shape
of fortresses, ships, animals, and birds. Paintings by the contemporary artist Carducho and Flemish wall hangings formed the decorative background of the proceedings.[16]

In France living "tableaux" were staged in Cardinal Mazarin's
famous gallery. The participating ladies of the court represented

figures in the Cardinal's mythological paintings, such as the *Parnassus* or *The Judgment of Paris*, and wore their costumes. Works of art and people enacted the same imaginative experience.[17]

Performances serving as frameworks of exhibits were planned and viewed by numerous people, and often by an anonymous general public. Under all circumstances the drama of the performance seems to have captivated the beholders.

It is the privilege of an owner to admit others to the sight of his treasures or to exclude them. Intellectual peers and congenial connoisseurs may receive preferential treatment; their comments can enrich the meaning of a specimen or awaken the awareness of a hitherto ignored detail of contents or form. Naïve persons impressed with an unaccustomed environment of glamour or oddity may spread rumors of unprecedented riches or feel confused and disappointed. In all cases the viewing of a collection is a favor that at any time can be curtailed or revoked.

In his efforts at reform of domestic policy Julius Caesar condemned hoarding by private individuals and himself set an example by dedicating his own collections to temples. His Dactylotheca, containing six collections of engraved stones, was consecrated to the temple of Venus Genetrix. Upon Caesar's death, however, the objects distributed by him among the public institutions were again seized by private collectors. "*Spectari monumenta sua voluit*" was the reputation enjoyed by Asinius Pollio, who, in contrast to other collectors of ancient Rome, wished his treasures to be appreciated by many people and not to be reserved for his own benefit. Another public-spirited collector of the Augustan era was General Agrippa, who threw his collections open to the public and appealed to other collectors not to hide their treasures in the exile of their villas, on the ground that the best of art should belong to the community, to the state, to everybody who could and wanted to enjoy it.[1] His words remained unheeded, and the collectors of Rome continued to regard the enjoyment of works of art and curios in their possession as their individual privilege.[2]

The Medici of Florence not only admitted visitors to their museum in the sixteenth century, if not before, but required of their servants a civil treatment of those who came. Lorenzo the Magnificent acknowledged that enjoyment of art sprang from a general human desire of an experience of excellence.[3]

An appeal to collectors to make their treasures accessible to visitors so that people would benefit from acquaintance with rare and beautiful specimens without incurring the dangers of travel into distant lands was made by A. Olearius in his catalogue of the collection of the Duke of Schleswig-Holstein and Gottorf, in 1674. The suggestion seems to have met with little approval, judging by the limited access to collections in the seventeenth and eighteenth centuries. The famous Dutch anatomist Frederik Ruysch was known to admit to his collection royal personages, princes, ambassadors, and generals,[4] and Mr. Townley in London opened the doors of his Roman

Villa in Park Street, Westminster, to "men of taste," to whom he personally acted as guide. The Tradescant Museum in South Lambeth in London, regarded as the most extensive European collection about the middle of the seventeenth century, was referred to in Thomas Flatman's contemporary *Poems and Songs*, in which he wrote the verse, "Thus John Tradeskin starves our greedy eyes – By boxing up his new found rarities." (Fig. 18.)

A notice which appeared in English newspapers September 17, 1773, and was signed by the noted collector Sir Ashton Lever, ran as follows:

This is to inform the Publick that being tired out with the insolence of the common People, who I have hitherto indulged with a sight of my museum (at Alkrington), I am now come to the resolution of refusing admittance to the lower class except they come provided with a ticket from some Gentleman or Lady of my acquaintance. And I hereby authorize every friend of mine to give a ticket to any orderly Man to bring in eleven Persons, besides himself whose behavior he must be answerable for, according to the directions he will receive before they are admitted. They will not be admitted during the time of Gentlemen and Ladies being in the Museum. If it happens to be inconvenient when they bring their ticket, they must submit to go back and come some other day, admittance in the morning *only* from eight o'clock till twelve.[5]

Considering the lack of formal education among the great masses in eighteenth-century England, their poverty, and the popularity of rough pastimes so strikingly illustrated by Hogarth, it is remarkable that people in great numbers wished to be admitted to a collection of stuffed birds, shells, fossils, and like things, and that many were prepared to pay an admission fee. Even a woman of more refined tastes, Susan Burney, remarked in writing to her sister, Madame d'Arblay, that she could hardly remember a dozen of names of the thousand she had heard while visiting Sir Ashton's collection. Ordinary mortals are not likely to have been favored by an interpretive service; on such occasions guides were guards first of all.

The desire of collectors to add to their treasures unlocked the doors of numerous private cabinets to artists. Lorenzo de' Medici provided a training ground for budding artists in his outdoor collection of ancient marbles.[6] Returning from a trip to Italy, Charles Lennox, later Duke of Richmond, in 1758 opened his house in London as a gratuitous school of drawing for impecunious students; they were offered opportunities for a close study of paintings, ancient sculpture, and casts.[7]

The great masses, both in ancient Greece and Rome, had access only to exhibits available in the temples and in the streets of their towns.[8] The situation remained unaltered in the Middle Ages and

Figure 18. An example of Fredrik Ruysch's anatomical preparations. From his *Thesaurus Animalium*, Amsterdam, 1735.

during the following centuries when, except for the few who owned private collections, people had no opportunity of seeing works of art and curios save in churches, where stress was inevitably laid on religious experience and respectful awe for the strange and rare rather than on unprejudiced observation. A similar mood obtained on the occasion of outdoor exhibitions of art in the course of religious festivals, with the emphasis shifting in later years to the display of paintings for discriminating art patrons and prospective buyers. Such shows for commercial purposes were held in front of San Marco in Venice and in the Colonnades in Rome.

When the English diarist John Evelyn wrote of the Ashmolean Museum in Oxford, opened in 1683, as "the first public institution for the reception of rarities in art or nature established in England," his semantics were of his era but not of ours. At its inception the Ashmolean Museum was governed by the interests of a small exclusive group of scholars of a private university. It was a research facility of the School of Natural Philosophy and was connected with the chemical laboratory housed on the floor below. Mr. Ashmole, the Tradescants' heir, had donated the Ark of Lambeth to the University, and the first people to view it in Oxford were the doctors and masters of the learned institution, who were preceded by the Duke of York.[9] When the public was admitted each person had to pay an admission fee in accordance with the time spent in viewing the exhibits.

When the first collections were established in America, the European distinction between "private" and "public" lost much of its definitiveness. In the early years of the republic, citizens were given access to collections owned by private individuals or by groups of people united by a common interest; the owners intended it to be so. A prosperous citizen could be motivated by the desire to share knowledge and enjoyment with his fellowmen, as an end in itself or in the expectation that a diffusion of information would further the prospects of the developing community. Some may have considered an admission fee to be a legitimate contribution to the maintenance of a shared facility, while to others the income may have represented the ultimate purpose; more often than not selfish and unselfish motives mingled, one leading to the other, and in either direction. P. T. Barnum, the notorious showman in the museum enterprise, who added to his success by exhibiting "educated dogs" and "industrious fleas," toward the end of his career endeavored to persuade the federal government of the advantages of a large public museum that would have been of no personal benefit to him.

The idealistic component should not be underestimated in an environment in which awareness of fundamental human equality was maturing at an accelerated pace. Enthusiasms were buoyed up after the freshly won independence from an oppressive regime, and the realization of human rights was moving beyond all precedent in human history.[10] Furthermore, knowledge was thought of not only as a means to material improvement but as a necessity in the process of molding the minds of citizens who were to be fitted for self-government, a condition for continued liberty. Jefferson considered it the fate of America to prove to what degree a society may venture to entrust its members with self-government.

When the apothecary John Speakman, the dentist Jacob Gilliams, and their friends began to meet in private homes and cake shops in Philadelphia, they wished to improve the condition of mankind by seeking knowledge themselves. The informal discussions of persons of limited knowledge eventually led in 1812 to the establishment of the Academy of Natural Sciences in Philadelphia. Sixteen years later the collections on the premises of the Academy were opened "for the gratuitous admission of visitors who were not members," in other words, to the public.[11] When the New York merchant Luman Reed in 1830 turned the top floor of his residence in Greenwich into a gallery of paintings he had acquired in Europe and admitted the public, he wrote in the catalogue of his collection: ". . . a picture gallery in a town is a source of refinement; nay, even more, a stronghold of virtue."[12]

An early example of a fruitful cooperation between public agency and private enterprise in America was the accommodation in 1802 of Charles Willson Peale's private collection of art, curios, and natural history in the Hall of Independence in Philadelphia. Peale was of course an accredited Patriot and owned one of the five scientific institutions in existence at the time when "Washington became President."[13] Yet even before him, in 1790, the Society of St. Tammany had obtained exhibit space in the City Hall of New York, where Indian relics and a small menagerie could be viewed gratuitously by members, and by others for an admission fee of 25 cents. The tradition continued when in 1810 John Scudder, allegedly an organ-grinder whose wanderings led to collecting, established his American Museum in the Alms House in the park of City Hall. Because it was considered an educational institution, Scudder was exempt from paying rent, and the proposal of the showman Barnum to collect materials for a national museum with the aid of governmental representatives abroad received favorable acceptance by President Andrew Jackson.[14]

It is significant that Charles Willson Peale, the founder of the first large collection in America, which enjoyed semiofficial status, in 1800 wrote in a letter to William Finlay:

In the first place I declare that it is only the arrangement and management of a Repository of subjects of Natural History, &., that can constitute its utility. For if it should be immensely rich in the number and value of articles, unless they are systematically arranged and the proper modes of seeing and using them attended to, the advantage of such a store will be of little account to the public.[15]

He was far ahead of his time when he painted backgrounds to exhibits of beasts and birds, forerunners of later habitat groups, and by the simulated general setting helped an uninformed public to grasp the meaning of exhibits. He showed insects under microscopes, and substituted sculpture for perishable hair stuffing as a basis for animal skins.

Peale's early realization that the physical admission of people to the view of exhibits does not necessarily mean an admission of their minds expressed his profound concern with the diffusion of knowledge. To this day his message awaits full realization, even though efforts in the United States have been both more numerous and more successful than in Europe.

Between the later eighteenth and the early nineteenth century a new public insitution came into being — the Museum — which both reflected and fostered changing ways of life. The ongoing process of large-scale industrial production of goods required an upgrading of the scholastic skills and general education of workers to substitute for those of small farmers and craftsmen whose competence had not necessarily required literacy and whose awareness was limited to their immediate environment. New expectations were awakened in the urban wage earners whose embitterment over new kinds of deprivation was sharpened by their exposure to a greater variety of available goods and to a mixed crowd of people.

The transformation of private collections into public museums, and the establishment of new museums, were symptoms of the acceptance by society of expanding human rights. Spokesmen arose among those holding power and among the unprivileged; ideas were articulated which represented what is known as the "Spirit of Enlightenment." The process of its development was very gradual, with numerous brakes applied to it, but it was palpable, and it quickened with the passing of years.

With regard to early public museums, three different areas are distinguishable: *Continental Europe, Great Britain,* and the *United States.* Each of these three main areas offered different preconditions for the new public institution.

Continental Europe

The French Revolution not only led to the first public museums in France but accelerated events in other Continental countries. In general terms, the public museum on the Continent was established under duress; under the immediate threat or in fear of a violent eruption of discontent of populations. One might call it a palliative, since the discontented did not demand access to collections but higher wages and greater justice in matters of taxes.

The opening of museums to the masses was a symbolic act representing a confirmation of their claim to participation in life's offerings. In the majority of cases a private royal collection was opened to the public, with restrictions that varied from one country to another; in the course of decades it became administratively transformed into a public institution.

France. The nucleus of the Louvre museum in Paris was Francis I's collection assembled in his Palace at Fontainebleau, known to the great public only from accounts and rumors about the "Merveilles de Fontainebleau."[1] Work on the Louvre palace had been gradually carried on since Francis I began to replace a gloomy medieval structure. Minister Colbert wished to direct his king's attention from the pleasure house at Versailles to a mansion that would add to royal glory; he believed that posterity would consider fine buildings as an expression of a prince's greatness, second only to victories in battle. The great enlargement of the royal collection and its transfer to the Louvre under Louis XIV were also due to the influence of the minister, who wished to contribute to the training of contemporary artists by providing them with an opportunity of studying good pictures, and thus to further the interest of the country. True to the spirit of mercantilism, M. Colbert regarded a country's independence from foreign import as the most favorable economic solution, and it appears that as a staunch rationalist he ranked works of art among other goods.[2]

Under Colbert's guidance the royal French collection grew considerably. The sale of the royal English collection after Charles I's decapitation in 1649 provided a unique opportunity for purchases. The French Crown acquired a number of works from London and others later as a part of the collection of the French banker Jabach. On his return to Paris from London, where he had figured among the galaxy of European connoisseurs, Jabach found himself in financial difficulties which forced him to part with several of his newly acquired paintings, with some Correggios among others, which originally had belonged to the Dukes of Mantua. The minister and the banker were old friends, but where business was concerned, M. Colbert did not allow sentiment to deflect his judgment. He proposed the purchase of a certain part of the collection only — the paintings and drawings — refused to consider the engraved stones, the jewels, busts, and many other valuables, and suddenly postponed all discussion of the deal. In a letter to the minister written on March 10, 1671, Jabach cried: ". . . *je Vous conjure du fond du coeur!*" As creditors became increasinly pressing, 108 paintings and 5542 drawings were sent to the Louvre, in return for a comparatively small sum of money. At the end of his reign Louis XIV possessed 1478 pictures by old masters of the French, Italian, German, and Flemish schools, thousands of drawings, and a fine collection of ancient Greek marbles and bronzes brought home by the ambassador in Constantinople, the Marquis de Nointel. The collections of Cardinal Mazarin and of the Abbé de Marolles were presented as gifts to the King.

It was not, however, the mere increase in the number of objects that characterized this period of the Louvre; the collections began to form the background of intellectual and artistic activities. In

1692 L'Académie de Peinture et de Sculpture was installed in the palace, and it was decided that the Salon de Séances should be used for an annual exhibition of paintings and sculpture. Occasional exhibitions were held first in the Salon and later in the Grande Galerie of the Louvre. Toward the end of Louis XIV's reign a change of policy occurred: the royal collections were moved to the King's private quarters at Versailles. The transfer was regarded both as a deprivation for the French people and as a potential danger to the pictures. The demand for their return was not dampened by the passing of several years and was voiced in a pamphlet written by an anonymous author, Lafont de St.-Yenne, and entitled *L'Ombre du Grand Colbert*.[3]

In 1750 Louis XV decided to return 110 pictures to Paris, this time to the Palais Luxembourg. Since the early seventeenth century, artists had been admitted for study at Fontainebleau; now the Palais Luxembourg was opened to the public on two days of the week, the other days being reserved for artists. The concession to the public is said to have been instigated by Madame de Pompadour, Louis XV's mistress, but it was of short duration. Her enemies at the court did not wish her to gain in popularity and argued that royal collections were to be reserved for the pleasure of the King and the nobility.[4]

Thirty-five years later the paintings were once again dispatched to the King's residence at the Louvre and Count d'Angiviller, director general of buildings, planned to collect the finest pictures and statuary and exhibit them in the Grande Galerie. In the ninth volume of the *Encyclopédie*, Diderot had described a museum at the Louvre that would resemble the *Mouseion* of Alexander the Great — a temple of the arts and sciences in which collections would be combined with communities of scholars. Yet even d'Angiviller's more modest plans were shelved. Private views were unwelcome to the authoritarian regime.

Following upon the Revolution of 1798, the Republican government decided to revise d'Angiviller's plans for the Museum in the Louvre, which was opened in 1793. The public was admitted on certain days of each "decade" — ten days being the republican unit replacing the week. In addition to the paintings collected by French royalty and brought to France by Catherine de' Medici and other royal brides, it contained works of art confiscated from churches during the Revolution.[5]

A commission known as Conservatoire du Muséum National was put in charge of the arrangement of the Louvre as a public museum. Paintings were exhibited in the Grand Salon from 1796 till 1798, and in 1799 the Grande Galerie was reopened to the public, though the plans of reconstruction were upset by an ever increasing influx of new specimens, the trophies of Napoleon Bonaparte's victories throughout Europe. Whenever the Grande Armee invaded another country, the Louvre had to prepare for another exhibition hall to be opened. On the anniversary of the battle of Jena in 1807, the Rotonde d'Apollon was formally opened, and a guide book was published entitled *Trophées d'Art conquis par la Grande Armée dans les Campagnes de 1806–7.* The effort to bring some order into the arrangement deserves appreciation. Paintings were separated from sculpture, and both were arranged according to the nationality of the artists and alphabetically. (Figs. 19 a, b, c, d).

The Musée Napoléon in the Louvre was one of the problems with which the Congress of Vienna in 1815 had to deal when the affairs of Europe, so gravely unsettled by Napoleon's rise and fall, had to be reordered. The grandiose museum ceased to exist; a considerable quantity of objects which had been carried away by the Bonapartists from other countries were restored to their previous owners, where their origin was ascertainable.

After a brief period of inconspicuous existence collections in the Louvre began to grow once again. In 1827 Louis Philippe's collection of hundreds of Spanish paintings was made accessible. The revolution of 1848 caused the museum in the Louvre to be struck from the royal civil list and to become national property.

Austria. The first public museum, again a legacy of imperial collectors, illustrated the international character of the Hapsburg Empire, whose banners at some time flew over German, Slav, Hungarian, Italian, Spanish, and Flemish territory. The works of art and curios amassed by Hapsburg princes in Vienna, Prague, Innsbruck, and Antwerp, and drawn from a wealth of talent in the Italian, Dutch, and Spanish domains, were united in the seventeenth century in Vienna by Emperor Ferdinand II. There were, in addition to more recent acquisitions, remains of the once famous Chamber of Treasures of the princes of Burgundy, with whom the Hapsburgs were related by marriage; it consisted of goldsmith work of the highest quality and of curios.

Early in the eighteenth century it was decided to transfer a part of the imperial pictures from the residence in the "Burg" in Vienna to the Stallburg palace (Fig. 20) to relieve the storerooms in the residence, but the Stallburg too proved too small for the display of all available pictures.[6] Another transfer took place, to the Belvedere palace, where, in 1781, the public was given access to the hoard, a policy dictated by the period of enlightenment.[7]

At the Stallburg, pictures were cut into such shapes as would form a continuous wall covering, and would fit the shapes of doors. At this particular time, in the earlier eighteenth century, the Hapsburg princes and their coteries seemed to crave spectacular luxury more than a more subtle enjoyment of single masterpieces. The text above the picture of the interiors in the catalogue of 1735 reveals a defensive attitude toward apparent criticism by contemporary scholars, who were informed that for all their learning they had no comprehension of sublime Imperial Majesty. At the Belvedere the style of presentation was radically changed. The engraver C. von Mecheln, who was in charge of the new arrangement, laid stress on a systematic presentation, "educative" rather than "enjoyable." He liked to compare a gallery with a library and had paintings hung in rigid rows and sculpture of small size packed into cases. A contemporary writer on European museums, the Frenchman Viardot, who visited museums in many countries, expressed his appreciation of the arrangement in the Belvedere by stating that there was a division between pictures by Northern and Southern artists. M. Viardot wrote: "Thank heaven . . . in the Belvedere the disorder is not as great (as in other galleries). One cannot say that the confusion is tantamount."[8] Contrary to Viardot, a domestic critic profoundly disapproved of Mecheln's display. Herr von Rittershausen maintained that sensitive people were kept away from the pictures. He felt that the "purpose of a gallery is not to offer historical knowledge but to develop taste and to awaken the noblest instincts of the heart."[9]

The benefit derived by the public from the collections in the Belvedere for some time remained limited by the expense connected with a visit. A group of viewers had to pay twelve gulden to the curator; admission to the Imperial Treasure Chamber was granted for twenty-five gulden.

Russia. The nuclei of two main museums were formed by two rulers surnamed "the Great," by Peter and Catherine.[10] Peter's collection grew out of his interest in science. The breadth of his personality and his vigor in westernizing Russia led to the accumulation of fine works of art, a symbol of a ruler's might in his period. He had inherited from his forebears a *guardaropa* containing armor and arms, precious clothing, jewels, and plate. These origins gave to the later Kremlin Museum the name of a Museums of Arms. To the customary curios Peter added jewelry of solid gold that had been

Figure 19a. A glimpse of the annual exhibition of artists of the Academy in the royal residence at the Louvre. A drawing by Gabriel de St. Aubin, of 1757, conjures up the intimate atmosphere of the event. (By courtesy of the Louvre Museum.)

Figure 19b. Artists were among the first commoners admitted to the art collections of princes and other private owners of works of art. Before the opening of museums to the public and the establishment of art schools, private collections offered the only opportunities for seeing paintings and sculpture of high quality. It was a give-and-take arrangement: the artists who were admitted were expected to produce copies of great masters' works and to improve their own skills. The representation of the Grande Galerie in the Louvre by Hubert Robert was presumably painted after 1799. (By courtesy of the Louvre Museum.)

Figure 19c. An art show at the royal residence at the Louvre in 1699 for the exclusive pleasure of the king and his guests who share a common repertoire of ideas and sentiments. Anonymous engraving in the Bibliotheque Nationale, Paris.

Figure 19d. With the French Revolution came the public museum: a confrontation of large and heterogeneous groups of people with miscellaneous works of art. The new situation created impedances in the flow of communication. Museums are now trying to remove barriers to human understanding and empathy.

The engraving after a painting by Monsaldy shows crowds at the Louvre in the year VIII of the Republic (1800). By courtesy of the Bibliothèque Nationale and the Louvre Museum.

Figure 20. The Imperial collections in Vienna at the time of their accommodation in the Stallburg. From Stampart's and Prenner's catalogue of 1735.

In this presentation works by great masters served as a decorative setting of the image of "sublime" majesty in the minds of ordinary mortals.

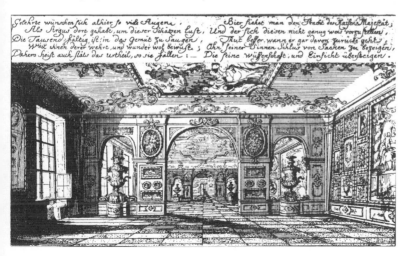

sent to him as a present by a miner in Siberia. He was hardly aware of the significance of the objects found in prehistoric tombs, which are now among the most precious items of the Hermitage Museum, but he was captivated by their beauty and issued a ukase for the preservation of Siberian monuments.

His practical concern with harbors and ships, and his first stay in Holland, resulted in the purchase of Flemish pictures, especially of marine pieces. His ambassador in The Hague, Count Kurakin, and his commercial agent in Amsterdam, Osip Solonyov, were buyers at auctions and from dealers. They sent hundreds of pictures home, but apparently Peter wished to choose paintings himself. During his second trip abroad, in 1718, he visited artists' studios and attended auctions, until he owned a surplus of paintings, more than needed to decorate the new imperial residence Monplaisir in the park of the palace of Peterhof. Some of his acquisitions were stored, and others were sent to the *Kunstkammer*, which is sometimes also referred to as *Schatzkammer* ("Treasure Chamber") and as the first public museum in Russia. It was not a public institution in the present sense of the term; Russia was not yet ready for a public museum.

The German princess who by her marriage to a tyrannical and short-lived Czar became one of the noted rulers of Russia ranked as one of the great art collectors of the later eighteenth century. Catherine invited Diderot, the editor of the *Encyclopédie*, to come to Russia, where he could continue his work, which was in danger of being prohibited in France because of its irreligious spirit; as a muse of liberty she won the praise of the philosopher Voltaire and Diderot's later assistance in enlarging her art collection, but at home she was no liberal and grew more reactionary with the passing years, and as she witnessed the challenge to the political status quo by two revolutions, in America and in France. She was prepared to improve the education of the Russian nobility by having them introduced to French literature, but the Treasure Chamber in the Kremlin, also known as The Armory, remained closed under her rule. Its opening had been discussed years before at the time of the founding of the University of Moscow in 1755, but had been squashed by court circles. It was only in 1806 that the people of Russia obtained the privilege of getting a glimpse of objects illustrating a thousand years of Russian history.

It is difficult to identify Catherine's motives as a collector. Was she a genuine connoisseur who experienced intense emotions in confrontation with paintings of quality? Or was an art collection to add to her fame? She continued Peter the Great's ambition to raise Russia to equal partnership with other European powers, if not to surpass them.

Distinguished people in Western Europe assisted the Empress in her activities in collecting objects of art. In Paris Diderot gave advice; in Italy Anton Raffael Mengs, Angelica Kauffman, and other artists watched for opportunities for the purchase of pictures and sculpture; Sir Joshua Reynolds was Catherine's English counselor. With the aid of these helpers she succeeded in acquiring some complete famous European cabinets: the select collections of Crozat in Paris, Count de Bruehl in Dresden, Prince Giustiniani in Rome, Robert Walpole in England, and Hope in Amsterdam. When Frederick the Great of Prussia experienced financial difficulties after the lost Seven Years' War, some 225 pictures purchased for him by the Berlin merchant Gotzkowski were redirected to Catherine. Thus the collections at the Hermitage came to contain about 1700 paintings, mostly by Italian and Flemish artists, with only a few Russian ones.

After his visit to Russia in the early nineteenth century the French traveler Viardot wrote: ". . .où l'on a compile' des tableaux et on se perd dans un labyrinthe." There was no principle of order, neither chronological nor geographical; works of great quality were next to copies; valuable pictures were hung opposite windows, where they suffered from too much light and became almost invisible.

In the fashion of the eighteenth century Catherine set up a luxurious retreat for herself in the Hermitage, a small building connected with the Winter Palace of St. Petersburg. It came to house the most exquisite pieces of her collection; the corridor connecting it with the Winter Palace was decorated with copies of Raphael's *Loges de Vatican*. In this milieu worthy of any sovereign of Western Europe she entertained special friends and conferred in privacy with foreign diplomats. She displayed the fashionable spirit of enlightenment by liberalizing the rules of admission to the Hermitage. Under Peter the Great only members of privileged classes were received and entertained like guests, with coffee and wine. Under Catherine the public was theoretically admitted, but in practice remained in most cases debarred. First of all there was a physical hurdle: whoever wished to enter the monarch's premises had to present himself, or herself, in an outfit worn at court functions, and only a small minority of potential visitors possessed such luxuries. Furthermore, there were mental barriers to be surmounted of which neither Catherine and her courtiers nor the citizenry are likely to have been altogether aware.

Spain. The Prado in Madrid also evolved from former royal collections. For some time young artists of promise *("de acreditada conducta y aplicación"*), as well as distinguished Spanish and foreign connoisseurs, were granted permission to view paintings in royal palaces, badly hung and lit as they were, but of a quality reflecting the connoisseurship of several Spanish monarchs. Charles V had been brought up under the tutelage of his aunt Margaret, Governess of the Netherlands, whose collection at Malines was superb. According to Velazquez, Philip IV had an unmistakable taste in matters of art. The advantage of putting a selection of fine paintings on view in a single palace was suggested by writers on art in the eighteenth century, though they did not go as far as proposing that a special building in the sense of a museum should be chosen. The idea of a public museum began to be shaped under the successive Kings Charles III and Charles IV and gained in strength during the French invasion. The Bonapartes were propagating popular enlightenment as a means of propaganda for themselves.[11]

A royal decree of December 20, 1809, issued by the "intruder-king" Joseph Bonaparte, proclaimed: "There shall be founded in Madrid a Museum of Paintings which shall contain collections of the various schools, and for this purpose the pictures necessary shall be taken from all the public buildings and even from our palaces." Confiscations from suppressed religious houses and sequestered private collections yielded further loot of which only a part remained in Spain. Many fine pictures were dispatched to France or remained in the hands of French generals in Spain, some to be sold in England after the downfall of Napoleon. The graceful task of bringing the plans for the foundation of a museum to a conclusion and of opening the Prado in 1819 was left to the legitimate Spanish King. After his return from France and his remarriage, Fernando VII wished to refurbish the royal palace, and the removal of pictures was welcome. The museum in a separate building was to be a gallery of paintings and sculpture for the teaching and profit of pupils and professors; it was to satisfy the noble curiosity of natives and foreigners and to add to Spain's glory. It was a public museum, but the spirit in which it was created does not appear to have been truly "of the people and for the people." Madrazo's illustrated catalogue of the early Prado, his *Collección lighographica de los cuadros del Rey de España,* Madrid, 1826, by its title already indicated that the museum was a private royal collection. The submissive devotion to a master who permitted ordinary men to view his inherited treasures was expressed in the odes adorning the catalogue. There it was stated:

¿Que fuera' Ay triste' Sin tu dulce influjo,
Gran Rey, ese edificio suntuoso
quo encierra el portentoso
Caudal a Te debido?

The choice of a building created problems which were solved without much judiciousness. First the royal residence Buena Vista was to serve as a decorative shrine, but later it was decided to house the paintings in the Prado, a building which originally had been erected for the purpose of a Museum of Natural Science and was not particularly suitable for the accommodation of paintings (Fig. 21).

Contemporary critics praised the building of the Prado for its "sumptuousness, wealth and ornaments," its columns, cupola, and the size of its rooms, some of which extended in length to 141 feet and were 31 feet high. The *majestuosa empresa* involved the expenditure of considerable sums of money. While problems of lighting and similar technicalities did not receive much attention, the moral perils resulting from exhibiting paintings of nudes constituted a major problem. In 1845 the English traveler Richard Ford wrote about "the peccant pictures" of the Prado, which were kept in a reserved gallery so that visitors could hardly get access to some of the works by Titian and Rubens, considered as lascivious and disquieting. Foreigners wishing to visit the Prado had to produce their passports, and even Spaniards were admitted on one or two days of the week only, on Wednesdays and Saturdays, except on rainy days.[12]

Germany. In contrast to the majority of early European museums, which developed out of the adventure of a private collection, or of the haphazard combination of several ones, the public museums of Berlin were from the beginning based on a plan.[13] A royal treasure chamber existed as in other capitals, but the Thesaurus Brandenburgicus was not chosen as the public museum-to-be, possibly on account of the general intellectual climate in Prussia.

In the aftermath of the Napoleonic wars the classical idealism of the period, of which the aged Goethe had been a representative, obtained dominance. In this atmosphere men like W. v. Humboldt, the statesman and scholar, desired that the growing generation of Germans should combine the best qualities of all Europeans and grow into "ideal world citizens." The museum was regarded as one

Figure 21. The central gallery of the Prado Museum in Madrid in the later nineteenth century shows some of the changes that occurred in the transition from private royal collections to public museums. A. F. de los Rios' *Guia de Madrid, Manual del Madrileño y del Forastero*, 1876. (By courtesy of the Prado Museum.)

among other educative means of molding the new type of German. Hence the national museum was to be made to plan: it was to illustrate the evolution of the European mind. Whereas a collection that had grown slowly and according to the fancies of individual owners (such as the Museum of Dresden, the former private gallery of the Princes of Saxony) would contain Italian paintings of the sixteenth and seventeenth centuries, and little else, or Flemish and German schools only, the Museum of Berlin was to be a well-balanced selection of works of art representative of all periods and schools of Europe.

The first visitors admitted to a Prussian gallery, toward the end of the seventeenth century, were students of the academy of art who were granted the privilege of viewing the pictures in the royal residences. In 1797 Frederick Wilhelm II gave order that the best pictures in all royal residences should be assembled for the benefit of artists in the castle at Berlin. In 1810 an edict followed ordering the foundation of a public museum. In its preparation experts were sent to London and Paris to study collections and museums abroad; diplomats and scholars received orders to purchase works of art in Italy.[14]

The Altes Museum in Berlin was one of the earliest museum buildings erected for its purpose. In 1797 plans for its construction were submitted to Frederick Wilhelm II by A. Hirt, professor of ancient art in Berlin. In his memorandum Hirt encouraged the building of large halls and long corridors, and stressed the importance of good lighting; he warned of unnecessary decorations. Paintings were to be accommodated on the higher floor and statues downstairs. The arrangement of the pictures was to be according to schools of painting. Hirt's proposal did not gain royal favor and was shelved, but interest in a museum was reawakened by the return of works of art which had been carried away by Napoleon. Schinkel was entrusted with the design of the building; its imposing cupola and colonnades in classical style attracted the public before the exhibits were set up.[15] The Old Museum was opened in 1830. In spite of all planning, it proved to be too small, and contrary to expectations, the interiors were too ornate.

Of greater originality was the earlier reconstruction, by Schlueter, of the old *Kunstkammer* in the royal palace in Berlin.[16] It was intended to arrange each room as an entity, in contrast with the kaleidoscopic incoherence of preceding private collections. Various means were used to create a wholeness. In one room pilasters and mirrors created a uniform background; in the cabinet of ancient statues the walls were as white as the marble figures. Shells and corals appeared in the allegorical frescoes on the ceiling of the natural history room. Combined, the backgrounds resulted in a conspicuously ornate atmosphere; they drew the attention of viewers away from the actual specimens.

The desire was to facilitate access to the collections, but the small objects kept in built-in cupboards were stored rather than exhibited. In order to be viewed they had to be taken out and shown to conducted groups. The accessibility was further reduced by the fact that only the room of coins, which served as the curator's office, was equipped with a stove; in the remaining rooms no provision was made to protect visitors against the cold of the Northern winter.

Italy. The unification of the country was achieved in the late nineteenth century and was preceded by fragmentary units in the form of city states, of several separate republics, or of foreign rule over parts of the area. In Florence the splendid private collection of the Medici was opened to the public in 1739 as the Uffizi Gallery, the name being derived from the building that once had been used as a governmental office, but the history of the papal collections in Rome would seem to be the most significant example of the evolution of a public museum in Italy.

In the grounds of the Vatican, the papal residence which underwent great architectural changes in the Renaissance, a pavilion formerly erected by Innocent VIII appeared to Julius II (1503–1513) as the proper setting for some of his fine ancient statuary. The little structure became known as the Belvedere, owing to the view it afforded over Rome, and was enlarged according to plans drawn by Bramante (Fig. 22). It was connected with the main palace by a gallery, and the courtyard was adorned with eight niches which were to hold statues. Other statuary stood among the orange trees and flower beds around the central fountain. To some of the Popes the Cortile, serene and remote, with its fragrance of orange trees, the sound of the fountain waters, and the beauty of ancient statues, was a place of rest and refuge from affairs.[17] Leo X (1503–1521) opened the Antiquario delle Statue to the people of Rome. Twelve paths led to the Cortile, which was one of the great sights of Europe, housing as it did the unique *Laocoön,* an Apollo statue, and a few other marble figures of outstanding quality.[18]

In contrast to their predecessors, Pius V and Sixtus V were hostile to ancient relics, which may have seemed to them carriers of pagan magic forces. Apparently they wished to free themselves from heathen menace when they gave away a considerable number of

Figure 22. As art patrons and collectors some of the Popes vied with lay princes. The
beautiful outdoor setting for statuary was painted by Hendrik van Cleve, a visitor from the
Netherlands, who was in Rome before the year 1551. His picture of the Belvedere is
likely to be a panoramic view telescoping reality.

statues. Some were sent to the Capitol in Rome; Emperor Maximilian II was presented with twelve busts of Roman emperors; the Medici in Florence received twenty-six statues, but desired to get more. They dispatched an ambassador to the Vatican to inquire — or to request — their due in the "process of clearance" that was going on in the collections of his Holiness. Fortunately the Cortile had been closed to the public by Hadrian VI, and the niches holding statues were boarded up with roughly hewn doors. For almost two hundred years they lay in obscurity, and remained known only through engravings and casts. When the English traveler Evelyn visited Rome in 1645, he found matters in this state. For some time the Antiquario in the Belvedere had been under the supervision of M. Mercati, physician to the Pope and director of the botanical garden of the Vatican, and to the doctor the value of the statuary lay in its material, marble being a fine variety of stone.

Under Clement XIV the Antiquario woke to new life. The Cortile ceased to enshrine the fine statuary, which was bound to suffer from permanent exposure to the weather, and only some pieces of decorative sculpture and sarcophagi holding plants remained; statues of outstanding quality were assembled in a newly erected gallery. The Museo Pio Clementino was opened to the public in 1773, and was enlarged by succeeding Popes.

The ornate arrangement of art collections in princely houses guided the principle of presentation in this early museum: the walls were in sumptuous Pompeian red, too conspicuous and too light-absorbing to be a favorable background for sculpture or paintings; columns of alabaster with gilt capitals and benches of porphyry drew attention away from the white marble figures. The desire for costly material surpassing the available funds, alabaster was imitated in paint in some of the architectural parts.

Another feature of this early public museum was its limited accessibility. In his account of the Vatican collection the German traveler Volkmann wrote as follows:

The famous statues and the new museum are now under the supervision of a guardian and it is most difficult to find him. Once he starts on a tour with a group of visitors he shuts the door of the museum and then one can lie in wait for hours, or it may happen that one has to give it up and leave the Vatican without having viewed anything. It is advisable to visit the Vatican in the company of a person familiar with the place, so that one gets access to all the interesting things therein.[19]

The Netherlands.[20] Unlike most European countries, there were no treasures accumulated over centuries in a cabinet or gallery of an authoritarian ruler — inherited from his ancestors and acquired by marriage or by war. After their liberation from Spanish control in the late sixteenth century, the Netherlands became a Republic of United Provinces under a Stadholder, each province guarding its fargoing independence; within each province were the towns which since the Middle Ages had been wielding considerable power. Added to this balanced network of social forces was the wealth derived from international trading, Amsterdam being the largest commercial city in Europe about the time New Amsterdam was founded in America. Accordingly there were numerous art collections, limited in size but in most cases of excellent quality. Owing to the existence of these decentralized resources, the two great museums, the Rijksmuseum in Amsterdam and the Mauritshuis in The Hague, could both expand and reach a level of excellence soon after the idea of public museums surfaced in the late eighteenth and the early nineteenth centuries.

Some of the source-collections had in a sense always been public; they were owned by municipalities, governmental offices, and other collective agencies, and consisted to a large extent of group portraits of persons entrusted at different periods of time with the leadership of communal affairs. The custom was introduced by the Civic Guards, who were in charge of the military defense of their townships before the advent of artillery and later continued as social groups dispensing honorary duties, holding gatherings on their premises (doelen) and occasionally feasting together. The most famous group picture of a Civic Guard is the *Nightwatch* by Rembrandt, commissioned in 1638 by the municipality of Amsterdam on the occasion of the first visit of a queen in the Republic, of Maria de' Medici of France, and like many other paintings of similar character was later transferred to a public museum, this particular one to the Rijksmuseum. By whomever commissioned, corporate pictures became municipal property once they were hung on the premises of the corporation.[21]

Civil Guards followed the example of the military ones in having periodically corporate group portraits painted and hung in their chambers. At one time the Syndics, or Governors of the Cloth Guild, employed the services of Rembrandt; from their Court Rooms the painting was transferred to the town hall of Amsterdam, which later lent it to the state. Similarly the Guild of Surgeons and the Governors of numerous charitable institutions (old men's and lepers' homes, orphanages, hospitals, and so on) had at various periods their administrators represented, until whole series decorated their halls, each the work of a great painter. Furthermore there were paintings in the conference rooms of the Lords of the Admiralties as well as of the directors of the East and West Indies and the Levant Companies. They represented personalities and views of the distant colonies of the Netherlands and became the property of the state when the companies were wound up.

The corporate portraits were discontinued in the later seventeenth century, and single family portraits came to the fore, commissioned by aristocratic families and in increasing numbers by wealthy middle-class merchants, one generation after another following the custom. In his *Book on Painters* published in Haarlem in 1604, Carl van Manders mentioned numerous private cabinets containing a variety of works of art, which were assembled and auctioned away as the financial fates of trading families rose and fell. Eventually many of these treasures — portraits, landscapes, and genre pictures by Rembrandt, Hals, Ter Borch, and other great masters — were bequeathed or sold to museums. They were mostly of the woof and warp of their townships, their provinces, or the country as a whole, each being another periphery of strong bonds of loyalty. Stadholder William V, Prince of Orange, was one among other collectors, but he had the good fortune of acquiring in 1768 the cabinet of Van Slingelandt, chief tax collector of Holland and West Friesland, reputed for owning the finest art collection in the country.[22]

When Napoleonic troops in 1795 occupied the Netherlands, they followed their customary strategy of seizing art treasures and dispatching them to Paris as war trophies. The cabinet of paintings of the Stadholder was the obvious first target; what remained of the collection suggested to some influential people that a national gallery should be established, public museums and galleries being topical issues at the time. It was opened in 1800 at the Huis den Bosch at Haarlem, and further pictures were located in other palaces or were purchased. Visitors paid a few pennies for admission and were guided around by an artist, apparently in response to the interest shown by the public. A catalogue was issued in 1801.

Hardly was Louis Bonaparte made King of Holland in 1806 when he began to make preparations for a Royal Museum in keeping with the example set by the grandiose Musée Napoléon in the Louvre in Paris. It superseded the short-lived National Gallery, which on Louis' orders was moved to Amsterdam. Both King Louis and the infant Royal Museum were accommodated in the town hall, which soon became crowded with pictures; the political events were precipitating financial calamities, and auctions offered favorable opportunities for the acquisition of paintings.[23] Other accessions were works by contemporary artists whose exhibitions had proved to be very successful.

With the collapse of the Bonapartes and the return in 1813 of the last Stadholder's son as King William I, the Royal Museum was set up in the Trippenhuis, a fine former private residence. In 1817 it was opened as the Rijksmuseum, which rapidly expanded as purchases and legacies began to follow each other. Simultaneously with the preliminaries to the Rijksmuseum in Amsterdam, preparations were made in The Hague for the Mauritshuis, which came to contain some paintings of the initial National Art Gallery in Haarlem and others returned from France after the Congress of Vienna. It was opened in 1821 and first shared its building with the Royal Cabinet of Curiosities, which was later removed. So were the contemporary pictures, which in 1838 were set up as a nineteenth-century museum in Haarlem.

Great Britain

In contrast to most other European countries and capital cities, the British Isles and London possessed no royal collections which could be simply transformed into public museums. The marvelous art collection of Charles I of England had been dispersed after the brief but intense revolution in the seventeenth century.

"The art of reigning was the only art of which he was ignorant," wrote a contemporary author soon after the execution of Charles, who had been renowned throughout Europe for his scholarly interests and for his informed and fastidious taste.[1] After a visit to his collection in London, the painter Rubens, himself a man of the world and a connoisseur, wrote to a friend: "I must confess that from the point of view of painting, I have never seen such a quantity of pictures by great masters."[2]

Charles' predecessors on the throne had done little as collectors. Travelers reported having seen a few portraits of English and foreign sovereigns, some battle pieces and allegorical paintings in the palaces at Whitehall, Windsor, and Hampton.[3] Charles inherited a modest collection — which at the time of Henry VIII's death contained 150 pictures — and developed it in style; his *grand coup* was the acquisition of the entire gallery of the Dukes of Mantua, mostly paintings by Italian masters. A thousand paintings and hundreds of ancient statues were left at the time of his death and were sold between 1650 and 1653 at public auctions at which owners of private collections in other parts of Europe were the bidders.[4]

In eighteenth-century London artists received scant opportunity to develop their talents by the study of great masters of the past.[5] Charles Lenox, heir of the Duke of Richmond, freely admitted artists to his gallery and outdoor collection of casts in Whitehall; he had been inspired by the example set by the Medici in Florence. His concern was, however, not shared by many other persons of wealth and station, who continued to enjoy their treasures in the seclusion of their country homes. But even if a gentleman favored artists with the permission to view his collections, the expenses of travel by stagecoach into the country were often prohibitive, and tips for the servants of collectors had to be considered. In 1761 The Society of the Dilettanti proposed to establish a collection of casts that would be "beneficial to the publick," but their plans did not materialize. In 1768 the Royal Academy was organized, and its first exhibitions were held in 1769.[6] In the late seventies John Wilkes M.P. advocated in the House of Commons the establishment of a National Gallery of Art, but England was not yet ready for an expensive, large-scale effort devoted to the arts and allowed Sir Robert Walpole's collection to be sold to Russia.

A few decades later art was recognized as a potential source of profit in commerce, and the House of Commons appointed a "Select Committee on Arts and their Connexion with Manufactures" which acknowledged "that a greater cultivation of the arts would advance the humble pursuits in industry, and that . . . in many despotic countries far more development had been given to genius" than in Great Britain.[7] The Select Committee referred specifically to the absence of "public and freely open galleries."

The foundation of the British Museum in London, the first public institution of its kind in England, has its origins in a passage in the will of Sir Hans Sloane, the famous physician, which ran as follows: "Whereas from my youth I have been a great observer and admirer of the wonderful power, wisdom, and contrivance of the Almighty God, appearing in the works of his creation, and have gathered together . . . books . . . natural and artificial curiosities . . . and the like . . . Now, desiring very much that these things, tending many ways . . . to the . . . use and improvement of the arts and sciences, and benefit of mankind, may remain together and not be separated, and that chiefly in and about the City of London, where they may, by the great confluence of people, be of most use. . . ."[8] In such words Sir Hans requested his trustees to appeal to Parliament that his collection should be made a public museum, in return for a payment to his heirs of the sum of £20,000, which was one fourth of the money he himself had spent on it. With the acceptance of the offer by an Act of Parliament, in 1753, the British Museum was founded and was opened to the public in 1759.

Though it had been Sir Hans's wish that the museum should be of the greatest possible benefit to mankind, the British Museum was for some time not easily accessible. In 1785, after a visit to England, the German historian Wendeborn wrote that persons desiring to view the British Museum had first to present their credentials at the office and that it was only after a period of about fourteen days that they were likely to receive a ticket of admission.[9] Sometimes months passed before people who had applied for a ticket were informed that the investigation into their credentials had been completed and that it was their turn to visit the museum. They had to present themselves in an anteroom between eleven and twelve o'clock in the morning, receive tickets if found to be "not exceptionable," and could now join one of the groups under the supervision of an attendant. Eight groups, of not more than fifteen persons each, were admitted in the course of a day. Conducted groups rapidly traversed the exhibition halls; requests for information were frequently rebuffed by the guides, the labeling was scarce, and the first synopsis of the contents was printed in 1808.[10]

The general public was admitted on four days of the week, from Monday through Thursday, and on Fridays select companies. On certain days the museum was reserved for students of the Royal Academy. The Statutes declared that men of letters and artists were to be the main users of the museum. The admission of other people was considered to be "popular but far less useful," and children below the age of ten were not eligible as visitors.

The first museum building, on the site of the present one, was the former private residence of the Duke of Montague and had been built toward the end of the seventeenth century in the style of a French château by architects sent for the purpose to England by Louis XIV (Fig. 23a,b). While one critic stressed that the "grand staircase had the magnificence becoming the residence of a nobleman . . . and the painted figures created a perspective that filled and satisfied the mind," another found that the discordant styles of the French mural paintings, representing allegorical figures, landscapes, and flowers, produced a garish splendor, and together with the heavy carved and gilt furniture, resulted in a cumbrous magnificence.[11]

Originally the British Museum consisted of three departments: of Manuscripts, Medals, and Coins; of Natural and Artificial Productions; and of Printed Books. In Dr. Hans Sloane's collection Artificial Curiosities had been a mere appendage, but accessions preceded the opening of the museum — the Harleian Manuscripts and the Cotton Library — to which later were added Sir William Hamilton's Italian Collections.[12] The early nineteenth century brought an extraor-

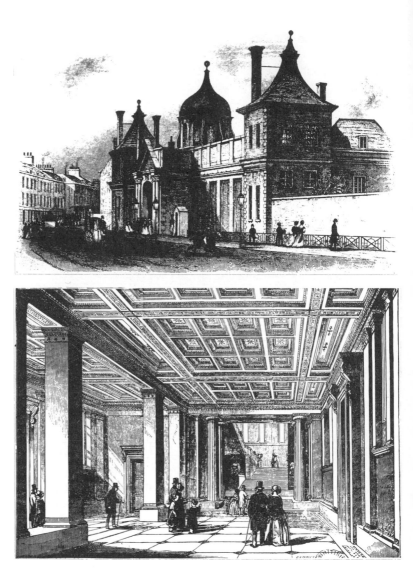

Figure 23a. The British Museum in London in its original building known as Montague House, a former aristocratic private residence in French style. The museum was opened in 1759. (By courtesy of the British Museum.)

Figure 23b. With fast-growing collections a new building was needed for the British Museum, which is here represented in its appearance in 1862. The country was powerful and enjoyed the wealth brought by the Industrial Revolution. Rules regulating the admission of visitors were becoming more generous, but the taste for grandiose architecture survived. (By courtesy of the British Museum.)

dinary influx. The year 1802 saw the arrival of the Egyptian collections made by French archaeologists attached to Napoleon Bonaparte's army, and surrendered by the French to Sir Richard Abercrombie's troops at Alexandria. The parliamentary grant of £16,000 for the extension of Montague House was hardly obtained when classical antiquities were added from Mr. Charles Townley's cabinet.

In 1816 the Elgin Marbles were acquired, and in 1823 King George III's Library. Another extension, known as the Quadrangle, was completed in 1838, when further accessions led to a worse congestion than ever before. The Assyrian antiquities brought by Layard and Rawlinson, and Sir Charles Newton's excavations from Halicarnassus, had to be stored in the basement, and the rooms over the King's Library which originally had been intended to house a collection of pictures were devoted to minerals and geological specimens.

The reactions of visitors to the early British Museum may be represented by the two following paragraphs..

Toward the end of the eighteenth century a visitor wrote: "The British Museum contains many valuable collections of natural history, but with the exception of some fishes in a small compartment, which are begun to be classed, nothing is in order, everything is out of its place; and this assemblage is rather an immense magazine, in which things have been thrown together at random, than a scientific collection."[13]

A little book entitled *A Visit to the British Museum*, of 1838, gave an account of a Mr. Edward's impressions for the benefit of his sons and nephews. He described the Entrance Hall, with its statue of Shakespeare, the Indian Idols, the ornament from a Hindu Temple, and the skeleton of a hippopotamus; the adjoining staircase, which was decorated with paintings illustrating Ovid's *Metamorphoses* and the picture of a llama, the South American beast of burden. The upper floor opened with a room of artificial curiosities and productions of uncivilized tribes and nations and was followed by another with skeletons of quadrupeds. The eighth room on the first floor housed models of ships, Oriental bronzes, pottery, and Roman antiquities, and other rooms were devoted to "animal creation" and various aspects of natural science. In the Gallery of Antiquities the objects were arranged according to their material, as "terra-cotta," "marble," "stucco," "bronze," and so on. An Egyptian sarcophagus inspired Mr. Edwards to a dissertation on granite and other minerals.

An important museum in Scotland, the Edinburgh Museum of Science and Art, developed from the seventeenth-century collections of two physicians, Sir Andreas Balfour and Sir Robert Sibbald.

The United States

Significant events and trends in museum developments at the time of their origins appear as a continuum from the late years of the British colonies to the early decades of the republic. In comparison with the Old World, especially with the European Continent, several American characteristics stand out: the fecund force was private initiative and not public authority; those who took initiative represented a wide spectrum of intellects, of social and economic backgrounds; work by committees was important, as Tocqueville well recognized as a trait of life in the United States; confidence in the future remained undaunted by failure, as one short-lived museum led to another, the new often absorbing the preceding one, which in this manner continued its existence; interest in natural history, and science in general, dominated the attention paid to art.

In 1773, three years before the Declaration of Independence, the first public museum of America was founded in Charleston, South Carolina, and it exists to this day. As may be seen from Powell's *South Carolina Gazette*, of March 22, and April 5 and 12, 1773, the Charleston Library Society made the following announcement:

Taking into consideration the many advantages and great credit that would result to this Province from a full and accurate Nature History of the same, and being desirous to promote so useful a design, they have appointed a committee of their number to collect and prepare materials for that purpose . . . they do now invite every gentleman who wishes well to the undertaking . . . to cooperate with them . . . to procure and send to them the natural productions, either animal, vegetable, or mineral . . . with accounts of the various soils, rivers . . . of the different parts of the country.

The accounts that were invited were to explain the uses and the virtues of the articles either in agriculture, commerce, or medicine. The document declared that a museum had been fitted up to receive the specimens.

The emphasis was on the practical application of the natural sciences to the mundane affairs of the community, and the purpose of the museum was clearly stated. This approach continued over many years and may be best stated in the words of the naval surgeon Dr. Edward Cutbush, the moving spirit and first president of a much more ambitious later organization, the Columbian Institute, established in Washington, D.C. in 1816 for the Promotion of the Arts and the Sciences. In one of his addresses inviting governmental support for the private organization depending on small contributions, he referred, in 1817, to a museum for the reception of natural curiosities, in connection with the intended scientific work:

The extensive limits of our country afford numerous opportunities for discoveries and improvements, in every branch of natural sciences. . . . How many minerals which might serve, not only to enrich the cabinets of the curious, but minister to the wants of our growing population! What an infinite number of substances may present themselves as objects of new trade and commerce, or for the supply of the necessary materials for the various domestic arts and manufacturers. . . .

Later in his address Dr. Cutbush spoke of agriculture that "can only be improved by the assistance of the chemical philosopher."[1]

Another strain in this address is the deistic reference to the wisdom and goodness of the creator displayed in the sublime view of the order and the different parts of our system; and another is the ardent pride taken in the genius of the republican institutions which "has infused so much strength and activity into the mind," and which supplies "the superlative happiness to live in tranquility, under an inestimable form of government."[2]

When the energies of the Columbian Institute ebbed, it was superseded in 1840 by the National Institution for the Promotion of Science, later to be known as the National Institute, with Mr. Joel R. Poinsett, Secretary of War, as its central figure. Mr. Poinsett urged the formation of a national museum in Washington as a depository for the mounting collections, first of all of natural history and ethnology, which arrived in response to the appeals for cooperation which the National Institution had sent to members of Congress, army and navy officers, consuls and citizens, and which were brought home by the exploring expeditions. In his "Discourse on the Objects of Importance of the National Institution" on its first anniversary, Mr. Poinsett specially referred to the large collections brought together by the seventh expedition, under Lieutenant Wilkes, to the Pacific, a part of which had arrived and was "packed away in boxes in a room in the Philadelphia Museum." He continued, "I can not believe that after all the labor, pains and expense incurred in procuring them, these specimens are not to be brought to Washington to be arranged and exhibited here."[3] One of the last acts of Poinsett as Secretary of War was to persuade James Kirke Paulding, the Secretary of the Navy, to order the collections to be brought to Washington.

The Patent Office became the depository of a substantial part of the collections accumulated in Washington (Figs. 24 a, 24b). Although its main original mission had been to receive and exhibit models of inventors, it grew to a National Cabinet of Curiosities and came to house an extraordinary miscellany of objects.[4] In 1844 officers of the National Institute gave an account of their deposits,

Figure 24a. The Patent Office in Washington, D.C., for many years served as a depository of collections owned by the government of the United States. (By courtesy of the Smithsonian Institution.)

Figure 24b. Exploring expeditions were adding to the growth of the national collections of the United States. "Plan of the National Gallery Containing the Collections of the Exploring Expedition," in the eighteen-fifties. (By courtesy of the Smithsonian Institution.)

PLAN
OF THE
NATIONAL GALLERY,
CONTAINING THE COLLECTIONS
OF THE
EXPLORING EXPEDITION.

The United States
109

which consisted of minerals, works of art, portraits of distinguished Indians, Indian curiosities, Bedouin war instruments, skins of birds and quadrupeds, botanical specimens, jars filled with mollusks, fishes and reptiles, insects and shells. The quantities of specimens were considerable; for example, more than seventy thousand insects, many thousands of fossils, and even more numerous minerals.

The account was made in response to an accusation that the collections of the Institute were "of very trifling extent and value," and that the Institute was "unworthy the patronage of the Government."[5] During its nearly eighteen years of custodianship of museum materials belonging to the nation, the Institute had to face various difficulties. The collections under their care were not at all times welcome at the Patent Office. On one occasion, in the fifties, a Commissioner of Patents is supposed to have lightened his burden by sending a collection of fossil vertebrates to a bone mill in Georgetown, where they were transformed into commercial fertilizers.

A bulletin of the Institute, of November 25, 1846, informed its members that "more than a thousand boxes, barrels, trunks, etc., embracing collections of value, variety, and rarity in literature, in the arts, and in natural history, remain on hand unopened. . . . For the preservation, reception, and display of these, the Institute has neither funds nor a suitable depository."[6] Henry Theodore Tuckerman, a visitor to Washington in 1849, wrote: "In the National Institution like nearly all of our scientific and literary establishments, as yet in embryo, sea quadrupeds from the arctic zone, birds of rare plumage, the coat in which Jackson fought at New Orleans, the rifle of an Indian Chief, plants, fossils, shells and corals, mummies, trophies, busts, and relics, typify inadequately natural and bold adventure."[7]

The lofty goals which the National Institute set itself were commensurate with the talents of many of its participants; they were rooted in the farsighted enthusiasms that characterized many of the early American leaders; the responsibilities, however, would have overwhelmed any group of individuals lacking regular financial support. The ideology, the successes, and the failures of the National Institute offered valuable directives to those who came after them. In 1846 the Smithsonian Institution became the governing body of the national collections.

Several precedents provide both inspiration and warnings to later museums. The oldest was the Cabinet of the American Philosophical Society in Philadelphia. A cabinet or museum was a natural part of an eighteenth-century academy, but it could not keep its place among the gradually maturing public museums. The specimens — from fossil bones to coins, from Central American antiquities to Indian artifacts, and so on — were passed on to agencies specializing in one or another area. The Philosophical Society showed wisdom in recognizing its priorities.[8] In the early nineteenth century the American Antiquarian Society pioneered by promoting interest in anthropology, especially with regard to Central America, even if its Cabinet housed the customary mixture of natural history and of art. When the end of its mission came, the Society perceptively affirmed it.[9] In the later nineteenth century, people realized the extent of the demands made by collections of objects on their keepers; those who felt unable to attend to extensive collections and who were more inclined toward research and serious discussion than to peep shows saw their future in fieldwork, in the study of records, and in publications.

Charles Willson Peale, soldier-patriot, artist and collector, went farther than any of the early owners of private museums open to the public before he too was overtaken by failure, owing to the flux of economic circumstances.[10] By his championship of democracy Peale lost his patrons among the members of the mercantile class who had employed him as a portrait painter, but he was quick to notice that visitors to the art gallery in his home at Third and Lombard Streets took interest in his shells, minerals, and mounted birds. In 1785 he set out to form a collection of natural history which was to be no less than "a world in miniature," containing every object in nature or in art which might be "curious or instructive," and calculated "to delight the mind and to enlarge the understanding." The Peale Museum, which at times was called the American Museum or the Philadelphia Museum, grew to about one hundred thousand items, ranging from insects to Indian artifacts, from casts of ancient statues to models of new machinery. The establishment gained semiofficial status when it moved in 1794 to the building of The American Philosophical Society, and in 1802 to the old State House, now known as Independence Hall. While leasing facilities in the Philosophical Hall, Peale rendered much needed services as a curator, although he was referred to as librarian.

In 1801 Peale led an expedition to Ulster County, New York, where uncommonly large animal bones had been discovered. He had for many years been fascinated by fossil bones, since designing such bones for a visiting surgeon in Philadelphia,[11] and together with his son Rembrandt had made efforts to find a complete fossil skeleton. At last he found a skeleton of a mastodon which he named a mammoth and which he exhibited in his museum (Fig. 25). The direct confrontation with the evidence of a beast that had roamed the continent and had totally disappeared prompted doubts in the immutability of creation as described in the Book of Genesis, but it opened up new perspectives of knowledge. About 1810 Peale's Museum in Philadelphia reached the peak of its development; it enjoyed fame.

When the elder Peale formally retired, his son Rubens became the manager of the family enterprise. The situation apparently called for new means of fund-raising. Rubens Peale specialized in experiments in "natural philosophy," an object of contemporary fascination. Visitors watched as electricity generated sparks, and some were willing to have shocks administered to themselves; metals were melted in a special blowpipe. Gradually the intended great School of Universal Knowledge in the form of a museum, akin to the grandiose *Encyclopédie* of the French philosophers and to the Temple of Learning of which Bacon had dreamed when he wrote *The New Atlantis*, deteriorated to such tricks as the "Unaccountable Rotating Cylinders" and stuffed monkeys dressed like human beings and in postures suggesting the pursuit of various trades. In the end the collections of the Peale Museum in Philadelphia were dispersed. Rembrandt Peale established in 1814 the Peale Museum in Baltimore; after some successes and more numerous vicissitudes, he saw its residue acquired by P. T. Barnum. The building, the first museum building in America, served diverse and at times rather uncongenial purposes before it was restored as a museum in the thirties of this century.

William Clark's Indian Museum in St. Louis was unique: it supposedly was the first museum west of the Mississippi; it was founded by the national hero Clark, who together with Lewis had opened up trails into the uncharted West; and his exhibit hall fulfilled a definite purpose. As the governor of the Missouri Territory he conducted his negotiations with Indian chiefs in a hall studded with beautiful buffalo robes, wampum, blankets, saddles, and a variety of other products of Indian skill. He set a mood for communication in his Council Chamber. Apart from Indians, there were numerous other visitors who stopped in St. Louis to take their bearings before venturing out farther West.[12]

In the early history of American museums the impetus came from many sides and with a good deal of dissonance among the participating elements. Next to a Cutbush, a Poinsett, a Charles Willson Peale, and the scholars who started the collections of curiosities

and minerals at Harvard and Princeton, there were men of lesser
fame who came and went having made their contribution to the evolution of museums. In Washington, D.C., John Warden and the painter
C. Boyle were exhibiting natural history specimens. In New York a
succession of colorful characters started, kept intact, and increased
a collection of the Society of St. Tammany. John Pintard, city inspec-
tor and a man who was instrumental in founding the New-York Historical Society, was followed by Gardiner Baker, by the less learned
but competent John Scudder, and of course by Barnum, a collector
of derelict museums — with other collections being absorbed in the
process. From a private association's one-room cabinet, the collections grew to an "American Museum" occupying several floors of a
building on Broadway that went up in flames[13] (Figs. 26a,b). In 1791
Daniel Bowen began to exhibit curiosities in Boston, first in his
American Coffee House on State Street and later in a schoolhouse
where the exhibition assumed the more ambitious name "Columbian
Museum." There was the New England Museum of 1818 owned by
shareholders, and the Boston Museum of 1841.[14] The popularity
of museums, of which the French visitor Eugène Ney wrote in a rather
uncomplimentary manner, extended west. When the steamboats
made their appearance on the Ohio River in 1811 and Cincinnati
became a Midwestern boomtown, the growing city got its Western
Museum.[15] Like museums of the period on the East Coast, it began
in the name of science and came close to being a circus in the
style of Barnum, but it proved durable enough to last almost half
a century.

These and similar enterprises offered informative specimens of
natural history or of historical souvenirs next to questionable paintings and undisguised entertainment for the less sophisticated, in the
form of wax figures, exotic animals, stuffed and alive, ventriloquists
and curious mirrors. With the arrival of new immigrants in rising
numbers, a variety of tastes had to be satisfied if the owner of a private museum wanted to survive the year in which he started, but the
number of literate persons who sought to advance themselves and
their country by self-education was remarked upon by eighteenth
century travelers from abroad. And the plurality of early museum
efforts in the United States should be considered together with
other sources of information that was sought with the help of public
schools, of pamphlets on a variety of social problems, and platform
speakers. The American Dream of those years was compounded of
secured access to seemingly unlimited land resources, of the

Figure 25. *Exhuming the First American Mastodon,* 1806 – 1808, by Charles Willson Peale. The Peale Museum, Baltimore. Gift of Mrs. Harry White in memory of her husband. (By permission of the Board of Trustees of the Museum.)

Figure 26a. The American Museum in New York's City Hall Park. Lithograph from a drawing of 1825. (By courtesy of the Prints Division of the New York Public Library. Astor, Lenox, and Tilden Foundations.)

Figure 26b. Another prelude to the modern public museum: the showman Barnum's museum on Broadway. Lithograph by Deroy after August Köllner, entered in 1850. (By the courtesy of the Prints Division, The New York Public Library. Astor, Lenox, and Tilden Foundations.)

chance of every individual to become a member of any social and economic group, and of faith in education as a power promoting human welfare.

It was in more than one sense a new dawn in the pilgrimage of man on earth. The names of Locke and Hume, of Voltaire and Rousseau, were known to an intellectual minority only, but the spirit of the great social philosophers was diffused throughout the country. Originally generated in the Old World, it began to be applied to ways of living on American soil. News of almost miraculous events lifted the spirits of downtrodden Europeans of many tongues and gave them courage to dare the crossing of the Atlantic and to reach out for an unknown future. Among the immigrants were many indentured people who pledged years of humble work in return for a passage; men escaping the draft; landless peasants and urban workers seeking to throw off the chains of rigid class societies in which very few could escape the social and economic station into which they were born. There was a wave of rising human expectations, and museums were among the means that were to meet the demand for information.[16]

Natural history exhibits had priority in the orientation of the citizens in the new country; they contained directives to available natural resources.[17] Art mattered less; the casts after ancient Mediterranean sculpture which the Scottish painter John Smibert had brought over from Europe in 1728 had been appraised at £4 after his death in 1752. There was no general awareness of the importance of casts and engravings after famous European paintings which for some time constituted the only artwork available in America, but John Singleton Copley, the first great American-born painter, received his education in part from Smibert's collection of casts and engravings.[18] About the turn of the century James Bowdoin was in Europe buying pictures which in 1811 he would leave to the college in Brunswick, Maine, which bears his name. The Common Council of the City of New York encouraged their citizens to visit the exhibitions of art dealers, and the city hall came to house a collection of casts of old sculptures and of portraits of national leaders. To John Trumbull, army officer and artist, goes the credit for arranging the first exhibition of old European masters in the United States, in 1804. The response, however, was discouraging; the pictures found no buyers and had to be shipped back to Europe. Trumbull's own paintings of men and events of the Revolution received greater recognition and led to the establishment of the first college gallery in the United States, at Yale in 1832. In 1805 the Pennsylvania Academy of Fine Arts came into being; the New-York Historical Society, founded in 1804, became the repository of artistic bequests; in 1844 the Wadsworth Athenaeum in Hartford, Connecticut, was opened, to mention some of the important landmarks in the development of art appreciation which in those years had to compete with the attraction exerted by the historical contents of works of art.

In 1839 the American Art Union of New York, lately the Apollo Club, started its activities leading up to a distribution among its members of engravings from American paintings.[19] At the exhibitions in the Union's gallery on Broadway laboring men became conspicuous; membership cost $5.00 and rose close to 20,000 subscribers, one of whom was the fortunate who won an original painting at the annual "distribution" in the old Tabernacle. This yearly event caused, however, the termination of the entire enterprise; in 1853 the authorities declared the distribution to be a lottery. Another effort to spread interest in the arts was made by Secretary of War Poinsett, whose broad interests enabled him to be simultaneously the director of the National Institution, that rudimentary National Museum. He proposed in the 1840s that copies of all congressionally commissioned pictures, statues, and medals be distributed to all the populous plains and fertile valleys of the land; the proposal was never realized.

As in the field of museums dedicated to science, which had to contend with more spectacular offerings, the early art museum had an aggressive competitor in the Panoramas, an importation from Germany via England, which was providing some of the excitement now made available on television.[20] Huge, no doubt quickly fabricated, murals, often sent from one place to another, represented such dramatic matters as coronations of emperors, distant Jerusalem, or the Niagara Falls. They were in their own way "happenings" that transported viewers into fabulous environments and in return earned fortunes.

Early Museums: Summing Up

The German poet Johann Herder recorded his memories of visits to museums in verses that in roughly rendered prose run as follows:

All is silence — Am I in this desert to meet you, beloved Rome: — All those figures which once elsewhere I fondly greeted. . . . Here that fragment of a statue, there a bust, sacred limbs cruelly dismembered — all patched and stored in this lumber-room: in a museum! Fear and misery are haunting me.[1]

In the introduction to the catalogue of his collection to be sold in public auction after his death, the French poet Edmond de Goncourt expressed the wish that the objects of art which had contributed to his happiness should not be buried in the cold grave of a museum.

With regard to Europe, Sir Frederic Kenyon summed up the situation when he stated in a lecture which later appeared in print:

It was not . . . in the eighteenth, nor yet in the earlier part of the nineteenth century that museums can be said to have taken any noteworthy part in the national life of any country. They began to be of service to scholars. . . . Artists as well as scholars began to profit. But for the general public museums were just collections of curiosities . . . with little guidance for the inexpert and no help to enable him to assimilate this mass of strange and unrelated material.[2]

In the United States collections of natural history or of inventors' models had an immediate, practical purpose. People were breaking new land, were eager to learn about crops they could raise on a soil and in a climate that were new to them, to get acquainted with the native animals of their neighborhood, or to get ideas that would bring profit in manufacture and trading.[3] Such incentives hardly existed in Europe, where landless peasantry predominated and where urbanization was more advanced than in America. A museum of natural history in Europe was of academic interest to those who cared for knowledge as an end in itself, and to others it was a collection of oddities.

Furthermore, there was a fundamental difference between Europe and the United States in the attitude of people toward change — toward change of any kind. While Europeans generally feared it, resisted it, were indifferent to it, or did not even conceive of the possibility of change in situations of life that were thoroughly familiar to them, the inhabitants of the United States were attracted to novelty as a possible directive to improved techniques of living.

The motivation to learning was greater in the United States than in the Old World, but the early museums did not capitalize on it to any great extent. The buildings in which collections were housed in America were less intimidating than the palatial European structure;[4] architectural megalomania did not yet exist, for lack of funds, if for no other reasons. The selection and presentation of objects were, however, equally ill conceived on both sides of the Atlantic. A visitor had to be well informed about topics presented in a museum to add to his knowledge or to feel stimulated to further thought: the communication contained in exhibits was obliterated by the visual noise that assaulted viewers who faced a screen or a case, or who walked amidst incongruous objects. More often than not a museum hall was an alien land in which people were addressed by a visual equivalent of several tongues unknown to them and issuing simultaneous messages. Yet exposure of people to experiences was equated to transmitted communication.

The priorities in the lives of visitors to those museums radically differed from those of private collectors, princes, or scholars; in their great majority people worked to exhaustion to earn inadequate food, clothing, and shelter. They had little time and energy left to visit a museum unless it held out the promise of useful information or of recreation that required little effort. Human motivations to seek sights had not altogether changed since crowds in ancient Greece or Rome had visited temple collections. Tokens of historical events of relevance to the living, rare and costly things, especially if associated with famous persons, retained their magnetism, even if the belief in a unicorn horn as a magic wand and in a piece of a mummy as a panacea had lost its power. Responsiveness to art was blunted by more urgent practical concerns and could hardly be expected but from exceptional individuals in the absence of a general cultural environment in which sensitivity is fostered without precepts.

The regulations which limited the physical access of visitors to early museums were not always the major factor in curtailing the intended use of the new public institution. The minds of most visitors remained debarred from the experience even when they were physically admitted. Visitors were alienated by the perpetuation of arrangements inherited from cabinets and galleries of private collections of past centuries, which were not only automatically continued but which often degenerated into incongruous combinations of storage room, palace, and studio. What they saw had little relevance to their lives, and the effect of intrinsically interesting, beautiful, and rare objects effected but a brief outburst of excitement; in this respect museum resources could not compete with shallow entertainment.

When d'Alembert urged the systematization of the early Encyclopédie, he defined its state by saying, "It is a Harlequin's coat where there is some good stuff but too many rags." The early museum may have justified a similar description.

For the sake of convenience, and to some extent for palpable reasons, three periods of reconstruction of museums will be distinguished, one developing around the middle of the nineteenth century and suddenly brought to a close by the outbreak of war in 1914, a second between the two world wars, and the third beginning around 1945 and leading up to the present. In the United States the end of the Civil War seems to mark the beginning of the first era of reconstruction.

With regard to all three periods, only essential trends can be indicated within a single volume; an appreciation of numerous individual efforts is beyond the scope of this survey.

First Period: Up to 1914

In a search for functions fulfilled by museums, a consideration of qualitative developments seems more promising than of numerical growth which often may have extraneous causes of little significance to core problems.[1] During the first period of museum reconstruction several aspects became conspicuous: a trend toward specialization of contents; the effects of a series of international expositions on museums; the changing role of the United States from a back-bencher in museum matters to a position of prominence; and a beginning concern with the presentation of materials for the benefit of a growing public.

Specialization was dictated first of all by overextension and congestion in some large institutions. Where a limitation in size was decided upon, or dictated by the limits of the available accommodation, specimens illustrating one subject matter were brought together to form a separate collection. In 1883 the Natural Science collection of the British Museum was moved from the headquarters in Bloomsbury to another part of London, to Kensington, which developed into a center of specialized museums. In 1899 the South Kensington Museum became known as the Victoria and Albert Museum and was devoted exclusively to arts and crafts; the Science Museum split off as a separate establishment.

Even within a single building objects were grouped more carefully according to their subject matter. The Department of Oriental Antiquities and of Ethnography of the British Museum was in 1861 divided into three separate units. Greek and Roman relics formed one part; coins and medals formed another; ethnography was lumped together with objects referred to as Oriental, British, and Mediaeval Antiquities. In 1866 the Oriental Antiquities split off, containing Egyptian and Assyrian specimens. At the Ashmolean in Oxford archaeology was separated from natural history and was moved to a separate building on Beaumont Street. In Berlin the overcrowded Neues Museum of 1841 was relieved of its paintings, which in 1905 were set up in the new Kaiser Friedrich Museum. In the United States historical societies, which often served as the guardians of donated or bequeathed objects, passed on natural history specimens and works of art to specialized institutions as these came into being. Around 1870, at the time of the foundation of the two great museums in New York, of art and of natural history, the earlier dream of a small universe under a single roof had dimmed, and specific types of museums occupied the minds of people.

National, Nationalistic, and Historic Museums were variations of one theme.

England's National Gallery in London, founded in 1824 after many adversities in the course of its preparatory period, expressed the self-assurance of a world power.[2] Its contents awakened no associations with English or British history, but the high quality of its paintings of international origin gave witness to the community's standing. When H. Balfour in his presidential address to the Royal Anthropological Society in 1904 encouraged the establishment of a museum that would preserve and display objects illustrating ways of life of the past in the British Isles, he repeated a plea made before by others for a national museum, but the idea never materialized.[3]

The situation differed in other areas of Europe where communities were striving for political independence or sought symbols of lost greatness. Hungary drew strength from the existence of a National Museum erected from contributions of the rank and file of patriots by means of a tax imposed voluntarily upon themselves by a group of Hungarian landowners. In fact, the National Museum of Budapest played a role in Hungary's struggle for liberation from Austrian rule and it was from the steps of the museum that the poet Petöfi, in March 1848, declaimed his "Up, ye Magyars!" which inaugurated a new phase in the fight for independence. Similarly, the National Museum of Prague began mainly as a collection of artistic, literary, and scientific antiquities, testifying that Bohemia, at the time a province of Austria, had once been an independent cultural unit. In Rumania a museum building was started in 1912 to house collections that were to keep citizens aware of their historical legacy and would fulfill a responsibility toward future generations. All these museums were symptoms of conditions that led to the First World War, in which the Austrian empire split up into a number of independent national entities. The Norsk Folkemuseum in Oslo signaled the Norwegian struggle for independence from Sweden.

In Germany symbols of national unity preceded the political union of separate states. When Humboldt's aspiration to educate the Germans to be "complete Europeans" was superseded by Schlegel's patriotic yearnings, a plan for a National Gallery was conceived which was to embody the essence of the Teutonic spirit. It was to be a collection of paintings by German artists of all periods and schools. Voices condemning the idea of a "patriotic storehouse" were raised and the journal *Dioskuren* proclaimed that to be German did not mean to be Prussian, and that Prussia had no claim to nationalism since it was no nation at all. Yet the patriotic tendency prevailed against all arguments, and the Pinakothek, the former private gallery of the princes of Bavaria, with its collection of old masters of different national origin, was opened in Munich in 1836 as a museum of preponderantly Germanic paintings. The Bavarian sovereigns gave a further expression to their nationalistic leanings by founding in 1867 a museum of National Archaeology. Another representative German National Museum was founded in 1852 in Nuremberg, to illustrate all aspects of German life throughout the centuries.[4]

In Rome, the establishment of the Museo delle Terme followed the unification of Italy to a single kingdom in 1871.

After numerous mishaps, Spain enjoyed political independence but was merely a worn monument of a grandiose past; it needed sources of moral strength. In 1867 Queen Isabella II laid the foundation stone of the Biblioteca Nacional y Museo that was to illustrate the glories that had been Spain's between the seventh and the sixteenth century. The Peninsula was recovering from a century of Bourbon rulers controlled by France and from sufferings endured during the Napoleonic invasion; the disintegration of the Spanish world empire was in its terminal stages, and the country was enfeebled by endemic civil wars.[5]

The Scandinavians were among the first to realize the vanishing of rural traditions under the impact of industrialization and urbanization, of phenomena of an age that affected them as other areas of Western man, and began to rescue the memory of the past in their indoor and open-air folk museums. The first such museum, Skansen near Stockholm, opened in the nineties, and became a model for similar establishments far beyond Scandinavia.

It is difficult to pinpoint the time when the United States National

Museum came into being; in a modest form, if compared with its later expansion, disparate parts of it existed for years before the Regents of the Smithsonian consented in 1857 to the transfer of the governmental collections hitherto kept at the Patent Office to the first Smithsonian Building in the romantic style of a turreted Norman castle.[6] The totally unexpected bequest by James Smithson, an English chemist who had never set foot on American soil, gave body to ideas and ideals cultivated over decades.[7] The Columbian Institute presided over by Dr. Edward Cutbush had gone out of existence, and the National Institute, which drew its inspiration from Mr. Joel R. Poinsett and his associates, turned moribund in the forties, but the visions of these men remained viable.[8] Indeed, Mr. Poinsett had been clearly aware of the significance of the Smithson bequest for the establishment of a museum in the capital and had struggled for its control by the National Institute, which for over eighteen years had been the custodian of museum materials belonging to the nation. He advocated a union of the Smithsonian with the National Institute, but Congress eventually decided to separate governmental property from a private organization.[9]

While the collections under the care of the National Institution, later to be known as National Institute, were known as the "cabinet," the term "national" became attached to the cabinet of curiosities of the Patent Office with the passing of the Hough bill of 1846, which concerned the organization of the Smithsonian Institution. The accumulating natural history specimens were until 1851 known as the Museum of the Smithsonian Institution. As George Brown Goode wrote in his account of the genesis of the U.S. National Museum, it was the offspring of the marriage of the National Cabinet of Curiosities with the Smithsonian Museum.

In this comparison of national museums as reflections of their countries or nations, the institution of the United States suggested a national awareness, and even a desire to strengthen this awareness by means of a museum, but it was free of all aggressive nationalistic posture, and it was directed to the future in contrast to the emphasis on the history of the past in some of the national museums in Europe.

When Mr. Poinsett expressed his hope for a national museum he also spoke of the light of science it would shed over the land. Access to a sampler of its natural resources was of the utmost practical importance to a new nation expanding over a vast continent. A committee of the National Institution stated the need to explore the country's resources and to have every state in the Union represented in a national cabinet established at the seat of the central government. The scheme was to unite all persons and parties because it was national. Because it was national it was to receive support from all. It was to elevate the national character and to add to national fame, but in comparison with circumstances fostering the foundation of National Museums in European countries, the emphasis in the U.S. National Museum at its beginnings appears to have been on practical purposes serving the physical advancement of the nation.

Models of new technical inventions were collected during the period in many countries, but in the United States the project not only had a larger scope but it also documented what men of humble beginnings could achieve in a free country. Courage and a spirit of enterprise and inquiry were writ large in the collections brought home by several governmental expeditions, going westward in the United States and beyond. Further, a National Museum was to contribute to the process of uniting different states, people of different backgrounds and of different climates. The amalgam of a nation was still in the making.

The growth of the collections introduced supernational elements: the evolution of organic life from primitive fossils of the Cambrian era to man, and human ways of living in a variety of cultures (Figs. 27a–e).

Smithson's bequest stipulated that the money he left the United States, in fact his entire estate of $508,318.46, be used for an institution in Washington that would serve "the increase and diffusion of knowledge among men." When after eight years of debate Congress accepted the bequest, a museum was written into law, but wide scope was left for the interpretation of the ways in which knowledge was to be increased and disseminated, and what functions the museum was to fulfill.

The first Secretary of the Smithsonian Institution, the noted physicist Joseph Henry, interpreted the increase and diffusion of knowledge desired by Smithson as research and as a dissemination of published research among scholars and scholarly institutions. He was well aware of the importance of a museum as a means of public education, but did not wish to encumber the Smithsonian with its custody. The Institution under his direction was to serve the advancement of knowledge and needed collections of objects as study aids of scholars.[10] His reserve toward the maintenance of large accumulations of objects was not unwarranted. If they were to be properly maintained, they would drain funds away from the pri-

Figure 27a. James Smithson as student in Oxford in 1786. Portrait by an unknown artist. Why did an Englishman who never set foot on American soil leave his entire estate to the United States for the advancement and the diffusion of knowledge? (By courtesy of the Smithsonian Institution.)

Figure 27b. The original building of the Smithsonian Institution, which looks somewhat fragile in C. A. Wood's drawing of 1865, and which was to become the nucleus of a cluster of great museums which to this day keep on expanding in both size and numbers. (By courtesy of the Smithsonian Institution.)

Figure 27c. The Great Hall in the original building of the Smithsonian, around 1860. (By courtesy of the Smithsonian Institution.)

Figure 27d. The formation of a Gallery of Art was among the earliest plans of the Smithsonian Institution; it was to give encouragement to artists who needed free exhibition space. Portraits of North American Indians by J. M. Stanley occupied a prominent place in the gallery, which was so severely damaged by a fire in 1865 that the remaining objects were dispersed among local institutions. In 1909 the new Museum of Natural History offered space for art collections until their move into their own home, in 1968, when the remodeled Old Patent Office Building was ready to house them.

The picture of the Gallery on this page appeared in the *Guide to the Smithsonian Institution and National Museum*, in 1863. (By courtesy of the Smithsonian Archives and of the Secretary of the Smithsonian Institution.)

Figure 27e. Behind the scenes of the early Smithsonian — and behind the scenes of every large museum at any time — collections keep growing. They are bound to outgrow space, manpower, and funds unless museum workers counteract the explosion with such questions as: What are our goals? What are our priorities? Do we control our materials, or do they control us? (By courtesy of the Smithsonian Institution.)

mary purpose of research; if they were neglected, they would easily share the fate that befell many of the specimens collected by the Columbian Institute and the National Institute — they would be ruined or lost. Baird, the second Secretary, had organized his private museum before coming to the Smithsonian, but the chief museologist of the Smithsonian — in fact one of the very few great museologists of all times — was George Brown Goode. By training an ichthyologist, this extraordinary man could in many ways contribute to the shaping of museums in our days.

Ethnological Museums represented another type of specialized institution.[11] Implements of peoples of primitive material culture, their garments, idols, and other objects created and used by them had fascinated people for centuries before the foundation of ethnological museums proper; they were particularly suitable for serving as "curios" which fascinated people by their strangeness and oddity. David Murray quoted a description of the Danish king's collection at Copenhagen in the seventeenth century which contained the following passage: "In one of the rooms there is nothing but the garments, arms and utensils of Indians, Turks, Greenlaenders and other barbarous nations which for their number and variety entertain the eye." In his *Museographia* the German eighteenth-century author Neickelius wrote between a reference to the wild ox of India and another on Indian indigo about "savage peoples such as are the Hottentotes, the Greenlaenders and others similar to them by their horrid appearance."

The motives that led to the establishment of ethnological museums in the nineteenth century were distinct from earlier curiosity and superstitious beliefs. Two lines of thought influenced their evolution. Anthropologists approached the problem scientifically and set out to illustrate the evolution from primitive life to civilization. In England, General Pitt Rivers began in 1851 to form his Ethnographical Museum, which was opened at Bethnal Green in 1874. He laid stress on the common article of everyday use, as distinct from the odd and curious, and his collection illustrated stages in the development of objects. The *Annual Return* for 1845 of the British Museum stated that "a large gallery was opened to the public for the reception of the ethnographical collections." These collections had been exhibited before in a different arrangement and had been known as "curious objects."

In France men like Jomard, Hamy, and Siebold led to the establishment of the ethnographical collections at the Trocadero. It was a common practice of English and French scholars to present ethnography in connection with archaeology; the geographer Siebold recommended ethnology as a supplement indispensable to the historian, the philosopher, and the student of natural science. A new scientific spirit was superseding the ancient idea of black men being a different species from white men and by nature designated to be slaves. A spirit of enlightenment, of the Rights of Man, and of inquiry unfettered by superstition, documented itself in the growing interest in ethnology.

A simultaneous influence of entirely different origin encouraged the creation of ethnological museums in the interest of imperialistic policy and of the control exercised by civilized nations over peoples of primitive material culture. In his foreword to the *Handbook to the Ethnographical Collections of the British Museum* of 1910, Sir Hercules Read reminded his fellow citizens of the responsibilities of the leader-nation of an empire, and of the need for ethnographical collections illustrating the manners of life of native peoples. Such collections, he wrote, would help to avoid blunders in the administration of the colonies and would assist merchants in the choice of wares for export. Holland, another modern colonizing country, started in 1837 its Rijksmuseum voor Volkenkunde in Leyden and opened in 1865 a Colonial Museum in Haarlem, housing ethnological objects. The interest in ethnology in the United States was fostered by the presence of the Indians, but was by no means limited to home territory. One of the earliest museums in the United States, belonging to the Salem East India Marine Society organized in 1799, was devoted to natural and artificial curiosities, and especially to those acquired by shipmasters beyond the Cape of Good Hope and Cape Horn. The collections illustrating indigenous cultures of Polynesia, Micronesia, and Melanesia were housed in Marine Hall on Essex Street in Salem, which was dedicated in 1825. With the decline of the Salem trade around the middle of the nineteenth century, fewer shipmasters went as far as the Cape of Good Hope, and others were not admitted to the Salem East India Marine Society. The ensuing problems were solved by George Peabody, a philanthropist born in New England who became a banker in London; he provided funds for a reorganization of the collections and the establishment of the Peabody Museum in Salem.[12]

The International Expositions inaugurated in 1851 in the Crystal Palace in London offered incentives for the establishment of new museums and the use of new manners of display (Fig. 28). Developing technologies for the mass production of goods being in the focus of these expositions, they had a direct bearing on *Museums of*

Figure 28. New York City was quick in following the example of the first world exposition held in London in 1851. Representation of the New York Crystal Palace. Wood engraving by J. W. Orr. (By courtesy of the Metropolitan Museum of Art.)

Science and *Museums of Arts and Crafts*. Prince Albert, Queen Victoria's consort, believed that international exhibitions would provide the needed survey of technological development which all Western mankind shared. He inaugurated a contest in fairs among the European countries, and between Europe and the United States, each overshadowing the preceding one in scope and in splendor, and all acting as a powerful intellectual stimulus to visitors, from mechanic to art lover, from merchant to social reformer.[13] Each international exposition raised the awareness of people of new advances in technology and of an environment in which machines reaped crops and made furniture, while people could light their nights with electricity and annul distances by talking over telephones and using automobiles for travel. Innovations which only a century before would have appeared as phantasies were becoming everyday reality. Furthermore, the expositions offered an unprecedented opportunity for individual countries to reassess both others and themselves against the background of rapidly changing technologies and ways of life. Europeans obtained a more respectful opinion of the United States.

The Great Exhibition in London spurred enthusiasm and contributed to funds needed for the establishment of the Victoria and Albert Museum. In Philadelphia the original building of the Museum of Art as well as some of its contents were a legacy of the Centennial Exposition; in Chicago the Natural History Museum was established in the former Palace of Fine Arts of the World's Columbian Exposition of 1893; in San Francisco the De Young Memorial Museum of Art found its first home in one of the pavilions of the California Midwinter Exposition of 1893 – 1894. Exhibits of foreign countries displayed at international expositions supplied specimens to new and existing museums. The Philadelphia Centennial of 1876 provided the United States National Museum with additional loads of materials, and the Columbian Exposition at Chicago sparked the idea of the Commercial Museum in Philadelphia, which in this manner acquired for $10,000 materials valued at half a million — samples of raw materials and of finished products from around the globe, and of considerable interest to both manufacturers and consumers.

In matters of display the expositions set an example by showing sequences from raw materials to articles of use, and by exhibiting working machines turning out products in the presence of onlookers. There was only a step from there to the participation of visitors in handling machinery, which indeed came into use in the Deutsches Museum (of Science) in Munich and to some extent in the Science Museum in London, which were both conceived before the First World War.

Museums of Natural History experienced both successes and setbacks during this period and had to look for visitors among new sections of the population. The publication of Darwin's *Origin of the Species* in 1859 dampened the interest among amateurs whose religious feelings were offended; they were attracted to specimens of natural history in museums as divine manifestations and not as illustrations of natural selection. With the gradual ascendancy of laboratory biology in universities, the descriptive botany and zoology dealing with entire organisms in museum collections took second place. This general trend did not prevent a fundamentalist, who opposed Darwin's ideas, from becoming a major force in the establishment of natural history museums in the United States. The Swiss zoologist Louis Agassiz, who in 1848 became a Harvard professor, lectured indefatigably on matters related to the "Plan of the creation," and his enthusiasm for study by direct observation and of entire organisms communicated itself not only to his students and other audiences but also to Mr. Francis Calley Gray of Boston, a descendant of a pioneer maker of shoes in Lynn, Massachusetts.[14] Agassiz's dream of a museum that would be a "Library of the Works of God" approached realization when Mr. Gray in his will bequeathed $50,000 for the establishment of a museum of natural history that would be connected with the University of Harvard. The Gray Museum of Comparative Zoology was opened in 1860. One of Agassiz's students was Albert Smith Bickmore (a dissenter from his mentor's ideas with regard to the theory of evolution), who became a driving force behind the foundation of the American Museum of Natural History in New York as well as its director in the first wing of its present building of 1877 (Figs. 29a,b). From its origins this museum combined research activities with concern for the dissemination of knowledge. Slide-illustrated lectures introduced adult education, and emphasis was laid on the presentation of natural history specimens in the form of habitat groups, of animals and birds shown in small numbers and in lifelike postures in a simulated natural environment that was painted and furnished with rocks and plants.

This trend in *presentation* gains in interest if considered in the context of a dialogue conducted at the time in museums on both sides of the Atlantic. In accordance with the rising status of science, many people favored a presentation of museum objects of any kind in an "analytical" manner, considered to be scientific. According to the adherents of Museological Darwinism even specimens of archaeology or crafts were to be arranged as a consultative library of objects progressively subdivided into orders and genera, an approach satisfying the needs of students but not those of laymen, who hardly noticed subtle differences between items in a series, and who were repelled by monotony. The opposite school of thought favored a "synthesis" of appropriate objects to a meaningful whole, in the form of habitat groups of animals or of period rooms in which works of art were shown together with furniture and other things of everyday use, all belonging to the same era. Complete interiors in the style of the fifteenth, sixteenth, and seventeenth centuries were shown in 1888 in Nuremberg, in a museum housed in a former monastery, and then again in the early years of the twentieth century in the Kaiser Friedrich Museum in Berlin. The Scandinavian open-air museums carried the idea further and offered complete environments of authentic old buildings, of workshops in action, with attendants in national costumes, folk music, and habitat groups of regional animals. On the whole, however, presentation in the manner of "synthesis" remained an exception in Europe, while it became widely accepted in later years in the United States, where communication with the general public was more eagerly sought than in the Old World. It was an American museologist, George Browne Goode, who stated that an efficient educational museum may be described as a collection of instructive labels, each illustrated by a well-selected specimen.[15]

In matters of interpretation, of using museums as mediators between research and general education, museums in the United States were on the way to becoming innovators. They also introduced a new manner of establishing institutions and of maintaining them. It was done by a team composed of wealthy individuals, a large number of subscribers making small contributions, of committees of private citizens and public authorities. When Mr. F. C. Gray bequeathed $50,000 to the Museum of Comparative Zoology at Harvard, the State Legislature of Massachusetts contributed twice the sum, and the rest was raised by public subscription. On some occasions a museum began with an idea in the mind of an individual who provided some of the needed funds as a bait for others who would pursue a community project by contributing cents or thousands of dollars as well as volunteer labor. In this manner the Toledo Museum of Art came into being, with substantial seed money coming from the glass manufacturer E. D. Libbey. Worcester had to wait almost ten years before an idea of Stephen Salisbury III, together

Figure 29a. A general view of the interior of the main room of the American Museum of Natural History in New York appeared on the occasion of the opening of its new building in *The Daily Graphic*, December 22, 1877. (By courtesy of the American Museum of Natural History.)

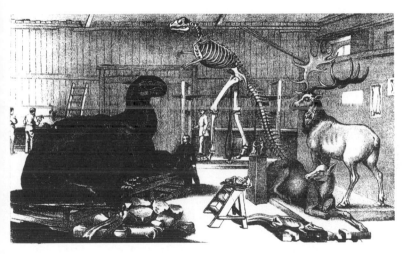

Figure 29b. Similar impressions can still be gained behind the scenes of contemporary museums. In 1868 the "Central Park Museum" in New York had no alternative but to establish its own paleontological studio. But should expeditions for the purpose of a hunt for large taxidermy specimens still be counted as priorities of a museum? Who is to benefit from the sight of another static elephant or zebra, and what can a costly exhibit of this kind communicate that could not be more dynamically conveyed by a film taken in the natural habitat of the animal and shown on the television screen? The presumed realism of large habitat groups has a kinship with a Victorian drawing room: both represent canned life.

The provision of animals for taxidermy, and taxidermy itself, are areas of museum work that lend themselves well to centralization, with ample scope for individual needs (By courtesy of the American Museum of Natural History.)

with his dollars, rallied sufficient cooperation of other citizens to translate an idea into a fine art museum. The city of New York declared a museum to be as important and beneficial an agent in the instruction of people as any of the schools or colleges; it granted land for both the Metropolitan Museum of Art and the American Museum of Natural History, and issued stock on behalf of them, being empowered to do so by the state legislature.

The nineteenth century had run half its course when the United States could still boast of only three art museums — the Philadelphia Academy of Fine Arts, the Boston Atheneum, and the Atheneum in Wadsworth, Connecticut — but this condition was not to last. James Jackson Jarves wrote in 1864 that it was becoming a mode to have a taste, and that private galleries in New York were almost as common as private stables. Toward the end of the century the Fogg Museum began to train art experts, and American connoisseurship ripened quickly under the guidance of such cognoscenti as Charles Eliot Norton and Bernard Berenson. Collectors were prepared to correct errors they had made in days of naïveté and to replace works of art of indifferent quality and fakes by authenticated pieces. There was redundant wealth — "with which our prosperity threatens to possess us," as the Reverend Dr. Bellows from All Souls Church in New York put it in 1869 at a preparatory meeting of the Metropolitan Museum of Art. There was as yet no restraining income tax, which was considered to be unconstitutional; and the Tariff Law of the first decade of the twentieth century exempted works of art over one hundred years old (Fig. 30).

Circumstances spurred the daring of entrepreneurs and were uncommonly favorable to the breeding of unscrupulousness, but to all appearances many of the new millionaires retained some of the concern with civic matters that had characterized the fathers of the early republic. Many, if not most, of their conquests in the markets of art, in which they were outbidding competitors, would sooner or later be channeled into museums, as gifts, legacies, or loans. The private collectors were also setting standards of taste for millions of museum visitors. The propagandist for Italian masters was Isabella Gardner; the Henry O. Havemeyers were early buyers of Spanish paintings; Charles Long Freer developed an unerring eye for quality in Far Eastern art. The list could be continued at some length. The alchemy that kept a Charles Freer indifferent to the condition of his underpaid immigrant workers while he was piling up millions by manufacturing railroad cars, and at other moments released an extraordinary sensitivity to an Oriental vase, is beyond the scope of

Figure 30. View of the Metropolitan Museum of Art from the Cesnola Galleries in 1882.
(By courtesy of the Metropolitan Museum of Art.)

our considerations; so is the amalgam in the strikebreaker Henry Clay Frick of ruthlessness with delight in delicate paintings by Boucher. But neither of these men had the desire to keep their treasures beyond the brief span of an individual lifetime, in contrast to tycoons and conquerors of the past who sought immortality in heirlooms guarded by dynasties. Everybody is their heir who enjoys the museums they have left in Washington, D.C., and in New York City. In fact, Mr. Freer had to exercise patience while waiting for the Smithsonian's acceptance of the gift of his gallery. John Pierpont Morgan, one of the main patrons of the Metropolitan Museum of Art and for years its president, seems to have followed a grand strategy as collector and as administrator; he wanted an art museum for America containing the best of all countries and centuries, and making it unnecessary for Americans to seek such sights in Europe.

The charisma of the United States that in the forties had attracted the gift of the Englishman James Smithson still exerted power in the seventies when the Italian nobleman Louis Palma di Cesnola offered his voluminous collection of classic antiquities to the Metropolitan Museum that was in the making.[16] Cesnola had served in the Union Army and as a reward had been appointed consul in Cyprus, where, in the style of the time, he proceeded to open up thousands of ancient tombs, which yielded objects of Greek and Oriental origin. The British Museum was a bidder for the purchase of the collection, but Cesnola chose to pass it on for a lower price to the United States; he threw in years of volunteer labor in sorting and cataloguing the objects, until, in 1880, the museum could afford to appoint him as a salaried director. Up to that time all work at the Metropolitan had been done by committee members and other volunteers.

On the whole, in the first period of "reform," between the middle of the nineteenth century and the First World War, museums went further in admitting human bodies than human minds to their resources which remained incomprehensible to the majority of people. Acquisitions were made in a haphazard manner, and were largely derived from donations. The style of presentation may be best described in the words of four writers of the late nineteenth century:

The orderly soul of the museum student will quake at the sight of a Chinese lady's body encircled by a necklace of shark's teeth.[17]

They [the museums] have not made it their business to tell any particular story . . . and the fragmentary stories they do tell are so incompletely and unsystematically set forth that they are unintelligible.[18]

A museum is a place where every separate object kills every other, and all of them together the visitor.[19]

Criticism as well as constructive ideas came from George Brown Goode, who considered historical museums as being even less developed as science museums and as representing mere chance accumulations. He wanted all types of museums to be transformed from bric-a-brac cemeteries to nurseries of living thoughts and to retain their vitality in a continuous process of evolution.[20]

Complaints continued in the new century. A paragraph by the architect Russell Sturgis in the *Dictionary of Architecture and Building* (New York: Macmillan, 1901), vol. II, p. 1000, stated:

It is noticeable that no special pains have been taken by the directors, guardians, or builders of museums to agree as to the essential characteristics of those buildings. Such agreement as the librarians of Europe and the United States have sought to reach might have proved of great benefit to the managers and to the public. The earliest museums especially built for that purpose are as good as the latest . . . the latest-built ones are as likely to prove failures as those of half a century ago . . . architectural spendour . . . has generally interfered greatly with proper lighting and showing of the objects exposed.

Architects did not succeed in bringing about vital innovations in museum architecture during the later nineteenth and the early twentieth century, but the functionalism of Louis Sullivan's Transportation Building at the 1893 Chicago Exposition was a prologue to later developments in museum architecture. Sullivan and his associates demanded that a building should have a form fitting its function and be a plastic expression of democracy. They challenged their contemporaries to "throw off the ancient tunic" of architectural styles of the European past. The radical change did not occur immediately, but the comparative simplicity of ancient classicism won over the romanticism of Romanesque architecture. In less ambitious ways the display halls of many international expositions counteracted the legacies of temples and palaces. The new building of the Boston Museum of Fine Arts, of 1909, offered a model for the use of daylight in a museum building.[21]

The housing of collections remained one of the most frustrating aspects throughout the period leading up to the First World War. The National Museum in Munich, founded in 1867, was housed in a building which originally had been intended as an Institute for the Deaf and Blind and then had been found unsuitable for the purpose. The structure was of inferior quality as may be gathered from the collapse of ceilings, which caused injury to visitors and damage to exhibits. When the much discussed Imperial Museums of Vienna were completed in 1881, the palatial buildings, with their copious Renaissance decoration, proved too small for the specimens to be accommodated. The site would have been large enough, but according to tradition, the rooms and corridors had been made so spacious, and above all so high-ceilinged, that the practical purpose of the museum was almost defeated. The building designed to hold the Art Gallery and Museum of Glasgow, which was completed in 1901, was, to quote a contemporary description, an "ornate structure in the spirit of the French Renaissance." There was an abundance of carved surfaces and a floor of variegated white, black, and yellow marbles, and the great hall was impressive by its mere height of eighty feet. The Victoria and Albert Museum was hardly established in its new building, in 1908, when criticism was voiced, especially of the shortcomings of the building, of the lack of provision for offices of keepers, bad lighting, and the uniform type of cases.

The concessions to the public made during this period affected mainly the physical admission of visitors. Museums were open daily, in many instances on Sundays as well as during the week. Admission fees were low, if they existed at all. Before the end of the century several British museums offered special exhibits for children, mainly specimens of natural history, models, and pictorial material; isolated efforts of similar kind were made on the Continent, but they were all modest if compared with the vigorous activities in the United States, where education was considered a primary function of public museums.

Improving transportation brought greater numbers of visitors to museums and enabled larger institutions to send loan exhibits to smaller ones, to schools and associations of people interested in certain topics. The South Kensington Museum in London inaugurated in 1855 its Circulation Department, which loaned specimens first to schools of art and later to schools in general. The German Museum of Applied and Commercial Arts (Deutsches Museum für Kunst in Handel und Gewerbe) in Hagen, founded in 1912, conducted a campaign for discriminative design. It collected specimens illustrating that good taste could go together with machine production and offered exhibitions for loan. In 1912 fifty exhibitions arranged by this itinerary museum were shown in forty-two towns, of which eight were outside Germany.[22] In the United States, where road traffic was developing at a fast pace, museums in out-of-the-way country places experienced an influx of visitors. According to an American museum authority, in 1895 the ratio between motorcars and house museums was 20 to 40; in 1910 there were 500,000 cars and 100 house museums.[23] The use of railway trains for the accommodation of agricultural exhibits by the expanding agricultural colleges in America and their extension services deserves to be specially mentioned as a symptom of quick adaptation to needs of primary importance and of creativeness in using facilities for new purposes. Hundreds of thousands of farmers benefited from such demonstrations set up in several railway cars making thousands of stops at the end of the nineteenth century and in the course of the following two decades.[24] Such experiments remained, however, rare exceptions in all countries.

In 1903 the curator in charge of a great European museum faced halls in which elephants seemed to walk into tapestries and ancient paintings. A few years before World War I the German author Edward Fuchs, himself a great collector, declared, with special reference to the public collections in Berlin in the era of William II, that "the contemporary museums give but a fragmentary idea of the culture of past epochs . . . they show them in a festive attire and only rarely in their everyday appearance."

A multiplicity of reasons kept museums ill adjusted. When shaping new institutions and even concrete objects of use, the human mind has difficulties in wrenching itself altogether from precedent, however irrelevant to the purpose at hand. Early automobiles bore a striking likeness to vehicles pulled by horses, and public museums have been particularly slow in cutting their navel cord from private collections of the past: being less exposed to the pressure of public opinion than hospitals and even than schools, museums had a built-in static element. Furthermore there was the braking force of prejudice militating against a diffusion of knowledge, of greater strength in Europe than in the United States, but nowhere totally missing; where social mores made such attitudes unbecoming, they were submerged in the depth of minds, sometimes unknown even to the people who nurtured them, and they surfaced when occasion permitted. From a long-range point of view, obsolete attitudes underwent a very gradual erosion.

Only in exceptional cases was the purpose of a specific exhibition or of an entire museum clearly defined. The era was even less prepared to choose means that were likely to fulfill set goals; the pitfalls of communication, in museums or otherwise, were rarely thought of. It was still taken for granted that physical exposure of human beings to information in whatever form would metamorphose to understanding in their minds. The agriculture exhibits mentioned before are a striking example of consummated communication due to the clarity of purpose for a specific public. The raising of crops and of livestock was a matter of life or death, and the seriousness of the situation turned people away from routines, viable or not, and toward such untraditional methods in relation to exhibits as demonstration and discussion. On the occasion of another topic of urgency, of urban development in the era of mounting industrialization, the immediate consequences were less palpable to great numbers of people and may be even to the town dwellers to whom Sir Patrick Geddes addressed himself. His proposal for a *Civic Museum* illustrating the development of towns and cities did not materialize. Its potential for furthering "civic sense and civic consciousness . . . and to serve as an incentive to action" remained untapped.[25]

With the outbreak of World War I, European museums became dormant, and activities in the United States slowed down.

Second Period of Reform: Between the Two World Wars

Four theaters of action can be distinguished during this period: the Russian Soviet Socialist Republics; the fascist States, Italy and Germany; the United States; and those areas of Europe that may be summed up as "Liberal Europe." The object of this essay is to consider these areas for the goals set in their museum programs and the extent to which aims were met with chosen means.

Soviet Russia. The period of revolutionary social change offered unprecedented opportunities for a reform of the public museum.[1] The Commissariat in charge of the "Enlightenment of the People," which came into existence with the 1917 Revolution, established a Central Office for the Care of Objects of Art and Archaeology (*Otdjel po djelam musejev i ochranjenije pamjatnikoff iskusstwa*); in 1921 a central office controlling all museums was set up. The tasks confronting these authorities were formidable indeed.

The museum workers who met in a conference in 1930 considered museums as aids in the struggle for a reorganization of society that was going on in their country. The new philosophy of life that was accepted by the community called for a reshaping of individual minds. What was said with regard to the Hermitage Museum may be considered as a general museum program:

Its ⌊the museum's⌋ mission is to help the great masses of the workers of the Soviet Union to form right ideas of the various forms of culture created by different classes of society in the course of the development of civilization; to help them to select in this uninterrupted series of evolution of society all that may be of value and may be made part of the cultural heritage of the proletariat.[2]

Three kinds of collections were to be reshaped into public museums. The vast holdings of some existing large institutions were to be changed from overwhelming hoards to displays of significant meaning for large numbers of people. Among them were the imperial collection of paintings in the Hermitage in Leningrad, the Rumyanzov Museum of history, prehistory, and ethnography, and the Tretyakov Museum of Russian Art. Only a minority of specialized students could benefit from the informative and aesthetic values of those stores. There were numerous smaller museums in the far-flung country which resulted from past efforts of private societies, interested in natural science, ethnography, or archaeology, which were in need of adequate accommodation and maintenance. In Czarist times even the Academy of Science had lacked funds. Finally, there were numerous private collections whose owners had fled abroad at the outbreak of the Revolution.

In 1917 the estimated number of museums had been 114, in 1934 it was 738. The regional museums showed the greatest numerical increase. Other favored subjects were public health, technical science, and history related to the recent Revolution and to social problems in general.

When Catherine the Great had joined the band of royal collectors in the eighteenth century, pictures were to provide first of all a decorative background and to be the symbols of a powerful ruler. Later on some order was introduced according to the quality of paintings and their chronology, but the new Russian museology called for a different set of criteria in the Hermitage.[3] The guiding principle was to regard all objects which were human products, be they tools, pottery, paintings, or machines, as records of human existence under certain conditions of society — "slave-owning," "feudal," "capitalistic," or otherwise. The French Department was reorganized first. Furniture, sculpture, textiles, and samples of other crafts came to join the paintings which before had alone filled the Hermitage, and were grouped in a series of rooms illustrating phases of French history and the contribution made by different classes of society in the process of historical evolution. There was the France of royal absolutism, with large Gobelins in academic style, costly inlaid furniture and silversmith work, and the France of the feudal and moneyed upper classes coming to the fore with disintegration of the absolutist regime, their style equaling the former in luxury but with louder and livelier accents in paintings and accessories. Other period rooms were related to the French middle class, which once had been the ally of kings against feudal aristocracy and later took up battle against royalty. German culture was presented at the time of the Peasant War and in the period of industrial capitalism, and so on. Another series of rooms was devoted to Oriental cultures.

The Museum of Fine Arts in Moscow was renamed Museum of Descriptive Art, objects of art, like any other products of man, being considered as records of human attitudes and behaviors under varying conditions of society. In the Museum of Modern Art in Moscow, paintings of realistic, impressionistic, and expressionistic styles were exhibited as illustrations of conflicting elements in a bourgeois society of the imperialistic era. Some museum workers put the informative value of paintings so high as to deny to masterpieces of art all claim to special appreciation; others utilized the emotional appeal of art in their ideological campaign. They considered their work as an experiment in progress.

A distinction was made between exhibits for laymen and study collections for students. Presentations in the style of synthesis were favored for the general public, with works of art shown in an environment of objects of everyday use of the period, and wherever possible in combination with lectures and concerts related to the topic of an exhibit; students were offered chronologically arranged collections of specimens. Accordingly, different staff members were employed for the two sections of visitors, and specialists in education enjoyed the same status as experts in a field of science or of art.

Emergency conditions called for a leveling up of education among the great masses of the population, which up to now had to a large extent been illiterate. Instruction was focused on immediate concerns, political and economic.

The range of topics covered by museums of informative character was impressive. There were the numerous provincial museums devoted to local natural science and history. There were museums of science, planetaria, and anthropological collections. Hygiene museums were often known as Museums for the Protection of Mother and Child. A research institute in Moscow dealing with animals used in transportation combined the practical study of animal husbandry with paintings showing horse traffic in past epochs. The Museum of Reconstruction of Agriculture offered a survey of the evolution of agriculture, from its primitive stages to the precapitalistic and capitalistic eras, as petty-peasant farming, and finally as socialized work on the land. The historical part served as an introduction to current problems in farming. A part of the exhibits on view in the museum, models of agricultural machinery and of different breeds of cattle, was loaned to collective farms and agricultural academies.

Many of these museums were the primary laboratories of scientists-to-be and maintained close collaboration with the schools. Opportunities were offered for visitor participation: models of machines waiting to be set in motion; studios for amateur artists; projects in which children would gather specimens for local collections.[4]

The museum workers of the U.S.S.R. had definite views with regard to the ultimate goals of museums in the United States and in the European countries outside the Russian sphere of influence: they were to contribute to the maintenance of the socioeconomic status quo. According to these views, an endeavor was made to create an image of the past as something immutable, in contradiction to the continuous flux and change of life. Art was supposedly given priority, in the belief that the appeal of aesthetic qualities would consolidate conservative attitudes.

The Fascist States. Of museum work undertaken in fascist Italy two new foundations in Rome stand out as characteristic efforts of the period: the Museo dell' Impero Romano, inaugurated in 1926, and the Museo Mussolini, opened in 1938.

The catalogue of the Museo dell'Impero Romano authoritatively stated that the museum owed its existence to the enthusiasm for ancient Rome generated by fascism throughout the Italian nation.[5] Collecting was organized on a large scale, and requests went out to all thirty-six provinces of the country to search for and to deliver to Rome any kind of record of the ancient past. In this manner statuary, reliefs, photographs, maps, and a variety of archaeological material were assembled in considerable quantities. Their artistic quality was not more valued than the information they conveyed on Roman customs and manners, with regard to the clothing and the arms of the legionaries who had conquered three continents, and to the ships that had carried Roman sailors to victories. Domestic utensils of ordinary men and women in ancient Rome were found worthy of as much attention as the principles upon which the administration of the empire had rested.

The newly made collections were temporarily housed in the **Terme** of Diocletian but were a part of the Italian National Museum founded in 1876 as a projection of Italian nationalism. At the time of the fiftieth anniversary of Italy's unification, in 1926, the new imperialism to which Mussolini aspired was expressed in the catalogue of the Museo dell' Impero Romano:

When in future the finally collected materials are exhibited in a building worthy of them, not only students but the educated general public and especially the growing generation of boys and girls visiting the exhibitions will realize with admiration what the Romans achieved in Gaul and in Spain, in Britain and in the Orient, in Asia and in Africa. In all minds the museum will evoke a vision and a consciousness of what the Roman Empire once represented, and what it still represents in the history of human civilization.[6]

The Museo Mussolini[7] was opened in 1938 and was provisionally accommodated in a building which once had served the San Ambrogio convent. The classical archaeology was related to Rome, the *urbs*, the focus of the *imperium*. A passage in the catalogue explained that "the museum is dedicated to the man who himself has devoted to the urbs his indomitable, passionate spirit and his untiring labours."

The purpose of the fascist Italian museums was the education of the masses. It was a special kind of education, a subordination of interests to a single master idea: Italy's political mission to regain the position of a world empire, as dictated by the destiny of Rome. No provision was made, however, to bring the archaeological exhibits nearer to the understanding of the general public and of children, who were declared to be important visitors. By introducing all exhibits as part of the life history of the country—almost chapters of every Italian visitor's family history—a sentimental mood was aroused. Viewers were overwhelmed by the wealth of relics of ancient Rome—*their* Rome—and reasoning powers were dimmed by a continuous emotional appeal. The aim of these museums, as of other mass media, was the molding of men into devotees and willing fighter-slaves.

In addition to these activities, guided by a political program, the reorganization of the gallery of paintings in the Vatican, the Pinacotheca Vaticana, ought to be mentioned.[8] An effort was made to bring systematic order into the grouping of the paintings, with representations of sacred themes being shown separately from portraits and other lay subjects. A definite improvement was achieved in the room containing pictures by foreign masters where up to this time eighteenth-century English artists and medieval Germans had been close and incompatible neighbors. The infatuation of the fascist Italians with quantity as a measure of grandeur led to the addition of rooms in the Pinacotheca and to an increase in the number of pictures from 282 to 463 items.

In August 1933, the museum workers of Nazi Germany met in a conference at Mainz and resolved that their first duty was to be true servants of their epoch—of an epoch dictating that "museums should with all their powers contribute to the shaping of an amorphous mass of population into a nation."[9]

Two types of museums, closely connected with each other, were characteristic of the Nazi period: the Fatherland Museum (*Heimat-*

museum) and the Army Museum (*Heeresmuseum*). Few kinds of museums can have gripped the imagination of the general public more than the Fatherland Museum. Newspapers offered prizes for the best description of their value to the citizen, and people described how their museum fortified them in times of difficulties and of doubt, and how it made them realize the continuity of history in which the individual was but a link in a chain.[10] The Fatherland Museum was regarded as an important aid in the education of the growing generation, which was to be imbued with faith in the common destiny of all Germans and with the will to maintain the unity of nation and country. In the history curriculum emphasis had shifted from international events and recent periods of history to prehistory and early German history.

In the Fatherland Museum in Hanover a "prehistoric workshop" (*Vorgeschichtlicher Arbeitsraum*) was set up in a disused school building.[11] Every child spent two days of his school career in this workshop-museum and was made familiar with the life of his prehistoric ancestors by handling objects they had produced and used in their daily occupations, as well as by making objects modeled on ancient ones. The ultimate aim was not merely to impart facts to children but also to kindle enthusiasm in them for what was known as the Germanic Race.

The Army Museum was an accentuated form of the Fatherland Museum. In 1935 a German author wrote that "In a period of invigorated fighting spirit army museums deserved special attention." The aim of these museums was to glorify a certain type of man — the soldier, the "guardian of the people" — and by his glorification to generate throughout the population a certain spiritual and intellectual attitude, which in fact was a preparedness for war.[12]

A distinguished German art historian, K. Koetchau, stated in 1933 that the time had arrived for museums to serve the people rather than students. Translated into more explicit terms, museums in Nazi Germany were declared to be one among other means of propaganda. Fatherland and Regional Museums illustrating the Germanic past came to dominate other types of collections which by their contents did not lend themselves to topical political phraseology.[13] Even the National Gallery in Berlin followed the slogan of the day and arranged a series of exhibitions entitled "German Art Since Dürer," with stress laid on the Teutonic element. Authoritative speakers openly demanded that German money should be spent on German art and that purchases of works of art by foreign masters were of secondary interest.

In these circumstances the informative value of museums was

more appreciated than any other qualities. A foreign critic wrote in 1937:

In certain countries in which all forces of the nation converge on political action, the museum regards as its major task to act as a means of pedagogy; it fulfills a political role at the expense of esthetics and sensitiveness. . . . In these museums of social pedagogy the work of art is regarded as a historical record and is exhibited together with auxiliary material such as casts, copies of other paintings, maps and graphs.[14]

Problems of display which in years preceding the Nazi period had occupied many people in Germany were now approached with mild interest only. The reconstruction of the National Gallery in Berlin proceeded on familiar lines; the ceilings of the "Cornelius rooms" were lowered, and a triple glazing was introduced to diffuse the top light evenly.[15] On other occasions the exhibition of a few selected specimens was recommended instead of a monotonous series of objects, a docile repetition of effort of the past. Paintings were presented in combination with music of the period, with concerts played in the room of the appropriate exhibition.[16] On such exceptional occasions rhythm, in its twofold expression in paint and in sound, was valued for its own sake, and for once propaganda seemed forgotten.

The United States. "The American Museum is . . . neither an abandoned European palace nor a solution for storing . . . national wealth. . . . It is an American phenomenon developed by the people, for the people, and of the people." Such was the definition used by a distinguished American expert in drawing a comparison between museums in Europe and the United States.[17]

If expressed in numbers the progress made by museums in the United States between the two world wars was impressive.[18]

A main characteristic of museums in the United States during this period was the increasing emphasis laid on education and the widening scope of the educational function. This prevalent concentration on a single function was, however, not unanimously shared by all experts. The conflicting views will be presented in the following paragraphs.

. . . activities of the museum are far more important than its housed specimens . . . it is the primary task of museums "to lure our word-drugged minds" to the contemplation . . . of concrete objects.[19]

If critical intelligence is to survive in a civilization flooded with propaganda and intellectual authoritarianism, the longing for first-hand information must be kept alive. . . . Books and lectures were referred to as hypnotic processes of education allowing the

individual to submerge his own reason in a common judgment. . . .[20]
. . . the staff of the early museum was chosen for its scholarship
and not its social consciousness. Thus scholarly work achieved a
place of prominence in museums far out of proportion to its relative
importance. . . . Briefly, the purpose and the only purpose of museums is education in all its varied aspects, from the most scholarly
research to the simple arousing of curiosity . . . one thing is certain
and that is that museums must shift the emphasis from scholarly
work to . . . popular education. Needless to say the latter may be
increased without diminishing the former.[21]

(The purpose of museums is to afford) . . . to our whole people free
and ample means for innocent and refined enjoyment, and also
supplying the best facilities for practical instruction and for the
cultivation of pure taste in all matters concerned with the arts. . . .
Here then is the final and basic justification for museums . . . to be
the midwife of democracy.[22]

. . . the conclusion may well be drawn that museums in the United
States are a definite educational force, contributing to the economic and cultural life of their communities.[23]

The word "education" is a very ambiguous one, and the parent of
much misunderstanding.
We are misled into thinking educational effort the panacea for all
the ills of society.
Our faith in the machinery of instruction becomes unconsciously
inflated beyond all reason.[24]

Critics who doubted the power of instruction as an all-purpose nostrum raised strong objection to the didactic bias in art museums
which was blamed on the "atrophy of perception in Anglo-Sax-
ons" — on their absorption in effort and their aversion to pleasure.

. . . a work of art is not a specimen, not primarily an historical document, but a source of pleasure, analogous to, say, a musical composition. The major purpose of the National Gallery is to allow each
painting, piece of sculpture, or other object of art to communicate
to the spectator, with as little interference as possible, the enjoyment it was designed to give.[25]

The critical comments with regard to the use of art museums represented the reaction of some experts to the widely held opinion
that objects of art were social documents and that their historical
contents were to receive as much attention as their aesthetic qualities. This approach was to meet the needs of a general public that
still had limited education and as little aesthetic experience as any
population of an urban, industrialized environment which in its
hasty growth had allowed the spread of ugliness. References to the
background of life in which works of art had been created were to
bridge the gap between objects which are accessible only to sensitivity and human beings alienated from beauty in any form. Implied
was an emphasis on people as sociological beings.

The promotion of education in museums led to an increase in numbers of people attending lectures and gallery tours, which in their turn added momentum to the campaign. In 1935 sixty thousand people participated in guided tours in the Metropolitan Museum of Art in New York; on a single Saturday morning 1000 persons attended a morning lecture at the Toledo Art Museum in 1937.[26] Notwithstanding these symptoms of success in terms of attendance figures, the museum atmosphere was not free of malaise. A demand was voiced for a replacement of offerings to the "heedless masses" by efforts directed to specific groups, and preferably to established ones that had achieved a certain degree of coherence based on common interests, social or professional. There was an awareness of a gap between expended efforts and results, and attendance figures may not have been considered by everybody as reliable indicators of successful performance. To some the gap between financial investment and results may have ranked highest; others may have been mainly concerned with the benefit people actually derived from visits to museums — from drawing lots in a kind of cultural lottery.[27]

The doubters appear to have been in a minority, if we can judge by the continuing efforts of museums to increase attendance without probing into the qualitative gains of visitors. Conducted tours, lectures, and museum clubs offered information on a wide range of subjects and were open to the general public and to groups united by a common interest — in insects, in design, or otherwise. Their appeal was supposed to reach a miscellaneous variety of human beings — housewives, factory workers, salesmen of specific goods, pupils of certain school grades, or immigrants in the process of "Americanization."

In search of contacts with people outside museums, liaison officers of large institutions visited factories and workshops which might benefit from loan collections as source materials for design patterns and color schemes to be applied to contemporary arts and crafts, machine-produced or handmade. Temporary loans — entire collections or single specimens — were exchanged between museums, or were made available to schools, libraries, associations, and even to individuals.[28]

The desire to use the public museum as a means of dissemination of knowledge brought to the fore methods of selection and presentation of exhibits which were developed beyond all precedent, even if some approaches had originally been devised in Europe. There were the Period Rooms and the Dioramas, or Habitat Groups, show-

ing a few specimens — paintings or models of machines or zoological specimens — as parts of a total environment, as distinct from the
more or less coherent and monotonous series of objects. The Period
Rooms of the Pennsylvania Museum of Art in Philadelphia were
among the most accomplished representatives of their type and
style. On an even wider basis synthesis found realization in complete architectural settings: as early as 1909 in the Japanese Court
in the Museum of Fine Arts in Boston, and on a much grander scale
in The Cloisters in New York, opened in 1938.[29]

Numerous historic House Museums and Trailside Museums of
natural history or of archaeology, closely related to their location,
expected the motorist on the expanding highways. They represented
a trend toward small museums outside urban centers and were
harbingers of new ways of adult education in an era of more plentiful leisure. A suggestion was made that the Historic House may
develop to a vacation resort where a few days could be used to better advantage than being whiled away; where visitors could come
face to face with a past gone by and yet present in the architecture
of a building, in furniture, paintings, and objects of everyday use;
where people would be stimulated by such sights and could add
information obtained from a small appropriate library. Facilities for
accommodation and meals would be available but would not be the
dominant attractions.[30]

The "total environment" exhibit reached its largest scope and
highest degree of excellence in the outdoor museum of Colonial
Williamsburg in Virginia, and it included facilities for visitors who
wished to stay for longer than a few hours.[31] In the course of generations the elegant small capital of the oldest and wealthiest British
colony in America lost color, as indifferent facades came to cover
up eighteenth-century features, and an instant slum of shacks and
gasoline stations cropped up with munition workers in need of accommodation during the First World War. The vision of a reconstructed Williamsburg arose in the mind of the Reverend W. A. R.
Goodwin and came to be shared by John Rockefeller, Jr. Thus began the metamorphosis of a town: extensive preparatory studies,
architectural plans drawn up in accordance with old documents,
the demolition of hundreds of structures of more recent years, the
rehabilitation of original ones still in existence behind defacing cam-
ouflage, and the erection of entire buildings on authentic foundations. Scholarly accuracy was the set criterion, and the undertaking
required an investment of $80 million.

In 1934 the first visitors entered an enclave of serene beauty

— streets lined with fine eighteenth-century houses and spacious gardens, with workshops in which craftsmen were working at old trades, and inns serving appropriate dishes. In the stillness of a preindustrial environment, costumed guides provided information in installments as people wandered from one place to another. It was here that Washington, Jefferson, and other patriots had sat in the House of Burgesses. Here they had feared an attack by the British from the sea and had decided to move the capital of the rebel government to Richmond.

In spite of the unavoidable artificiality of an open-air museum the evocative power of Colonial Williamsburg is remarkable. It shows some elements of the quintessence of the early United States; in the fashion of museums in general it does not include other aspects of the era — the manner in which less privileged people lived.

Another large open-air museum of the period between the two world wars is Greenfield Village near Dearborn, Michigan, established by Henry Ford.[32] The village consists of buildings which originally did not belong together, and it lacks in this respect the integrity of Colonial Williamsburg, but it illustrates a definite educational program. Ford believed that education ought to teach people to look ahead by looking back, and he had a profound faith in the qualities of the pioneers who had shaped the nation, in their self-dependence and their creative capacities to cope with unprecedented problems; he had doubts whether the schools were sufficiently related to agriculture and to industry. Ford's Museum of Industrial and Domestic Arts at Dearborn and the Edison Institute, which houses collections, are related to the outdoor installation extending over two hundred and sixty acres in Greenfield Village; the three units supplement each other. Henry Ford trusted the effectiveness of learning by direct confrontation with objects people had used. In his view an experience of this kind could in an hour provide a truer impression of human ways of living than could be had in a month of reading.

The tradition of private initiative in establishing and maintaining museums continued in spite of the federal income tax, which had come to stay in 1913. Those with very large incomes now needed a shelter from the rising estate and inheritance taxes which were to maintain a measure of "cradle equality" in the United States.

Among numerous fine projects of those years three stood out: Colonial Williamsburg; the Museum of Modern Art, New York; and the National Gallery in Washington, D.C. The different ways in which they challenge and inform human thought and feeling rule out a comparison with regard to precedence in terms of quality.

The Museum of Modern Art began its official existence in 1929 and moved in 1939 from rented quarters to its present building on Fifty-third Street, but the impulse to its establishment began early in the century.[33] At the Armory Show in 1913 modern art definitely declared its arrival in the United States; the exhibition was organized by the attorney and collector John Quinn, with the assistance of other crusaders, and in the face of vigorous opposition. Originally American avant-garde artists, alienated from the sedate National Academy of Design, were to be provided with an opportunity for a representative display of their creations, but in the end modern European paintings occupied a good deal of space on the burlap-covered partition walls under the uncongenial roof of the 69th Regiment Armory. The press mostly ridiculed the show and called it pathological, but pictures purchased on the occasion signaled the spread of interest in modern art. When the Metropolitan Museum in 1921 ventured to exhibit post-Impressionist paintings, with some of the loans coming from Quinn's collection, anonymous sponsors of a circular were quick in perceiving a link between degenerate art and a Bolshevist attempt to destory the social order in the United States. In consequence Quinn refused to leave his unwelcome paintings to the Metropolitan; they were sold in 1927, after his death, and their dispersal spurred action that led to the foundation of the Museum of Modern Art. The John Rockefellers, Jr., and members of their family offered both financial backing and genuine understanding.

The influence exerted by the Museum of Modern Art has been inestimable. It has honed the sensitivity of innumerable men and women to contemporary artistic expression as well as to the qualities of well-designed simple furniture and such ordinary domestic utensils as coffee cups and spoons. At a time marked by the human struggle for adjustment to a physical environment changing rapidly in the wake of unprecedented technological novelties, the Museum of Modern Art has helped innumerable people to get glimpses of tomorrow's perception of shapes and colors. Other museums have followed in its trail.

In 1941 the National Gallery opened its doors.[34] It represented the largest gift a nation ever received from an individual. The donor, Andrew W. Mellon, did not wish the museum to bear his name, if for no other reasons because a National Gallery was more likely to attract future donors. The paintings he contributed were of supreme quality; Van Eyck, Rubens and Rembrandt, Botticelli, Raphael and Titian were in the company of other great masters. Purchases had been facilitated by the depression, by the financial needs of the U.S.S.R. that sent westward pictures of the Hermitage to be exchanged for funds needed by a newly developing industrial economy, and of course by Mellon's financial capacity. The art collection he donated was valued at $50 million , with $15 million added for an endowment and a building. Before the completion of the marble shell that extended over eight hundred feet and was far too spacious for the Mellon collection, other donors began to announce their contributions. Samuel Kress gave up his plan of building a museum and donated many of his paintings to the National Gallery; the Widener, the Dale, and the Rosenwald collections added works of such excellence as demanded by Mellon when making his gift. Another of his stipulations concerned the prevention of any undue influence of the traditional emphasis on science of the Smithsonian Institution with regard to its new bureau, where art was to be cultivated. The gallery is governed by an independent board of trustees.

In the now traditional manner of museums in the United States the support by a few wealthy individuals went together with contributions from the rank and file of citizens. The following quotation was taken from a guidebook of the Metropolitan Museum of Art of 1944:

We extend to you a most cordial invitation to become a member of the Metropolitan Museum of Art. In this way it is possible for you to take an active part in increasing the value and extent of our general services and educational activities. Your membership in the Museum represents the thoughtful public support without which no public institution can prosper. . . . The Museum offers to its Members not only the satisfaction of aiding an institution of established and far-reaching usefulness but also a growing number of special services and privileges which include . . .

While the drums were beaten to keep museums in the limelight of public awareness, work of a different temper but of no minor long-term importance was carried on in other quarters. The idea of the multiplicity of the functions of museums became more widely accepted, judging by the provision of study collections in some museums, which fundamentally differed from the exhibits for the general public. The approach was reflected in the recommendations made by architects, who considered that a museum building ought to consist of several distinct parts, each serving a specific purpose — permanent and temporary exhibitions, study rooms, storage facilities, and so on — which were lacking in a monolithic block.

The desire to assess the motivations of people to visit museums, and the relationships between different kinds of exhibits and results in terms of learning and enjoyment, began to assume articulate thinking when psychologists turned their minds to museums. The initiative was taken in the later twenties by Edward D. Robinson, professor of psychology at Yale University. His premature death may have caused the promising beginnings to peter out in the thirties; it is much to be regretted that the published observations of Robinson and associates have been little taken notice of in practical application.[35]

The intellectual climate in museums at the end of the period between the two world wars was poignantly described by Francis H. Taylor in his short but substantial book *Babel's Tower*. The two alternatives he perceived were "temples of learning and understanding" and "hanging gardens for the perpetuation of the Babylonian pleasures of aestheticism and the secret sins of private archaeology."[36] His statement left considerable scope for interpretation, which became more specific in the years that followed.

The museums of the United States made great strides during the years between 1914 and '40 plus, but the period ended in a mood of a dilemma. If translated into articulate words, it was as much, or more, a time for meandering questions than for definite answers: What indeed were the primary functions of museums? Did all museums have to follow the pattern of a uniform purpose? If museums did not exist, would people of the twentieth century feel the need to invent them?

Liberal Europe. In this context the title designates territories not necessarily connected with each other geographically or by way of administration, yet united by the fact of not having been engulfed in a nonliberal doctrine during the period between the two world wars.

The new start in European museum work after the 1914–1918 war was heralded by a number of reports taking stock of conditions, of assets as well as of shortcomings, and suggesting ways of reconstruction.[37] In addition to statements concerned with museums of a single country, international opinion was voiced through the International Museums Office founded in 1926 and affiliated with the Institut de Co-opération Intellectuelle in Paris, which organized conferences and offered a platform for international opinion in its journal *Mouseion* and in the symposium entitled *Muséographie*.[38]

International museum experts concurred that the very wealth of European museums was a liability. At the time of its opening, the Prado in Madrid had contained 300 pictures; a century later its contents amounted to about 3000 items. In 1793 the original museum in the Louvre in Paris housed 650 objects; the catalogue of 1933 listed 173,000 items.[39]

In large museums a number of previous private collections appeared in incoherent combinations; objects were presented in monotonous rows, and labeling was scarce.

Various remedies were recommended to instill vitality into the barren wealth of the European museum: (1) cooperation between museums, which would relieve the large museums of their surplus and offer new opportunities to provincial establishments, (2) centralization of administration on a national basis that would facilitate cooperation, (3) division of the large museum into three main parts: exhibitions for the general public, galleries for students, and storage rooms, (4) clearly defined goals for each museum, and in small museums a limitation of contents to a specific topic, preferably related to its locality.

The situation of European museums after the First World War may be summed up in the words of an English expert:

Until the end of the period brought to a close by the War, the prime energies of those responsible for their direction were devoted to acquisition. Collecting mania was prevalent. . . . A new orientation makes the intelligent use of the art gallery's and museum's recources even more important than their increase. . . . Our principal task, in short, is to make the man in the street conscious of his possessions, and to help him to use them.[40]

In practice the recommended far-reaching reforms found realization on a small scale and in a halfhearted manner only.[41]

Changes were undertaken in numerous museums, but as a rule they concerned details, mostly with regard to display. Spacious halls were divided into bays and exhibits were "thinned out"; through wider spacing single objects received greater emphasis. Preference was given to plain backgrounds, in paint or cloth. Wherever possible cases were made inconspicuous and built into the walls. The sequencing of objects, on a chronological or geographical basis, gained in clarity.

Critics were aware of the pioneering efforts made in a few institutions but continued to stress the general absence of progress:

It may be accepted as a fact that the uses and functions of museums and art galleries are not generally appreciated.[42]
Drift, neglect, decay—these are the material features of the majority of our provincial museums and art galleries.[43]

A few enterprising museums made information available that was of special relevance to the epoch and to the rank and file of citizens. Subject matter ranged from agriculture to airways, from refrigeration to noise abatement, from healthful diets and hygiene for the expectant mother to human labor under preindustrial and industrial conditions, from problems of population to those of production and consumption of raw materials.

The cataclysm of the First World War, after an extended era of comparative peace, aroused a sense of uncertainty with regard to man's knowledge of himself—among the vanquished and the victors of the war, and the Musée de l'Homme at the Trocadéro in Paris took a new approach to ethnology: white man's ambitious sense of superiority over those who used less advanced tools was replaced by an interest in the species man in general. The emphasis was on the study of ways of life of different peoples, their ways of controlling forces of nature around them and within themselves; on the relationships among individuals, and between individuals and the community. Even in museums of science and technology human problems often became central. In previous times, objects — machinery or minerals, or paintings — had been shown as ends in themselves and not in relation to their functions in the lives of human beings. Man and his man-made environment were featured in a growing number of museums of ethnology and of folk museums — the first stressing life in communities of primitive material culture still in existence outside white man's world, and the latter illustrating ways of living in Western man's preindustrial environment.[44]

In a temporary exhibition, "The Sahara," at the Musée de l'Homme, a complete experience was called up by a combination of prehistory, geology, geography, botany, zoology, and ethnography. The Wellcome Medical Museum in London, primarily addressed to students, testified that synthesis was not necessarily limited to popular education. Survey exhibits illustrated human diseases from their causes to their pathological symptoms, treatments, and methods of prevention. Photographs and dioramas supplemented specimens and together presented a consecutive story, with certain objects acting as high spots of a dramatic sequence. Verbal information varied from short labels to literature contained in files within a particular bay.[45] "Relationships," in form of comparison or of evolution, were the keynotes in the presentation of information in the Museum of Social Science (Gesellschafts und Wirtschaftsmuseum), Vienna.[46]

On a small scale synthesis was used in numerous museums of Liberal Europe. On the whole, units based on concepts were more cultivated than realistic habitat groups. Popular concepts were the migration of birds or animal locomotion; or the productive capacity of a geographical area, in terms of raw materials or manufactured products.

The museum of the Imperial Institute in London specialized in showing steps in industrial processes by appropriate samples of those stages, the raw materials that were used, and photographs or dioramas of people at work and while using the finished articles. The Institute's aim was to present exhibits that would arrest, hold, and intrigue the visitor's attention, and strike some chord of experience in his mind.

Concern with the transmission of information to laymen led to facilities for visitor participation. The science museums in Munich and London expanded opportunities for the handling and operating of machinery. The Hygiene Museum in Dresden offered courses in dietetics and first aid. The Palais de la Découverte in Paris pioneered by organizing regular science demonstrations for the general public in their museum.

Museums of art, and arts and crafts, were more conservative than institutions devoted to the sciences or to ethnology, but exceptions existed. The Barock Museum in Vienna, housed in a palace of the period, combined paintings, sculpture, and furniture of baroque style. The result was an articulate expression of the essence of Austrian culture, that combination of sophisticated court manner, Roman Catholic mysticism, and a singularly artistic temperament of people at the watershed between the West and the East. Even to the uninitiated the Barock Museum was likely to impart a message. As a well-informed critic of this museum wrote, "it had transcended the limitations set to museums in the nineteenth century, which were means of exhibiting single objects of art . . . it represented an artistic creation in itself."[47] It was indeed an orchestrated whole, without period rooms and costumed wax figures, and yet filled with the atmosphere of an epoch, of a locality, and of the dominant social groups of the culture.

In a more explicit manner art was connected with its social background in a temporary Rembrandt exhibition in Amsterdam where simple pictorial charts illustrated economic and social conditions of the period. Photographs of the master's paintings were part of the historical records; originals were shown in local museums.[48]

In spite of a number of isolated pioneering efforts, the Public Museum of Liberal Europe at the time of the outbreak of the Second World War had not developed to an institution of vital importance to society. Halfhearted measures, lack of clearly defined goals, and stagnancy prevailed. The men who proposed reforms were not vested with authority to put their ideas into action, and those in positions of authority were often amateurs in matters of museums. Furthermore, or first of all, the welding and propelling influence of public opinion was missing. Even when citizens disapproved of their museum or museums, they had no means of exerting pressure that might be conducive to changes. European museums were mostly supported by public funds and were governed by impersonal bureaucratic routines. Without directive forces from either inside or outside, many of these museums seemed to exist in a vacuum. They were far less subject to criticism than literature, dramatic art, or concerts; there were no established standards of performance as in schools. Neither visitors' books in which the attendance is supposedly registered nor the stricter control of the turnstile at the gate of the museum which mechanically records the number of visitors is a true indicator of performance. At their best they record the number of warm bodies entering the premises.

It was only on the rare occasions of controlled experiments that the motivations of people to visit museums could be grasped and that their reactions to the experience became known and recorded. Statements made by close to one hundred persons I interviewed toward the end of the Second World War in Cambridge, England, were as follows:

1. With regard to their motivations to visit museums:

The exhibition is more vivid . . . more living than a book.

I like to see real objects . . . to use my own judgement.

It is easier to grasp things in a museum than in a written or told description.

I like to see things of ancient times — where we came from.

I like to see the beginnings of things . . . flint implements . . .

To see ancient things . . . and to see development . . . and to compare things . . . gives solace and solidity.

To see human development gives you a feeling of eternity.

I like to see the texture and color of objects of art . . . they give the atmosphere of a whole country . . . a whole century . . . I like to feast my eye on a single beautiful thing.

The emotional side comes first . . . the painter sees the more essential features . . . and shows them like a magnifying glass.

2. With regard to conditions existing in most museums:

Museums, as they generally now are, are wasted. A wretched use is made of them — they say nothing.

They are generally bad . . . physically tiring . . . they demand a mental strain even from those positively interested in a matter.

There should be more space . . . things should be less crammed.

If only there were fewer things . . . less distractions . . . less examples of one kind.

So frequently in exhibitions the exhibits are just put in rows with a card saying where they came from, and one goes out feeling considerably more muddled than when one went in.

It needs patience to sort out the jumble . . . one should ruthlessly throw out all repetitions.

There were some beautiful things, but one would not bother to look at all the bits.

The exhibition left questions unanswered. What is the purchasing power of those currencies . . . how is it used . . . ? By what sort of people?

We were given plenty of facts but no information — very little in the way of dates to connect them.

The more I looked at it the less connection I saw. The objects should be connected by photographs of surroundings and of the people to whom the objects belong.

Jumping from one thing to another . . . it is hard to keep one's mind on anything . . . It is quite chaotic . . . an attack of measles.

If we judge by these statements, museums offered to people experiences they did not find elsewhere: the direct confrontation with authentic objects and even with copies or models of authentic specimens, resulted in a speedy and forceful communication. Value was found in the variety of museum materials. A far greater variety can, of course, be found in books, but even a single visit to a museum of medium size may make people more acutely aware of the extraordinary spectrum of phenomena on earth if some samples of them are seen in a few adjacent rooms. There is a difference between an input that is varied to the degree of creating confusion and a sampler that can be mentally digested. The visitors distinguished between the potential and the actual qualities of museums. They unanimously appreciated their potential qualities, but were critical of many actual aspects; in fact, laymen were more severe critics than experts.

The authorities in charge of European museums desired to render service, but as long as the functions of their institutions remained vaguely defined, a playground existed for the expression of leanings which on occasions of more stringent reality remained repressed or were adjusted to circumstances. The miragelike existence of some museums would occasionally awaken retrogressive attitudes, and people would seek satisfaction in experiences of hoarding and boasting — in palacelike museum buildings as symbols of respectability, and in accumulations of objects of high or of indifferent quality. In addition to the "palace-fallacy," the "laboratory-fallacy" persisted — the assumption that what was good for specialists would be equally beneficial for the general public.

The uneasy brief intermission between two world wars did not offer sufficient opportunities to Europe to correct long-established faults in museums, or even to perceive all of them, and the period of respite was hardly conducive to the realization of unprecedented projects. One such project was a museum attached to The Mundaneum, the planned international intellectual headquarters in Geneva. Le Corbusier was commissioned to design the architectural installation. The museum was to be in the form of a stepped pyramid, and the exhibition illustrating the evolution of human culture was to begin at its top and to end at the exit of the building into the street where visitors would view the final installment of the development in which they were all participants.

During the summer months of 1939 a temporary art exhibition was offered by the Municipal Museum in Geneva. It was an event of great significance: for once Europe's international cooperation was successful. Famous works of art belonging to Spain and menaced by the Spanish Civil War had been salvaged by the efforts of a committee and were given shelter in Switzerland. When the danger passed they were returned to Spain: some 1300 pictures, unique tapestries, historic relics, manuscripts, and a long list of other irreplaceable objects. Hopes rose. Man seemed to be making progress in his evolution from brute selfishness to peaceful cooperation, but disenchantment was not far off.

Third Period of Reform: from 1945 to the Present

An account of this period could be given from a variety of points of view: these are years of search and conflict, of gestation, achievement, and deadlock such as museums have never known before. Since my personal comments are largely reserved for the final chapter, and the following pages are to reflect the opinions of those who took action in the events, it seems best to proceed according to groups which to a considerable extent imply different collective memories and varying immediate needs.

Europe is to receive precedence owing to the destruction suffered by its museums during the Second World War. In *America* three distinct museological areas have been forming – the United States, Canada, and Mexico. Third, there is an *Area of New Expectations*, which includes a miscellany of locales, past experiences and ceilings of expectation. Under the aegis of UNESCO's Museum Section and of the International Council of Museums (ICOM), a superordinate *Inter-Nation Group* is budding. Of all these multifarious efforts only some of the main phenomena and trends can be presented in this general survey.

Europe. The small peninsula to the west of the continent of Asia looms large in the minds of men owing to its achievements that encompass several millennia. It is a jigsaw composed of a number of countries or nationalities, each a self-contained unit molded by centuries and differing from its neighbors. There are many breaks in this jigsaw, and the parts do not fit smoothly into any overall picture. The current divide deepens between the Communist countries and those of a different persuasion.

Museums in some parts of Europe suffered considerable losses in the course of the Second World War,[1] but their renewal has been remarkable,[2] not merely in terms of increased quantities of both museums and visitors but also with regard to the quality of architecture and display — with Italy in the lead in some respects and the Soviet Union and its associates in others.

Western Europe. The following aspects received special attention and challenge further thought:

Where should museums be located? The Louisiana Museum north of Copenhagen in Denmark highlighted the attractions of an establishment outside a big city, in the park of an old residence, but voices were raised against the sterilization of public museums in cultural parks. In the city of Lund in Sweden, an art gallery was built close to the marketplace. A well-informed and perceptive critic recommended that museums might be built in such places of daily confluence of the general public as in shopping centers.[3] Indeed, in 1968 the first subway museum, Musée Métro, became available in Paris, with Assyrian, Egyptian, and Roman antiquities installed in marble vaults and niches and flanking the booth of the station master.

Should museums exist in isolation from each other or other institutions, or share a site with others? The combination of a teaching institution with a museum is of old standing, but with the international trend in museums toward popular education goes the idea of a Cultural Center embracing a museum, or museums, a library, an archive, a theater, and a concert hall. When the German city Pforzheim replaced its destroyed museum, it combined on one site two museums, of history and of jewelry, which is a local industry, and a civic archive. Louisiana, although framed by an isolating landscape, is a part of a recreational area. In West Germany survives the idea of the "Museum Insel" (Museum Island). With the prewar one being now cut off from the West, two new complexes of museums are in the process of development, at a cost of 180 million DM, one devoted to Western cultures and the other to those outside Europe. The Stiftung Preussischer Kulturbesitz (Foundation for Prussian Cultural Properties), which started its activities in 1962, has chosen the sites near the Tiergarten and in Dahlem with the view of a reunited Berlin. The complex at the Tiergarten includes a building housing the national library, a music building, and several museums, with St. Matthew's Church serving as focus.

What kind of architecture? A summary answer can best be given by way of exclusion: museum buildings ought not to look like temples or palaces; they ought to fit the human scale and intone a mood of relaxation and enjoyment rather than of awe. In Louisiana members of the anonymous public wander around without meeting uniformed guards, sit on comfortable chairs, and drink coffee in the library. The Danes have also shown originality in the use of museum architecture in their zoological museum of the University of Copenhagen. Contrary to all tradition they accommodate their research collections, laboratories, and storage facilities on the main floors, while the exhibits are shown on the upper floors.

The widely expressed verbal revolt against large, monolithic structures was on some occasions put into realization in the form of several pavilions. Pforzheim may serve as one example. On the French Riviera, the collector and art dealer Aimé Maeght was instrumental in building a gallery of contemporary art, designed by the Spanish architect Sert, in which studiolike rooms and patios form a meandering continuum of enclosed and open spaces. They frame the work of some of the greatest contemporary painters and sculptors—a Bracque, a Miró, a Giacometti, and their peers. A room is often reserved for a single artist's creations; the roofs serve as platforms for sculpture. There is a conference hall and a chapel.

In a larger building it is recommended to break the space up into several environments differing in size, in ceiling height, and in illumination. A fine example of this approach translated into practice is Ignazio Gardella's Pavilion of Contemporary Art, in the Gallery of Modern Art in Milan, where visitors move through five different spaces within an overall enclosure of two stories. Italy has shown creative subtlety in adapting ancient convents and palaces to a new use as museums. In the San Lorenzo Cathedral in Genoa four underground circular rooms of different diameters were added which enshrine unique contents: the Cup of the Holy Grail, the Golden Casket containing the ashes of St. John, vestments and reliquaries which reflect human aspirations above common everyday matters throughout centuries. Each of the main exhibits is housed in a room of its own which seems to echo, to modulate, and to condense the perennial message of the objects.

Are museums moving toward a new humanistic attitude? The traditional attitude in museums, especially in European museums, was object-oriented; less attention was paid to the human beings who visited the establishments purportedly existing for human use. There has been a change in this direction, a change in process, and European countries participate in it in varying degrees. There is still a reserved attitude on the part of museum officers toward the general public, especially in Germany and in England, but in hardly any place in Europe would a curator find it politic to say openly that "if the public at large took to visiting museums, it would be the end of everything," as a French curator was reported having stated in 1940.[4] Yet some of the new European museum buildings show a concern with the capacities and limitations of the human eye, brain, and nervous system in perceiving exhibits, and not only physically but at some depth of meaning. Backgrounds tend to be plain, and specimens are better spaced. In the Museo Correr in Venice, Carpaccio's picture *Two Courtesans* becomes a new experience when one faces the familiar painting in isolation from a crowd of other pictures, casually leaning on an easel. Brazil's new art museum in São Paulo has gone even further in making backgrounds inconspicuous: the easels which support paintings are of transparent plastic.

A number of experimental methods have been tried in Europe to avoid the well-known phenomenon of museum fatigue, which begins in the feet of a viewer and creeps up into his head. The common principle of such efforts was to move the exhibits in front of a seated and static viewer: exhibits were mounted on moving belts and drums or were placed on a horizontal bridgelike background, moving in turnstile fashion between narrow drums. In the Nederlands Postmuseum in The Hague visitors are seated while watching an automated demonstration of procedures related to mail services — to the designing and printing of stamps, the sorting of mail, and so on. The fourteen available tapes include information about weather reports and the work that goes on in a telephone exchange. Moving lights direct the eyes of the viewers to the changing focus of the operations, which are accompanied by a variety of sounds and by series of sequential slides, and of course by a taped interpretation.[5] In the Atomarium of the Tekniska Museet in Stockholm seated visitors watch science demonstrations related to atoms of matter; they are presented with one model at a time or with a demonstration illustrating a single concept. The involvement of visitors in the presented information by providing opportunities for the manipulation of machinery and the handling of objects has been gaining wider recognition, and no doubt keeps up the alertness of people.

The growing recognition of the potentialities and limitations of the human creature has initiated a search for multisensory approaches to the museum visitor. In a Swedish Forestry Museum a large tree is fastened by its roots to the ceiling; visitors can view it, touch it, and smell the tree as well as a variety of wood samples. Sound linked to exhibits is a generally familiar matter; at the International Labor Exhibition in Turin in 1961, people viewed display panels illustrating increase in production, which went by them on an overhead moving belt, while they listened to the sounds of factories. The Institute of Contemporary Arts in London, an intrepid leader of living art, declared recently on the occasion of their move to respectable quarters that they will not show exhibitions but exhibit shows; they will mix all arts. The *animal humain* has indeed been too long alienated from the use of all its senses.

Sales desks, guided tours, and refreshment rooms have appeared in European museums where they did not exist before World War II, or hardly existed. They too indicate a new deference to the layman where previously the scholar was king.

Are museums changing their topics? The change lies largely in the emphasis, and here again the lay visitor is appealed to, and it seems implicitly admitted that no single individual can be omniscient. In museums of different kinds the new emphasis is on contemporary matters. In the Museum of Science and Industry in Munich it is an adopted policy to give larger scope to contemporary advances in science than to its historical development. In numerous ethnographical museums stress is often laid on preindustrial ways of life of the locality of the museum rather than on curios originating from distant lands and from cultures which for long periods of time were considered by white men as being primitive or savage. In the Musée de l'Histoire de France in Paris the topic of an exhibition was The Feudal Society;[6] when discussing such topics as Medieval Cities or The Reformation in France, visiting school pupils handle actual specimens or copies of fragile objects. In a variety of ways man is the focal point of the presented information, his dependence on the natural phenomena of his environment, and his achievements in taming such forces.[7] This frequently leads to the use of art and archaeological collections as illustrations of human history, more often of social and economic than political events.[8] The prevalent historical approach had found vocal opposition among museum workers who wish to retain the claim of single exceptional objects, be they of art or of archaeology, to be considered on their own merits and with a recognition of the aesthetic enjoyment they stimulate in people.[9]

Two world wars and ongoing revolutions stirred in 1948 the staid Museum of Natural History in Vienna to express the human urge for peaceful living in an exhibition Mankind, a Single Family. It was a sermon against racial prejudices and theories of "master races." About the same time, the Galliera Museum in Paris staged an exhibition illustrating man's stuggle for life and liberty on earth. In a new museum in Copenhagen, the Frihedsmuseet, human liberty is the exclusive fundamental theme.

Science and technology are high on the totem pole of museum topics, and they tend to fulfill a gamut of functions. They excite the curiosity of young people and their interest in becoming scientists and technicians, without whom the wheels of a modern industrial society would stand still; they generate appreciation among adult citizens, whose scientific literacy was left low during their school years before the steep upswing of scientific developments in more recent decades, and whose power on a country's decision has to be reckoned with where politicians react to pressures of public opinion; and they are likely to assuage concerns of people about science and technology growing too big and strong, and overriding humane concerns.[10] A comparatively small private museum named Evoluon, in Eindhoven, Holland, illustrates progressing technology as allied to man's fate on earth.

Helsinki has for many years had a Museum of Finnish Architecture. It promotes contemporary architecture by frequently changing exhibits, by a specialized library, and by acting as an information center. The Swedish Museum at Lund attracted crowds of visitors with its First International Exhibition of Erotic Art.

Centralization and decentralization are in the process of being identified for their compatibility and their propriety on different occasions.

With the increase in financial subsidies granted to museums by their national governments, there has been a strengthening of a central authority over museum matters. In accordance with an Edict of 1945 the Musées de France may give assistance to all museums in France, public and private, by offering guidance in such matters as the making of inventories, the planning of projects and the like. In Great Britain, the Area Museum Services (or Councils) established in 1963 – 1966 obtain grants from the central government on a fifty-fifty basis. Their specialists in conservation, display, and other aspects of museology serve institutions of an established region. In Denmark two Acts of Parliament, of 1956 and of 1964, permit grants to both cultural and art museums, and empower the central government to supervise museums by established experts.[11] Centralization is imaginatively applied by the Kunsthalle in Cologne, where a temporary exhibition, The Roman on the Rhine, was staged from loan materials of fifty-nine museums and by an interdisciplinary team of thirty-eight subject matter specialists and nine display experts. It was found helpful to keep the Kunsthalle a neutral ground, not directly related to any other establishment.[12]

Decentralization has been gaining recognition in the form of small museums specializing in local matters, of natural history or related to the man-made world. In Norway a preference has been shown to avoid the term "museum" and to name a small local collection a "hamlet center" (*bygdetun*); essentially these hamlet centers are diminutive folk museums. This trend goes together with centralization in other respects; in 1953 the Norwegian Parliament created the post of State Director of Museums. Similarly, Denmark cultivates local history museums, which are strengthened by the country's first Museum Act, providing state grants to individual institutions under the supervision of a state commission.[13] The Netherlands have had a crop of regional or specialized ethnographical museums and seek their aid in obtaining better insight into a common core of human behavior.

Great Britain can chalk up a first among the various, and variously fractured, Western European efforts in training museum personnel. In 1966 the University of Leicester instituted the first university department for training entrants into the museum profession.[14]

The examples selected for an illustration of Western European museums established since 1945 do not represent the average institution in any of the countries referred to. They are indicative of trends and of the direction of a process. There is hardly a point of time in this era of rapid changes that could be considered as the "present"—there is a fluid condition in which a congealing past, or pasts, meet head on with symptoms of tomorrow, and after-tomorrow, in a state of turbulence characteristic of new beginnings.

Some further references to European museums will be made in the account on museums in the United States, when a comparison of conditions will appear to be desirable.

Eastern Europe. In spite of precautions taken in Soviet Russia at the beginning of the Second World War, overwhelming losses were suffered by museums. Of the 122 museums governed by the People's Commissariat of Education, 114 were plundered or partially destroyed. While some museums had to be closed, others carried on their work in new ways:

Some museums organized exhibitions and lectures connected in one way or another with questions of the country's defense. Nearly all the regional museums were engaged at that time in the search for mineral resources in their localities which could be used for the needs of industry, public health, etc.
A number of museums collected materials from the battle-fields, so that now not only the main military-historical Soviet Army Mu-

seum but all history and regional museums have on display tens of thousands of documents and relics. . . .[15]

At a recent count 900 state museums existed in the Soviet Union, apart from thousands of others in schools, institutions of higher learning, and industrial and other enterprises. Attendance was estimated to have surpassed sixty million. In the national republics museums exist in hundreds; they are often in areas in which in Czarist times a museum had been a rarity.

Museums continue to enjoy the high regard they have been accorded since the early days of Communism, when the first People's Commissar for Education, Anatoly Lunacharsky, declared the museum to be "a grandiose memory book of mankind." If lectures given recently at the Hermitage are indicative of the general attitude of both museum workers and citizens to their museums, there exists a collective emotional attachment to these institutions.[16] They glory in their possessions, and the pride they take in the People's Treasures may account not only for high attendance but for an apparent absence of vandalism. In one of the lectures reference was made to a letter received by the administration of the Hermitage in which a visitor anxiously inquired about the progress in the restoration of a painting he had found missing in the museum.

The Research Institute of Museology, founded in 1937, has enlarged its activities. The Institute promotes the role of museums as a prime source of knowledge about both nature and society, and their collections as embodiments of material and spiritual culture from prehistory to the present. Workshops and publications on such disparate aspects as conservation and display spread the Institute's theories about the functions of museums among the rank and file of museum workers.[17]

Among the outstanding events of more recent years has been the opening to the public of the entire Kremlin as one large museum complex,[18] the establishment of the first Cosmonaut Museum, in Kalouga, the hometown of K. E. Tsiolkovsky, the erection of a new building for the Armed Forces Museum, and the new State Picture Gallery and Exhibition Hall of the Union of Soviet Artists on the Moskva embankment. Glass was chosen for the outer surfaces to merge in appearance with the river, an effect which lends lightness to the colossal structure covering almost 18,000 square meters. To facilitate the orientation of visitors, the museum is divided into five distinct circuits, each with an introductory room. Moving stairways and resting rooms are to prevent fatigue. Although in its exterior a monolith, the gallery is a combination of five subunits. One can well imagine that the exterior grandeur calls forth joyful pride in Russian viewers, especially in contrast to their limited and sober private quarters; once inside the building and focusing on single exhibits and sequences of objects, visitors find the measurements scaled down and comprehension facilitated to a pair of human eyes and a human brain.

As in some Western countries a trend has appeared on some occasions toward a combination of a museum with other facilities. In Poland, a new National Park Museum in Bialowieza, housed in one pavilion, is combined with two other pavilions serving as a hotel and a tourist shelter. In another locality in Poland, in Wilanow, the visitor to historical interiors, which once belonged to the Counts Potocki, has sport grounds at his disposal.[19]

In the choice of exhibition topics Communist museums provide wide scope to an illustration of social and economic conditions at different times of history, with special reference to modern times and to concerns shared by the majority of citizens. A variety of museums serve this ultimate goal: Homeland and History Museums, Ethnography and Folk Museums, and even Museums of Prehistory. A socioeconomic approach has been increasingly noticeable in the West, but its pitch has remained lower. The reverberations of revolutions of a mere two generations ago are stronger than the echoes of events two centuries ago, and overlaid by other mass experiences. Consequently the themes extend in the East to outspoken Museums of the Revolution, or of revolutions that took place in the past. Czechoslovakia presented the story of the Hussite Revolution in the later Middle Ages, and the National Museum in Belgrade held up the memory of the struggle for liberation in Serbia. The Ukrainians have erected two buildings to commemorate the defense and liberation of Sevastopol in two wars, in 1854–1855 and 1944; large panoramas provide an overall picture to which documents and personal effects of heroes are added. In Poland the traumatic memories of the Nazi extermination camp in Auschwitz (Oświęcim) found expression in a gruesome open-air site museum.

Even in museums of science and technology, economics and sociology are bound to receive greater stress in societies in which dramatic changes occurred in the course of a few decades owing to a diffusion of educational opportunities, and where a greatly enlarged bank of talent speeded up the development of science and technology. In Eastern Europe scientific and technical museums often serve as popular colleges and their use by adults is more than a pastime.[20]

The numerous Memorial Museums, related to political and military heroes as well as to writers, artists, and actors, may have two aims. They belong to the group of museums which keep the memory of the early revolutionary days alive, and they hold up models of excellence, of individual and national achievement.

Centralization exists by the very nature of a central government which dictates uniformity in fundamental respects, first of all in the emphasis on a political philosophy which remains supreme. By a systematic decentralization of efforts – in the form of local and regional museums, of traveling exhibitions, of museum trains and museum ships, which reach out into small villages in all parts of the huge territory, the diffusion of the central philosophy is strengthened; at the same time more numerous individuals are exposed to an educational upgrading. In Poland, the Silesian Museum in Wroclaw established museological Cooperation Centers which assist schools, factory clubs, and houses of culture in a certain area in obtaining exhibits. The Centers organize exhibitions and provide transportation as well as other facilities. The Silesian Museum itself acts as a center of publicity for museums in general by exploring new ways of making people aware of museums; they install samples of their work in showcases in railway stations and post offices, make ample use of publicity by means of newspapers and radio, and have even staged an art exhibition on Museum Advertising. General knowledge competitions with prizes for winners alert the public to the existence of their museum; questionnaires on museum work, prepared jointly with the departments of sociology and psychology of the local university, serve as another tool for image-building, and at the same time provide museum workers with better insights into the reactions of the public and into the effectiveness of their exhibits to put messages across to viewers.

An original centralizing effort is a Republic of Sculpture in Poland, in Orońsko near Kielce, where nature provides wood, granite, marble, and sandstone. Homes and a beautiful park are available to talented sculptors who spend their summer months in congenial company and in the tranquillity of the countryside; their patrons are local industries and trade unions. A Gallery of Modern Sculpture is a part of the project which has encouraged other localities to follow their example.[21]

An important decentralization occurred when the Hermitage Museum sent collections of paintings to the capital towns of national republics, to Kharkov, Odessa, Omsk, Alma Mata, and so on. A kind of decentralization that appears to be effective is the custom of dealing with specific audiences; of combining the topic of an exhibition with the vocational pursuits of a group of people; or of timing an exhibition in accordance with a seasonal event. Groups of people from a factory or a farm receive special attention during their Sunday visit in museums, and the guide fits his (or more often her) communication into an existing background of associations instead of darting around in a vacuum. What is shown and said is of relevance to the audience. At some museums special days are reserved for builders or for farmers, or for young readers. The Technical Museum in Prague arranged an exhibition of "Technology in the Service of the Woman." A similar situation is created when workers visit their factory museum that specializes in objects related to their trade. In the Ukraine a traveling exhibition on wedding customs is sent to villages at a time of the year when weddings are customarily celebrated.

Decentralization may also result from a growing awareness of the function of specific museums. Some Communist museums concentrate on research in departments established for the purpose. The Moravian Museum in Brno, Moravia, a part of Czechoslovakia, established in 1962 a Department of Genetics, named after the pioneer scholar Gregor Mendel. It deals with the uses of genetical techniques in plant cultivation, livestock breeding, and public health, and it acts as a consultation center. A separate pavilion of the museum is devoted to anthropology and includes scholars of geology and paleontology.[22] Poland found its pilot project of an educational museum in Gorzów so successful that it replicated it in other localities. In keeping with the trend to small regional museums, these educational museums deal first of all with regional natural science and history, but they go beyond it to illustrate principles of science in general, from the structure of matter to the origin of life, and they connect the sciences with the evolution of human history. Their personnel are trained first of all in learning and teaching procedures.

A widening of the forces that shape museums has led to what is known as People's Museums. Their main characteristic is volunteer work. In fact, these museums are brought into being by volunteers, often retired persons, and are maintained by them, on a very small or on a larger scale. Sometimes a group of individuals working in a village or in a factory take up the initiative in forming a collection of local interest, and they learn by preparing materials they wish to communicate to others. They are in their own fashion distant heirs of the *curiosi* of earlier centuries who for their satisfaction pursued a variety of intellectual interests and shared this with others.

America. A separate volume would be needed to do justice to the museums in all parts of the huge continent. It seems best to concentrate on three countries where museological activities during the period under review were most lively and productive of new directives, in the form of questions if not of solutions — in the United States, Canada, and Mexico.

To the south of them exists a wealth of museums, first of all of anthropology, archaeology, and history, but economic conditions are rarely conducive to the ferment and renewal we know in the North. The Latin-American countries have, however, something to offer that is lacking to the north of Mexico: they are a great open-air museum containing richly decorated buildings of the times of Spanish rule, palaces of viceroys and churches, and remains of the great Mayan culture which in sophistication equaled peaks of European or Asiatic creativity. Almost any collection enshrined in one of these ancient buildings resounds with echoes and acquires a captivating power.[23]

The United States of America. In quantitative terms the museums in this country have been progressing in great strides. According to the Statistical Survey by the American Association of Museums, of 1965,[24] a new museum was founded every 3.3 days between 1960 and 1963, in comparison with new establishments following each other every 10.5 days between 1940 and 1949. The increase in attendance in 1962 surpassed that a decade earlier by 122.1 percent, and escalated steeply in the second half of this period of time. The director of the Association described the situation in 1961 by stating: "In 1932 there were over eleven museums for every million of population, in a total population of approximately 134 million for the United States and Canada. Today, there are more than twenty-one museums for every million of population, in an estimated total of 194 million for the United States and Canada."

In 1966, the association's executive officer illustrated the phenomenal growth of museums by referring to the rise in new museum buildings and in the capital invested in them: between 1957 and 1965 the number of new buildings doubled the number of structures erected during the preceding six years; the annual capital outlay tripled.[25]

Such symptoms of an excellent state of the art ought to be considered together with the views of professional observers:

While we bask in the glory of staggering attendance records we actually know very little of what the figures really mean. For instance, how many individuals are involved? It seems clear that art museums, on the average, receive more visits from the same persons over a given length of time, than do the museums of natural history. . . .

The grossness of a purely quantitative self-esteem may also backfire in the end. It should not be forgotten that the Roman circuses likewise enjoyed excellent attendance records. The question is not how many arrive, but how well are they served by what they find when they get there. Of this we know very little indeed. . . .[26]

When reflecting on the lively temper of American museums, which at times produces chameleonic effects, some main trends claim attention. They concern the contents of exhibitions, their styles of presentation, and administrative organization:

An increasing interest and changes of taste in art museums

An increasing concern with ecology, in both museums of natural history and of anthropology

An awareness of minority groups

Manners of display tending toward a Total Environment

A museum-school marriage

A new emphasis on research

Multi-track versus one-track establishments

A widely spread malaise with regard to existing conditions in the presence of physical progress.

Museum Contents. The curve illustrating the number and the vitality of art museums is rising. In gross figures the attendance in 1962 doubled that of 1952. The Smithsonian Institution, which in the past favored the sciences, in recent years has been taking the initiative in expanding toward the arts. At last the National Art Collections have been transferred to a separate building, the old Patent Office, after remaining for decades in the shadow of mounted beasts and of rocks in the Natural History Museum.[27] Further, the current Secretary, S. Dillon Ripley, a biologist by training, took action to secure for the nation an exceptional collection of modern art; the Hirshhorn Museum, a new Bureau of the Smithsonian, will bear the donor's name.

The Kress Foundation has continued the policy of the Kress brothers, great patrons of the National Gallery, in channeling the family's art treasures into public museums; gifts were distributed among museums and galleries in seventeen states.[28] The Kresses collected mainly works of art by European masters of past centuries, but a more recent emphasis is on contemporary and avant-garde art as well as on so-called primitive art created by natives of

Africa or the Pacific Islands. This tendency, together with a notice-able liking for folk art, especially American folk art, suggests that American collectors' appreciation has widened in scope beyond old European masters of established reputation who formerly mo-nopolized their attention; it does not imply a disregard for old works of quality. In 1967 attendance at the Metropolitan Museum of Art in New York rose to the unprecedented peak of near 4,700,000 visi-tors. To some extent the record figure, surpassing by a million that of the preceding year, is likely to have been due to the dramatic dis-play methods of the new director, Thomas P. F. Hoving, who on a single Sunday succeeded in attracting 62,000 people, but even a figure close to four million visitors before Hoving's arrival at the Metropolitan indicates that New Yorkers and visitors are well aware of their art treasures.

In museums of natural history, ecology has been receiving intensi-fied attention. Among notable ecological exhibits I have seen in recent years, or have read about, the following stand out: The Web of Life, No Place to Play, and One Does Not Live Alone, in the Cran-brook Institute of Science; Does Environment influence Culture?, and Dynamics of Life, at the Milwaukee Public Museum; Design for Ecology – The Oakland Museum Views the Environment. For San Diego's two-hundredth anniversary celebration its Natural History Museum prepared a Hall of the Desert and exhibits on the Sea and the Shore. The museum at Texas Technological College in Lubbock, which will require several years for its completion, is devoted to the illustration of arid and semiarid lands. The Museum of the North on the campus of the University of Alaska, in a building inspired by the ancient Indian community house of the region, the circular Bara-bara, is to serve as a lexicon of ecology under certain conditions of soil and climate, in a land where men at times of simple technology survived in a continuous severe contest with their natural environ-ment. The underlying philosophy of the Sonora Desert Museum near Tucson, Arizona, is what Graham Netting has called an "Ecol-ogical Symphony." In the case of the Desert Museum it is at times a symphony of both sight and sound: some of its animals, which have the freedom of coming and going at their own behest, give tongue to their condition.[29]

The small site museums of numerous national and state parks have for years been pioneers in designing interdisciplinary ecologi-cal displays.[30] Metropolitan natural history museums have as yet not fully attended to their function in creating that awareness of man's involvement with nature that daily urban experience does not generate, as Albert E. Parr put it.[31] The perception of relationships between different areas of life rather than of isolated parts of it is in keeping with the growing general concern with the maintenance of a balanced natural environment, yet the traditional training of biologists as specialists may slow up the realization of projects. One could well think of museums as an avant-garde in the teaching of ecology from grade school to continuous education, while universities emphasize specialization in depth. And it is interesting to note that some botanical gardens and zoos now consider ecology as the way of structuring information.[32]

Significant changes are to be expected in anthropological exhibits. The Dutch anthropologist and museum specialist Hermann Frese has well defined the need for a sociological approach to many problems of anthropology. The display of artifacts is not enough; we need displays calling up in our imagination the life of the people who once used the objects, and the *faits sociaux totaux*.[33] Frese finds that the apparent lag in the development of cultural anthropology in museums in the United States is due mainly to the advances made in American universities, and to a tenuous relationship between universities and museums, in contrast to the cooperation between some universities and museums in Europe, in Canada, Australia, and New Zealand.

Stephan Borhegyi of the Milwaukee Museum urged the development of anthropological exhibits to "magic mirrors in which the diversities of human behavior and their causes" are reflected, and in which the man in the street can perceive himself. Sterile displays featuring "savages" should be replaced by illustrations of pressing current issues, first of all racial problems.[34] The Dickson Mounds of the Illinois State Museum point to the function of anthropology in maintaining a perspective of the past. Facing hundreds of Indian skeletons in their graves, viewers have an opportunity to sense the kinship among all members of the human species. Irrespective of the time and place in which we live, we share not only the finiteness of life but also arthritis and dental cavities. Some of the Mounds go back to the centuries before the arrival of Christopher Columbus on this continent, and they embody traditions antedating the birth of Jesus Christ. There are far more recent chapters of human existence which now rapidly slip away into oblivion and which call for preservation of surviving artifacts in museums. In his report for the year 1966 the president of the outdoor museum known as Old Sturbridge Village wrote, p. 24:

New England will become of even greater public interest and study.

The destruction of the New England picture villages will accelerate as our Atlantic seaboard cities expand into the megalopolis of the future. Only in places like the Old Sturbridge Village will it be possible to preserve period buildings with their proper furnishings and in their proper settings, free from the distracting sounds and sights of the contemporary world.

A somewhat increasing interest in Health Museums and health exhibits may be attributed to a spreading awareness of the importance of the prevention of illness. One must, however, not discount the impact made by the first Health Museum in the United States, in Cleveland, Ohio, under the direction of Bruno Gebhard, M.D., who combined sober knowledge of medicine with the missionary zeal of a pioneer.[35]

The Smithsonian's Museum of History and Technology, which in 1964 moved under a new roof covering some fourteen million cubic feet of space along two city blocks, represents a novelty in the sense of a sharpening definition of a museum's function: contrary to the general trend toward an emphasis on contemporary science, the Museum of History and Technology continues to represent the historical development of science.[36] The National Armed Forces Museum Park on the Potomac is to serve as a Science Museum of a special character. Among other matters it is to illustrate the contributions made by the Armed Forces to the advancement of knowledge in the sciences.

The National Art Museum of Sport, about to be completed in Madison Square Garden Center, New York, is a first of its kind, and may come to be considered among Americana by people from other countries. The American Museum in Britain, at Claverton Manor in Bath, Somerset, established in the sixties, suggests an attractive manner of introducing one culture to another.[37]

The Philadelphia Panorama, in the city's Civic Center, deserves to be mentioned for dealing with city and regional planning, one of the most urgent problems of our era. The William Penn Memorial Museum in Harrisburg, Pennsylvania, excites the imagination by the very fact that its topic is an *Idea*, or a cluster of related ideas; it is a shrine in which a never-ending celebration in low key is going on proclaiming human liberty and human rights.[38]

In contrast to the perennial topic of the permanent exhibition at the Penn Memorial Museum, the Riverside Museum in New York has set itself the task of placing on museum walls a visual record of events that are part of the current news. They began with a display named "Eyewitness: Czechoslovakia, 1938–1968," in the form of photographs.

Museums and Education. The Association of American Museums reported in 1961 that 79 percent of the museums were offering organized educational programs, in comparison with 15 percent in 1932,[39] yet the demand for such services appears to have lost some of its missionary fervor during the period between the two wars. It may be that a saturation point in the supply of educational facilities in museums was reached; or that children, to whom much of this work is addressed, are now offered alternative facilities. Since the use of museum resources for children has occupied me for many years, I shall deal with this aspect at a greater length in the Appendix and also offer my own evaluation. According to statistics of the American Association of Museums, the number of Children's Museums slipped from their first place among other types of museums in 1948 and 1950 to the seventh place. The Natural Science for Youth Foundation contradicts this appraisal and holds that many Children's Museums now drop the word "children" in their appellation in order to satisfy the desire of preadolescents to grow up fast to members of the general public.[40] Their claim is supported by the attendance figures in actual children's museums, which more than doubled between 1952 and 1962.

Any children's museum would be hard put in rivaling the science displays and demonstrations such as are offered for example by the Franklin Institute in Philadelphia or the Cranbrook Institute of Science in Michigan. Cranbrook has in recent years established a room called the Atomarium, somewhat analogous to a Planetarium, where atoms are shown in action. A Scintillation Viewer makes the radioactive decay in pitch-blende visible as tiny flashes of light. Another institution noted for its demonstrations for young people is the Boston Science Museum. There is, of course, the need for acquainting young people with simple, fundamental laws of nature, with the aid of unsophisticated and inexpensive equipment, but this is being done increasingly in the schools from the elementary grades up.

In recent years museums and public schools have occasionally established a close cooperation which dims the identification of both partners. A few institutions have undergone a name change, from "museum" to "center." Most of these activities went into high gear when federal funds became available via the Office of Education.[41] The largest establishment of this kind in the United States is the Lawrence Hall of Science, a memorial to the physicist Ernest Lawrence, and a part of the University of California at Berkeley.

To keep matters in perspective in this overall survey it seems desirable to allow three critics to express their perception of the vaguely defined field of museum education:

Whenever we speak of the "educational activities" of museums we seem to refer only to the functions of a teaching staff giving verbal instruction in lecture halls and among the exhibits. . . . But if the exhibits themselves, unaided by docents, lecturers, guidaphones or other audial verbalizers, are not the principal vehicles of museum teaching, there is little reason for the museums to remain in business. (A. E. Parr)[42]

The need for evidence of the effectiveness of educational offerings in museums in addition to the recurrent statements advertising their existence was voiced by numerous observers, and with great vigor by Wilcomb E. Washburn.[43]

The most serious hazard is that of reform in museum education being imposed from without, rather than being developed from within. . . . I suggest that we must first clarify for ourselves the objectives in education through museums, for in my view this has not yet been done. . . . Perhaps it is enough for the moment if we recognize the absence of clarity, and if we set ourselves the task of seeing clearly both the immediate and long-range objectives. . . . We must define our (the museum's) uniqueness. . . .
We know virtually nothing of those factors which do and do not make exhibits effective as communication. Yet we are here discussing education through museums. . . . (Duncan F. Cameron)[44]

Mr. Cameron rightly stresses the need for a clarity of purpose in museums, which so often remains but dimly defined, but not everybody would agree with regard to our total ignorance of the factors which enhance or diminish the capacity of exhibits to serve as media of communication, though one may safely say that we do not avail ourselves of the limited knowledge that exists. Cooperation between museum practitioners and psychologists, specializing in visual cognition, in learning and human communication, has as yet to be fully established. There have, however, been some new developments initiated by practitioners which deserve attention as directives to the future. There are some new programs in which education is perceived in a much broader context than as a reflection of school curricula, and where emphasis has been laid on learning rather than on teaching.

The Smithsonian's Branch Museum in the southeast of Washington, D.C., in an unused theater building in Anacostia, is a "storefront" museum which serves mainly the black citizens of the area They have participated in its establishment, and they cooperate in the setting up of programs. The number of exhibits is kept very limited, and preference is given to things that permit manipulation, actual physical interaction between object and person. The Smithsonian has also staged temporary events on its Mall, in the mood of a fiesta, around features that were to encourage students to complete their high school education, and to instill discouraged and angry people with new hope. Staff members of the Exhibit Division of the Smithsonian demonstrated techniques of silk-screen, model-making, and dry-freeze preservation of organic specimens. On another occasion craftsmen from distant parts of the far-flung country were brought to Washington to demonstrate their old folkways; for once attention was diverted from modern technology to the hands of Eskimos carving things in ivory and to simple folks from the South who in the presence of spectators turned cornhusks and strands of wool into dolls. Another time it was a kite-flying competition that went together with a workshop for the making of kites, and a lecture on the origins, the uses, and the technology of kites.[45]

Of even more recent date is the Bedford Lincoln Neighborhood Museum in New York City, operated by The Brooklyn Children's Museum, but serving children, teen-agers, and adults. Known among children as "Muse," the museum retains its integrity by offering objects of a variety, and it uses the objects as stimuli to activities as well as motivations to paying attention to interesting objects and to their use as sources of information and further stimulation. A junior advisory council, whose members are seven to seventeen years old, assists the museum staff in setting up programs addressed to their age peers. By offering workshops ranging from art to astronomy and aviation, and from creative writing and jazz music to the sciences, the Bedford Lincoln Neighborhood museum assumes features of a cultural center.

The philosophy of a multitrack establishment catering to the interests of a great variety and to all age groups is evident in the change of the name of the former municipal Rochester Museum of Arts and Sciences to The Rochester Museum and Science Center, now chartered by the New York State Board of Regents. Its "School of Science and Man" offers classes for youth and adults. The museum in Rochester is directed by W. Stephen Thomas, one of the internationally active leaders in museum matters, and its recognition of the need for extensive facilities for continuous learning is of significance.

A new and fully fledged cultural center is the Roberson Center for the Arts and Sciences in Binghamton, New York. One of their temporary themes, The Shoemaker's Story, illustrated their philosophy and procedures. To an exhibit of footwear from ancient times to the present were added samples of raw materials, of tools and of machinery used in the making of shoes; the medical viewpoint of the effects of footwear on feet was included; and a ballet production touched off associations with the ballerina's toe slipper, choreography, and ballet music. The center is customarily drawing both materials and talents from a variety of sources, and it directs its offerings to diverse sections of the community. Exhibits are only a part of the mosaic; there are theatrical productions and television programs; there are workshops for teachers; a Young People's Art Center and a Scientific Talent Development Laboratory establish ties with the school-going population, and classrooms are entered by means of circulating exhibit packages. A Vocational Information Center is addressed to school leavers.

The Roberson Center appears to be an embodiment of a spreading interest in Cultural Centers; in the inclusion of a museum or gallery within a complex of other establishments, of theaters, concert halls, meeting halls for diverse civic purposes. The celebration of the tercentenary of New Jersey in 1964 saw the maturing of a museum and library complex, an important part of a new state cultural center in Trenton.[46] The desire to attract growing numbers of people to museums and galleries expresses itself also in the installation of show windows in the outside walls of some museum buildings; for instance, in The William Penn Memorial Hall in Harrisburg and in the Milwaukee Public Museum, Wisconsin.

Numerous museums show a shift from the traditional object-oriented institution to one in which objects are means serving various human needs. Increasing provision is being made not only for cultural minorities but also for physically handicapped persons.[47]

Museums and Research. Research was never abandoned in museums, but after an initial phase of supremacy, its role narrowed during the period between the two world wars when a vociferous crusade was on for museums to be first of all instruments of popular education. Without any demand for a restriction of the museum's function in diffusing knowledge, the emphasis on research was strengthened in recent years.[48] For obvious reasons University Museums have been among the promoters of research, and they do not apologize for their evaluation of priorities in their setting.[49] The director of the University Museum of Colorado stresses the need for authentic, tangible specimens to develop insights in a person into the total human condition and to act accordingly.[50] With the progressive tendency in universities to stress molecular and cellular biology, the function of the natural history museum dealing with total organisms ought to come to the fore again, instead of being weakened by the interest in suborganic parts that is cultivated by universities. A currently favored approach to descriptive biology is in the form of Biosystematics, with entire populations of a species representing the object of study instead of individual organisms. The Los Angeles County Museum of Natural History pursues a plan for an enlargement of its collections for the study of biosystematics; if fully developed, this project could serve students of a rapidly growing number of new colleges in the West which are in no position to establish and to maintain worthwhile study collections. A natural history museum can act as a center serving small colleges of an extended area, with the aid both of collections of complete organisms and of specialized experts in these matters. While the need for centralized facilities in science for pupils of elementary schools and of high schools has been clearly recognized, the same concept just begins to dawn with regard to college undergraduates.[51]

The casual visitor to museums is rarely aware of activities outside the exhibit rooms. In some of the large museums only a few percent of the collections are on show, and the rest are stored for later use in exhibitions and more often for research. The American Museum of Natural History in New York has about one tenth of its collections on display.[52] Similarly, the Guggenheim Museum in New York exhibits only about 10 percent of its paintings; the rest are in storage or on loan. The architect Philip Johnson suggests, as a rule of thumb, that one third of the display area should be reserved for display. The Annual Report to Members for 1966 issued by the American Museum of Natural History in New York gives an idea of the diversity of disciplines in which museum scholars endeavor to advance the frontiers of knowledge: "What happens if you put contact lenses on a far-sighted fish to give it normal vision? What is the mysterious power called instinct? What is the secret of a bird's built-in time clock? What will be the cultural impact of the space age?" The director's Annual Report for 1966–1967 lists on thirty pages research projects conducted by paleontologists and by biologists dealing with existing organisms, preserved and living, from micro-organisms to large vertebrates, by specialists of animal behavior and by anthropologists.

The hottest (or should-be hottest) current issue is *ecology*, the study of the interdependence of all living things among themselves and with the inorganic environment. It is not a novel issue but one that has rapidly assumed dramatic importance to man's well-being and survival on earth, and it is of course closely allied to the generally mounting concern over the abuse of natural resources which became a pathological condition on earth with increasing industrialization and mechanization of ways of living. A most articulate proponent of both research and education in ecology in museums is the Smithsonian's S. Dillon Ripley. His thinking sums up a mosaic of projects in a variety of museums, in the form of research and of education by means of exhibits. In Mr. Ripley's words, the inhabitants of planet earth are developing a new "environmental awareness" that "grew out of the human population explosion and contamination of our ecosystems with radioactive fallout, smog, and pesticides," of "the recognition that man has the power to affect irrevocably the nature of his world . . ." and that "the construction of livable environments of the present and future must be based on the discovery and application of ecological principles."[53] Ecology does not limit itself to the effects and reactions of inorganic substances but includes the behaviors of organisms which are both affected by and are affecting social conditions. This extends to an interlocking of biology and anthropology, and to human ecology.

The natural history museum is outgrowing its former limitations. It is leading to the "museum of man and nature."[54] The topic of an ecological study may be the breeding of an animal species in the tropics or problems of cultural infiltration studied with the aid of archaeological and ethnohistorical materials.[55]

The concern with man's further fate on earth expresses itself in many ways. Are we in danger of eroding our natural resources as well as our memories of the past? On the occasion of the Bicentennial of the Smithsonian Institution, the noted French anthropologist Claude Lévi-Strauss urged an intensified study of native cultures in various parts of the globe which are disintegrating faster than radioactive bodies; he warned that with the recession of numerous cultures, which took centuries or millennia to develop, we are losing unretrievable images of ourselves. The University of Pennsylvania Museum has for many years been one of the centers of anthropological research stocking up a record of man, of his variability and his sameness,[56] but both the successes and the failures of this century have made anthropology and ethnology matters of urgency. "Just as basic research in nuclear physics altered the course of human progress, so research into the basics of behavior will give man the tools to carry himself out of the Stone Age, sociologically," wrote the director of the Museum of Natural History, New York, in his Annual Report for 1966 – 1967.

The style of fieldwork has been changing. It has been recognized that unselective collecting reaches a point of diminishing returns and has to be replaced by a carefully prepared search for selected specimens which fill gaps in existing stores and facilitate analyses of patterns in organic diversity—of plants or men. The number of found new specimens would appear to be of less significance than the number of notebooks filled in advance or in the course of an expedition. This work has to be continued after the return of the expedition, when accessions are catalogued; the research of tomorrow depends on the recording and the maintenance of museum materials today.[57] Foresight has been shown in recent years with regard to the safeguarding of museums at some indefinite future when another armed conflict — another violent outburst of irrationality in man — may once again endanger and destroy treasured articles kept in museums of different kinds.[58]

A sense of loss over the disappearance and the decay of material evidence of past human endeavor by the mere passage of time or, more dramatically, during interludes of war and as a side effect of the building of highways, dams, and other structures claiming a piece of the earth's surface led to accelerated salvage work of Indian and other archaeological remains and to a refining of techniques of preservation.[59]

Education versus Research. When it comes to a choice of a museum's primary function and of appropriate manners of display, from the architectural style of the building to the presentation of exhibits, the key word of this period in the United States is experimentation. During the "Second Reform," between the two world wars, the dialogue between representatives of mass education and the minority of others was predominant, but now, in the course of the "Third Reform," there is the hum of voices as from a Tower of Babel, and it seems to be rising in pitch. Concern with a condition abounding in dilemma and paradox is becoming more articulate; my personal suggestions are offered in the final chapter: "A Twelve-Point Program for Museum Renewal."

The University of Michigan at Ann Arbor draws a clear line between its several research museums and an exhibit museum for the general public. In other institutions the demarcation line exists but is not expressed in architectural form; the cooperation between the two functionally differing units varies in fluidity. At the Franklin Institute in Philadelphia activities devoted to the advancement of knowledge appear to be made available readily to the museum that interprets science to the public — from the way the heart works to adventures into the universe. The point of gravity in an institution decides on the ratio in the combination of the twin functions, research and education, and the museums' third function, that of a depository, may be entirely ruled out or be developed in varying degrees.

Experiments in Presentation. Art museums engaged in avant-garde experiments in display are open to visitors of all backgrounds, but their location and style are likely to attract in the first place the attention of somewhat sophisticated individuals. The Guggenheim Museum in New York is a large circular shell in which visitors descending a gently sloping ramp along the walls are more exposed to the cumulative experience of many paintings than to any one in isolation; the building serves as a frame and creates unity. Frequently exhibited works of art assumed new roles and called up new associations of thought and feeling when presented in the exhibition "In the Presence of Kings" at the Metropolitan Museum of Art; their inclusion under a common theme spurred new impressions and insights. Subunits, colors, and lights suggested to the visitor where he might best establish communication with exhibits, by stopping or moving in certain directions, instead of getting drained of energy in an effort of receiving a message. P. F. Hoving's experimentation with a face-to-face comparison between antipodes, put pop art, complete with a piece of an automobile tire and spaghetti, next to a painting by Poussin. The new Kimbell Art Center in Fort Worth plans to make its own films of paintings by old masters, and use close-ups and scene-cuts to bring a Rembrandt picture closer to new ways of perception.

In some museums, actual works of art, ancient or contemporary, disappear altogether on occasion, and what is offered is dematerialized "Light/Space/Motion." This theme was sponsored by the Art Centers of Milwaukee and Minneapolis; Kansas City's Nelson-Atkins Gallery presented a Magic Theater with an Electronic Cathedral in which a wealth of changing lights and light-reflecting surfaces created illusions of weightless unreality reinforced by sounds activated by a person's movements.[60]

The search for ways of establishing communication between museum objects and people by exposing them not only to sights but to a stimulation of all human senses is spreading. There is the talking label and the music akin to a work of art. The Toledo Museum of Art deserves the credit for having early encouraged this trend. At the Walters Art Gallery in Baltimore visitors wander around and look up at a work of art while they listen to a concert; at the Boston Museum of Fine Arts a special performing group plays on some of the ancient musical instruments of the museum, and visitors with appropriate qualifications may play one of these treasured instruments. In a number of museums instruments in showcases are connected with periodically playing records.

A cohabitation of the visual arts, of drama and ballet, is becoming accepted; and drama in close confrontation with static works of art is being tried. In the Metropolitan Museum a contemporary play was acted in front of modern paintings; in Williamsburg, Paul Green's symphonic drama *The Common Glory* was staged, which tells Thomas Jefferson's story by a combination of acting, dancing, and music.

Another budding or maturing museological feature in the United States concerns the establishment of introductory centers for visitors, another approach to a facilitation of communication or learning. In this respect the site museums in National Parks have been early trailblazers. Among others, the Metropolitan Museum is planning a "visitors' center" manned by multilingual students who will assist people in choosing routes, newcomers or specialists who wish to go directly to certain exhibits.

Specialization and Centralization. The diversified tasks in museums call for knowledge in many disciplines or skills of increasing specialization. No single individual can be an expert in "museology." If he aspires to work at a professional level, he has to limit himself to a well-defined section of museum work. (Compare p. 216). John E. Anglim, chief of the U.S. National Museum's exhibit section, summed up the need for exhibit laboratories which would supply a number of institutions in a region with biological and mechanical models, taxidermy work, silk-screen graphics, and assistance in the restoration of objects in different materials.[61] No individual museum except some of the very large ones can afford to maintain a permanent staff of such and similar experts.

The demand for specialists in many fields leads to the need for an adequate provision of training facilities for a variety of museum personnel. A. W. Crompton of Yale's Peabody Museum of Natural History wrote: "It is, I think, time that we recognized that the functions of maintaining collections, designing exhibitions, and running sophisticated research programs cannot be carried out by a single person."[62]

Discontent with existing museums and art galleries expresses itself in many forms in the United States, and elsewhere. Artists declare that traditional, static paintings and sculpture no longer provide full satisfaction to the human eye and mind. Composer La Monte Young triggers changes in light patterns by amplifying his breathing with the aid of an instrument applied to one of his nostrils. Robert Israel chooses transparent vinyl as his medium and inflates it in a variety of huge shapes, which could be viewed at the Whitney

Museum in New York. Nobody considers such experiments as final solutions, but they indicate that a quest is on for new art forms and new kinds of art museums.

If some museums of natural history cover their walls with what impresses one as magnified pages of textbooks, or if they dilute their identity in a symbiosis with schools, they join the questers.

A few years ago art museum directors of the American Association of Museums conducted meetings devoted to their specific problems and to a redefinition of some of their functions. On a later occasion executives of industry and business met with museum leaders at Aspen, Colorado, to search for answers to fundamental questions that can be summed up in a single sentence: "A Museum —What Is It?"

In a confrontation with elusiveness, questions sometimes begin to pall, but they surface again in other quarters, and the quest for a definition of the functions of museums in American society continues.

The National Museum Act passed by Congress in 1966 is an expression that all is not well in our large, costly museums and that legislators are determined to offer improved museums to citizens. The Act strengthened the capacity of the Smithsonian Institution to assist smaller establishments by centralized stores of information, by the advice of expert consultants, by publications, and in ways still to be decided upon. The attention paid to museums by Congress endows these institutions with status and underlines their responsibilities.[63]

In a letter of June 20, 1967, the President of the United States requested the Federal Council on the Arts and Humanities to study museums and to report to him. He asked: "What is their present condition? What are the unmet needs of America's museums? What is their relation to other educational and cultural institutions? I hope that the Council will recommend ways to support and strengthen our museums."[64]

After two lengthy conferences of a group of representative museum leaders and a study of numerous individual institutions, the report was sent to the White House in November 1968 by Mr. Roger L. Stevens, chairman of the Federal Council on the Arts and Humanities, and was soon after published under the title *America's Museums: The Belmont Report*.[65] The document emphasizes the need of museums for federal financial support. It gives account of the quantity of services rendered by American museums, but is equally concerned with the need for improvements in quality; especially with the setting of standards, with the training of museum personnel, and with research that would clarify the characteristics of effective exhibits. Specific references to the Belmont Report will be made in the final chapter of this book.

Canada. A phenomenal numerical growth of museums has occurred here since the end of the Second World War, with 650 provisional listings in recent years following upon the recording of 385 institutions only a few years before.[66] The celebrations of the Centennial in 1967 have no doubt been a strong stimulus to the development of museums, but would not seem to have been the only activating force.

Newfoundland, the youngest and most easterly of the ten provinces, may serve as an example of the thematic challenges that exist in Canada. Its museums illustrate such disparate momentous episodes as the way of life of an extinct Indian tribe, the Beothics, the landing of Cabot in 1497, and the sagas of the medieval Vikings and of modern aviation.

The new establishments include Marine Museums and Pioneer Museums, a twenty-mile dinosaur trail connected with a paleontological museum in the badlands of Alberta and restorations of gold-rush ghost towns, and a number of museums devoted to mining and forestry. According to reports of close observers, the Historical Museums under the supervision of the National Parks Branch of the Federal Department of Indian Affairs are shifting their emphasis from military and naval history to other aspects of the Canadian past.

Museological events of a scope beyond all precedent are still in a stage of drafting and building. The new $30 million Centennial Centre of Science and Technology in Toronto is to illustrate man's progress toward a better life.[67] Contrary to some older institutions it is more oriented toward the present and the future than the past. Contemporary science and technology have been allotted the claim to 70 percent of the contents, while their historical precedents may occupy only 20 percent; 10 percent of all communications will be extrapolations into the future. To keep in step with the present rate of progress in science and technology, about 1.5 percent of the exhibits are expected to be brought up to date every year. The enlargement of the National Gallery in Ottawa is to be a part of a cultural complex including an opera house and theaters. The different functions of the Gallery — administration, research, educational services, and conservation — are to find architectural expression in diversified units.

The institution which for many years has been in the lead of museums in Canada, the Royal Ontario Museum in Toronto, is steadily continuing its work. Among its planned ventures is a credit course in museology to be offered jointly with the University of Toronto.[68] Research work in progress, including underwater archaeology, is being reported in the *Archaeological Newsletter* of the museum.

The recent evolution of Canadian museums gains in importance when considered in the perspective of the past. The private museum established in the twenties of the nineteenth century by the sculptor Pierre Chasseur in Quebec was later acquired by the government for $2000; in the thirties and forties one-room museums of science budded as appendages of Mechanics Institutes. It took one hundred years to raise the number of Canadian museums to 91. Governmental authorities were slow in perceiving the potential of museums as media of education, and the five-thousand-mile expanse across Canada was fractured into isolated islands until the meshing of subcultures by air travel. With the jetliners came a stimulating influx of tourists.

Mexico experienced its museum expansion in the sixties; Mexico City alone was enriched by five museums.[69] In the largest institution, the National Museum of Anthropology, as well as in the other museums, devoted to history, to folk art and industry, to natural history and to pedagogics, the goal is to raise the cultural level of the population, including that of the large and less privileged masses, by exposing them to information concerning their country's past — its wealth of human talent, its creativeness in the arts, and its courage in overcoming perils and aggression.

When Mexicans enter their museums in Chapultepec Park, they tread the ground on which the long departed Aztecs once settled. This is the first step in an education that is to enrich the minds of citizens and to alert their emotions; knowledge about the past is to give emphasis to directives into the future; the message is to accelerate the maturing of a democratic way of life. The implied lessons are many, but they are not school texts writ large by means of objects on walls. The extension into the past far beyond the white man's arrival and into a period of prehistory measured by a grand geological clock provides the living with an opportunity to stand taller. Racial prejudices are likely to shrink as people watch the changes of cultures with the ticking of time — from the skeleton of the Man of Tepexpan, one of the oldest known fossil men of America, who rests in the trench in which he may have been buried at the end of the last ice age some 10,000 years ago, to a variety of Indian cultures and especially to the splendor of the Mayas, and so on to life under despotic Spanish Viceroys and to the existence of men of freedom.

The museums are employing a variety of means to put their messages across to a heterogeneous public. They utilize architectural features to magnify the chances of reaching human minds; in a new gallery of the National Museum of History visitors look out into the park through windows in the outside walls and on the opposite inside walls they are offered windows into 150 years of their history in the form of sixty dioramas. To receive a continuous story they walk along a descending ramp: there are no unrelated objects to distract attention from the chosen theme, and the alternation of vistas into the park and the dioramas provides a restful change of visual and mental focus.

In the National Museum of Anthropology the visitor is first exposed to a brief survey of all available exhibits in the Sala de Resumen, where he receives information in the form of models and photographs, and of sound. If he decides to view things by himself instead of joining a guided tour, he is now in a position to decide where to go, or to go first, instead of rambling into the unknown of twenty-five exhibition halls; he can walk directly from a central patio into the hall of his preference without getting physically and mentally fatigued during a run through a number of halls.

The Section of Cultural Diffusion of the anthropological museum invites people to view the exhibits in greater detail and with deepening understanding by joining a program *Visite el Museo con nosotros,* which consists of twenty visits in the company of a specialist in anthropology or history. In the educational department, which is working mainly with schools, teachers act as guides. Groups of schoolchildren visit after having received in school preparatory information, as a rule in the form of a slide-illustrated lecture. In the museum they listen to a brief talk and are then free to view exhibits on their own in a single hall related to their school studies. Finally they are supplied with materials for a creative reaction to their experience in the museum; they draw and sculpt.

The National Museum of Pedagogics, administered by the Ministry of Education, reinforces and keeps updated what teachers have studied during their training: the history of education in Mexico and plans for future developments as well as comparative pedagogics. They are given instruction in producing teaching materials, in improving their skills in crafts, and they have access to a specialized library. Marionettes are often used for demonstrations.

The National Museum of Folk Art and Industry not only exhibits finished articles but keeps native crafts alive, and revives those that wilted away because of lack of recognition, by giving assistance to craftsmen of superior talent. Those who in previous years had to live below the starvation line by paying 80 percent to 250 percent interest to lenders who commissioned their work now receive funds for materials and have workshops and tools put at their disposal in the museum. The National Foundation for Folk Art and Industry cooperates in the sale of quality products. On occasion entire families work on local crafts and avail themselves of the outlets offered by commercial centers in the provinces.

All visitors to the Museum of Anthropology, young and old, casual and studious, are offered concerts of ethnographic music. Records of Mexican music are on sale.

The museum devotes its energies to both education and research. It is closely related to the National Institute of Anthropology and History which supervises excavations and reconstructions on a variety of sites which precede Site Museums. On one such site, in Tepexpan, was discovered the Pleistocene fossil man. The Linguistic Section of the museum contributes to the rescue of vanishing cultures by making records of vestiges of tribal languages; of vocabularies and grammars. Comparative Linguistics opens up insights into the "genetics" of different alphabets. Some of these studies are reflected in exhibits for the general public — on writing in general, on the Mayan alphabet, and on language and culture.

Two novel Mexican approaches to museums should be of considerable interest, not only to museum workers but to everybody concerned with means of fostering understanding between different cultures or subcultures, to city planners, sociologists, and educators involved in the education of underprivileged groups. Their Border Museums near entrance points to the United States are to supplement the insight into Mexico on the part of visitors from North America who often do not go far inland and get merely acquainted with the noisy, gift-shop atmosphere of Mexican towns. Other museums with a clearly defined purpose address themselves to Mexicans: there are the traditional small regional museums, which are designed in the awareness of the still widely spread illiteracy among agricultural workers; and there are museums destined to serve as focuses of rehabilitated communities, such as Tlatelolco, a part of Mexico City, which sank into decay after a period of prosperity in pre-Columbian times. A new Cultural Center, including a museum and a reconstructed Aztec temple, is to stimulate in the neighborhood sentiments of pride in a common past and a constructive attitude toward the future. The project is a part of the redevelopment plans of Mexico City.

The Area of New Expectations

For all the profound differences separating the cultures combined in this account, they all have a significant feature in common: a reawakening to full partnership in life on earth after centuries and millennia of debilitation under oppressive foreign regimes. Their liberation came when their European masters found themselves weakened after the Second World War, and in the course of socio-economic changes due to rapidly advancing technology. People around the globe may learn a great deal from museums established in recent years in such areas. Why do newly emerging societies wish to have museums?

Africa. As Jean Gabus, the imaginative Swiss museologist, who served as adviser to some African museums, wrote,[1] a museum of ethnology can be much more than a collection of objects: it may be a collection of wisdom, of concepts of morality and order embodied in objects and striking chords in the minds and hearts of people. In this sense humanistic African museums — of ethnology, archaeology, or native arts and crafts — fulfill the function of strengthening the social cohesion in their communities. Natural history museums are projections of man's natural environment and may suggest to him ways of adapting himself to it and controlling it in a more systematic manner than by dangerous hit-or-miss procedures in nature's laboratory without walls. The emphasis on technological and scientific museums is but another endeavor to enlarge human capacities.[2]

In tropical Africa, Nigeria has shown considerable interest and skill in establishing museums, with governmental support as in the rest of the African continent. First of all there is a desire to preserve what is left of ancient regional culture and to present it to citizens. The Nigerian National Museum in Lagos, established in 1957, is open from 7 A.M. to 7 P.M. In Jos a technological museum is in the process of growth, and it is devoted to aspects of new technology as well as to traditional crafts, to pottery, wood-carving and brass work. It is a multitrack institution that includes an open-air theater and a dancing area; it trains museum personnel and sends out traveling exhibits. In the Uganda Museum in Kampala some of the attendants are trained in the use of native musical instruments and make the fine collection of instruments resound; visitors too may perform, provided that they know how to handle instruments; musical talent is widespread in Africa. Archaeology and ethnology are cultivated at the Chad National Museum, in Fort Lamy in the Republic of Chad, with the Chad Institute for Humanistic Studies encouraging the work. In Senegal several museums condense a view of African Negro culture. In Dahomey the history of ten reigns of Dahomean kings is illustrated in old buildings. Ghana plans a series of regional museums which are to further the study and the understanding of African civilizations. Their National Museum is in Accra.

Kenya's Natural History Museum in Nairobi has for some time enjoyed the reputation of being the largest museum of its kind in tropical Africa, and may for some time remain the only one of its scope. Senegal has a Museum of the Sea in Gorée. The interest in museums in all sciences is increasing.

In many of its parts Africa is moving in the course of years across distances of time which other societies transversed in the course of centuries. In this situation of challenge that is fraught with perils and rewards, museums contribute to a keeping of balance between the past and the present. They have special means to inform illiterate people and members of linguistic splinter groups. Occasionally contrasts are conspicuous: attachment to ancient prejudices and customs may be found next to sophistication. A visitor may associate in his mind a museum with a temple and leave an offering before an exhibit. On the other hand some university departments were quick in realizing the need for visitor studies in museums, as for example, those conducted by a staff member of the sociology department of the Makerere University College in Kampala, and for training facilities for museum personnel. Such facilities received assistance from UNESCO and exist in Jos, in Nigeria; they deal with such diverse aspects of museology as museum architecture, taxidermy, display, and preservation, the latter being of accentuated importance in the tropics. In Cameroon the University of Yaounde stresses the training in the subject matter represented in a museum.

The examples referred to illustrate a far greater number of museums which exist in Africa from Tunis down to South Africa. In a brief summary one may say that museums play a definite role in the independent African countries, not only in the struggle for survival but in a deliberate search for an African Personality.

Owing to historical precedents, the Arab Republic is a world of its own within Africa. The Museum of Egyptian Antiquities in Cairo offers, however, another illustration of European dominance in past centuries when French and English generals, diplomats, collectors, and dealers were excavating and exporting antiquities on a large scale. Gradually laws restricting such activities were introduced in Egypt, which in fact accumulated a vast store of its ancient creations by permitting foreigners to keep only one half of their acquisitions. The other half went at no cost to Egypt. With passing years the laws became stricter. The West may, however, claim to have inspired Cairo in more recent years to establish a Science Museum.[3]

Asia. The museums of *Israel* are psalms in stone, sacred songs in varying moods, from meditation to jubilance laced with memories of grief.[4] Collections of archaeology obviously receive preference on a soil dotted with relics which illustrate thousands of years of human civilization on a high level of philosophical thought and of ethics. The personalities and the events of the Old Testament are palpable in this land. Like other museums in the country, the Israel Museum in Jerusalem is composed of a group of pavilions, each of its own architectural character that fits the temper of the contents. There is the Bronfman Biblical and Archaeological Museum, the Bezalel National Art Museum, and the Shrine of the Book housing the Dead Sea Scrolls, which revived the knowledge of the Jewish Revolt against Rome. After lying hidden in a cave for 2000 years, they were discovered in 1947 by Bedouin shepherds.

The subterranean sanctuary, with only a portion of its double parabolic dome emerging above the ground from a pool of water, symbolizes the emergence of the State of Israel after centuries of dormancy. The black basalt wall arising from the cavern below the upper plaza, in contrast to the white dome, accents the heavy burden which lay on Israel for more than 2,000 years. . . . The subterranean caverns forming the Shrine itself are symbols of the caves in which the scrolls lay hidden. . . .[5]

The viewing areas of the dome serve the display of the scrolls; related archaeological materials—fabrics, locks, keys, and specimens of glass illustrating Judean life two millennia ago—are exhibited in a separate chamber. Letters written at the time of Bar Kokba are kept in the Shrine. In the event of an emergency the cylinder around which the Scrolls are displayed can be lowered deep into the ground.

The Israel Museum is notable for its location on a hillside and in the close proximity of governmental buildings. A series of five terraces gives coherence to architecture and landscape and offers a framework for a collection of contemporary sculpture.[6]

There is a notable museum of archaeology in Tel Aviv, and small-scale museums exist in numerous collective settlements known as Kibbutzim. Collections of antiquities from countries of the Near East are shown in museums, and there is a Museum of Japanese Art in Haifa believed to be the only specialized museum of its kind outside Japan; it is under the direction of a Japanese expert.

A museum of entirely differing character, combining aspects of natural history and modern technology, is the Dagon Grain Museum in Haifa, founded by Reuven Hecht, head of a large firm specializing in the storage and transportation of grain.

In this brief sampler of museums of Asia reference will be made to examples illustrating two different, and in fact opposite, trends related to what they have been learning from us and what we ought to learn from them.

There are the science museums which have been growing in numbers, and which are still quite insufficient in comparison with the areas and the numbers of people to be served. They are the West's main museological gift. *India* has several museums related to science, technology, and industry; for example in Bangalore, Calcutta, and Pilan. It may well be that the facilities for children in some Indian museums have been inspired by museums in the United States.

Ahmedabad in India opened in 1963 a Gandhi Memorial Museum located near the Sabarnati Ashram, where Gandhi lived from 1917 until 1930 when he set out on his march and vowed that he would not return before India achieved independence from Great Britain. It is a museum of spare contents, but the inconspicuous things it contains are of the highest significance to Indians. Gandhi's Prayer Platform has its place in this shrine-museum, which in the main consists of mental associations and of a fitting atmosphere created by the simple architecture of square rooms and patios, which are square open spaces, all of the same size, twenty by twenty feet. The roofs are pyramidal. There is a pool, and steps lead down to the Sabarnati River.

An interesting museum building was in recent years erected in *Pakistan* to house the Mohenjo-Daro Museum;[7] it preserves the archaeological remains of an ancient Indus Valley city.[8] *Kuwait* may at this time have completed its proposed National Museum that is to embrace the humanities and the sciences, and to engage on large-scale educational activities.

Further references to museum activities in newly developing nations will be made in the following account dealing with international agencies concerned with museums and with efforts of individual institutions specially devoted to cooperation between nations.

The Internation Group. This group is represented first by UNESCO's section of Museums and the International Council of Museums

(ICOM), two closely related agencies with headquarters in Paris. Their manpower and funds are in no relationship to their responsibilities. Much of the work is done by volunteers, by museum workers connected with national subgroups or committees.

Agencies concerned with museums at an international level are confronted with the same superhuman tasks as other cultural or educational organizations oriented to the whole earth as a unit: they endeavor to put some measure of evenness into the working of the man-made system of the planet, which is racing in some parts and in other parts has maintained the slow pace of past ages, or has even slowed up owing to the progress in technology elsewhere, to the population explosion, or to the effects of the admission of a colonial community to full partnership among nations. The interest in museums illustrates a deep concern with the leveling up of education. Further, there is an unprecedented realization of man's shortcomings in controlling his own attitudes and actions owing to a lack of understanding of the springs of human behavior. This intensifies the desire to salvage all remaining material evidence of human ways of living, anywhere and at any time. In terms of pigeonholed disciplines this means new approaches to ethnology, folklore, and archaeology in museums;[9] it also leads to an emphasis on the diffusion of basic information on a global scale of matters of science and technology.[10]

In order to make a dent by their endeavors, the international agencies have to keep citizens around the globe and their governments aware of the potential contributions of museums to human well-being. Societies engaged on making a new start after a period of dormancy receive special attention. International museum crusades have been conducted, and the holding of museum weeks has been encouraged.

To promote knowledge about the use of museums, conferences and seminars are held periodically in key locations which by themselves show up the smallness of our planet, and with changing panels of professional participants. UNESCO's first Museum Seminar was held in Brooklyn, New York, in 1952; ICOM held a conference in Baghdad, Iraq, in 1967, and in Cologne, Germany, in 1968.

Traveling exhibitions have proved successful and have led to a clearer understanding of problems involved in the moving of quantities of objects, to some extent valuable ones; in repeated installations in quarters lacking in uniformity and sometimes in basic necessities; and in using the same exhibit for communication with members of diverse cultures and subcultures. One traveling exhibition of the fifties visited twenty-six countries in the course of four years and was viewed by 1,200,000 people. Consultants are sent as special advisers to countries and to specific institutions. Publications are issued: the quarterly magazine *Museum*, and *ICOM News*, and occasionally more extensive statements on specific topics. An International Center for the Study of the Preservation and Restoration of Cultural Property was established in Rome in 1949.[11]

In participating in "Freedom from Hunger Campaigns" museums declared their preparedness to add an edge to a current theme of highest priority by harnessing the power of museum materials which as a rule stay aloof from demands of the present. In the National Museum in New Delhi two exhibitions proclaimed human solidarity and the perennial aspects of hunger. Photographs of Indian stone sculpture and actual prehistoric and anthropological specimens rekindled memories of times of survival by food gathering; the need for surpluses received attention.

In a paper "The Museum Seminar: a Stimulus and an Example," Grace McCann Morley pointed to the significance of brief international encounters serving as germinal operations.[12] They may spell disenchantment among people who wish to see immediate results, but their long-term effects must not be underestimated. The measure of the chain reactions that radiate from such high-intensity events depends on numerous circumstances, and to a considerable extent on the quality of the input—of the participating minds, of the relevance and the clarity of their contributions, and of their capacity to communicate not only with their colleagues at the conference table but indirectly with larger sections of humanity.

Numerous regional conferences have followed some of the international meetings. The Museum Seminar in India in 1966 effected the publication of museological articles in India, not only in the daily press but in a magazine addressed to cultural leaders.[13]

With Europe's painful efforts to achieve a degree of unification went a series of exhibitions issuing from the Council of Europe, which were to give dominance to personalities in the past who projected an image of a European spirit rather than that of any nationality. Charlemagne was one of the selected figures; he had struggled against fragmentation almost one thousand years ago.

Some individual museums have taken initiative in sharing exhibits with other countries. The Science Museum known as the Palais de la Découverte in Paris, a pioneer in science education by means of demonstrations, sent science exhibits to countries in Europe and Latin America, in Asia and Africa;[14] the Deutsches Museum in Munich, an even earlier pathfinder in science education, engaged lately on similar activities. The Carnegie Museum in Pittsburgh has a foreign-visitor program and offers fellowships to trainees from abroad.

International agencies have been taking considerable interest in the use of new *scientific techniques* in museums; in some cases they were instrumental in establishing laboratories or in assisting publications, and their urgency in these matters spurred the activities of others.[15] The uses to which science can be put in museums are numerous: the basics in the preservation of objects and their restoration are the two best-known aspects;[16] there is the dating of objects their codification and registration; the separation between genuine and faked articles. The material composition of objects is studied with increasing accuracy, and so are ancient techniques. A number of specific examples will point out the variety of work which is going on in museum laboratories and is likely to gain momentum in years to come. Such laboratories are being founded in various parts of the globe.[17]

Carbon-14 dating has been in use over a number of years with regard to materials which once formed a part of living organisms. With the passing of time radioactivity decreases, and it is necessary to develop ways of measuring very low levels of radioactivity.

The fluorine-dating test concerns the number of fluorine ions originating from the groundwater and stored in the form of fluorapatite in bones buried in the earth.[18]

When a piece of clay is fired, its radiation is reduced to zero; by making a radiation count of a piece of ceramics, the radiation accumulated since its last firing gives a clue to the age of the object.[19]

Paints contain impurities, and paints used by individual masters — by Rembrandt or Raphael — are supposedly characterized by their chemical imperfections. A fleck of paint bombarded with neutrons in a reactor provides an "atomic fingerprint" and contributes to a file of genuine pictures by famous artists, which become standards of comparison for pictures of questionable origin.[20]

Gamma radiography serves as a means for identifying the material composition of ancient Buddhist figures in bronze, for giving insight into the techniques used in producing them, and for locating repairs made in the past.[21]

Electronic instruments are in use for such diverse purposes as the location of archaeological underground remains and the prevention of loss due to theft in museums. An appropriately located television control room can replace numerous human guards in exhibit rooms, and is less conspicuous to visitors. In the new Museum of History and Technology in Washington, D.C. facilities exist for the televising of objects in all halls and without a great deal of preparatory work.

The effects of light, of air pollution, and of drastic changes in temperature or humidity on museum materials are of interest to all museum workers or collectors. Metal and stone are not sensitive to light, but paintings are, especially watercolors, and textiles are so to a high degree. For some time bright lights in museums were considered as signs of progress, and artificial lighting was given preference; currently concern exists with the deleterious effects of ultraviolet radiation.[22]

Computers are to serve a variety of purposes in museums and may, in the view of some people, save museums from extinction due to an ongoing accumulation of materials requiring more than all available energies for simple tasks of maintenance and leaving the knowledge the specimens represent unattended. At a symposium "Museums Today" at the annual meeting of the American Association for the Advancement of Science in December 1967, Donald F. Squires, deputy director of the Museum of Natural History, Smithsonian Institution, contributed a paper "The computer comes to the aid of museums." According to Mr. Squires, museums have the alternative of serving as warehouses or as "institutions that dredge the informational content from the specimens, to be interpreted, analyzed, or synthesized as bits of a mosaic which fill important gaps in the total picture of man's knowledge." He described museums as links of modern communications and providing cross-linkage between specimens, their documentation, and the literature about the objects.[23] Another staff member of the Smithsonian, Wilcomb E. Washburn, head of American studies, has written about the need of scholars throughout the country, if not on an international level, to have easy access to a library of objects projected on a video screen in their studios.

Under present conditions we lack a system which would convert objects into widely available information with the aid of a machine-based retrieval procedure. Without such aid, the scattered collections of hundreds of small museums serve hardly any scholarly purpose, and the holdings of large museums outgrow human capacities. To illustrate his point Mr. Washburn described the rise in the number of objects in the United States National Museum: from 55,389 specimens of natural history and ethnology in 1860, the figure rose to 4,819,836 in 1900, and to 55 million in 1964. While discussing the special needs of scholars, Mr. Washburn is fully aware that museums have more than one function to fulfill and that they ought to display objects which cannot be more adequately described in writing or by visual image.[24]

Other museum tasks assigned to computers are related to the identification of antiques and to their separation from fakes. A computer brain is expected to detect an inconsistency in the intricate pattern of a coded mark on a piece of Sèvres porcelain, which remains elusive to the human eye.[25] A computer in the museum lobby may engage in a dialogue with a visitor and may record the things people liked best or liked least, and what they would like to view on the occasion of future visits to the museum; it may provide requested information. With children it is expected to play games such as ones on color relationships or on the names of famous statues.[26]

The finale is concerned mainly, and yet not exclusively, with museums in the United States, with which I am currently most familiar.

Some important directives into our museological future have gained in clarity in the course of the decades since the end of the Second World War — concern with the preservation of relics sheltered in museums, an increasing recognition of the need for the sharing of facilities by a number of institutions, first of all in the form of traveling exhibitions; the wish to get better insight into the motivations of people to view displays of objects — but in their sum, efforts have remained too scattered and halfhearted to hold out the promise of significant improvements in a situation that is widely recognized as unsatisfactory. Have we not been paying attention to detail mainly and to problems that are conducive to immediate action, with action being sometimes mistaken for a solution — another project, another committee, and maybe another wing to a building — without probing far enough into the ideological background in which all human actions and institutions are embedded? Without concentrating on strategies based on fundamentals and on priorities? Without evaluating the results of our actions, as if we were afraid of facing them?[1]

1. *The term museum.* International Council of Museums (ICOM) succinctly defined a museum as an establishment in which objects are the main means of communication. If we agree with this definition, an establishment in which objects are not used at all or are not used as main carriers of messages are not museums, whatever their qualities may be otherwise. A place in which people are exposed to changing lights or to a galaxy of light and sound unrelated to objects may offer a new kind of symphony or a carnival, according to its quality, but it is not a museum. If a few objects provided by a museum or by any source are used in a club or a recreation center among other items on the program, such as dancing or discussions of current problems and of vocational opportunities, the place still retains its identity. The term museum is neither better nor worse than the term club or center. We dim the outlook on our goals if we instill terms with connotations of borrowed status.

There is considerable scope for a combination of objects with

6

A Twelve-Point Program for Museum Renewal

other media, with brief motion pictures illustrating a single concept or with appropriately designed (and not overdesigned), suitably sized and placed graphics, but objects have to remain the stars of the cast.

2. *Museums are man-made institutions* in the service of men; they are not ends in themselves. While a recent letter from the White House requested an inquiry into the unmet needs of America's museums, I propose to vary the question, and to ask, "What can museums do with regard to unmet needs of people?" Within this very wide area every individual museum may decide on its share of intended accomplishment, and of resources required to reach its goals. Few individual institutions, if any, can be all things to all men. Even a very large museum will have to decide how much of its energies and financial resources is to serve the community of scholars or the general public, or specific sections of the public. Purposes have to be clearly defined in keeping with now existing needs. Proposals for the use of modern technology in making museum specimens available to scholars on video screens and in restricting the display of objects should be taken very seriously; they may be the key to the further existence of museums.[1] Dormant collections of innumerable small museums would in this manner become viable resources of thought. Scholars need not lose the unique experience that comes from the seeing and touching of actual specimens: all that has to be done is a distribution of the hoards of duplicates in the catacomb-like storage rooms of some very large and some not so large institutions to places in which they can serve human beings. Small, well-documented, collections could be kept in colleges which have no similar resources and in public libraries. Mr. Wilcomb Washburn reminded us that up to 1870 the Smithsonian Institution systematically distributed specimens.

A restriction in the number of materials displayed for the enjoyable education of the general public need by no means result in a lowering of their benefits; it may, indeed, lead to experiences of greater quality. There are signs that we are outgrowing the period of enchantment by statistics indicating growth in quantities and that we are on the way to the more mature appreciation of quality.[2] We need balanced mental diets in museums befitting the capacities of human minds seeking more than the satisfaction of a fleeting curiosity.

3. *Museums are not islands in space;* they have to be considered in the context of life outside their walls. The truism becomes a verity under present conditions of accelerated change and at a time when

every institution has to take measure of itself as a means to legitimate survival. Since public museums have developed from private collections, from recesses reflecting the moods and idiosyncrasies of select individuals and of bygone cultures, they are specially in need of considering their viability in terms of their capacity to enhance the overall potentialities of individuals and of society in years to come.

4. *The museum's uniqueness.* It is the three-dimensional reality and the authenticity of objects that matter, and the stimulation they offer to eye and hand. Most of man's traffic with his environment in the course of his perplexingly brief existence on earth has been directly through the senses: historically, written language is an invention of yesterday, and spoken language is comparatively new if we consider it as a means of communication in the context of the entire organic sector on earth. New evidence that emphasizes the effects of sensory deprivation on human beings confirms by implication the importance of visual and tactile stimulation.[3] So far museums have not availed themselves at all of findings made in psychological laboratories, although precisely these insights endow museums with genuine status: they begin to reveal one of the fundamental causes of the attraction exerted by museum materials on people. A wide field for experimentation opens up for a generation of museum workers interested in core problems rather than in fringe effects. What can a museum do that no other medium of communication can do, or cannot do at the same level of excellence?

Anybody is likely to welcome on occasion an encounter with the "First Signal Environment" of objects as a relief from overloads of symbolic communication, and such encounter is even more craved by people who are only functionally literate and who are one of the main current concerns of educators in a wide sense of this term.

A recognition of the importance of systematically developed environments of "things" inside museums leads far beyond their walls, into architecture and landscape design, into the appreciation of the physical appearance of objects of everyday use and into city planning. In all these cases we deal with a relationship between human beings and three-dimensional, concrete parts of the environment, complete with color and light.

The quality on which the museum's uniqueness rests implies a warning against the use of materials lacking object-concreteness. An exhibit which consists exclusively or largely of written sentences on screens is an alien body in a museum, however large the letters may be. Its existence may be due to a misunderstanding or to a self-betrayal of which those perpetrating it need not always be aware.

Another quality that endows museum materials with a high potential as a medium of communication is the opportunity they offer to present a number of facts simultaneously and in a context. Here again the museum worker has allies in psychological laboratories if he cares to turn to them. Information-in-a-context is easier and faster apprehended than unrelated items; it is easier recorded in human minds; and it is retrieved from memory with greater certainty. The assumption that the cumulative meaning of a number of appropriately selected items is superior to the sum of messages embodied in them is widely accepted in theory but is rarely put into practice in exhibits — sometimes because of a dearth of materials and more often because of their thought-scattering overabundance. When Kenneth E. Boulding wrote of the museum's function of providing developed images of the world, he may have considered the exhibit's aspect of simultaneity of impact of a number of items.[4]

Information-in-a-context is particularly important when knowledge is to be diffused among increasing numbers of people lacking background information and requiring aids to form mental associations.

4. *What is the museum's interpretation of "education"?* Is it our sole desire to feed information into people, or do we understand education to be a process of wider scope: a tuning of people to their best ability to think judiciously and to feel humanely? To realize new relationships between phenomena on earth, and between their own behaviors and what happens around them? And to develop a wider gamut of understandings and of appreciations, and — why not say it — of satisfaction with the fact of having been born and of being alive?

Obviously a museum exhibition can merely offer skeleton information and may light up interest with regard to a single point or to a few points, but if such impact is achieved with the help of the somewhat primordial forces of objects, a greater number of people may gain the necessary momentum to explore further by means of abstract media, first of all by verbal communication, oral or written. I venture to propose that the criterion of "good" education is its capacity to propel human beings along their evolutionary trajectory; in this case from the building of concrete models of the world to the use of more complex and abstract terms.

5. *What are the priorities among museum topics?* Smörgasbord-style exhibits drawn from accidentally available museum stores reveal a strange alienation of museum staffs from the human emergency situation of unprecedented rapid changes in ways of living. A

parade of rocks, ancient timepieces, mounted birds, and exotic costumes had validity in a private cabinet of the seventeenth century where it represented a sampler of current knowledge. Each item was of relevance to the elite of scholars and amateurs who owned or viewed such things. Today's man, even the proverbial man of the street, has easy access to incomparably greater and more varied stores of information brought to his home by the mass media; the traditional museum offerings pale in comparison with the stimulation he receives otherwise — unless museum resources are presented to the layman in a context of either current issues or of perennial human affairs.

Modern man is not merely stimulated by his daily input of information, but he is overstimulated and fatigued by his exposure to a great deal of irrelevant input which is a fallout of our selling-buying culture. Most educational and recreational settings could cut down on their fatigue-without-return element, and a freewheeling institution like a museum is specially in need of self-imposed brakes. Museum people might do well to heed Kenneth Boulding's advice in his book *The Image* that we ought to seek a significant minimum curriculum rather than to try to expand our offerings.

Two basic questions may help in establishing priorities among topics in museums: how relevant is the subject matter or its presentation to man at this time of his history, and does the topic lend itself to a message based mainly on objects? Numerous topics of modern science may not lend themselves at all for presentation in exhibits, or in so grossly simplified models only as to defeat purposes implied in education — the conveyance of accurate information and the sharpening of the judgmatic capacity of people. An oversimplified model may encourage infantilization.

There are too many rather than too few topics that would pass the test of the two proposed basic questions — how often, if ever, do we ask them in museums?

Where are the exhibitions dealing with proposed model cities and other urban developments, together with illustrations of effects of environments on the socioeconomic life of human beings? Where are the exhibitions on facets of the population explosion on earth and of food production? UNESCO encouraged museums to deal with Hunger, but the situation calls for ongoing appeals to human awareness and for powerful communication; archaeological specimens of tools used in food production are important items, but they contain only fragmentary parts of the message.

Where are our museum exhibits which would contribute to the

ongoing discussion of dissent and of aggression as parts of the congenital human endowment? We have among us scientists of a philosophical bent whose ideas await illustration in exhibits. They consider harmonious cooperation among groups as being favored by natural selection; to them aggression need not be of the essence of living but may turn into an obsolete and destructive feature of existence; they perceive the human being as fundamentally ethical owing to his capacity to foresee the consequences of his action.[5]

We see in museums the work of iconoclastic artists who replace paint and stone by changing lights, but their expression of dissent would gain in meaning if it were presented among other forms of dissent expressed by other groups of the population. Who expressed dissent in the past? And dissent from what? And why? And by what means? Relics and graphic interpretations of faded passions exist, and so do records of historical events that began with small actions of individual dissent from a majority. Is there any palpable thread of dissent running through human history, irrespective of any particular nation or country? How is religion or economics, political history, education, or any other aspect of civilization related to an individual's confrontation with the ruling mores of his day? Exhibits of this kind would help us to perceive better the continuities of human existence beyond the brief span of individual lives as well as changes in rationality and in humaneness, be they progressive or retrogressive.

What do people mean when they talk about the gulf between generations? How similar or dissimilar were two succeeding generations during various phases of the past? In appearance and in ways of life?

The current interest in ecology, including human ecology, can hardly be overestimated in its potential values: it is apt to multiply insights into peaceful group living, which biologists may sometimes achieve without the almost unavoidably inherited inhibitions which obstruct so much of the endeavor of humanists. Yet topics from biology alone do not exhaust the overall subject of human ecology.

"Futurism" has as yet not entered the halls of museums, but ample literature exists that can assist museum workers in lengthening their vistas toward the year 2000 and beyond.[6]

With leisure time becoming an increasingly prominent part of the lives of great numbers of people who in the past knew little leisure, exhibits on ways of using abundant time should receive attention; they may help us to understand what is meant by "leisure" as contrasted with "work." There is more to such exhibits than a case filled with baseball or golf equipment. We want to know what motivations came to the fore when people played certain games, and what satisfactions were sought, and perhaps found. Are volunteer workers engaged on a political campaign or on a community project, working or enjoying a leisure-time pursuit? What general human traits may be found in a comparison between the recreational activities of preindustrial natives of a South Sea Island, the ancient Greeks, and ourselves?

Since many of us at present live under conditions of hyperactivity and of stress, we would benefit from considerations of different forms of recreation as means of correcting ecological imbalances in our inner environment. Frequently museums offer opportunities for additional hyperactivity, which may attract some people, or many people on some occasions, but there are others who would appreciate or learn to appreciate a Silence Room. Even the Freer Gallery, my personal favorite, is too loud as long as one finds oneself engulfed by exhibits on all four walls of a room. Where is the museum where visual chamber concerts would be offered, with a few works of art stemming from different cultures being orchestrated with a beautiful crystal, a rare map, a photograph of excellence, or an exquisite flower arrangement? One such experience can hardly be equated to another, but noise and rush and small talk are alien to all of them.[7]

It is the unique privilege of man to act as a pilot in his evolutionary process, if he wishes to do so, and if he constrains himself to a distinction between advancing and retarding, or distorting, trends.[8] Are we as much concerned with the effects of noxious impressions on our minds as we are with air pollution? In the as yet to be created area of therapeutic man-made environments, museums could act as pioneers.

6. *Who is who in a museum?* You may be one of those who felt thoroughly disenchanted while visiting a museum whose director had fascinated you by his papers you heard at conferences or read in journals. You began to question whether you were in the right place: what you saw did not tally with what the director had said or written. He had advocated exhibits of musical instruments that would make entire cultural eras come to life — and you came face to face with a miscellany of musical instruments attached to long labels and crowded in a case, stamp-book style. You had listened to a rousing call to museum workers to interpret current racial problems in halls of ethnology — and what confronted you was yesteryear's habitat group of figures of Indians dropping to their knees

before gun-toting white men taking control of a piece of the American continent. You expected to get an insight into events below the earth's crust which preceded a recent earthquake — and you walked along tedious cases of rows upon rows of igneous, sedimentary, and metamorphic rocks. Even if you kept your thoughts to yourself, the director is likely to have pointed to the villain of the story: the curator immured in his study and unavailable for comment, who had insisted on such presentation as you saw.

Subject-matter specialists have an inherited brief in many museums to judge what is to go into an exhibit case, even if some of them may prefer to be exempted from the task and to limit themselves to an advisory role. The diffusion of knowledge among laymen is as a rule outside their interests and competence, but their voices should be heard for the sake of offering to the public authenticated information. They should be members of a team composed of scholars of specific disciplines, of communicators with thorough knowledge of the psychology of human communication, and of designers; a consensus among the three is necessary. At present, communicators have as yet not entered the realm of museums, and a condition of imbalance exists due to the dominance of either the curator or the designer (compare Point number 8 in this section).

When a deadlock occurs between a curator and a member of the education department or a designer, one emphasizing the substance or the "what" of an exhibit, and the other the "how" of the presentation (educators and designers by no means representing the same museum staff species), the director is often called upon to act as a decision-maker, to solve a phantom problem that cannot be solved. Furthermore, the director's delicate relationship with the museum's governing board, trustees, committee chairmen, and big givers encourages compromise. Big gestures may be made in solving marginal problems, but the tensions and rifts that unavoidably exist in an organization lacking defined areas of authority have to be kept under wraps. How an individual director will survive under such circumstances, to what degree he himself will erode, depends on the predominant ingredient of this unenviable character of many parts — a manager with traits of a power-loving executive, a smooth public relations officer, a fund raiser, and maybe a scholar turning sour in the process of trading his former delight in intellectual pursuits for more palpable comforts. On occasion a member of the education department, a figure borrowed from the school classroom, climbs on the status and income ladder and reaches the chair behind the director's desk. This does not necessarily add to the nimbus of educators among their museum colleagues: every-body is ready to dabble in an area often thought of as being more nebulous than it is in fact. Although the planning of exhibits is even less trammeled by principles than what goes on in the name of education in museums, and is often a free-for-all, the exhibit designer has in recent years established a position for himself. In fact he often oversteps the bounds of his competence.[9]

We have to consider anew what categories of competence a specific museum requires as its human resources; some of the traditional figures may be unnecessary in an institution of certain goals and in a certain locality, while new talents may be called for. There is an urgent need for communication specialists using the museum environment, and mediating between the subject-matter expert, the museum curator or his equivalent in a university acting as adviser to a museum, and the designer. A practitioner of educational routines is no equivalent for a communication specialist grounded in theories pertinent to his task and gleaned from diverse fields of scholarship, from neurophysiology to a variety of psychological thought.

If museums wish to reach a level of professional competence and to become functioning public institutions to the limit of their potential, a task analysis of each staff member must become routine procedure, and his authority in decision-making must fit his competence and his task. A bad fit in this respect is a source of unending trouble. Furthermore: a single line of authority from the income-top down is obsolete in any kind of organization, and every organization has to create its own specific and most fruitful lines of interaction.[10]

7. *Exposure is not enough.* One of our blind spots, in all manners of educational environments, is the assumption that the exposure of people to experiences necessarily results in learning and stimulation. In public schools this pious belief is contradicted by an almost incredibly low achievement by large numbers of people, and by a variety of dropouts and malcontents.[11] In museums, I witnessed comparable results under experimental conditions. This is an area in which research has to go into high gear after a good deal of reflection in many quarters. Unless we undertake this difficult, challenging, and often tedious task, we may just as well close much of our far-flung museum enterprise.

A museum, every single museum hall, every individual exhibit is a man-made environment; it is not a natural phenomenon resisting change; it can be changed. Before exposing large numbers of people to any such temporary, small-scale ecological niche, we have to test its effects on appropriate sample populations. The now generally accepted hit-and-miss procedure has a colossal and quite unnecessary margin of waste.

8. *Who are the testers?* To some people the answer is easily at hand: get a hard-nosed psychologist. But what if the mind behind that rocky nose is totally immersed in a single, perhaps momentarily fashionable, psychological dogma that does not take into account the needs of a museum environment? If a plant physiologist is needed to counsel people on the growing of plants in a semiarid soil, an oceanographer specializing in deep-sea fishes is not likely to be called. Psychology may be less diversified than biology, but it is diversified enough to lead to farcical situations unless, once again, competence in relation to specific tasks is considered very carefully.

Vision being the human sense acting as the main message receiver in a museum, a psychologist specializing in visual perception is needed; more than one may indeed be called for, since perception begins with the physiological capacity of the human eye and leads to the interpretation by the brain of what the eye perceives. Communication is in the early stages of becoming a special area of study, and the testing of the degree to which a message in any medium is communicable is of utmost importance. Motivation psychology has its uses, if those who practice it are familiar with the New Look school of motivation and do not completely disregard laws of visual perception. Since the viewing of exhibits is as a rule a voluntary occupation and is not linked to grades and other extraneous rewards, exhibits are an excellent opportunity for studying intrinsic motivations to man's congenital desire to seek information. A hundred-dollar bill cannot motivate a human being to read letters placed behind his back as a rabbit might do could he read, nor can anybody repeat and remember words spoken at great speed and out of context; the same applies to communication by visual means.

Another hazardous area for the selection of exhibit testers is the market survey. It may indeed be interesting to confront the motivations of museum visitors and of patrons of stores.

9. *Determine your visitor population.* It is one of the assets of museums to offer their facilities to everybody who wishes to come, be it for study or a few fleeting glances. Unforeseen interests may germinate under a variety of circumstances. Yet the probable margin of waste is the broader the more heterogeneous and anonymous the public is. All means of communication cater to somewhat defined consumers; most communities have several newspapers;

public libraries provide popular books while specialized ones serve professional groups; there is a difference between a college library for undergraduates and a graduate library in a university. Why should museums not address themselves to specific segments of the population? Some might choose to do so at all times, or a few times in the year, apart from the offerings for everybody; and there would, of course, be no reason for excluding anybody while making a presentation with the view of the needs and interests of specific groups. I remember with pleasure an exhibition not intended for me and entitled "How to Look at Sculpture" in the Junior Museum of the Metropolitan Museum of Art.

A segment of the population which deserves special attention is our growing college population. Apart from collections illustrating the subject matter of their studies, there ought to be temporary interpretive survey exhibitions with stress laid on interdisciplinary relationships, and if possible with reference to current conditions of life. At this stage of life people make it their business to learn, or to receive information and to reflect on it; college youth is more interested in learning than others who give preference to empirical experience; and the demands of college courses and of examinations almost preclude wide, interdisciplinary reading.[12]

A special organization would be needed to plan, to prepare, and to circulate such campus exhibits, preferably on a regional basis, and serving a number of colleges. With an advisory committee drawn from the subscribing colleges, from both faculties and students; and wherever possible, with students being employed under professional guidance in the preparation of the exhibits, during school vacations if not otherwise.

10. *Problems of funds and of identity.* Museums are experiencing grave financial problems. Old endowments are being debilitated by diminishing purchasing power; large-scale donors are becoming scarce; and museums have as yet less access to public funds than other institutions. Admission fees lead to special problems in view of the fact that a nonprofit organization exempt from taxes may not be allowed to charge admission, yet it is the payment of the individual museum visitor for the service he receives which in my opinion holds out the greatest promise. The gist of the Belmont Report is an appeal for federal funds.[13] Since museum attendance in the United States has risen close to 300 million visits a year, or has passed this figure, and since museums have to turn down requests for services, it would seem logical to expect a financial contribution from individual visitors and from organizations based on memberships

and associations. A federal contribution between $35 million and $60 million for the first year could be doubled or tripled if each person paying for one of the 300 million museum visits would leave the token fee of 50 or 75 cents at the gate in the case of adults and less for children.

We live in a culture based on selling and buying, and a comparison with societies in which museums are state-supported has to include a reference to the loss of individual freedom that often is a part of the package. The time is not propitious for additional demands for federal support; there are other and awesome priorities. Further, would federal support in the sum of $35 million or even $60 million truly solve any of the fundamental problems of museums due to overextension or would it merely serve as a first-aid band?

There is no reason whatsoever to doubt the willingness of the public to pay for admission to museums; a visit would still be a bargain if compared with a ticket to a movie theater or to a concert. Visitors would, however, probably expect better evidence of the quality of a museum's offerings than they do now when few are aware of the indirect contribution they make to a tax-supported institution; a direct cash transaction tends to arouse alertness which in its turn may lead to a judiciously critical attitude which is now missing. And it is missing because of the absence of professional critics of museum exhibits whose interpretation would be made available in newspapers and magazines read by great numbers of people. Books, films, and sports are regularly reviewed; critics of drama and of music are established figures. They are important informal educators who quicken insight and refine sensitivity. Strangely enough some museum workers oppose the reviewing of exhibits. Their arguments are not persuasive and seem to be based on anxieties; they themselves may not be altogether convinced of the value of their displays or they may struggle to maintain the unquestioned authority of little feudal lords in their relationship with the anonymous public. Yet a stipulation of standards, which the Belmont Report rightly demands, can only be hoped for in a continuing process of rational analysis shared by many people. In the sciences, which have progressed in leaps, blunt and often abrasive criticism is considered to be a forward-moving force. René Dubos, of the Rockefeller University, wrote:

All important human activities have given rise to a highly sophisticated profession concerned with the criticism of their values, achievements, trends and potentialities. The professional critics . . . play an essential and creative role even when they do not themselves contribute directly to the fields of activity they evaluate.[14]

Currently American museums sometimes run the hazard of losing their identity by courting donors of substantial funds and affluent people in search of status symbols. Occasionally an exhibit hall that is more stunning than informative is used as an advertisement that may attract the attention of a person of means and induce him to underwrite a research expedition; in the process of this enticement thousands of anonymous visitors are admitted free of charge to the exhibit hall and leave it without deriving any benefit from the experience.

In order to please buyers of expensive museum memberships, gala openings of new exhibitions are reserved for them; a great deal of effort is sometimes expended on not altogether needed temporary displays which offer opportunities for more frequent gala openings – a special form of cocktail party.

Some business corporations favor the soft sell by means of museum exhibits, preferably related to their work. They are not merely prepared to pay for them but to show favor in some other form. For example, by giving to the research division of the museum a contract which they may have otherwise placed in another laboratory, even though the research staff of the museum may be as competent as others. A loss of identity may also occur when a museum decides to enter a close partnership with a school system for the prime reason of obtaining access to public funds earmarked for education.

The risks of cheapening museums by accepting token fees at the museum door seem less than indirect bargains. Admission fees should not discourage low-income people from visiting museums; there are ways of attracting visitors from economically or culturally underprivileged backgrounds. One might, for example, offer a certain number of free admissions to various organizations at certain times of the year and in this manner arouse interest even among people who previously paid no attention to museums. Those whose earning capacity is severely curtailed by the style of our economy, students and senior citizens, should be given special privileges.

Individual admission fees to museums should, of course, not prevent public authorities from supporting specific projects, especially concerning research and clearly identified problems under the heading of education.

Our resistance to admission fees in museums stems from a general dislike or fear of changes of custom, or from a widely spread adjustment to times gone by. The numbers of dis-timed people are far greater than of the better known displaced ones.

11. *What do we mean by training in museology?* By its extensiveness "museology" is a vacuous term. What relationship is there between taxidermy and learning processes, or between security measures in museums, the preservation of tempera paintings, and the capacities of the human eye to view things? (Figs. 31a, b, c) To acquire meaning the term has to be subdivided into a number of fields.

Most of the existing courses are held in museums of art, of anthropology, or of natural history, with stress laid on identification and on skills of preservation.[15] The National Endowment for the Humanities supports museum internships and fellowships, and the Smithsonian Institution appears to be aware of the many facets of training for museum personnel. My personal experience in conducting sessions with graduate students added to my conviction that young people are ready to pursue the study of communication by exhibits.[16] A few other museums are beginning to consider the need for an inclusion of the psychology of perception and of communication in the training of museum personnel. If plans are put into practice, it will be essential to offer workshops in addition to classes. A person has to go through the experience of selecting a theme, of writing an outline of an exhibition, of having the joys and frustrations of collecting materials, and of using them for a display.

Any such training ought to include prospective critics of museum activities who are not active members of the profession.

12. *The life and death of organizations.* John Gardner is credited with having stated that "most ailing organizations have developed a functional blindness to their own defects. They are not suffering because they can't *solve* their problems, but because they won't *see* their problems." Pauline Tompkins, president of Cedar Crest College, referred to Gardner's statement and added herself:

. . . there are climactic times when developments within society stretch the capacity of existing institutions to cope with them. Such times require a qualitative reassessment, a breakthrough to new concepts, what Harrington describes as the "audacious use of the social imagination" to engineer radical change in institutions and to articulate new goals.[17]

In my estimation the main problem museums have to perceive is the need for a *change from an emphasis on hardware to an emphasis on software*: let us call a moratorium on the expansion of buildings and on the acquisition of additional gadgetry until we know more about the benefits people derive from what is going on in museums, or what could and should go on.

Let us delete all statistics which boast that a new museum is

founded every 3.3 days. Do we always know what kind of misfits
are created in addition to institutions of excellence? What meaning
have rising attendance figures as long as they are not compared
with increasing populations? With changing levels of general education? Or with increases in the demand for other media of education
and information?

 We have to recognize that a museum is not an all-purpose nostrum
and that an instant museum is not likely to be a museum of quality.[18]
It should be a fascinating goal to search for the specific, intrinsic contributions these institutions can make to human well-being.
We may then at last be in a position to give an answer to the question "Would we invent museums if we did not have them?"

Figure 31a. An arrangement of paintings that ignores the capacities of the human eye and brain: it creates an oversupply of visual impressions.

Figure 31b. Another transgression of basic requirements of visual perception: a display of statues in which the viewer cannot concentrate on any single object without having others crossing his field of vision.

Figure 31c. Symphony or cacophony? Where, my eye, are you to travel first? In what direction? In what sequence? Up and down it goes, from one side of the hall to the other, and back again — and to what end?

The Term "Museum" and Some Other Terms of Similar Meaning

In Greece the claim of a place to the name Μουσεῖον — the Muses' realm — depended on its general atmosphere rather than on concrete features. It was a place where man's mind could attain a mood of aloofness above everyday affairs. Elements of a sacred temple and of an educational institution seem to have mingled in Greek Schools of Philosophy, in Pythagoras' school in Southern Italy, and in Plato's Academy, where the study of Philosophy was regarded as a service to the Muses.[1]

The emphasis shifted from the religious and ethical to the intellectual side in the Hellenistic Museum of Alexandria, that great namesake of our museum, which in fact was more akin to a research institute than to a museum in the present sense (Fig. 32).[2] A collection of statues of thinkers, of votive donations, of astronomical and surgical instruments, and of such products of nature as elephant tusks and hides of rare animals was part of the equipment. The association between the Museum of Alexandria and our later museums is based not only on the collecting of specimens but also, or first of all, on the encyclopedic scope of interests. At the Museum of Alexandria inquiry extended to all available realms of knowledge. The subjects of research, discussions, and lectures ranged from religion to medicine, from myths and philosophy to zoology and geography, and in each case the compilation was on a grand scale. Myths were collected into a lexicographic body; a survey of all existing geographic information was attempted, together with a summary of philosophical thought. This great stocktaking of knowledge was indicative of a state of peace and wealth under the Ptolemies, and of a desire to speed the progress of civilization by means of the power of knowledge.

Learning of encyclopedic character was again connected with the term Museum on occasions when books were published under this title. Whatever the subject matter, a book entitled Museum was a compilation that supposedly contained a representative selection of information on a single subject, if not all available data. How widely the topics of the musea in print varied can be seen from a few examples. The Museum Metallicum, published about 1600 by the famous naturalist and collector Aldrovandi of Bologna, was supposed to contain all information on metals. Dr. M. B. Valentini's Museum Museorum appeared in 1704 in Frankfurt and offered a survey of "all materials and spices for chemists and their customers, and also other artists." A Poetical Museum, containing songs and poems on almost every subject, was published in 1784 in Lon-

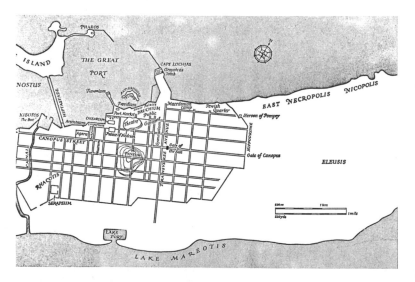

Figure 32. Map of Alexandria at the time of the Ptolemies when the "Museum" was a center of learning and research of importance to the entire civilized world. The Museum was located off the main artery, the Canopus Street. From Claire Preaux, "Alexandria under the Ptolemies," in *Cities of Destiny*, ed. Arnold Toynbee. (By courtesy of Thames and Hudson.)

don, and a *Museum of Dramatists*, composed of plays from English dramatists, followed at a comparatively recent date, in 1906[3]

Pliny's *Natural History* was an encyclopedia in the Greek meaning of a "complete circle of learning."[4] In the Middle Ages an all-round conception of knowledge may have been at the basis of such works as the *Etymologies* of Bishop Isidore of Seville in the seventh century, or in Roman Lull's *Ars Generalis* in the thirteenth. It seems noteworthy that the sixteenth and seventeenth centuries, which engendered interest in encyclopedic learning, were also periods unusually fertile in the creation of collections of "Naturalia" and "Artificialia" containing an almost unlimited variety of specimens of nature, objects of art, mechanical inventions, and religious idols.[4]

The term Museum reappeared in fifteenth-century Florence, where Cosimo de Medici's collections of codices and curios was referred to in such manner. In subsequent centuries the term Museum was used among other terms, all related to private collections, but it is hardly possible to connect specific terms with collections of a certain kind, in terms of contents or otherwise. The term gallery, which at present is often associated with a collection of paintings and sculpture, as distinct from the *mixtum compositum* of a museum, was and is also used to indicate a collection of miscellanea.[5] Francis Bacon, in the *New Atlantis*, distinguished between a "gallery" for statues and a "closet" for various rarities.[6] For architectural reasons the term gallery appears connected with collections of objects of art rather than curios, since paintings and statuary require special lighting such as can be provided by a corridorlike room with much window space between and opposite the specimens. Part of the extension of the Medici Palace in Florence in the sixteenth century, built by Vasari for Cosimo de Medici and known as "Galleria delle Statue," was a narrow corridor with large windowpanes. "A long narrow room, well lit on both sides" (apparently on the two long sides) was the description of a gallery in Zeiller's *Itinerarium Germaniae*, of 1632.[7]

In his book *L'Idea della Architettura Universale*, of 1615, Scamozzi proffered the explanation that the gallery was an architectural invention of the North, and especially of France, where it had originally served as an entrance hall to the residences of distinguished personages and later came to be used for housing collections.[8] In fact, the hall-like structure of the gallery became a feature of palaces only in the late sixteenth century, and subsequently became prevalent. Princely abodes ceased to serve as citadels and became ornate, and often boastfully conspicuous, residences. On some occasions, an art collection would be referred to as a gallery although housed in rooms differing in shape from a corridor.

The term *pinacotheca* too allows of more than one interpretation. The word *pinakothekai* derives from *pinas*, for plank, Greek paintings being executed on wood. In ancient Greece the word implied a collection of paintings, or sculpture, or rather the room in which they were exhibited. Vitruvius described the "pinacotheca" as one of the apartments of a great house at the time of Augustus, and as architect, gave directions with regard to its shape (Fig. 33a). Pliny used the same term when referring to galleries of paintings in private homes.[10] A catalogue of 1694 of a collection of a variety of things at Gothenburg, was entitled *"Catalogus . . . rerum curiosarum tam artificialium quam naturalium in Pinacotheca Olai Bromelii."* Neickelius, the author of the eighteenth-century *Museographia*, alternatively used the words gallery and pinacotheca for collections of paintings.

Other terms connected with the room in which specimens were housed by private collectors were "cabinet," often used in English, French, and German, or "Chamber" and "Closet" (*chambre* in French and *Kammer* in German). Very often these words appeared hyphenated with others specifying the character of the collections, such as a "Cabinet of Coins" or a "Chamber of Rarities." When Henry, Prince of Wales, was given his own establishment, Inigo Jones was appointed Surveyor of Works and built in 1611 at Whitehall a room for the collection of pictures known as the "Cabinet Room."[11] An implication of these terms seems to be the privacy into which the owner or the student of the collection may retire for the contemplation of the specimens. The connotation of privacy similarly underlies the term *Penetralia*. Alfonso, Prince of Aragon and master of Naples in the mid-fifteenth century, kept his Flemish paintings in a remote room of the palace and referred to it as Penetralia.[12]

In Dr. Johnson's view a Museum was a *Repository* of learned curiosities; he stressed the aspect of preservation as Leibnitz had done when referring to a *Conditorium*. [13] Originally, the term Conditorium had been related to dead matter, and especially to the ashes remaining after the cremation of people.

The term *Guardaropa* was of an entirely different character. It was used to indicate a storage place of valuable personal belongings, and it was a familiar term among Renaissance collectors.[14] Vasari chose the word *Anticamera* for the storage place of works of art.

A combination of private studio, storage accommodation, and an opportunity for decorative display seems implied in the term *Scrit-*

tojo. The inventory of the contents of the Medici Palace in Florence, of 1493, referred to the Scrittojo next to the Sala Grande where, in a fine case, the most valuable things were kept, such as jewels, vessels of semiprecious stones, and a unicorn horn.

The contents of the collections led to the use of a few specific terms. There was the Rarotheca, which is self-explanatory, further the Cimeliarchium and the Thesaurus, if specimens of exceptional material value were implied. The Cimeliarchium originally indicated the place where jewels were deposited, whereas the Thesaurus may have meant not merely a stored treasure but a secret hoard; in ancient Greece subterranean chambers under some of the temples were referred to as thesauri. According to Roman law a thesaurus was a treasure which had been hidden so long that all circumstances relating to its deposit were forgotten.[15] Later collections termed Thesauri may have contained articles of various kinds. In their seventeenth-century "Thesaurus," the Princes of Brandenburg kept coins and gems, and an assortment of varied objects classified as "Artificialia" and "Naturalia."[16]

On many occasions several terms were declared to be of identical meaning. Zedler's *Universal Lexicon* identified both the "cabinet" and the "Kunst-Kammer" with the "museum," and in the *English Dictionary* of 1737, by Nathan Bailey, the museum was defined as a "study" or "library." In his *Museographia* Neickelius referred to a Chamber of Rarities as "Schatz-Raritäten-Naturalien-Kunst-Vernunft Kammer" (Chamber of treasures — rarities — objects of nature — of art and of reason).[17]

Ways and Means of Acquiring Specimens

In ancient Greece as well as in the Middle Ages, and probably up to the dawn of the nineteenth century, the work of the living artist was regarded as second to none. The esteem in which ancient statuary was held in the Renaissance did not dampen the enthusiasm for contemporary creation. A personal relationship existed between patron and artist, and acquisitions were made by commissions. Princes installed in their castles studios for artists, visited them and watched them at their work. They discussed the contents of pictures to be painted and even the style of presentation, and they corresponded with artists on such subjects.[1]

Exchanges of gifts took place, and for a variety of reasons: as an expression of congeniality, as a bribe, or as a boastful gesture. When Charles I, as Prince of Wales, in 1623 visited Spain and his intended bride, the Infanta Maria, he attended gatherings of "Aficionados." On the occasion of his visit to the house of Don Geronimo Fures y

Muños, whose cabinet was noted for drawings and paintings by Italian masters, he received several pictures and weapons as gifts. When Charles's marriage to the Infanta was reconsidered, some of the fine paintings offered to him by his royal host and prospective brother-in-law, Philip IV, were unpacked and remained in Spain. Among them were Titian's *Danae* and *Europa*. Other royal gifts were taken home by Charles and were sold in the public auction following his decapitation. Titian's *Antiope* was sold to the French banker Jabach for £6000. Gian Bologna's bronze group of Cain and Abel later adorned the Duke of Buckingham's garden near York House; it had come to Spain as a gift from the Grand Duke of Florence to the Spanish King's minister Lerma.[2] One of the great scholar-collectors of the seventeenth century, Fabri de Peiresc of Aix, in France, took delight in presenting other students and collectors with antiquities, specimens of nature, and books, which were likely to further their special interests.[3] His unselfish passion for learning made him offer his Egyptian antiquities to Pater Kircher.

On some occasions great works of art were involved in a barter trade of a special kind. When the *Laocoön* was brought to light in 1506 in the process of building operations, the owner of the plot of land, a certain de'Freddi, derived considerable benefit from the incident; the Pope who acquired the statue appointed the man's son as a customs officer at the Porta San Giovanni, a post which brought a revenue of 600 ducats yearly, and later as a scribe in the papal archives[4] (Fig. 4). With the increase in building activities in Rome in the late fifteenth and sixteenth centuries new treasures came to light. "When the cardinal Domenico Grimani entertained in 1505 representatives of his state he showed them a great number of statues of marble and many other ancient things which had all been unearthed in the *vigna* while the foundations for his palace were laid," reported a contemporary author quoted by Burckhardt (translated from the German by the author).[5]

The Gonzaga, Este, Medici, and other princelings vied for the favors of the French King and the Spanish-Austrian Emperor and felt comforted when their seigneurs accepted a good-looking bribe. On the occasion of Charles V's visit in Bologna, in 1529, the Duke of Este received a letter from one of his agents who conducted negotiations with the Emperor's adviser in Italy, Francisco de los Cobos, who wrote: "I implore your Highness to present him with the most beautiful ones [paintings]." A second letter from Cobos to the Duke's agent amounted to strict orders: "Under all circumstances I must get this picture."[6] The coveted picture was a portrait of the

Duke of Este by Titian, and indeed a few weeks later the painting decorated the Emperor's studio. It was not merely the loss of a much valued painting that pained the Duke, but anxiety that the gift might call forth the Pope's displeasure. "What would the Pope say if he knew— (of the Duke's portrait being in the Emperor's personal rooms)," asked Casella, on the Duke's behalf. Cobos knew his answer: "It would certainly anger him to think that His Majesty carries in his heart the image of the Duke as his loyal servant." The Este knew that their claim to the rule over Modena and other territory depended on the Emperor's contentment.

From the Duke of Mantua, Charles V received Corregio's *Danae and the Shower of Gold, Leda and the Swan* and *Jupiter and Io.* When the Emperor came to Mantua, in 1532, the Gonzaga staged a series of entertainments and opened to the illustrious guest their *Guardaropa* containing a precious collection of armor and paintings. Charles's interest in Titian's portraits goes back to that visit. At a later date a Grand Duke of Florence intended to win French sympathies by presenting the monarch with a small statue of Louis XIII on horseback, made of pure gold, but a crisis between Florence and Genoa affected his plans. Spain's weakened powers still cast a spell of authority over European affairs, and the Grand Duke added to his courtesy by begging from the Spanish ambassador in exchange for the statue a portrait of Philip IV — so as to enjoy the sight of the adored master's countenance as a substitute for the much missed conversation with him.

At a time of limited facilities for travel, ambassadors abroad acted as agents for their royal masters and fellow countrymen. The Earl of Arundel, Charles I's emissary to the Continent in 1636, sent paintings home from Vienna, the Netherlands, and other places. Sir Thomas Roe, Whitehall's envoy to the Porte, interested himself in Greek antiquities on behalf of the Earl of Arundel and the Duke of Buckingham.[7] He reported home that manuscripts were not available, but that antiquities in marble were unesteemed . . . and to be "procured (especially at Delphos) for the charge of digging and fetching." He wrote that "Mr. Petty (one of Sir Thomas's helpers) hath raked togither 200 peices, all broken, or few entyre." The ambassador's ambition was to obtain statuary from the Porta Aurea in Constantinople. The Sultan's Treasurer was reluctant to part with sculptures made fast to the walls with iron pins, but eventually granted a "Firman" (government permit) to the British representative in Constantinople allowing him to take away stones with old inscriptions. In this manner the Earl of Elgin acquired statuary from the Parthenon in Athens which is now one of the great treasures of the British Museum.[8] His claim that he saved a legacy of ancient culture from destruction was not unfounded under the conditions of the Turkish administration which either ignored the Greek remains or considered them "enchanted." In return for what they gave away, the Turks received from the British an "old booke of prophesy" which they desired.

In times of war collectors' items changed hands at an accelerated rate. "Sulla's treatment of Athens was harsh and alien to the Roman character . . . but he committed yet another outrage at Alalcomenae by carrying off the very image of Athena," wrote Pausanias. Emperor Nero robbed five hundred statues of gods and men in the sanctuary of Apollo at Delphi, and Roman generals carried off monuments of piety and art from Corinth; Pausanias added an apology: "It is known that Augustus was not the first to carry off votive offerings and images of gods from his vanquished foes, but that he only followed a long-established precedent"[9] (Fig. 33b).

Philip IV of Spain and his men equaled in violence the ill-famed Roman Consul Verres. The Spanish Viceroy at Naples gave order to arrest the Prior of the Dominican monastery who had denounced his abbot to Rome for having sold to Spain pictures of the monastery. To avoid the prior's fate, Pater Clemente Stapoli of Palermo personally delivered paintings claimed by Philip's agents. A poem by the Venetian poet Marco Boschini survived as a record of the sadness among Italians when they watched carriages filled with paintings taken from residences in Naples and ready to leave for Spain.[10]

France had gained from the loot of soldiers of Francis I, who brought fine works of art from Italy as booty, but the Napoleonic art plunder throughout Europe surpassed all precedent.[11] When the French invaded Italy, confiscations were to be confined to public property, but all influential individuals who showed opposition to Bonaparte were despoiled of their ancient heirlooms. The Colonna, Borghese, Barberini, and Chigi were forced to dispose of their pictures in order to prove that they had no other means of satisfying the invader's demands for money (Fig. 34a).

Empress Josephine took personal advantage of the situation; the fine gallery of Cassel was one of the complete collections of which she took possession, keeping for herself a few selected objects and using the rest for presents and for sale. After Napoleon's downfall, representatives of Hessen were among numerous other claimants for the restoration of property and called at the palace of Malmaison, a residence of the former empress. They were informed that their pictures were in Russia. Czar Alexander declared he had purchased the paintings for a sum of 940,000 francs and considered himself to be their rightful owner. A considerable part of the Bonapartist booty was, however, returned to its owners.

An excellent survey of the acquisition of works, both by violent and peaceful means, in the course of the Napoleonic wars is contained in the *Memoirs of Painting* by W. Buchanan, an art dealer of distinction, who sent agents to different countries.[12] His representative in Spain during the Peninsular War was the artist G. Augustus Wallis, who wrote between October 1807 and January 1808:

All seems to be fear and confusion . . . every payment here from the bankers is half paper and half money and the exchange not at all favourable. I lost 30% on some two days past . . . nothing but talk of French and Spanish armies and fleets arriving . . . many old things are in the possession of the old families, and are very little regarded. . . . In going to Loeches, twenty miles from Madrid, to see the famous pictures of Rubens . . . the people took me for a Frenchman, and with great difficulty I got off with my life.

The bulk of the booty was destined for Napoleon's grandiose museum at the Louvre and for the provincial museums in France in which the emperor took interest. When the Duke of Wellington pursued the French in the East of Spain, Joseph Bonaparte was forced to take to flight at Vittoria near Pamplona and to forsake the spoils he was carrying in hundreds of carriages (Fig. 34b). One of the Duke's biographers wrote about the encounter: ". . . in the carriage of Joseph who escaped capture narrowly, we found Correggio's beautiful painting "Christ in the Garden."[13] Another artistic gain for England was the Egyptian antiquities collected by the French Army and taken by the British when the French capitulated near Alexandria before Sir Ralph Abercrombie.

Injury to works of art was hardly avoidable under such and similar conditions of acquisition. A picture of the Madonna by Raphael came to be known as *La Vierge Coupée*. The painting had been cut to pieces on the order of Marshall Soult to facilitate its removal from a Spanish church; later on it was shipped to England, piece by piece, and was sold in installments.

Revolutions may have affected collectors' items even more than wars. The sale of Charles I's collections of art on order of Parliament in 1653 drew a crowd of important collectors to London. Among those who sent representatives were Christine of Sweden, Catherine of Russia, Philip IV of Spain, and the Austrian Archduke Leopold Wilhelm. Cardinal Mazarin was represented, and so was the French

Figure 33a. A gentleman's private Pinacotheca in ancient Rome. From Vitruv's *De Architectura*.

Figure 33b. Who took what, when, and from whom? In his *Geschichte der Abführung Vorzüglicher Kunstwerke . . .* , of 1803, the German author F. K. L. Sickler limited himself on the page reproduced here to the listing of art plunder committed by the ancient Romans, but the catalogue could be expanded to an international scope.

Tabellarische Uebersicht

aller von den Römern erbeuteten und abgeführten Statuen.

Kunstwerke, Statuen und Gemälde.	Ort, wo sie erbeutet wurden.	Ort wohin sie abgeführt wurden.	Zeit in welcher dieses geschah.	Krieg in welchem die Abführung vorfiel.	Volk oder Männer durch die sie erbeutet wurden.
1. Juno regina.	Veji in Hetrurien.	Rom.	J. d. W. 3558	Kr. g. d. Vejenter.	R. Furius Camillus.
2. Zweitausend Statuen.	Bolsena in Hetrurien.	R.	3620.	Kr. g. Hetrurien.	R. Postumius.
3. Venus victrix.	Tuxium in Samnien.	R.	3650.	Kr. g. d. Samniter.	R. Fabius Fabricianus.
4. Jupiter Imperator.	Präneste.	R.	3658.	Kr. g. d. Latiner.	R. T. Quintius Dict.
5. Eine unbestimmte grofse Menge von Statuen.	Capua.	R. Colleg. Pontif.	3664.	Kr. g. d. abgefallnen Städte Grofsgriech.	R. Appius Claudius und Fulvius.
6. Mars und eine unbestimmte Menge von Statuen.	Tarent.	R.	3712.	Kr. g. d. abg. St. G. g.	R. Fabius Maximus.
7. Hercules ein Coloss aus Gold.	Tarent.	Rom Capitol.	3712.	Kr. g. d. abg. St. G. g.	R. Fabius Maximus.
8. Jupiter Jmperator oder Urius.	Macedonien.	Rom Capit.	J. n. R. Erbauung. 558.	Kr. g. Kö. Philipp v. Macedonien.	R. T. Q. Flaminius.
9. Die neun Musen.	Ambracia.	R. Temp. d. Hercules.	566.	Kr. g. Aet. und Cephallenien.	R. Fulvius Nobilior.
10. 285 broncene u. 230 marmorne Statuen.	Ambracia u. ganz Epirus.	Rom.	566.	Kr. g. Aetolien u. C.	R. Fulvius Nobil.
	Städte Klein-	R.	566.	Kr. g. d. K. Antioch.	R. L. Scipio.

Figure 34a. Napoleon Bonaparte's troops looting the Gallery of Parma in 1796. Drawing by Meynier, Musée de Versailles. From C. Saunier, *Les Conquêtes Artistiques de la Révolution et de l'Empire . . .* (Paris: Laurens, 1902).

Figure 34b. The acquisition of an art collection on a battlefield. Confrontation between Joseph Bonaparte and the Duke of Wellington at Vittoria, Spain. On the request of Spain the Duke kept the works of art, which he first wanted to be returned to their previous owner. (By courtesy of the Duke of Wellington.)

banker Jabach. The memorandum-book of a certain R. Symmonds, a contemporary connoisseur, which is now in the possession of the British Museum, offers an account of the event by an eyewitness.[14] He tells of the Spanish ambassador's anxiety to secure objects for his master and of his acquisition for £2000 of the famous *Sacra Familia* by Raphael, originally painted for Federico Gonzaga, and enthusiastically acclaimed by Philip, who named the picture *La Perla*. In 1651 a shipload of precious paintings landed in Coruña, and eighteen mules pulled the treasures from the coast up to the royal palace in Madrid.

A few generations later another dramatic situation arose; the French Revolution opened the doors to many palaces throughout the Continent. The sale of collections from France, Italy, and Spain in London created a taste for the acquisition of works of art "which had been almost dormant in England since the days of its illustrious patron and protector, Charles the First," as Mr. W. Buchanan put it. In his *Memoirs of Painting* (pp. xiii, xiv) he wrote:

. . . during the conflicting storms which ravaged the continent of Europe, Great Britain alone presented a bulwark to which foreign nations looked with awe and respect; and although at war with her politically, they still confided in her honor and in her strength; they transmitted their moneyed wealth to her public funds and their collections of art to private individuals, either for protection or to be disposed of for their use.

Sudden changes in ownership occurred during religious revolts. Philip II prided himself on having rescued numerous images of religious character from the iconoclastic Netherlands. One of the objectives of Parker's (first) Society of Antiquaries in England in 1572 was to preserve ancient documents and objects of archaeology menaced by destruction through the dissolution of religious houses. The Pinakothek in Munich was among the galleries that profited from the secularization of clerical property in territories occupied by Napoleon Bonaparte.

The potential adventures that could befall single works of art may be illustrated by two examples. The three Corregios commissioned by Federigo Gonzaga and later used by him to bribe Charles V were separated from each other when Philip II presented them as gifts to people at his court. They were reunited when Rudolph II purchased them, and together they sailed to Sweden among other artistic loot gathered up by Gustavus Adolphus, who captured Prague. After a brief stay in Sweden the Corregios were again on their way, this time accompanying Christina, the daughter and successor of Gustavus Adolphus, who disliked her royal task, resigned, and went to live in

Rome.[15] Her friend Cardinal Azzolini inherited the Corregios. After another change of hands, the pictures were sold to the Orléans in Paris, where the nudity of *Leda* and *Io* so offended the religious maniac Louis Orléans that he mutilated them. After their recovery with the aid of skillful restorers the Correggios found shelter in the residence of M. Laborde Mereville, whose gallery next to his palace in the rue d'Artois in Paris was not yet completed when the French Revolution broke out. Off went the three Corregios to London to add to the profits of *marchand-amateurs*.[16]

A chalice, known as the Royal Gold Cup, landed in the British Museum after numerous migrations.[17] The fine goldsmith work with enameled decoration was produced in the fifteenth century and was once the property of Jean de Berry, Duke of Burgundy, who presented it to King Charles VI of France. The Hundred Years' War played the chalice into the hands of the Duke of Bedford, who in his turn deemed it worthy of serving as a present to Henry VI of England. In 1604 James I gave the cup to the Duke of Frias, an agent in peace negotiations between England and Spain, and Frias passed it on to the Spanish convent Las Huelgas, where it first fell into oblivion and later disappeared. About 1880 the French art dealer M. Pichon acquired at a public sale a chalice which he regarded as good but modern work; he bought it for its metal value and sold it to England for 200,000 francs. He had not considered the international influence wielded by the clergy; rumors of the deal reached the convent at Las Huelgas, and the bull of excommunication against the unknown original trespasser on their property was declared annulled in return for a fair share in M. Pichon's gain.

The acquisition of ancient remains by travelers can be traced back to the fifteenth century, when the humanist Ciriaco of Ancona gathered inscriptions, statuary, and coins on his journeys in Greece and the Near East.[18] The traveler-collector was well represented in the sixteenth and seventeenth centuries, especially among scholars specializing in natural history or medicine; their curiosity often extended to archaeology and ethnology. Some scholars succeeded in forming several large collections in their lifetime and to sell them at a high price to other collectors, often titled persons.

In the seventeenth century the trade in art became organized. Paintings were still sold at fairs, in Paris, Leipzig, and other places, but the Netherlands increasingly became a Central European market.[19] Dealers had to obtain licenses from the Guild of St. Luke in Antwerp, and Dutch auctions were attended by an international clientele. Diplomats and artists acted now more often as advisers of great collectors than as their buyers. After Rubens' death a printed catalogue was sent to all important collectors in Europe. Philip IV of Spain was anxious to be among the first bidders and acquired ten paintings by the master himself and twenty-two other pictures for 127,000 Gulden.[20] Part of the Rubens collections went to the Duke of Buckingham.[21] In the eighteenth century the art dealer was generally an established figure, and his versatility was commented upon by Pope in the following verse:[22]

He buys for Topham drawings and designs,
For Fountain statues, for Pembroke coins,
Rare monkish manuscripts for Herne alone
And books for Mead and rarities for Sloane.

Museums and Children, or Children's Museums

Children's or Junior Museums, self-contained or forming a part of a larger institution, represent one embodiment of service rendered by museums and addressed to young people of different ages from preschool to high school. The same segment of the population, subdivided into age groups, is offered guided tours, lectures, and demonstrations. Such facilities are often synchronized with school hours and replace school sessions. Loan materials to schools are offered by some of the Children's Museums as well as by educational departments of museums for the general public.

In my experience, both as a museum practitioner working with young people and as an experimenter comparing results of different approaches, a preference for one or the other of these forms of museum service cannot be expressed without qualifications.[1] Either of them may open up specific opportunities for learning and enjoyment, and both may be totally irrelevant or even tend to pervert education.

Children's or Junior Museums are at present at crossroads which may lead either backward to no longer deniable obsolescence or forward to a new era of creativity.[2] This is one reason why careful and candid stocktaking is urgently called for. The need is emphasized by the fact that among all museums of poor quality, bad children's museums are the worst.

The history of children's museums commands respect. They have a niche among the pioneers of contemporary education. For decades they have been appealing to the child's otherwise neglected tactile sense in exploring his environment. Long before manipulative activities and the process of discovery were acclaimed by psychologists as motivations to learning, and were paid some attention in classrooms, junior museums kept children in rapt attention while handling rocks, calling forth rhythms from African drums, and conducting experiments with magnets or inoffensive chemicals. Young imaginations got excited on treasure hunts and along nature quiz trails. These are some of the brighter spots to which many others could be added, but they are often outbalanced by memories of shoddy, haphazard collections being presented to children in dismal, ill-lit rooms; of offerings which are disconcertingly meager and lacking in focus if compared with one of the numerous site museums in the National Parks or with a good televised science program, and even with experiences garnered at a high school science fair.

Children's and Junior Museums at present have to compete with facilities which did not exist in the past, and at the time of the pioneer institutions of their kind.[3] The number of summer camps where nature study is an important part of the program is increasing. Some school systems have camps to which pupils are taken in the course of their school year. Laboratory materials introduced into elementary schools, and of course into high schools, in both biology and physics, deal with many concepts which in previous years a child could see illustrated by objects and demonstrations in museums only. Materials related to social studies are being added to the science equipment. The first question administrators of Children's Museums ought to ask is how their offerings relate to other facilities in their area. Prior to the establishment of a new museum for young people, a careful analysis should be made of already existing opportunities for learning, which may bear a variety of names.

The second obvious question concerns the specific advantages of a Children's Museum if compared with a museum for the general public. Frequently it is a matter of finance, which is legitimate as long as the available funds can meet the minimum standards of a museum of any sort. This leads up to a pioneering task which Children's Museums may take up: the setting of standards for a new museum. Such standards exist with regard to libraries, but not with regard to museums. A public library has to have a minimum number of books covering a certain range of subject matter, and to employ people of appropriate and proven skills, to be eligible as a recipient of public funds, but the term "public" needs reconsideration in our era. Criteria of eligibility for access to public funds are important, but equally important are standards for any kind of man-made environment to which human beings are exposed.

Preschool children and probably children up to junior high school may feel attracted to a museum building of limited size and containing materials of a limited quantity, but this must not lead to offerings which are too restricted to provide information or to challenge thought. The search for standards in the use of museum resources for the benefit of students of different age groups, for gifted children and for slow learners, opens up new opportunities for experimentation. The people working in such settings ought to have knowledge of learning theories and to have given proof of their interests and achievements. A classroom teacher may develop into a fine museum worker, but there are considerable differences between a classroom that is a part of a large organization, and where set curricula are followed by thirty or more pupils, and a museum setting. There is no guarantee that a teacher will be the best person for utilizing the potential of a Children's Museum as we know it, or for expanding it to new horizons. It would be a wonderful opportunity for experiments which may in some cases be transferred to school rooms. Experiments can more easily be undertaken in the informal setting of a Children's Museum than within the framework of a large school system where each part affects numerous other parts, and where failure may have a wide margin of waste.

There are few more futile routines in our school-museum cooperation than the large-scale enterprise of sending school class after school class for an hour's or even a day's visit to a general museum, as a rule once in a year. Considerable differences in quality exist: in some cases the viewed exhibits and the talk given by a staff member of the museum are more or less synchronized with current school studies. The question remains how often they are sufficiently synchronized, if they are to form a part of the curriculum. There is also the problem, largely still unexplored, whether the viewing of an exhibit in a hall containing a number of them can be synchronized with a lecture for the benefit of human beings of any age. If the wandering eye receives a message which is at variance with that of the ear, confusion is likely to arise. This is, in my opinion, to be studied with special reference to children below adolescence, whose reaction to stimuli is fast and whose limited inhibitory mechanisms make it difficult for them to remain on the track of a single matter.[4]

In some cases the expense of the trip by school bus assumes such importance in the minds of authorities that several experiences are crowded into a day's outing: a guided tour, a lecture, a film show, a viewing of the entire museum without guidance, and possibly a visit to a nearby zoo or fire station. If the guided tour, the film, and the lecture combine to an interdependent whole, they are likely to reinforce each other, particularly if arranged in an appropriate sequence, but if they are unrelated fragments, they are likely to have a mutually debilitating effect, apart from offering slight fringe benefits. This should not be misunderstood as a proposal for strictly regimented visits of children to museums. In fact, I would recommend that a structured guided tour related to the school curriculum be followed up by a visit to a Gallery of Adventure where individual youngsters could view single specimens drawn from a variety of areas of knowledge — geology and paleontology, prehistory and archaeology, anthropology and history. It would be a worthwhile effort if only a few objects sparked an interest in the minds of a few children. To avoid a diffusion of thought, a gallery of this kind should be of limited size, with specimens being changed from time to time, and it should be reserved for youngsters at certain times of the week, for their own benefit and that of adult visitors. A small reference library would be helpful. A Gallery of Adventure might act as a learning environment of a special kind: it would challenge questions rather than offer answers.

From the point of view of administrative convenience guided tours of school classes have advantages, but the effects of the experience on children, once again the interests of human software versus hardware including office files, assume priority in an age that offers new opportunities for making man more human, more intelligent, more eager to enlarge his knowledge, and more sensitive.[5] Studies related to Children's Museum visits, which were made years ago and which in my opinion are still as relevant as they were at any time before, remain ignored.[6] They resulted in the following main directives:

Prepare children for a museum visit, and prepare them preferably in school.

Prepare fast learners several days, or even a week, before the museum visit; prepare slow learners on the day preceding the museum visit.

Ask pupils to search in the museum for answers to questions on a prepared questionnaire, and prepare such questionnaires preferably after a discussion with the pupils; they will be eager to search for answers to questions they raised themselves.

Wherever possible present a topic in comparison with another one — for example, Life in Ancient Egypt with Life in Ancient Greece. Children with undeveloped reading skills may benefit from an introduction in the form of a card game — even up to the eighth grade. Introductory lectures in the museum should be brief; a lecture-discussion at the end of the museum visit is helpful. So is a follow-up study in school.

In the course of my own experimental exhibitions for pupils of the seventh and eighth grade, the highest learning scores occurred when a limited number of objects was presented as an illustration of a coherent story—of Life in Prehistoric Times, or in Ancient Greece, or of early ways of Making Fire and Making Light. Opportunities for the handling of objects and for visitor participation were important. The following two Tables will supplement this information.[7]

Museum Resources as Learning Aids. *A comparison of six methods.*

	Methods					
Variable	1	2	3	4	5	6
Quantity of information	1-2-3 Limited quantity Less than 50 main items			4-5 Larger quantity More than 50 main items		Limited quantity as in 1-3
Coherence of communication	1-2-3 strong			4 weak	5-6 intermediate	
Facilities for touching and handling	strong	weak	3-4-5-6 none			
Facilities for participation	some	2-3-4-5-6 none				

Museum Resources as Learning Aids. *The effectiveness of six methods* expressed in terms of total mean scores achieved by homogeneous groups of students. Each method was tried with 75 students of junior high school age. The students came in groups corresponding with their scholastic achievements. To each method there were 30 low achievers (L.A.), 30 medium achievers (M.A.), and 15 high achievers (H.A.).

Methods	Total Mean Scores and Standard Deviations					
	L. A. T.M.S.	S.D.	M. A. T.M.S.	S.D.	H. A. T.M.S.	S.D.
1. Limited-quantity exhibit of stressed coherence. Facilities for participation and the handling of objects.	23.37	10.03	28.00	12.34	24.60	10.77
2. Guided tour in the same exhibition. Limited handling; no discussion	14.37	10.66	17.60	12.09	19.80	10.51
3. Undirected viewing of the same exhibition. No pupil participation.	6.50	10.74	14.23	13.26	14.33	6.03
4. Large-quantity exhibit of less stressed coherence. All materials in glass cases. No pupil participation.	2.63	7.44	−2.40	13.21	6.80	1.93
5. Guided tour in the same exhibition. No pupil participation.	6.43	9.36	6.57	16.44	7.53	7.56
6. Presentation of same topic in classroom *without* objects. Stressed coherence and pupil participation in discussion.	12.20	16.46	16.67	7.72	12.13	12.61

T. M. S.: Total Mean Score. S. D.: Standard Deviation.

Experiments — those made by others and by myself — stress the need for a situation of guided initiative in the course of children's group visits to a large museum.

Observations I had opportunity to make without control groups led to the conclusion that slow learners, who may be slow because of genetic or environmental drawbacks, benefit from a maximum of physical involvement; for example, in the form of dramatic play in which costumes are worn and specimens are handled.[8] A detailed account of these experiments and experiences will be given on some future occasion.

Extracts from Contemporary Accounts of Sixteenth-, Seventeenth-, and Eighteenth-Century Collections

From Sansovino's *Venetia, Citta Nobillissima e Singolare* (Venetia, 1663).

DE I PALAZZI PRIVATI
ET DE LORO ORNAMENTI LIB. IX. 393

. . . . *sopra esso
Canale, ch'è fiancheggiato da spatiosa fondamenta d'ambi le parti, si vede il Palazzo
del Conte Girolamo Cauazza, con facciata tutta di marmo, di vaga Architettura, &
se bene pare alquanto ristretto, nondimeno, ripartito di dentro in tre suoli, viene ad'haue-
re, oltre il commodo de mezadi, stanze alte assai riguardeuoli; quelle di mezzo, sondo
abbellite da portoni, e porte guarnite con fregio, & alette di marmo bianco, e nero, e con
Cartelle di paragone: Le Nape de Camini adorne de stucchi Eccellenti, e tutto il resto
corrisponde con politura senza pari, & con mobigliamenti ricchi, & honoreuoli quanto si
possono desiderare in Casa priuata; godendo il terzo suolo più alto, anch'egli pur degna-
mente fornito, la vista ampissima di due gran spatij di Laguna, sino à Monti Euganei.
Ma quello, in che egli si distingue da ogn'altro, è l'appartamento basso, aggiustato da detto Conte con ammirabile semitria, resi hauendo luochi di delitia, li destinati à gl'usi infe-
riori domestici; & illustrata con cinque ordini di cose rare, la Galeria per la quale se ve
entra. In effetto, nel metterui piede, resta rapito l'occhio, e l'animo insieme, dalla bian-
chezza non meno del Cielo, d'altezza straordinaria, & del d'intorno, lauorato à stucchi,
festoni, figure, & altre vaghezze, che dal corso di molti fori, dalla prospettiua dilettenuo-
le, cento passa andanti lontana, da gl'adobbi Nobili, che vi rilucono, e dalla varietà d'-
oggetti piaceuoli da tutte le parti, che si presentano. Dal lato destro, e sinistro ne Nicchi sono collocate Statue, e fra essi sopra modioni, teste, & busti. Vn poco più all'in giù,
ouati dorati di Cipresso, dipinti da migliori Pittori della Città, come dal Caualier Libe-
ri, Pietro Vecchia, Ruschi, & altri. Al di sotto d'una fascia intagliata, che fa diuisio-
ni, sono tramescchiati bassi rileui di prezzo; esquisite Teste antiche su piedestalli: Quadri
grandi di buone mani, sendone più alto quattro de retratti al naturale di Giorgione, con
particolar diligenza elaborati, & sotto le balconate, altri quadri d'intaglio, come anco de
Ottangoli pendenti dalla Cornice alta.
In Nicchio grande alla destra, e Loggiato Nettuno, à cui piedi si auuiticchia vn Del-
fino, & al piano stanno riposti due Leoni di marmo fino. Rincontro alla sinistra, fuori del
dritto corso della Galeria, doue giace vn Pozzo ottangolare, di pietra da Verona, circon-
dato da vasi di mirto; due rami di scala formano vn vacuo conuertito in Grotta dall'in-
crostatura di muri, composta di Capami, Giazuoli, & di conchiglie di mare di tante sorti,
e colori, che danno diletto per se stesse, per l'artificio, con che sono distribuite, & per gl'as-
petti diuersi, anche humani, che figurano; Et qui pure rimpetto al sudetto Nettuno è ca-
uato vn Nicchio tutto vestito di Madriperle, oue spicca vn gruppo di due statue Adone,
cioè, & Venere, che s'abbracciano, mirabilmente scolpito; chiusa rimanendo la Grotta, da
ferrata à gigli tutta dorata, perche niente manchi di leggiadro, e non commune, come li
sono li Banchetti di Veluto, e seggie simili, con portiere di doppio raso alle porte, che guar-
niscono gl'altri seguenti luochi ancora.
A Capo la Galeria, s'entra in vn Salato, con sei nicchi, sei porte, e quattro finestre,
tutto pure stuccato di bianco, con macchie tonde di marmo bianco, e rosso di Francia in
mezo a festoni. Sopra tauolini di paragone, e d'Ebano, rimessi d'Auorio, sono disposte
scolture antiche, & moderne; Bronzi di getto Eccellente, & altre rarità, in particolare
vn'Osso Scio intiero, con la gamba di Gigante, accreditato dall'ossatura stessa humana, di
grandezza strauagante. Nel vuòto d'una delle porte sono incassate molto artistamente
quattro gran lastre de specchi di sei quarte l'una, con fornitura di metallo dorato, le
quali restituiscono li oggetti, che si presentano, col vantaggio d'altretanto sfondro, in
modo, che ogn'vno, che non ne hà hauuto precedente notitia, resta sopraprefo, & bene
spesso ricerca per doue s'entra nell'altre stanze, da detti specchi oggettati. Inuentione
curiosissima, ritrouata dal detto Conte, che ha bauuto altri imitatori dipoi, con suario pe-
rò differente assai.*

R. Borghini, *Visit to El Riposo*, near Florence, a sixteenth-century account of a private collection, published in Milan in 1807, pp. 14–15.

..... da Firenze intorno a tre miglia, valicato il chiarissimo fiumicello dell' Ema a Vacciano. Siede il palazzo fra l'oriente ed il mezzogiorno riguardante, alquanto rilevato dal piano, sopra un vago poggetto, di sì diversi frutti, e di tante viti ripieno, che oltre all' utile, che se ne cava, è una maraviglia a vederlo. Quivi sono amenissime e fruttifere piagge: boschetti di cipressi e d'allori, che colle folte ombre destano in altrui una solitaria riverenza: acque chiarissime, che mormorando soavemente si fanno sentire: e pratelli di freschissima e minutissima erba coperti, e di molte maniere di vaghi fiori per entro dipinti e segnati. Ha il bene compartito palagio ampie sale, pulite ed ornate camere, luminose logge, acqua freddissima in gran copia, e volte piene di ottimi vini. Ma quello, che fa ciascuno intento a riguardare, sono le rare pitture e le sculture che vi si veggono; perciocchè vi è di mano di Michelagnolo il famoso cartone della Leda (1), e un altro pezzo di cartone pur del Buonarroto, delle guerre di Pisa, che si avevano a dipingere in Firenze nel palagio: di Lionardo da Vinci vi è una testa d'un morto, con tutte le sue minuzie: di Benvenuto Cellini il dise-

gno del modello del Perseo di Piazza: di Francesco Salviati quattro carte bellissime: del Bronzino due disegni della sua miglior maniera: del Botticello un bellissimo quadro di pittura: d'Antonello da Messina (1), che introdusse in Italia il lavorare a olio, un quadro, entrovi dipinte due teste: di Giambologna molle figure di cera, di terra e di bronzo, in diverse attitudini, rappresentanti varie persone, come prigioni, donne, dee, fiumi, e uomini famosi: e di molti altri pittori assai cose, che troppo lungo sarei a raccontarle, e particolarmente d'alcuni Fiamminghi paesi bellissimi. Ma di gran maraviglia a vedere è uno scrittojo in cinque gradi distinto, dove sono con bell'ordine compartite statue picciole di marmo, di bronzo, di terra, di cera: e vi sono composte pietre fini di più sorte, vasi di porcellana e di cristallo di montagna, conche marine di più maniere, piramidi di pietre di gran valuta, gioje, medaglie, maschere, frutte, e animali congelati in pietre finissime, e tante cose nuove e rare venute d'India e di Turchia, che fanno stupire chiunque le rimira. Appresso ad altre stanze, in altra parte del palagio, è un simile scrittojo tutto adorno di vasi d'argento e d'oro, ...

---

(1) Questo cartone di presente è in Firenze nel Palazzo dei Signori Vecchietti.

(1) Questo quadro pure è in Firenze nell'istesso luogo. La vita del medesimo Pittore si legge nel Vasari Parte II.

An account of the collection of the Archduke Ferdinand of Hapsburg in Castle Ambras, Tirol, by the French traveler F. M. Misson, who visited the castle in the year 1687.

160   V O Y A G E   D'A L L E M A G N E.   161

On nous a conduits d'abord dans une aſſez grande ſale, qui eſt une eſpece d'Arſenal, dont à la verité les armes ſont plus curieuſes qu'utiles. On nous y a fait remarquer, entre autres choſes, la lance extraordinairement grande & peſante, de laquelle l'Archiduc Ferdinand ſe ſervoit dans les tournois. Ils diſent que ce Prince * arreſtoit un carroſſe à ſix chevaux allant à toute bride, en le prenant par un des rayons de la roüe : Qu'il rompoit de ſes mains deux écus joints enſemble, & je ne ſçay combien d'autres choſes prodigieuſes, plus difficiles à croire que l'hiſtoire de Frederic.

Nous avons eſté de cette ſale dans une galerie où l'on voit pluſieurs Princes ſur leurs chevaux favoris, avec toute l'armure, & tous les ornemens qu'ils avoient dans les tournois. On y garde auſſi la peau d'un ſerpent, qui eſtoit long de quinze pieds, & qui a eſté pris auprés d'Ulm, ſur le bord du Danube. Au bout de cette galerie, on entre dans une chambre toute remplie de dépoüilles, & d'armes priſes ſur les Turcs. Un Bacha, & un Aga des Janniſſaires ſont repreſentez ſur leurs chevaux, avec le meſme equipage qu'ils avoient quand on les prit. Leurs habits ſont fort riches, & les barnois

nois des chevaux le ſont encore beaucoup davantage. Ils ſont chargez d'ouvrages d'or & d'argent, de pierres fines ; de damaſquinures, & d'autres enrichiſſemens arabeſques.

Aprés cela, on nous a menez dans une autre galerie, dans laquelle il y a un double rang ce grandes armoires, qui ſe joignent par derriere & par les coſtez, & qui occupent tout le milieu de la galerie, auſſi bien que toute la hauteur ; de ſorte qu'il ne reſte qu'un médiocre eſpace, pour ſe promener tout autour. Les trois premieres ſont pleines d'ouvrages d'albaſtre, de verre, de Corail, & de Nacre. Dans la quatriéme, il y a des Médailles & des Monnoyes d'or & d'argent. La cinquiéme eſt garnie de vaſes de Porcelaine, & de terre ſigillée. On voit dans la ſixiéme, pluſieurs petits Cabinets fort riches, d'une marqueterie bien travaillée ; & les layettes ſont remplies de Médailles, & de petits ouvrages d'agathe & * d'ambregris.

*On a écrit le meſme choſe de Leonard de Vinci, Peintre de Florence. On peut voir dans les Mémoires de Camerarius, un chapitre curieux & perſonnes extraordinaires robuſtes, To. 1. l. 2. ch. 5. L'Electeur de Saxe, & Roy de Pologne, maintenant regnant, (Sept. 99.) ne cede guere en plus robuſte de ces gens-là.

Ceux toujours fort petits ; Je diray ici deux choſes ſur cela.

La premiere eſt, que le ſuis comme je l'ay avancé. Ce n'eſt point une matiere d'examen ; c'eſt un fait, contre lequel il n'y a point à diſputer. La ſeconde choſe eſt, que les gens-là ſe trompent tous meſmes dans ce qu'ils connoiſent. M. Senchu de Rennefort, dans la deſcription de Madagaſcar qu'il publia en 1688, dit qu'on avoit trouvé dans cette Iſle un morceau d'Ambre-gris du poids de dix-huit onces. Garcias d'Orta & Medecin Portugois, dit en avoir vu un de quinze livres : & M. de la Nauche homme curieux & ſavant, parle de morceaux bien plus grands, dans le Traité qu'il en a écrit & cite ſes Auteurs, anciens & modernes. D'ailleurs, rien n'empeſche que cette matiere ne ſoit miſe en œuvre.

There followed an account of the contents of the remaining fourteen cases in which specimens were grouped according to their material or their kind: ancient weapons, natural curiosities such as plants and animals, objects made of wood, ivory, and feathers, manuscripts, keys and locks, semiprecious stones shaped into trees and animals, clocks, musical instruments, metals and minerals, vessels of a great variety, consisting partly of pure gold and studded with jewels, antiquities such as urns and idols. In addition to the specimens in the cases there were many others fastened to the ceiling and to the walls. After having described what he had viewed in the large hall which he referred to as "a kind of arsenal," M. Misson mentioned the library, the adjacent gallery, where ancient statues, busts, and other antiquities were housed, and several rooms decorated with costly paintings and wall hangings.

From E. Browne. *A brief account of some Travels in divers parts of Europe* (London, 1627), pp. 95–96. (With reference to the imperial collections in Vienna.)

The *Rarities* of the great Duke of *Tuscany*, The *Treasure* of *Loretto*, St. *Mark*, St. *Denis* in *France*, of the Duke of *Saxony* at *Dresden*, and others, were very satisfactory to me. Yet having a fair opportunity, I would not leave *Vienna* without a sight of the most noble *Treasury* or *Repository* of his Imperial Majesty; especially having heard so much thereof, and knowing it to be the *Collection* of many succeeding Emperours. I therefore took a fit opportunity to remain divers hours in it, and was extremely delighted. with the rich and magnificent Curiosities thereof.

In the first *Cupboard* or *Case* were many noble Vessels, turned and shaped out of *Ivory*, a *Cup* turned by the Emperours own Hand; another turned by *Ferdinandus* the Third. Gallant *Cups* of *Amber*; *Spoons* and *Vessels* of *Mother of Pearl*; many noble works in *Coral*; a fine *Galley* in *Ivory*, and *Cups* made out of *Rhinocerot's* horn.

In the second,

An *Elephant* of *Ivory* with a *Castle* upon his back, and over the *Castle* a *Ship*, with much other fine work in the same piece. Two fair *Pillars* of *Ivory*; good *Basso Relievo* in *Ivory*; a fair *Cranium* or *Deaths head*, and much other variety of *Ivory* work. A *Picture* in *Oyl* of *Ganimede*, by *Corvegio*.

In the third,

A fine *Picture* of an *old Man's head* in *Oyl* by *Albert Durer*: great Variety of *Watches* and *Clock-work* in *Silver*: a fine *Centaur* in *Silver*, which is a curious *Watch*.

In the fourth,

More *Watches* and *Clock work*; a gallant *Ship* of *Silver*, a *Triumphal Chariot*, a *Turk* riding and attended, a *Globe* and a *Sphere* in *Silver*, a curious *Landskip* in *Oyl* by *Corregio*, a *Cupid* by the same hand, with a fine Copy of it.

In the fifth,

A curious *Filigrane Handkerchief*, and two fair *Filegrane Plates* brought out of *Spain* by the Empress *Margarita*; an *Indian Basket* of an *Indian* sort of *Filegrane* mixed with *Birds*; a *Bason* of *Agate* finely wrought with silver *Craw-fishes* in it.

Evelyn, *Diary and Correspondence* (p. 21, n. 15). Entry of October 22, 1644 (with reference to the Medici Collection in Florence).

Under the Court of Justice is a stately arcade for men to walk in, and over that, the shops of divers rare artists who continually work for the great Duke. Above this is that renowned *Cimeliarcha*, or repository wherein are hundreds of admirable antiquities, statues of marble and metal, vases of porphyry, etc.; but amongst the statues none so famous as the Scipio, the Boar, the Idol of Apollo, brought from the Delphic Temple, and two triumphant columns. Over these hang the pictures of the most famous persons and illustrious men in arts or arms, to the number of 300 taken out of the museum of Paulus Jovius. They then led us into a large square room, in the middle of which stood a cabinet of an octangular form, so adorned and furnished with crystals, agates and sculptures, as exceeds any description. This cabinet is called the *Tribuna*, and in it is a pearl as big as a hazel-nut. The cabinet is of ebony, lazuli, and jasper; over the door is a round of M. Angelo; on the cabinet Leo the Tenth, with other paintings of Raphael, del Sarto, Perugino, and Corregio, viz. a St. John, a Virgin, a Boy, two Apostles, two heads of Duerer, rarely carved. Over this cabinet is a globe of ivory, excellently carved; the labours of Hercules, in massy silver, and many incomparable pictures in small. There is another, which had about it eight Oriental columns of alabaster, on each whereof was placed a head of Cæsar, covered with a canopy so richly set with precious stones that they resembled a firmament of stars. Within it was our Saviour's Passion, and twelve Apostles in amber. This cabinet was valued at two hundred thousand crowns. In another, with chalcedon pillars, was a series of golden medals. Here is also another rich ebony cabinet cupolaed with a tortoise-shell, and containing a collection of gold medals esteemed worth 50,000 crowns; a wreathed pillar of oriental alabaster, divers paintings of Da Vinci, Pontorno, del Sarto, an *Ecce Homo* of Titian, a Boy of Bronzini, etc. They showed us a branch of coral fixed in the rock, which they affirm does still grow. . . . In a press near this they showed an iron nail, one half whereof being converted into gold by one Thurnheuser, a German chymist. . . .

21st May [1644]. Visiting the Duke's repository again, we told at least forty ranks of porphyry and other statues [a detailed account of pictures and statues viewed in the gallery follows]. In the Armory were an entire elk, a crocodile, and, amongst the harness, several targets and antique horse-arms, as that of Charles V; two set with turquoises, and other precious stones. Then, passing the Old Palace . . . Here is a magazine full of plate; a harness of emeralds, the furnitures of an altar . . . in massy gold . . . in the middle is placed the statue of Cosimo II; the bas-relievo is of precious stones, his breeches covered with diamonds. There is also a King on horseback, of massy gold, and an infinity of such rarities.

Compare Fig. 7.

J. Ray, *Travels through the Low Countries, Germany, Italy, France, with curious Observations*, Natural, Topographical, Moral, Physiological, etc., made in 1663 (London, 1738). Extracts from his account of the Medici Collection in Florence, pp. 285–286.

The *Great Duke*'s gallery is in the old palace, a handsome pile of building. Under ground, as it were, in cellars, are the ſtables: above them fair *portico's* or cloiſters to walk in. Above the *portico*'s are ſhops for all manner of artificers to work in for the *Great Duke*. The uppermoſt ſtory is the *gallery* properly ſo called; where, in an open walk free for any man to come into, ſtand many ancient, and ſome alſo modern ſtatues, Round about on each ſide this walk, hang the·pictures of many Princes and other perſons, who have been famous in the world for learning or valour. Among the reſt we noted the pictures of of *Queen Elizabeth*, *King James*, *Oliver Cromwel*, and *Johannes Acutus*, before remember'd.

The chief rarities are lock'd up in cloſets, of which we ſaw four. The things which in our tranſient view we took more eſpecial notice of were, a huge terreſtrial globe, and a *Sphæra armillaris* bigger than that. A branch'd candleſtick including many little figures of ivory, or white wax appearing thro' the tranſparent amber: an engine counterfeiting a perpetual motion, like thoſe of *Septalius* at *Milan*. Several ſtone-tables, ſo curiouſly in-laid with ſmall pieces of precious ſtones of divers colours, as to compoſe figures of plants, fruits, and flowers, birds, beaſts, and inſects, ſo natural and to the life, that ſcarce any picture drawn by the hand can excel them. One of theſe, the beſt and richeſt that we have any where ſeen, both for the excellency of the workmanſhip, and coſtlineſs of the materials, being ſet with many rubies and pearls, they valued at 100000 *Florence Scudi*, which is more than ſo many *Engliſh* crowns. Several rich cabinets. That of the greateſt value, which they rated at 500000 *Scudi*, was rich ſet with gems of the firſt magnitude; a pearl of an enormous greatneſs, but not perfectly round; ſeveral topazes almoſt as big as wal-nuts, large rubies and emeralds, beſides other ſtones of inferior note, ſtuds of amethyſt, &c. Here we alſo ſaw the nail, pretended to be one continued body, half iron, half gold, part of the iron having been turned into gold by one *Thurnbaußerus*, an alchymiſt of *Baſil*, before·mentioned. . . . . .

There followed an account of the Armory, where the armor of many "great persons" and kings of Europe could be viewed next to armor and weapons from many distant lands. The Duke's wardrobe, or "Ar genteria," full of rich plate, and by-rooms containing stuffed animals and skeletons were described.

From F. M. Misson's description of the collections in the Great Duke's (of Medici) Palace in Florence. English translation (London, 1699), vol. II, p. 185.

The moſt precious and valuable Rarities are kept in the Octogonal Room, call'd the † *Tribune*, which is twenty Foot in diameter, and is cover'd with an arch'd Dome. The Floor is pav'd with ſeveral ſorts of Marble artificially laid together ; the Walls are hung with Crimſon Velvet, beautified with an infinite number of rare Ornaments ; the Windows are of Cryſtal ; and the inſide of the Dome is overlaid with Mother of Pearl. Nothing is admitted into this Place, but what is of great Value and exquiſite Beauty. You have doubtleſs read, in *Tavernier*'s Travels, the Deſcription of that lovely * *Diamond* which juſtly claims the firſt Rank among the Jewels of this Cabinet. Among other Rarities, theſe deſerve to be mention'd : an antique Head of *Julius Cæſar*, of one entire Turquoiſe, as big as an Egg ; a Cupboard full of Veſſels of Agat, *Lapis Lazuli*, Cornelian, and Chryſtal of the Rock, the whole garniſh'd with Gold and fine Jewels ; a large Table and Cabinet of inlaid Work, wholly compos'd of Oriental Jaſper, Chalcedony, Rubies, Topazes, and other Precious Stones, admirably well wrought ; a Collection of very rare Medals ; a prodigious number of antique Pieces of carv'd and engrav'd Work, very entire, and extremely well kept ; ſelect Pictures, ...

This Diamond weighs a hundred thirty and nine Carats and a half. 'Tis pity ſays Tavernier, that the Water or Luſtre of it approaches to a Citron-colour.

An account of some of the numerous "Collections of Curiosities" in Italy visited in the year 1663 by the English traveler John Ray and described by him in *Travels through the Low-Countries*, pp. 186 – 187.

From *Vicenza* we journeyed to *Verona*, a fair, large populous city, and thought to contain 70000 fouls. It is ftrong by fituation, and extraordinary fortified with walls, baftions, towers, bulwarks, and deep ditches full of water. Here we faw feveral cabinets of collections of natural and artificial rarities. 1. That of feignior *Mapheus Cufanus* an apothecary, wherein were fhewn us many ancient *Ægyptian* idols, taken out of the mummies, divers forts of petrified fhells, petrified cheefe, cinnamon, fpunge and mufhromes. A jafper ftone and an agate having chryftal within them. Stones having upon them the perfect impreffion or fignature of the ribs and whole fpines of fifhes. A *Catapulta* of brafs found 1656, about *Trent*. Several curious *entaglia's* or ftones engraved with figures of heads, &c. An ancient *Roman* gold ring. A good collection of ancient *Roman* coins and medals, as well confulary as imperial, befides modern medals. A ftone called *Oculus mandi, n. d.* which when dry fhews cloudy and opake, but when put into water, grows clear and tranfparent. An account of this ftone may be feen in the *Hiftory of the Royal Society*, brought in by Dr. *God-dard*. Among his medals we obferved a *Maximinian* and a *Dioclefian*, with this on the reverfe infcribed, *Veronæ Amphitheatrum*.

2. That of feignior *Mufcardo*, a gentleman of *Verona*, a civil and obliging perfon. He alfo hath a very good collection of ancient *Roman* medals, among which he fhew'd us an *Otho* of gold, and told us that thofe of brafs were all counterfeit, there having never been any found of that metal. Many forts of lachrymal urns and lamps, great variety of fhells and fome fruits and parts of plants petrified. Several exotic fruits and feeds: the ores of metals and minerals: gems and precious ftones in their matrices as they grew: *Lapis obfidianus* and a kind of ftone called *Adarce*. But becaufe there is a defcription of this *Mufeum* publifhed in *Italian*, I fhall not defcend to more particulars, but refer the reader thither.

3. The *Mufeum* of feignior *Mario Sala* an apothecary, containing only fome reliques of *Calceolarius*'s *Mufeum*, printed many years ago.

From *The Gentleman's Magazine*, vol. XVIII (London, July 1748).

Prince and Princess of Wales visit Sir Hans Sloane.

An Account of the Prince and Princess of Wales visiting Sir HANS SLOANE.

DR *Mortimer*, secretary to the Royal society, conducted their Royal Highnesses into the room where Sir *Hans* was fitting, being antient and infirm. The Prince took a chair and sat down by the good old gentleman some time, when he expressed the great esteem and value he had for him personally, and how much the learned world was obliged to him for his having collected such a vast library of curious books, and such immense treasures of the valuable and instructive productions of nature and art. Sir *Hans's* house forms a square of above 100 feet each fide, inclosing a court; and three frontrooms had tables set along the middle, which were spread over with drawers fitted with all forts of precious stones in their natural beds, or flate as they are found in the earth, except the first, that contained stones formed in animals, which are so many diseases of the creature that bears them; as the most beautiful pearls, which are but warts in the shell fish; the *bezoars*, concretions in the stomach; and stones generated in the kidneys and bladder, of which man woefully knows the effects; but the earth in her bosom generates the verdant *emerald*, the purple *amethist*, the golden *topaz*, the azure *saphire*, the crimson *garnet*, the scarlet *ruby*, the brilliant *diamond*, the glowing *opal*, and all the painted varieties that *Flora* herself might wish to be deck'd with; here the most magnificent vessels of cornelian, onyx, sardonyx and jasper, delighted the eye, and raised the mind to praise the great creator of all things.

When their Royal Highnesses had view'd one room and went into another, the scene was shifted, for, when they returned, the same tables were covered for a second course with all forts of *jew-*els, polish'd and set after the modern fashion; or with *gems* carv'd or engraved; the stately and instructive remains of antiquity; for the third course the tables were spread with *gold* and *silver ores*, with the most precious and remarkable ornaments used in the *habits* of men, from *Siberia* to the Cape of *Good Hope*, from *Japan* to *Peru*; and with both ancient and modern *coins* and *medals* in gold and silver, the lasting monuments of historical facts; as those of a *Prusias*, king of *Bithynia*, who betray'd his allies; of an *Alexander*, who, mad with ambition, over-run and invaded his neighbours; of a *Cæsar*, who inflaved his country to satisfy his own pride; of a *Titus*, the delight of mankind; of a Pope *Gregory* XIII. recording on a filver medal his blind zeal for *religion*, in perpetuating thereon the *massacre* of the *protestants* in *France*; as did *Charles* IX. the then reigning king in that country; here may be seen the coins of a *king* of *England*, crown'd at *Paris*; a medal representing *France* and *Spain*, striving which should first pay their obeisance to *Britannia*; others shewing the effect of popular rage, when overmuch oppressed by their superiors, as in the case of the *De Witts* in *Holland*; the happy deliverance of *Britain*, by the arrival of King *William*; the glorious exploits of a Duke of *Marlborough*, and the happy arrival of the present illustrious *royal family* amongst us.

The gallery, 110 feet in length, presented a most surprising prospect; the most beautiful *corals*, *crystals*, and figured stones; the most brilliant *butterflies*, and other *insects*, *shells* painted with as great variety as the precious stones, and feathers of *birds* vying with gems; here the remains of the *Antediluvian* world excited the awful idea of that great catastrophe, so many evident testimonies of the truth of *Moses's* history; the variety of animals shews us § great beauty of all parts of the creation.

Then a noble vista presented itself thro' several rooms filled with books, among these many hundred volumes of dry'd plants; a room full of choice and valuable manuscripts; the noble present sent by the present *French* king to Sir *Hans*, of his collections of paintings, medals, statues, palaces, &c. in 25 large atlas volumes; besides other things too many to mention here.

Below-stairs some rooms are filled with the curious and venerable antiquities of *Egypt*, *Greece*, *Hetruria*, *Rome*, *Britain*, and even *America*; others with large large animals preserved in the skin; the great *saloon* lined on every fide with bottles filled with spirits, containing various animals The halls are adorned with the horns of divers creatures, as the double-horn'd *Rhinoceros* of *Africa*, the fossil deer's horns from *Ireland* nine feet wide; and with weapons of different countries, among which it appears that the *Mayalese*, and not our most *Christian* neighbours the *French*, had the honour of inventing that butcherly weapon the *bayonet*. Fifty volumes in folio would scarce suffice to contain a detail of this immense museum, consisting of above 200,000 articles.

Their *royal highnesses* were not wanting in expressing their satisfaction and pleasure, at seeing a collection, which surpass'd all the notions or ideas they had formed from even the most favourable accounts of it. The Prince on this occasion shew'd his great reading and most happy memory; for in such a multiplicity, such a variety of the productions of nature and art; upon any thing being shewn him he had not seen before, he was ready in recollecting where he had read of it; and upon viewing the ancient and modern *medels*, he made so many judicious remarks, that he appear'd to be a perfect master of *history* and *chronology*; he expres'd the great pleasure it gave him to see so magnificent a collection in *England*, esteeming it an ornament to the nation; and expressed his sentiments how much it must conduce to the benefit of learning, and how great an honour will redound to *Britain*, to have it established for publick use to the latest posterity.

C. Saunier, "Les Conquêtes Artistiques de la Revolution et de l'Empire et les Reprises des Allies en 1815," *Gazette des Beaux Arts*, vols. 21 – 23 (Paris, 1899 – 1901).

According to Saunier's account based on contemporary documents, the initiative to levying war indemnities in form of works of art in the conquered countries came from men in authority in the governing body of the "Convention." Among the official statements of the year 1794 were the following: "By means of courage the Republic has succeeded in obtaining what Louis XIV was unable to obtain for enormous sums of money. Vandyk and Rubens are on their way to Paris and the Flemish School *en masse* will adorn our museums. . . . France will possess inexhaustible means of enlarging human knowledge and of contributing to the perfection of civilization." In a letter dated "II ventôse, an V [of the Republic]," the Minister of Justice, Merlin de Domaine, wrote to Napoleon that "the reclamation of works of genius and their safekeeping in the Land of Freedom would accelerate the development of Reason and of human happiness."

In the fifth year of the Republic works of art from the North were followed by transports from Italy, Commissar Thouin, who was in charge of the convoy, proceeding first in mule-drawn carriages and then in boats, announced his impending arrival in Paris in a letter addressed to the President of the Directorium in which he wrote as follows:

. . . Are the precious relics of Rome to arrive like loads of coal and to be put on the quai of the Louvre as if the cases contained nothing but soap? . . . I admit that the idea of such an arrival pains me. . . . Citizens of all classes of the population ought to be aware that the Government has given them consideration and that all will have their share of the great booty. People will be able to judge what a Republican Government means if compared with the rule of a monarch who makes conquests merely for the pleasure of his courtiers and the satisfaction of his personal vanity. . . . [Translated from the French by the present writer.]

In the month Thermidor of the sixth year of the Republic the entry of the conquered art treasures was triumphantly celebrated on the Champs de Mars, where, with pictures by Raphael, Titian, and other masters, the *Laocoön*, the *Apollo of the Belvedere*, and the *Venus of Medici* were among the ancient statues paraded on cars lined up in three rows (Fig. 2).

For several years workers at the Musée du Louvre, under the leadership of the director-general Vivant Denon, were busily engaged in sifting the arriving objects and arranging them. Credit is due to them for the devotion shown in the restoration of damaged specimens and in the effort of grouping them according to artistic schools and in a manner more systematic than was usual in museums of their period.

It ought also to be noted that there were voices, of Frenchmen of different political parties, who criticized the seizure of works of art throughout Europe and their concentration in Paris.

In 1815, after the battle of Waterloo, the French authorities tried to keep at least that part of the art treasures which was already catalogued and exhibited, but their efforts were in vain. The resistance of the officials of the Louvre museum against the allied authorities who came to claim their property may be gained from a passage in a letter of Vivant Denon's son, who wrote, "J'ai vu mon père arracher les tableaux du brancard où les commissaires étrangers les avaient placés, les reprendre jusqu'à quatre fois . . . les faire remonter dans la galerie, et les conserver ainsi a la fôrce de persévérance et d'energie. . . ."* When, at last, he recognized his helplessness in a contention with the leading powers of Europe and with armed soldiers knocking at the doors of the Louvre, Vivant Denon, at the time almost seventy years old, called out, "Qu'ils les emportent! Mais il leur manque des yeux pour les voir et la France prouvera toujours par sa supériorité dans les arts, que ces chefs-d'œuvre étaient mieux ici que qu'ailleurs."†

*"I have seen my father persistently removing. . . pictures from the carts on which they had been loaded by the foreign commissars. . . [I have seen him] carrying the pictures back to the gallery and trying to secure them by dint of will. . . ."
† "Let them carry them away! They have no eyes to see them! Masterpieces of art could be kept nowhere more appropriately than in France, the country which always will be leading in matters of art." (Translated from the French by the present writer.)

1. A museum—What Is It? (pp. 1–2)
(No Notes)

2. Preludes to Public Museums (pp. 3–4)

*Alfred North Whitehead, *The Aims of Education* (London: Williams and Norgate, 1950), p. 3.

[1]The opening dates of some of the main early museums were as follows:
British Museum, London, England, 1759
Charleston Museum, South Carolina, British Colonies in America, 1773
Belvedere, Vienna, Austria, 1781
Louvre, Paris, France, 1793
National Gallery of Art, Haarlem, Holland, 1800
National Museum, Budapest, Hungary, 1802
Pennsylvania Academy of Fine Arts, Philadelphia, United States, 1805
National Museum, Copenhagen, Denmark, 1807
National Museum, Rio de Janeiro, Brazil, 1818
Prado, Madrid, Spain, 1819
National Museum, Buenos Aires, Argentina, 1823
Colonial Museum, Wooloomooloo, Australia, 1828
Altes Museum, Berlin, Prussia, 1830

[2]For international surveys of private collections see:
Douglas and Elizabeth Rigby, *Lock, Stock and Barrel* (Philadelphia: Lippincott, 1944).
Francis Henry Taylor, *The Taste of Angels, A History of Art Collecting from Ramses to Napoleon* (Boston: Little, Brown and Co; an Atlantic Monthly Press Book, 1948).
W. G. Constable, *Art Collecting in the United States of America; an outline of a history* (London–New York: Nelson, 1964).
R. H. Hubbard, *European Paintings in Canadian Collections . . . With an essay on picture collecting in Canada* (Toronto: Oxford University Press, 1956).
Niels von Holst, *Creators, Collectors and Connoisseurs, The Anatomy of Artistic Taste from Antiquity to the Present Day* (London: Thames and Hudson, 1967).
Silvio A. Bedini, "The Evolution of Science Museums," *Technology and Culture*, VI, 1 (1965), pp. 1–29.
With regard to American collectors of more recent times see Aline Saarinen, *The Proud Possessors* (New York: Random House, 1958).
Great Private Collections, ed. Douglas Cooper (London: Weidenfeld and Nicholson, 1963), deals with individual collectors of the twentieth century. The motivation of people to "collect," and to collect specific things, is strikingly presented in the introduction by Kenneth Clark.
Compare Henry Heydenryk, *The Art and History of Frames* (New York: Heinemann, 1963).

Economic Hoard Collections (pp. 4–12)

[1]Homer, *The Iliad*, trans. A. T. Murray, The Loeb Classical Library (London: Heinemann; New York: Putnam, 1924), XXIV, pp. 230–239.
[2]H. Schliemann, *Ilios. The City and Country of the Trojans* (London: Murray, 1880). Compressed into a shapeless mass and under heaps of rubbish, ingots of gold, half-finished articles and vessels, weapons, caldrons and ornaments of gold were found by Dr. Schliemann at Hissarlick. The excavator regarded these objects as a part of the royal treasury described by Homer, which had been destroyed in the course of a conflagration and had remained buried for thousands of years.
[3]Dr. Schliemann claimed to have opened at Mycenae the tomb of Agamemnon, known as the Treasury of Atreus, which enshrined another collection of objects of gold, swords, goblets, diadems, buttons, and masks. Pausanias, who in the second century A.D. had visited Mycenae, referred to the places where Atreus and his sons had kept their treasures. Pausanias's *Description of Greece*, ed. J. G. Frazer (London: Macmillan, 1898).
[4]"It seems, in fact, chimerical as though men had agreed upon these metals (gold and silver) as a symbol for which they would strive and labour, fight and die. The myths, the Golden Fleece, Midas, the Rheingold, show us the desire for gold acting as a powerful impulse among quite simple societies. It entered into the ambitions of Darius and of Alexander, into the conflicts of Rome and Carthage." F. L. Nussbaum, *A History of the Economic Institutions of Modern Europe* (New York: Crofts, 1933), p. 95.
[5]"The Persian Empire and the West," ed. J. B. Bury, S. A. Cook, F. E. Adcock, *Cambridge Ancient History*, vol. IV (1960), pp. 40, 50, 101, 118, 264 ff.
"The Hellenistic Monarchies and the Rise of Rome," ed. S. A. Cook, F. E. Adcock, M. P.

Charlesworth. *Ibid.,* vol. VII (1928), pp. 778, 792.

"Rome and the Mediterranean," ed. S. A. Cook, F. E. Adcock, M. P. Charlesworth. *Ibid.,* vol. VIII (1930), pp. 307 – 309, 311.

T. A. Rickard, *Man and Metals* (New York-London: Whittlesey – McGraw-Hill, 1932), vol. I., pp. 278 – 279.

[6]W. S. Ferguson, *The Treasurers of Athena* (Cambridge: Harvard University Press, 1932), p. 107.

[7]Thucydides, *History of the Peloponnesian War*, Books II, XIII, 4, 5, trans. C. Forster Smith, Loeb Classics (London: Heinemann; New York: Putnam, 1926).

[8]The bullion of silver weighing 14,342 pounds carried in the triumph of Publius Scipio on his return to Rome in the year 207 B.C. was sent straight to the Public Treasury and so was, five years later, bullion weighing 123,000 pounds. See Rickard, *Man and Metals,* vol. I, p. 280.

Titus Livius, *The History of Rome,* Book XXXIV, XXI, trans. T. E. Page; Book XLV, XL, 1, trans. Alfred C. Schlesinger, Loeb Classical Library (Cambridge: Harvard University Press; London: Heinemann, 1951).

[9]Cicero, *The Verrine Orations,* trans. L. H. G. Greenwood, Loeb Classical Library (Cambridge: Harvard University Press; London: Heinemann, 1953); speech against Quintus Caecilius Niger, maintaining Cicero's own greater fitness to prosecute Verres, 3, 11.

Edmond Bonnaffé, *Les Collectionneurs de l'ancienne Rome* (Paris: Aubry, 1867).

[10]Cicero, *The Speeches,* trans. J. H. Freese, The Loeb Classical Library (Cambridge: Harvard University Press; London: Heinemann, 1956), In Defence of Sextus Roscius of Ameria, XLVI, 133.

[11]Cicero, *The Verrine Orations,* The Second Speech against Gaius Verres, Book IV, 1.

Compare Edmund Bonnaffé, "Trésor de Bosco Reale," *Gazette des Beaux-Arts,* Third Period, vol. XV, pp. 112 – 120.

[12]Cicero, *Letters to Atticus,* trans. E. P. Winstedt. Loeb Classical Library (London: Heinemann; New York: Putnam, 1939), I, 8 and 9.

Titus Pomponius Atticus left Rome for political reasons and resided from 86 B.C. until 65 B.C. in Athens where his educated slaves copied and translated Greek literature for the Roman market. In addition to being a successful publisher he provided Roman collectors with Greek sculpture and acted as their mentor. Megara, on the road from Athens to Corinth, was one of his quarries; its temples were in ruins, and statuary could be carried away without penalty.

[13]Nussbaum, *Economic Institutions,* p. 20.

[14]W. Sombart, *Der Bourgeois, Zur Geistesgeschichte des Modernen Wirtschaftsmenschen* (Munich and Leipzig: Duncker & Humblot, 1913), p. 32.

[15]Julius von Schlosser, *Die Kunst und Wunderkammern der Spätrenaissance* (Leipzig: Klinkhardt & Biermann, 1908).

Schlosser, *Die Schatzkammer des Allerhöchsten Kaiserhauses* (Vienna, 1918).

A. Weixlgärtner, "Die Weltliche Schatzkammer in Wien," *Jahrbuch der Kunsthistorischen Sammlungen,* New Series, vols. I and II (Vienna, 1927 – 1928).

[16]"En otro patio (del palacio) tienen su cuarto los infantes de Castilla, cerca de el está el guardajoyas. . . . Una flor de lis de oro media vara de alto y poco menos de ancho, bordada de piedras preciosas, que fué primero de duques de Borgoña, un diamante de tamaño de un real de á dos valuada en doscientos mil ducados, del que pendia la famosa perla llamada, por ser sola, la "Huerfana" (ó la Peregrina) del tamaño de una avellana, tasada en treinta mil ducados." R. de Mesonero Romanos, *El Antiguo Madrid* (Madrid, 1861), pp. 26 – 27. The palace was destroyed in a fire in the eighteenth century. Compare J. Evelyn, *Diary and Correspondence,* written 1641 to 1706, ed. Ernest Rhys, Everyman's Library (London: Dent; New York: Dutton, 1930).

On the seventeenth of October, 1644, with reference to the palace of the Prince of Doria at Genoa:

"The house is most magnificently built without, nor less gloriously furnished within, having whole tables and bedsteads of massy silver, many of them set with agates, onyxes, cornelians, lazulis, pearls, turquoises, and other precious stones. The pictures and statues are innumerable." Compare Appendix, pp. 244, 246, extracts from seventeenth-century descriptions of the imperial collection in Vienna and the Medici Palace in Florence.

See also Francesco Sansovino's description of the metalwork and jewelry accumulated in San Marco in Venice in his book *Venetia, Città Nobilissima e Singolare* (Venetia: Jacomo Sansovino, 1581), Lib. II, pp. 29 – 41.

[17]*Abbot Suger on the abbey church of Saint Denis and its Art Treasures*, ed. and trans. Erwin Panofsky (Princeton: Princeton University Press, 1946).

[18]Cesare Augusto Levi, *Le collezione Veneziane d'arte e antichità* (Venice, Ongania: 1900).

[19]J. Martinez, "Discursos practicables del nobilissimo arte de la Pintura," *Fuentes Literarias para la Historia del Arte Español*, ed. F. J. Sanchez Canton (Madrid: Centro de Estudios Historicos, 1930, vol. III, p. 37.

Velazquez: "Vuestra Majestad no ha de tener cuadros que cada hombre los pueda tener."

El Rey: "¿Como ha de ser esto?"

Velazquez: "Yo me atrevo, Señor, (si Vuestra Majestad me da licencia) ir a Roma y a Venecia a buscar . . . los mejores quadros. . . ."

[20]M. A. S. Hume, *The Court of Philip IV* (London: Nash, 1907). Carl Justi, *Miscellaneen aus Drei Jahrhunderten Spanischen Kunstlebens* (Berlin: Grote, 1908).

[21]". . . l'argent avait une place marquée dans toutes les combinaisons secrètes de l'éminent curieux (Mazarin)." A. Lemaître, *Le Louvre, Monument et Musée, depuis leurs origines jusqu'à nos jours* (Paris: Societé Française de Numasmatique et d'Archéologie, 1877), p. 253.

Compare Maurice Rheims, *Art on the Market*, Thirty-five Centuries of Collecting and Collectors, from Midas to Paul Getty, trans. David Pryce-Jones (London: Weidenfeld-Nicolson: 1961). For example, p. 234. Manet's *La Rue de Berne* brought 6000 francs in the nineteenth century and went up to 113 million francs in 1958. During the same period, wages in France went up over three times as much as the value of gold, which rose substantially. Yet the increase in the market value of Manet's pictures outdid both; if the one painting referred to above had remained an equivalent of gold, it would have fetched only one million francs.

Van Eyck's famous portrait of the merchant Arnolfini and his wife was purchased in 1842 by the National Gallery in London for £730. In the course of the following one hundred years the value of Van Eyck paintings increased to several hundred thousand dollars for a painting.

There have, however, also been phenomenal decreases in prices for works of art which ceased to appeal to the mood of a period. In the sixties of the nineteenth century a Murillo painting could fetch up to $50,000; around the middle of the twentieth century the Murillo slump reached a low of approximately one tenth of its former evaluation.

[22]*A Century of Baltimore Collecting, 1840 – 1940. Exhibition Catalogue*, Baltimore Museum of Art, 1941.

[23]Oliver Carlson and Ernest S. Bates, *Hearst – Lord of San Simeon* (New York: Viking, 1936).

[24]With regard to the sales in stores see two articles by Edward A Jewell in *New York Times*, January 28 and February 2, 1941.

Social Prestige Collections (pp. 12 – 17)

[1]Bronislaw Malinowski, *Argonauts of the Western Pacific* (London: Routledge; New York, Dutton, 1932), pp. 169, 173.

[2]Athenaeus, *The Deipnosophists*, or *The Banquet of the Learned*, trans C. D Yonge (London: Henry G. Bohn, 1854), pp. 315 – 323.

C. A. Boettiger, *Über Museen und Antikensammlungen* (Leipzig, 1808).

[3]L. Friedländer, *Roman Life and Manners under the Early Empire*, seventh enlarged and revised edition, trans. L. A. Magnus (London: Routledge; New York: Dutton, not dated), p. 45.

E. Curtius, *Kunstmuseen, ihre Geschichte und Bestimmung*, paper read before the *Wissenschaftlicher Verein* in Berlin and with special regard to the Royal Museum in Berlin, 1870.

[4]E. Law, *History of Hampton Court Palace in Tudor Times* (London Bell, 1885), pp. 33, 80.

[5]P. Dan, *Le Trésor des Merveilles de . . . Fontainebleau* (Paris: Cramoisy, 1642).

[6]Michel de Marolles, Abbé de Villeloin, *Mémoires* (Amsterdam, 1755). In his "Onzieme Discours," pp. 194 ff, and pp. 216 – 217, the Abbé wrote of outstanding contemporary seventeenth-century collections: "Ceux (cabinets) souffrent peu de comparison pour la magnificence des Cristaux . . . des Agates, des Calcedoines, des Coraux . . . des Ametystes . . . des Grenats, des Saphirs, des Perles et des autres pierres de grand prix qui y sont mises en oeuvre dans l'argent et dans l'or, pour y former des Vases, des Statues, des Escrins, des Miroirs, des Globes, des Chandeliers . . . et autres choses semblables."

Compare J. Evelyn, *Diary and Correspondence*, written 1641 to 1706, ed. Ernest Rhys, Everyman's Library (London: Dent; New York: Dutton, 1930).

Entry of March 7, 1644: "I set forwards with some company towards Fontainebleau, a sumptuous Palace of the King's, like ours at Hampton Court, about fourteen leagues from the city. . . . This House is nothing so stately and uniform as Hampton Court, but Francis I began much to beautify it; most of all Henry IV (and not a little) the late King. It abounds with fair halls, chambers and galleries; in the longest, which is 360 feet long, and 18 broad, are painted the Victories of that great Prince, Henry IV. That of Francis I, called the grand Gallery, has all the King's palaces painted in it; above these, in . . . excellent work in fresco, is the History of Ulysses, from Homer, by Primaticcio, in the time of Henry III. . . . The Cabinet is full of excellent pictures, especially a Woman, of Raphael. In the Hall of the Guards is a piece of tapestry painted on the wall, very naturally, representing the victories of Charles VII over our countrymen. . . .

"Having seen the rooms, we went to the volary. . . . There is also a fair tennis-court, and noble stables . . . In the Court of the Fountains stand divers antiquities and statues, especially a Mercury. . . ."

[7] J. de Zabaleta, "El Dia de Fiesta . . .," ed. G. L. Doty, *Romanische Forschungen*, vols. 41–42, pp. 147–400 (Erlangen, 1928).

J. C. Davillier, *Recherches sur l'orfevrerie en Espagne* (Paris: Quantin, 1879).

[8] *Descriptive Catalogue* of the statues, paintings, and other productions of fine arts that existed in the Louvre at the time the Allies took possession of Paris in July, 1815 (Edinburgh, 1815).

Compare further bibliography on the Musée Napoléon and on the acquisitions made by the Bonaparte family in the Appendix, pp. 290, 291, notes 9, 11, 12.

[9] Matthew Josephson, *The Robber Barons* (New York: Harcourt, Brace, 1962), pp. 339, 341–346.

[10] Herbert L. Satterlee, *John Pierpont Morgan* (New York: Macmillan, 1939).

"Mr. John Pierpont Morgan," Editorial on the occasion of Mr. Morgan's death, *The Burlington Magazine*, XXIII (1913), pp. 65–67.

Magic Collections (pp. 17–22)

[1] L. Thorndike, *The Place of Magic in the Intellectual History of Europe* (New York: Columbia University Press, 1905).

[2] C. de Morales, in his *Libro des las virtudes y propriedades de piedras preciosas* (Madrid, 1605), declared that the Bezuar stone was found in the kidneys of the cervicabra, a wild animal of Arabia which, after having been bitten by a serpent, produced a counteracting matter.

The Dutch sixteenth-century medical doctor de Boodt explained the word "Bezoar" as having evolved from the Hebrew "Beluzaar" and meaning "the master of poison." Compare A. Weixlgärtner, "Die Weltliche Schatzkammer in Wien," *Jahrbuch der Kunsthistorischen Sammlungen*, New Series, vols. I and II (1927–1928).

[3] Quoted by Thorndike, *The Place of Magic*, p. 16.

[4] J. W. Müller, *Das Einhorn vom geschichtlichen und naturgeschichtlichen Standpunkt* (Stuttgart, 1853).

Weixlgärtner, "Weltliche Schatzkammer," vol. II.

"(Unicorns) . . . of which I have seen many, both in Publick Repositories and in private hands. . . ."

E. Browne, *A brief account of some Travels in divers parts of Europe* (London, 1685), p. 101. (Printed for Benjamin Tooke)

What was considered as the horn of a magic beast was in fact a tooth of a narwhale — a tusk of a male cetacean, *Monodon monoceros*, of the family of Delphinidae.

[5] T. G. Pettigrew, *A History of Egyptian Mummies* (London: Longman, 1834).

[6] J. H. Zedler, *Grosses vollständiges Universal Lexicon aller Wissenschaften und Künste welche bisher durch menschlichen Witz und Verstand erfunden und verbessert wurden* (Halle-Leipzig, 1735–1754).

[7] Pausanias's *Description of Greece*, ed. J. G. Frazer (London: Macmillan, 1898).

W. Rouse, *Greek Votive Offerings* (Cambridge: Cambridge University Press, 1902).

J. Burckhardt, *Antike Kunst*, Collected Works, vol. 13, eds. Felix Stähelin and H. Wölfflin (Berlin–Stuttgart: Deutsche Verlágsanstalt, 1933), pp. 89–103.

[8] J. Calvin, *Traité de Reliques* (Geneva, 1601).

[9] Collin de Plancy, *Dictionnaire Critique des Reliques et des Images Miraculeuses* (Paris: Guien, 1821), vol. II, pp. 55, 62.

Idem, Abregé de l'Inventaire du Trésor de St. Denis (Paris, 1668).

Compare two seventeenth-century accounts of collections of relics in the Treasury of the cathedral of St. Denis in France by J. Evelyn in his *Diary* on November 12, 1643, and in San Marco at Venice by Francesco Sansovino, *Venetia, Città Nobilissima e Singolare* (Venetia, 1581), pp. 107–108.

Compare Appendix, pp. 244, 246, Extracts From seventeenth-century accounts of the imperial collection in Vienna and of Castle Ambras, Tyrol.

[10] F. L. Nussbaum, *A History of the Economic Institutions of Modern Europe* (New York: Croft, 1933), p. 25.

[11] Paul Lacroix, *Sciences et Lettres au Moyen Age et a l' Epoque de la Renaissance* (Paris: Fermin-Didot, 1877).

[12] *Viaje de Ambrosio de Morales por orden del Rey Don Phelipe II a los Reynos de León y Galicia y Principado de Asturias, para reconocer las Reliquias de Santos*, ed. M. Florez, 1765.

[13] G. Vasari, *Commentari del Ghiberti*, quoted by J. Burckhardt, "Die Sammler," *Beiträge zur Kunstgeschichte*, Collected Works (Berlin-Stuttgart: Deutsche Verlagsanstalt, 1930), vol. 12, p. 327.

J. Schlosser, *Die Kunst-und Wunderkammern der Spätrenaissance (Leipzig:* Klinckhardt & Biermann, 1908).

Collections as Expressions of Group Loyalty (pp. 22–39)

[1] ". . . da ganz Griechenland von Sagen und Liedern und heiligen Plätzen voll war. Alles hing an der kühnen Idee, dass Götter mit ihnen verwandte höhere Menschen, und Helden niedere Götter sei'n." Johann Gottfried Herder, *Ideen zur Philosophie der Geschichte der Menschheit*, ed. Gerhart Schmid (Darmstadt: Melzer, 1966), p. 340.

[2] Pausanias's *Description of Greece*, ed. J. G. Frazer (London: Macmillan, 1898), Book I, XXXV, 5–8; Book IX, XL, 11 ff.

J. Schlosser, *Die Kunst- und Wunderhammern der Spätrenaissance* (Leipzig: Klinckhardt & Biermann, 1908).

[3] The Elder Pliny's *Chapters on the History of Art*, trans. K. Jex Blake (London-New York: Macmillan, 1896), Book VII, 16.

[4] Tranquillus C. Suetonius, "The Deified Augustus," *Lives of the Caesars*, ed. J. C. Rolfe (London; Heinemann; New York: Putnam, 1928), Book II, 72, 3.

M. Solomon Reinach, "Le Musée de l'Empereur Auguste," *Revue de l'Anthropologie*, Series 3, *4* (1889).

[5] Quoted by David Murray, *Museums, Their History and Their Use* (Glasgow: Macl ehose, 1904), p. 3.

[6] Collin de Plancy, *Abregé de l' Inventaire du Trésor de St. Denis* (Paris, 1668).

[7] Compare E. Bonnaffé, *Les Collectionneurs de l'ancienne Rome* (Paris: Aubry, 1867).

[8] Pausanias's *Description of Greece*, ed. J. G. Frazer, (London: Macmillan, 1898). Introduction, p. XXXIX; Book 1, 1–3.

[9] Ibid., p. XXXVIII.

"Imagine yourselves at the Painted Colonnade; for the monuments of all your glories are in the market-place." Aeschines, quoted in Pausanias's *Description*, Book I, XV, 1. (Frazer's Commentary on Book I, p. 132).

[10] E. Tormo y Monzo, *Las Serias Iconicas de los Reyes de España* (Madrid: Junta de Iconografia Nacional, 1916).

Comparing the veneration of heirlooms in a primitive South Sea community and in Europe, B. Malinowski wrote in *Argonauts of the Western Pacific* (London: Routledge; New York: Dutton, 1932), pp. 88,89.

"When, after six years' absence in the South Seas and Australia, I returned to Europe and did my first bit of sight-seeing at Edinburgh Castle, I was shown the Crown Jewels. The keeper told many stories of how they were worn by this and that king or queen on such and such occasion. . . . I had the feeling that something similar has been told to me. . . . And then arose before me the vision of a native village on coral soil . . . and naked men, and one of them showing me thin red strings, and big, worn-out objects, clumsy to sight and greasy to touch. With reverence he also would name them, and tell their story. . . . Both heirlooms and *vaygu'a* are cherished because of the historical sentiment which surrounds them. However ugly, useless, and — according to current standards — valueless an object may be, if it has figured in historical scenes and passed through the hands of historic persons, and is therefore an unfailing vehicle of important sentimental associations, it cannot but be precious to us."

[11]U. Aldrovandi, *Le Statue antiche que per tutta Roma . . . se veggono* (Venetia: Giordano Ziletti, 1558).

    J. Burckhardt, *The Civilization of the Renaissance in Italy*, tr. S. G. C. Middlemore (Vienna: Phaidon Press; New York: Oxford University Press, 1950), pp. 75–79 89–145 ("The Revival of Antiquity").

    E. Müntz, *Les Arts à la Cour des Papes* (Paris: Aubry, 1898).

    A. Michaelis, "Geschichte des Statuenhofes im Vatikanischen Belvedere," *Jahrbuch des Deutschen Archaeologischen Institutes*, vol. V (1890).

    C. Hülsen, "Römische Antikengärten des XVI Jahrhunderts," *Abhandlungen der Heidelberger Akademie der Wissenschaften* (Heidelberg, 1917).

[12]". . . marmoreas (statuas) quinque tantum, quatuor in Constantini Thermis; duas stantes pone equos, Phidiae et Praxitelis opus; duas recumbantes; quintam in foro Martis; . . . atque unam solam aeneam equestrem deauratam." Poggio Bracciolini, *Historiae De Varietate Fortunae*, accomplished about 1450 (Lutetiae Parisiorum, 1723), pp. 20–21.

    F. Blondo, *De Roma Instaurata* (Venetiis, 1510), pp. 1, 33, 34.

[13]"Quando era a tavola, mangiava in vasi antichi bellisimi . . . A vederlo in tavola, cosi' anticho come era, era una gentilezza." V. Bisticci (Fiorentino), *Vite di Uomini illustri del secolo XV* (Milan: Hoepli, 1951), pp. 442–443.

[14]"Ed egli (Donatello) fu potissima cagione, che a Cosimo de Medici si destasse la volontà dello introdurre a Fiorenza le antichità que sono & erano in casa Medici." G. Vasari, *Le Vite de piu Eccellenti Architetti, Pittori, et Scultori Italiani* (Firenze: Lorenzo Torrentino, 1550), II Part, p. 347.

    Among the Renaissance artists who with great devotion studied the artistic remains of ancient Italy was Benvenuto Cellini, who wrote in his *Autobiography*: "While I stayed at Pisa, I went to see the Campo Santo and there I found many beautiful fragments of Antiquity, that is to say, mainly sarcophagi. In other parts of Pisa also I saw many antique objects, which I diligently studied." Referring to a silver box modeled upon an ancient sarcophagus, which he made for a cardinal, he wrote: "This was the first earning that I touched at Rome and part of it I sent to assist my good father; the rest I kept for my own use, living upon it while I went about studying the antiquities of Rome." *The Autobiography of Benvenuto Cellini*, tr. J. A. Symonds, The Classics (New York: Collier and Son, 1910), pp. 22, 28 Harvard, 38–39.

[15]Laocoön is a figure of Greek mythology and was considered to have been a Trojan priest of Apollo. He threw a spear into the side of a huge wooden horse filled with Greek soldiers, when the Trojans, against his advice, took the horse into their town and were defeated. The sculpture shows Laocoön and his two sons struggling with huge serpents which attacked them on the order of Athena, to whom the wooden horse had been dedicated. It was among the works of art which in antiquity adorned the Baths of Titus. In the course of the centuries the site became a vineyard and the sculpture lay buried. The memory of Laocoön, however, was kept alive by its description by Pliny the Elder, and humanists had knowledge of it before it was dug up.

[16]". . . quod multo damnabilius est etiam statuas, signa, tabulas marmoreas, atque aeneas, porphyreticos, et numidicos, aliorumque generum lapides extra Urbem in alienas Terras ac Civitates asportari." G. Marini, *Degli Archiatri Pontifici*, Appendice de' Documenti, No. xcvi (Rome, 1783), pp. 280–284.

[17]C. A. Boettiger, *Über Museen und Antiken Sammlungen* (Leipzig, 1808), pp. 6–7.

    W. Fränckel, "Gemälde-Sammlungen und Gemälde-Forschung in Pergamon," *Jahrbuch des kaiserlichen deutschen archaeologischen Institutes. VI (1891)*.

[18]Jocelyn M. C. Toynbee, "An Imperial Institute of Archaeology as revealed by Roman Medallions," *The Archaeological Journal*, vol. XCIX (London, 1942), pp. 33–47.

[19]J. Burckhardt, *Griechische Kulturgeschichte*, tr. F. Stähelin, Collected Works, vol. 8 (Stuttgart: Deutsche Verlagsanstalt 1930).

    L. Friedländer, "Touring under the Empire: Greece," *Roman Life and Manners under the Early Empire*, trans. L. A. Magnus (London: Routledge; New York: Dutton, n. d.), pp. 340 ff.

[20]Polemon Periegeta, *Fragmenta, collegit, digessit, notis auxit.* L. Preller (Lipsiae, 1838).

    Caput III, "De Historia atque arte Periegetarum," pp. 155 ff.; p. 156: "Pausanias et qui sunt eius similes, Polemo, Diodorus, Heliodorus, toti sunt in monimentis locorum describendis, signis, tabulis, delubris, inscriptionibus: haec antiquaria doctrina enarrantur, a causis historicis mythicisve repetuntur, ad memoriam et mores priorum temporum illustrandos revocantur. Nihil ultra curant, nihil omnem terrae naturam et figuram, nihil oppidorum situs . . . littorum flexus . . ."

    p. 157: "Periegetae autem nomen peculiariter pertinet ad eos, qui peregrinantibus ea,

quae per singula oppida spectaculo erant, praeibant atque interpretabantur."
  p. 164: "Erat igitur haec prima et praecipua artis periegeticae pars, fabulas . . . in promtu habere."
  p. 162: "Quamquam crediderim in insignioribus tantum urbibus, quae abundarent templis, donariis, ornamentis, periegetas proprio loco constitutos fuisse, in minoribus sacerdotes."
[21]Cicero, *The Verrine Orations*, trans. L. H. G. Greenwood, Loeb Classical Library (Cambridge: Harvard University Press; London: Heinemann, 1956), Book IV, 58.
[22]Friedländer, *Roman Life. . .*, p. 380.
[23]Changes in technology facilitated transportation and trade. If compared with later technological development, medieval changes were very slow, but they were nevertheless incisive: sailing vessels were superior to galleys depending on human muscle; the use of the horse for land-drawn vehicles became important with the introduction of a new harness which fitted the animal's chest and shoulders instead of his throat, and did not affect the windpipe.
  An entirely different aspect of technology affected the human mind. The grinding of lenses for eyeglasses added years of reading, even though only a minority of people could read.
  Compare Lynn White, "Technology and Invention in the Middle Ages," *Speculum*, XV (1940), pp. 141–159.
[24]"ecce . . . Caesar, quibus successisti, ecce quos imitari studeas et mirari; ad quorum formam atque imaginem te componas, quos, praeter te unum, nulli hominum daturus eram." Francesco Petrarca, *Le Familiari*, ed. Vittorio Rossi (Florence: Sansoni, 1933–1937), Lib. XIX, op. 3.
[25]According to D. Murray, *Museums, their History and their Use* (Glasgow: MacLehose, 1904), pp. 14, 15, there were 200 collections of coins in the Low Countries, 175 in Germany and more than 380 in Italy.
  Books were published featuring Roman emperors. In 1563 there appeared in the Netherlands Hubert Goltz's *Gaius Julius Caesar sive Historiae Imperatorum ex antiquis numismatibus restitutae.*
[26]A. Palomino de Castro y Velasco, "Museo Pictorico" (1715), in *Fuentes Literarias para la Historia del Arte Español*, ed. F. J. Sanchez Canton (Madrid: Centro de Estudios Historicos, 1934), vol. III, pp. 163 ff.
[27]J. Spon, *Recherches des Antiquités et Curiosités de la ville de Lyon, ancienne colonie des Romains et Capitale de la Gaule Celtique. Avec un mémoire des principaux antiquaires et curieux de l'Europe* (Lyon, 1675).
[28]"To whose liberall charges and magnificence, this angle of the world oweth the first sight of Greeke and Romane Statues, with whose admired presence he began to honour the Gardens and Galleries of Arundel House about twentie yeeres agoe and hath ever since continued to transplant old Greece into England." H. Peacham, *The Compleat Gentleman* (London: The Clarendon Press, 1906), p. 107.
  Mary F. S. Hervey, *The Life, Correspondence and Collections of Thomas Howard, Earl of Arundel* (Cambridge: Cambridge University Press, 1921).
  Lionel Cust, "Notes on the Collections Formed by Thomas Howard, Earl of Arundel and Surrey, *The Burlington Magazine*, XIX (1911), pp. 278–286; XX (1911), pp. 97–100; XX (1912), pp. 233–236 and 341–343.
[29]J. Sandrart, *Teutsche Academie der Edlen Bau-Bild-und Mahlerei-Kuenste ('L'Academia Tedesca, etc.)* (Nuremberg, 1679). The Appendix to Part II contains a biography of Sandrart, as told by himself to some of his pupils and published under the heading "Lebenslauf und Kunstwerke des wol Edlen und Gestrengen Herrn Joachim von Sandart . . . von desselben Dienstergebenen Vettern und Discipeln." A modern edition, by A. R. Pelzer, was published in 1925 by Hirth, Munich. The English translation of the quotation on p. 57 is from M. S. F. Hervey's book on the Earl of Arundel.
[30]*The Diary of Ralph Thoresby* (1677–1724), ed. Joseph Hunter (London: Colburn and Bentley, 1830), vol. II, pp. 31, 32.
[31]Adolf T. F. Michaelis, *Ancient Marbles in Great Britain*, tr. C. A. M. Fennell (Cambridge: Cambridge University Press, 1882).
  Lionel Cust, *The History of the Society of Dilettanti* (London: Macmillan, 1890).
  R. Cowdry, *A description of the Pictures, Statues, Busts, Basso Relievos and other Curiosities at the Earl of Pembroke's House at Wilton* (London, 1751). (Considerable portions of the collections of the Cardinals Mazarin and Richelieu as well as of that of the Earl of Arundel were at Wilton House.)
  H. Walpole, *Aedes Walpolianae*, or a Description of the Collection of Pictures at Hough-

ton Hall in Norfolk, the Seat of the Rt. Hon. Sir Robert Walpole, Earl of Oxford (London, 1752), contains interesting information as to the former owners of famous objects and to the import of works of art from Italy to England.

[32]Venetian merchants who shipped Crusaders to the Levant were instrumental in bringing Greek marbles to Western Europe. Ballast was needed to be added to the light cargo of silk and spices imported from the East, and the profit-conscious Venetians were not slow in recognizing the coming demand for marbles.

[33]A. H. Smith, "Lord Elgin and his Collection," *Journal of Hellenic Studies*, vol. XXVI, 2nd part (1916), pp. 163–372.

[34]J. T. Smith, *Nollekens and his Times*, ed. Wilfred Whitten (London: Lane, 1920), vol. I, pp. 213 ff.

"Museums and the Eighteenth Century," A Symposium held by the (British) South Midlands Federation of Museums at the Science Museum, London, October 1958. *Museums Journal*, 59 (1959).

[35]Hanns Flörke, *Studien zur Niederlaendischen Kunst und Kulturgeschichte* (Leipzig, 1908), p. 203.

[36]S. Pighius, *Hercules Prodighius*, seu Principis Juventutis Vita et Peregrinatio (Antwerpiae, 1587), pp. 235, 236–239. The account of the Ambras collection is part of a travel book which Pighius, a Dutch archaeologist, wrote for the enlightenment of his former pupil Prince Johann Wilhelm of Cleve.

The author of another sixteenth-century account of Ambras was Hainhofer, a cabinet-maker who supplied the archduke and other contemporary collectors with fine cases for their specimens, and who for the benefit of his own children at home wrote notes about things which impressed him during his travels. P. Hainhofer, "Reisen nach Innsbruck und Dresden," *Eitelberger's Quellenschriften für Kunstgeschichte"* (Vienna, 1901).

Compare in the Appendix, p. 245, a passage from the Frenchman Misson's seventeenth-century account of the collection of Castle Ambras.

See also A. Primisser, *Die Kaiser-Königliche Ambraser Sammlung* (Vienna:Vallishauser, 1827).

[37]Vincencio Carducho, "Dialogos . . . de la Pintura," *Fuentes Literarias para la Historia del Arte Español*, ed. F. J. Sanchez Canton (Madrid: Centro de Estudios Historicos, 1933), vol. II, pp. 63–115.

A. Palomino de Castro y Velasco, "El Museo Pictorico," *Fuentes Literarias . . . ,* ed. F. J. Sanchez Canton, vol. III, pp. 163 ff.

[38]A fifteenth-century collection of a townsman, a certain Jacques Duchie, of Paris, is contained in a *Description of Paris* by his contemporary Guilebert de Metz, which was published in 1855. Ed. Le Roux de Lincy, *Description de la ville de Paris au XV siecle*, pp. 67,68.

In the seventeenth century numerous collections could be found among members of the middle class. In a single page of his description of collections visited in Italy, the English traveler John Ray twice referred to apothecaries as collectors — see Appendix, pp. 247, 248. In his *Diary*, Evelyn referred to collections he had visited in France, which belonged to both titled persons and commoners. On February 27 and March 1, he wrote: "We returned to Paris. . . . I went to see the Count de Liancourt's Palace in the Rue de la Seine . . . (follows a detailed account of viewed paintings). The Count was so exceeding civil, that he would needs make his lady go out of her dressing-room, that he might show us the curiosities and pictures in it.

"We went thence to visit one Monsier Perishot, one of the greatest virtuosos in France, for his collection of pictures, agates, medals, and flowers, especially tulips and anemones. The chiefest of his paintings was a Sebastian, of Titian.

"From him we went to Monsier Frene's . . ." J. Evelyn, *Diary and Correspondence*, ed. Ernest Rhys, Everyman's Library (London: Dent; New York: Dutton, 1930).

Further information about French collectors in the seventeenth and eighteenth centuries, among the higher classes of society mainly, may be gathered from the *Memoires* of Michel de Marolles, Abbe de Villeloin, of 1657, later published in Amsterdam in 1755, vol. III, pp. 266 ff. Another important source with regard to collectors in Paris toward the end of the seventeenth century is Abraham de Pradel (alias Nicolas de Blegny), *Le Livre Commode* or *Trésor des Almanachs*, ed. E. Fournier (Paris: Daffis, 1878).

[39]Henry Steele Commager, *Search of a Usable Past* (New York: Knopf, 1967).

[40]Walter Muir Whitehill, *Independent Historical Societies: An enquiry into their research and public functions, and their financial future* (Boston: The Boston Athenaeum, distributed by the Harvard University Press, 1962).

[41]Douglas and Elizabeth Rigby, *Lock, Stock and Barrel* (Philadelphia: Lippincott, 1944), p. 270.

Collections as Means of Stimulating Curiosity and Inquiry (pp. 39 – 53)

[1]Ludwig Friedländer, *Roman Life and Manners Under the Early Empire*, trans. L. A. Magnus (London: Routledge; New York: Dutton), pp. 328, 368, 369.

J. Burckhardt, *Antike Kunst*, eds. Felix Stähelin and Heinrich Wölfflin, *Collected Works*, vol. 13 (Stuttgart: Deutsche Verlagsanstalt, 1934), "Die Anatheme, pp. 89 – 103.

Lucius Ampelius, *Liber Memorialis* (a cosmography assumedly written in the third or fourth century), ed. L. Annaeus Cl. Salmasius (Lugd. Bat.: Elzevirios, 1638). Ampelius wrote about the variety of objects, including works of art, which aroused the interest of people in ancient times. Under the heading "Miracula Mundi" (pp. 309 – 311), he listed the following sights:

"Amraciae in Epiro in pariete sunt picti Castor & Pollux & Helena, manu Autocthonis . . ."

"Sicyone in Achaia, in foro aedis Appolinis est. In ea sunt posita Agamemnonis clipeus & machaera, Ulyssis Chlamys & Thoracium . . . & arcus Adrasti . . .

"Ilio lapis quadrâtus, ubi Cassandra fuit alligata, quem si ante . . . fricueris, lac demittit, ex altera autem parte similiter si frices, ac si sanguinem demittit."

"Pergamo ara marmorea magna, alta pedes XL, cum maximis sculpturis."

[2]J. Schlosser, *Die Kunst- und Wunderkammern der Spätrenaissance* (Leipzig: Klinckhardt & Biermann, 1908).

[3]Pausanias's *Description of Greece*, ed. J. G. Frazer (London: Macmillan, 1898), Book IX, 21.

[4]Compare Condorcet's *Progrès de l'ésprit humain* (Paris, 1796). Condorcet and d'Alembert, forerunners of the sociologist Comte, distinguished between three consecutive phases in the development of the human mind, which they called "theological," "metaphysical," and "positive."

[5]C. R. Weld, *A History of the Royal Society* (London: J. W. Parker, 1848), vol. I, p. 2.

Henry Lyons, "The Royal Society of London," *Endeavour*, vol. II (1943), pp. 12 – 16; 52 – 55.

[6]F. L. Nussbaum, *A History of the Economic Institutions of Modern Europe* (New York: Crofts, 1933), p. 82. The same author wrote of the eight things "after which the learned and curious strive" – the stone of the philosopher, the liquor Alcobets, flexible glass, a perpetual light, the hyperbola in mirrors, the length of the degree, the squaring of the circle, and the perpetual motor.

[7]J. F. Denis, *Le Monde Enchanté; cosmographie et histoire naturelle du moyen âge* (Paris: Fournier, 1843).

P. Lacroix, *Sciences et Lettres au Moyen Age et à l Epoque de la Renaissance* (Paris: Fermin – Didot, 1877).

J. Schlosser, *Die Kunst- und Wunderkammern*.

Compare Appendix, p. 242, extract from a seventeenth-century account of the imperial collection in Vienna.

[8]Gerhard Händler, *Fürstliche Mäzene und Sammler in Deutschland*. Studien zur Deutschen Kunstgeschichte (Strassburg: Heitz, 1933).

A. Venturi, "Zur Geschichte der Kunstsammlungen Kaiser Rudolph II," *Repertorium für Kunstgeschichte*, VIII (1885), pp. 1 – 23.

In the eighteenth century, if not before, interest in "natural and artificial curiosities" extended beyond the sphere of scholars into the class of middle-class merchants. The following contemporary poem on the cabinet of a Frankfort citizen runs as follows:
"Das Wunderzeughaus voller Spur der unerschoepflichen Natur
Wo man ihr tiefverborgenes Wesen entdeckt und entziffert sieht
Hier sprach ich, kann man unbemüht, des grauen Alters Zustand lesen."
J. F. Uffenbach, *Gesammelte Nebenarbeit* (1733), p. 209.

Compare v. N. Holst, "Frankfurter Kunst und Wunderkammern des 18ten Jahrhunderts, ihre Eigenart und Bestände," *Repertorium für Kunstwissenschaft*, vol. 52 (1931), pp. 34 – 58.

There were others who castigated the collectors whose curiosity never seemed satiated. Jean de La Bruyère wrote in *The Characters: or The Manners of the Present Age*, translated by several hands (London, 1700), chap. "Of the Fashion," p. 29
"Curiosity is not an inclination to what is good or beautiful, but to what is rare and

singular; for these things which another can't match. 'Tis not an affection for those things which are best, but for those which are most sought after, and most in the fashion. 'Tis not an amusement, but a passion (often so violent) that it yields to Love and Ambition only in the meanness of its object."

In later years and in this country Nathaniel Hawthorne made fun of "A Virtuoso Collection," first published in *The Boston Miscellany of Literature and Fashion* and later in *Mosses From the Old Manse.*

[9]G. Agricola, *De Re Metallica*, English translation from the first Latin edition, of 1556, by H. C. Hoover (London, *The Mining Magazine*, 1912).

[10]J. Bronowski, *The Common Sense of Science* (Melbourne-London-Toronto: Heinemann, 1951), p. 55.

[11]Weld, *A History of the Royal Society* (London: Parker, 1948), vol. I, pp. 10 ff.

Nicolaus Pevsner, *Academies of Art* (Cambridge: Cambridge University Press; New York: Macmillan, 1940).

Comenius in England, translated from contemporary documents and edited by R. F. Young (Oxford: Oxford University Press, 1932).

[11]C. G. A. Harnack, *Geschichte der Kgl. Preussischen Akademie der Wissenschaften* (Berlin, 1910), vol. I, p. 5. "The Universities of Europe were born at the high tide of the Middle Age, and their institutions corresponded to the medieval view of transmitting the body of knowledge in fixed terms. The European Academies are an expression of the new spirit which was henceforth to obtain its power in the domain of life and thought." (English translation from Young, *Comenius*, pp. 2, 3.

The Platonic Academy at Florence, founded in 1470, was devoted to literary interest. Later, natural science received greater attention. The Societas Secretorum Naturae in Naples was founded in 1560, the Royal Society in London in 1660, and the Academie des Sciences in Paris in 1666.

[12]*Archaeologia* (London, 1770), vol. I.

[13]L. L. Cremonese, *Museo Cospiano annesso a quello del famoso Aldrovandi* (Bologna, 1677).

[14]*Museum Calceolarium* (Verona, 1622).

L. Moscardi, *Note overo Memorie del Museo* (Moscardi) (Verona, 1677).

Compare Appendix, pp. 247 – 248, a seventeenth-century account of contemporary Italian collections.

[15]P. Bonani, *Museum Kircherianum* (Rome, 1709).

G. Sepibus, *Romani Colegii Societatis Jesu Musaeum Celeberrimum* (Rome, 1678).

[16]*Museum Wormianum, seu Historia Rerum Rarorum* (Batavia, 1655).

[17]A. Olearius, *Gottorfsche Kunstkammer (Gottorf, 1674).*

[18]The *Catalogue of the Musaeum Tradescantianum* or *A Collection of Rarities preserved at South-Lambeth neer London,* by J. Tradescant, published in London in 1656, contained the following address to the prospective readers: "To the ingenious Reader: . . . That the enumeration of these Rarities (being more for variety than any one place known in Europe could afford) would be an honour to our Nation, and a benefit to such ingenious persons as would become further enquirers into the various modes of Natures admirable work and the curious Imitators thereof."

[19]Symposium "Museums and the Eighteenth Century," *Museums Journal,* 59 (1959), pp. 46, 47.

[20]"El intento de esta Academia es hacer una confección . . . de diversas profesiones . . . Peste es la ociosidad, y más rigurosa peste es la ignorancia . . . En estas juntas . . . todos somos maestros y discipulos." Rafal A. P. M. de Villena, *Un Mecenas del siglo XVII, el conde de Lomos* (Madrid: J. Rates Martin, 1911), p. 162.

Bronowski, *The Common Sense of Science,* pp. 46, 47, stresses the importance of empirical amateur workers for the progress of science in the seventeenth century.

[21]N. F. Levinson-Lessing, and the staff of the Hermitage, *The Hermitage Museum* (London: Hamlyn; Prague: Artia, 1964).

Ivan P. Trufanoff, "The Peter the Great Museum of Anthropology and Ethnology, Leningrad, USSR Academy of Sciences," *Museum, XX,* 2 (Paris, 1967).

Conspectus Aedium Imperialis Academiae Petropolitanae . . . bibliothecae et technophylacii . . . Petropoli (1744). (Description of the incorporation of Peter the Great's collections in the newly opened Academy of Science, with a few sketches giving an idea of the contents of the collections). (J. Bacmeister, *Essai sur la Bibliothèque et le Cabinet de Curiositées d'Histoire Naturelle de L'Académie de Sciences de St. Petersburg,* Petersburg (1776).

With regard to Czar Peter's visit in Dr. Ruysch's Cabinet compare A. Chalmers, *General Biographical Dictionary* (London, 1876), XXVI, p. 505.

22C. F. Neickelius, *Museographia*, ed. D. J. Tanold (Leipzig, 1727).

23"The Lucubrations of Isaac Bickenstaff, Esq.," *The Tatler*, No. 34, Tuesday, June 28, 1709.

"Being of a very spare and hective Constitution, I am forc'd to make frequent Journies of a Mile or two for fresh Air; and indeed by this last, which was no farther than the village of *Chelsea*, I am farther convinc'd of the Necessity of travelling to know the World. . . . I fancied I could give you an immediate Description of this Village, from the Five Fields . . . to the Coffee-House where the *Literati* sit in Council. . . . When I came into the Coffee-House, I had not Time to salute the Company, before my Eye was diverted by ten thousand Gimcracks round the Room, and on the Sieling. When my first Astonishment was over, comes to me a Sage of a thin and meagre Countenance . . . My love of Mankind made me benevolent to Mr. *Salter*, for such is the name of the eminent Barber and Antiquary . . . this personage would make a great figure in that Class of Men which I distinguish under the Title of *Odd Fellows*. . . . For he is descended not from John Tradescan, as he himself asserts, but from that memorable Companion of the Knight of *Mancha*. And I hereby certify all the worthy Citizens who travel to see his Rarities, that his double-barrell'd Pistols, Targets, Coats of Mail, his Sclopeta and Sword of *Toledo*, were left to his Ancestor by the said Don *Quixot* . . . down to Don Saltero. Tho I go this far in favour of Don *Saltero's* great Merit, I cannot allow a Liberty he takes of imposing several Names (without my License) on the Collections he has made, to the Abuse of the good People of *England* . . . one of which . . . may introduce Heterodox Opinions. He shows you a Straw-Hat, which I know to be made . . . three miles of Bedford; and tells you *it is* Pontius Pilate's *Wife's Chambermaid's Sister's Hat* . . . Therefore this is really nothing, but under the specious pretence of Learning and Antiquity, to impose upon the world."

Douglas and Elizabeth Rigby, *Lock, Stock and Barrel*, offer detailed quotations concerning exhibits in an American barbershop and in a whaling inn. These were taken from James Russell's description of a barbershop and from E. V. Mitchell's account of a whaling inn.

Survey of London, gen. ed. F. H. W. Sheppard (London: The Athlone Press for the University of London, 1963), vol. XXIX, pp. 266–270, concerning Bullock's Museum; vol. XXXI; p. 62, concerning various collections in eighteenth-century London.

24G. Brown Goode, "The Origin of the National Scientific and Educational Institutions of the United States," Memorial Volume to George Brown Goode, *Annual Report of the U.S. National Museum, ending June 1897*, Part II, pp. 263–354. The following quotation from a Memorandum by Adams, was taken from Dr. Goode's volume, pp. 268–269:

"In travelling from Boston to Philadelphia, in 1774, 5, 6, and 7, I had several times amused myself at Norwalk, in Connecticut, with the very curious collection of birds and insects of American production made by Mr. Arnold; a collection which he afterwards sold to Governor Tryon, who sold it to Sir Ashton Lever, in whose apartments in London I afterwards viewed it again. This collection was so singular a thing that it made a deep impression upon me, and I could not but consider it a reproach to my country, that so little was known, even to herself, of her natural history.

When I was in Europe, in the years 1778 and 1779, in the commission to the King of France, with Dr. Franklin and Mr. Arthur Lee, I had opportunities to see the King's collection and many others, which increased my wishes that nature might be examined and studied in my own country, as it was in others."

25Charles Coleman Sellers, *Charles Willson Peale* (Philadelphia: The American Philosophical Society, 1947), 2 vols.

Richard P. Ellis, "The Founding, History, and Significance of Peale's Museum in Philadelphia, 1785–1841," *Curator*, IX, 3 (1967), pp. 235–266.

26Thomas Jefferson, "A Memoir on the Discovery of Certain Bones of a Quadruped of the Clawed Kind, in the Western Part of Virginia," *American Philosophical Transactions*, IV (March 10, 1797), p. 246.

27F. V. Luther, "Jefferson as Naturalist," *The Magazine of American History*, vol. 13 (1885), pp. 379–390. Luther's paper contains Jefferson's letter to Mr. Innes, which was quoted in this chapter, p. 521.

28The Australian psychologist Paul R. Wilson recently published an account of an experiment he conducted with his students with regard to human judgment of the physical size of persons of differing status. When the students were asked to estimate the height of visitors, those introduced as professors were considered to be taller than lecturers;

people without any academic rank appeared to be shorter than the others. "Perceptual distortion of height as a function of ascribed academic status," *Journal of Social Psychology* (1968), part I, pp. 97 – 102.

Samuel L. Mitchell, *Discourse on Thomas Jefferson — More Especially as a Promoter of Natural and Physical Science* (New York: Cartill, 1826), p. 30. About the arrival of fossil bones in 1808, Mitchell wrote: "a consignment which arrived in the Potomac early in 1808 . . . was charged with expenses for transportation, etc. to the amount of three hundred dollars. The collection was probably the most extensive that was ever seen together in one display. As they lay on the floor of one of the great saloons in the President's house, the present narrator surveyed them in company with the owner."

Collections as Means of Emotional Experience (pp. 54 – 60)

[1]Herodas, *The Mimes*, ed. A. D. Knox after an earlier edition by Walter Headlam (Cambridge: Cambridge University Press, 1966), Mime IV, pp. 169 and 171.

[2]Compare J. E. Harrison, *Ancient Art and Ritual* (London: Home University Library of Modern Knowledge, 1914).

J. Murphy, *Lamps of Anthropology* (Manchester: University of Manchester Press, 1943).

[3]Pausanias's *Description of Greece*, ed. J. G. Frazer (London: Macmillan, 1898), Book V, xxiv, 9.

Ernst Curtius, *Olympia* (Berlin: Asher, 1890 – 1897).

[4]Pliny, *Natural History*, trans. E. Rackham, Book XXXV, xxxvi. 68 (Cambridge: Harvard University Press; London: Heinemann, 1952).

[5]Geoffrey Scott, *The Architecture of Humanism*, a study in the history of taste (London: Constable, 1924), p. 60.

[6]Susanne K. Langer, *Mind: an Essay on Human Feeling* (Baltimore: Johns Hopkins, 1967).

[7]Francisco Holanda, "Dialogos de la Pintura (1548), *Fuentes Literarias para la Historia del Arte Español*, ed. F. J. Sanchez Canton (Madrid: Centro de Estudios Historicos, 1923), vol. I.

[8]Crowe and Cavalcaselle, *Titian: his Life and Times* (London: Murray, 1877).

"Unveröffentlichte Beiträge zur Geschichte der Kunstbestrebungen Karl V und Philip II," *Jahrbuch der kunsthistorischen Sammlungen in Wien*, New Series (1933).

Karl Justi, "Philip II als Kunstfreund," *Zeitschrift für Bildende Kunst*, XVI (1881), pp. 305 – 312; 342 – 355.

[9]G. Gaye, *Carteggio inedito d'Artisti dei secoli* XIV, XV, XVI (Florence: Molini, 1839 – 1840), vol. II, p. 179.

[10]Morelli *(The Anonimo), Notes on works of art in Italy made by an anonymous writer in the sixteenth century*, trans. P. Mussi and ed. G. C. Williamson (London: Bell, 1903).

J. J. Volkmann, *Historisch-kritische Nachrichten von Italien* (Leipzig: Fritsch, 1777).

[11]". . . de que sirven las historias de las guerras de . . . hechas in pinturas y tapizerias, sino . . . para . . . que viendolas se animen . . . otros a ganar nombre y nobleza por caminos derechos, y no por . . . infames?," G. G. de los Rios, *Noticia General para la Estimacion des las Artes* (1600) Obras Completas (Madrid: La Lectura, 1916 – 1925).

[12]J. Burckhardt, "Die Sammler," *Beiträge zur Kunstgeschichte von Italien*, Collected Works, vol. 12, ed. Heinrich Wölfflin (Stuttgart: Deutsche Verlags Anstalt, 1930) pp. 293 – 496.

[13]J. Martinez, "Discursons practicables del nobilissimo arte de la Pintura," *Fuentes Literarias para la Historia del Arte Español*, ed. F. J. Sanchez Canton (Madrid: Centro de Estudios Historicos, 1934), vol III.

[14]"Il faut quitter tout cela!" Il s'arrêtait à chaque pas, car il était fort faible, et se tenait tantôt d'un côté, tantôt de l'autre; et jetant les yeux sur l'objet qui lui frappait la vue, il disait du profond du coeur: "Il faut quitter tout cela!," et se tournant, il ajoutait, "et encore cela! Que j'ai eu de peine à acquérir ces choses! Puis-je les abandonner sans regret? Je ne les verrai plus ou je vais!" Quoted by Francis Henry Taylor, *The Taste of Angels* (Boston: Little, Brown and Co; An Atlantic Monthly Press Book, 1948), p. 335. Compare:

H. E. P. L. Aumale, duc d'Orleans, *Inventaire de tous les meubles du Cardinal Mazarin* (1653).

Gabriel-Jules Cosnach, *Les Richesses du Palais Mazarin* (Paris: Renouard, 1885). Jean Vallery-Radot, "La Gallerie Mazarine et l'Exposition du Siècle de Louis XIV," *Gazette des Beaux-Arts*, Fifth Series, vol. XV (1927), pp. 129 – 147.

[15]Rose Kingsley and Camille Gronkowski, "The Dutuit Collection," *The Burlington Magazine*, vol. I (1903), pp. 381 – 386.

"The finest collectors look at their possessions with the feelings of an artist and relive, to some extent, the sensuous and imaginative experiences which lie behind each work," *Great Private Collections*, ed. Douglas Cooper (London: Weidenfeld & Nicholson, 1963), Kenneth Clark's Introduction, p. 13.

[16]*The Maryland Historical Magazine*, vol. 17, no. 4 (1922) and vol. 51, no. 1 (1956), quoted by Herbert and Marjorie Katz, *Museums, U.S.A.* (New York: Doubleday, 1965).

[17]Allan Nevins, *American Social History as recorded by British Travellers* (New York: Holt, 1931).

[18]Charles Francis Adams, *Familiar Letters of John Adams and His Wife Abigail, During the Revolution* (New York: Hurd and Houghton, 1876), p. 381.

The Presentation of Objects in Collections (pp. 60 – 74)

[1]L. P. Gachard, *Retraite et Mort de Charles-Quint au Monastère de Yuste. Lettres inédites d'après les originaux conservés dans les archives royales de Simancas* (Brussels: Commission Royale d'Histoire, 1854 – 1855).

[2]J. J. Volkmann, *Historisch-Kritische Nachrichten* (Leipzig, 1770) Vol. II., p. 435.

[3]Adolf Berger, "Inventar der Kunstsammlung des Erzherzogs Leopold Wilhelm von Österreich," *Jahrbuch der kunsthistorischen Sammlungen des allerhöchsten Kaiserhauses* (Vienna, 1883).

[4]Alma S. Wittlin, "Exhibits: Interpretive, Under-Interpretive, Misinterpretive," *Museums and Education*, ed. Eric Larrabee (Washington, D.C., Smithsonian Institution Press: 1968), pp. 97, 98. Being myself the author, I took the liberty of changing the tense.

[5]J. G. T. Grässe, *A Descriptive Catalogue of the Green Vaults* (Dresden, 1874). There was a Cabinet of Bronzes, a Cabinet of Ivories, a Silver-room, and so forth.

Compare Appendix, p. 243, a page from Browne's description of the imperial collection in Vienna.

[6]The table of contents of the *Catalogue of the Musaeum Kircherianum*, by Philippus Bonani, published in Rome in 1709, announced the following sequence: Idola et Instrumenta ad Sacrificia – Anathemata – Sepulchra – Fragmenta Eruditae Antiquitatis (stilli, anulli, sigillae . . . numisma . . .) Lapides, Fossilia, aliasque glebas – Apparatum'habet Rerum Peregrinarum (aves diversae . . . artefacta Turcarum, Persarum . . . Arma barbarorum . . . mumia) – Plantae Marinae, Animalia Marina . . . Terrestria – Instrumenta Mathematica – Tabulae pictae . . . Signa marmorea, Numismata . . . Animalia Testacea . . . etc.

[7]". . . due stanze . . . doue con triplicato ordine si retrouano, non poche statue . . . bassi relieui, e vasi . . . e buon numero di Medaglie antiche . . . e torsi 140 quadri grandi e piccioli di buone pitture," F. Scamozzi, *L'Idea della Architettura Universale* (Venetiis, 1615), vol. I, p. 305.

[8]Compare Appendix, p. 248, an account of the visit in 1748 of the Prince of Wales to the collection of Sir Hans Sloane. It is of interest to learn that in this great, if not greatest, collection of a scholar-connoisseur in England, which eventually became the nucleus of the British Museum, specimens were stored in cases and drawers and were put on show only when required for inspection and study; one set of objects was exhibited and then put away to make room for another.

[9]I. H. Hefner-Alteneck, *Entstehung, Zweck und Einrichtung des Bayerischen National-museums in München*, Bayerische Bibliothek *(Bamberg: Büchner, 1890), pp. 10, 11*.

[10]Carel Vosmaer, *Rembrandt Harmens Van Rijn, sa vie et ses oeuvres* (The Hague, 1877).

[11]Pausanias's *Description of Greece*, ed. J. G. Frazer (London: Macmillan, 1898), Book X, XXV.

[12]D. B. Major, quoted by G. F. Klemm, *Geschichte der Sammlungen für Wissenschaft und Kunst in Deutschland* (Zerbst: Kummer, 1837), p. 153.

S. Quichelberg, *Threatrum Sapientiae* (Paris, 1598).

[13]One such exhibition, at Bamberg in 1493, was described in a pamphlet entitled *Die Aufzuruffunge des hochwirdigen Heiligthums des Loeblichen Stifts zu Bamberg*. Another similar exhibition was performed in Wittenberg in 1509 and was announced in a pamphlet as *Die Zaigung des hochlobwürdigen Heiligtums der Stiftskirche zu Wittenberg*. The exhibition of treasures at San Marco in Venice was described by Francesco Sansovino, *Venetia, Città Nobilissima e Singolare* (Venetia, 1581).

[14]In his *Autobiography* Cellini referred to the musical performance in the Belvedere in which he played the "Soprano with his cornet." He wrote: "During eight days before the festival (The Ferragosto) we practised . . . then on the first of August we went to the *Belvedere*, and while Pope Clement was at table we played those carefully studied motets

so well that his Holiness protested he had never heard music more sweetly executed."
The Autobiography of Benvenuto Cellini, trans. J. A. Symonds, The Harvard Classics (New York: P. F. Collier and Son. 1910).

J. Burckhardt, "Die Sammler," *Beiträge zur Kunstgeschichte von Italien*, ed. Heinrich Wölfflin, *Collected Works*, vol. 12 (Stuttgart: Deutsche Verlags-Anstalt, 1930), pp. 476 – 477.

[15]C. Justi, *Miscellaneen aus Drei Jahrhunderten Spanischen Kunstlebens* (Berlin, Grote, 1908), vol. II, pp. 301 ff.

[16]Rafal A. P. M. de Villena, *Un Mecenas del siglo XVII, el conde de Lemos* (Madrid: J. Rates Martin, 1911), pp. 64 ff.

[17]Bibliothèque Nationale, Catalogue d' Exposition (Paris, 1927).

3. Early Collections and the Public (pp. 75 – 80)

[1]". . . there is preserved a speech of Agrippa, lofty in tone and worthy of the greatest citizens, on the question of making all pictures and statues national property, a procedure which would have been preferable to banishing them to country houses." Pliny, *Natural History*, Book XXXV, viii. 24-ix. Trans. E. Rackham (Cambridge: Harvard University Press; London: Heinemann, 1952).

[2]E. Bonnaffé, *Les Collectionneurs de l'Ancienne Rome* (Paris: Aubry, 1867).

A. Furtwängler, *Über Kunstsammlungen in alter und neuer Zeit*, paper presented to the Imperial Academy of Sciences (Berlin, 1899), p. 12.

[3]". . . perche grande è l'appetito nell' uomo di pascersi della vista di lavori prodotti da ingegni così nobili, così sublimi, dal Gran Duca è permesso a ministri, que anno cura di queste cose, che a chi vuol vederle siano cortesi; onde come altrui pare attentamente le consideri." M. F. Bocchi, *Le Bellezze della città di Firenze*, ed. M. G. Cinelli (Firenze, 1677), pp. 111 – 112.

[4]"His (Ruysch's) museum, indeed, both in the extent, variety and arrangement of its contents, became ultimately the most magnificent that any private individual ever accumulated, and was the resort of visitors of every description; generals, ambassadors, princes, and even kings, were happy in the opportunity of examining it." A. Chalmers, *General Biographical Dictionary* (London, 1876; revised edition), XXVI, p. 505.

Some of his distinguished visitors purchased entire Cabinets from the doctor who gained fame by his method of preserving specimens of natural history by injecting them with a chemical solution that remained his secret (Fig. 18). He hardly had sold one collection when he began to replace it.

[5]Quoted by S. Dillon Ripley in his article "A Cabinet of Curiosities," *Museum News, 40*, 3 (1961). Sir Ashton Lever's feudal manners persisted in a country which appeared to be advanced to the point of radicalism if compared with the traditional ways in other parts of Europe. Voltaire extolled the progressive social and political conditions in England in his *Letters concerning the English Nation*, published in 1734. The book caused an uproar, and the philosopher had to leave France for several years.

[6]"He (Torrigiano) was maintained in his youth by Lorenzo de Medici the elder, in the garden of that magnificent citizen on the piazza of S. Marco in Florence, full of ancient and modern sculptures, so that the loggia, the paths and all the rooms were adorned with good ancient figures of marble, with paintings and other masterpieces of the greatest artists of Italy and elsewhere. All those things . . . formed a school and academie for young painters and sculptors, and all others who studied design, especially young nobles." Georgio Vasari, *The Lives of Painters, Sculptors & Architects*, tr. A. B. Hinds. Everyman's Library (London: Dent; New York: Dutton, 1927), vol. II, p. 208.

[7]L. Cust, *The History of the Society of Dilettanti* (London: Macmillan, 1890).

[8]J. J. A. Ampère, *L'Histoire Romaine* . . . (Paris: Levy, 1862), vol. III, pp. 609 – 614.

L. Homo, "Les Musées de la Roma Impériale," *Gazette des Beaux-Arts*, Fifth Series, vol. XV (1919), pp. 21 – 46; 177 – 208.

[9]The opening of the Ashmolean Museum was described in the *Athenae Oxonienses*, vol. IV, p. 358, as follows: ". . . about 12 cart loads of rarities sent to Oxon by Mr. Ashmole . . . were first of all publicly viewed on the 21st day of May (1683) by the doctors and masters of the University."

F. Sherwood Taylor, "The Museum of the History of Science, Oxford," *Endeavor*, vol. I, 2 (1942), pp. 67 – 69.

[10]"The American Revolution was pitched on a moral plane. The patriots were concerned not only about mankind's good opinion, but, as Tom Paine felicitously phrased it, believed it to be in their power 'to make a world happy,'" Richard B. Morris, *The American Revolution Reconsidered* (New York: Harper & Row, 1967), Preface.

"Men . . . cherished faith in virtue and in the ultimate authority of justice and morality" during the period of American history which endeavored to transform natural law into constitutional law. Henry Steele Commager, *Search of a Usabie Past* (New York: Knopf, 1967), p. 34.

[11]One member expressed the hope that the museum of the association that began with a collection of minerals, would develop to an office filled with Nature's patents in which all may behold the wonders it had pleased the all-wise Creator to devise for the benefit and instruction of man. W. S. W. Ruschenberger, *A Notice of the Origin, Progress and Present Condition of the Academy of the Natural Sciences of Philadelphia* (Philadelphia, 1862).

[12]Luman Reed took great interest in contemporary American art and artists who received scant recognition at the time. Reed purchased their pictures, financed study trips to Europe, and commissioned paintings. At his request Asher B. Durand portrayed President Jackson.

[13]The other four scientific institutions being the American Academy in Boston, The American Philosophical Society, and the private Observatory of Ritterhouse. G. Brown Goode, "The Origin of the National Scientific and Educational Institutions of the United States," *Annual Report of the U.S. National Museum, ending June 30, 1897* (1901).

[14]For information about the museum of the Tammany Society and the men connected with it, consult the *New-York Historical Society Quarterly*, especially of April 1958 and of July 1959, with articles by R. M. and S. S. McClurg and by Loyd Haberly.

[15]Charles Coleman Sellers, *Charles Willson Peale* (Philadelphia: The American Philosophical Society, 1947), vol. II, p. 113.

4. Early Public Museums
Continental Europe (pp. 81 – 101)

[1]Christiane Aulanier, *Histoire du Palais et du Musée Louvre* (Paris: Editions des Musées Nationaux, 1947 – 1955).

A. Lemâitre, *Monument et Musée depuis leurs origines jusqu'a nos jours* (Paris: Societé française de numasmatique et d'archeologie, 1877).

P Dan, *Le Trésor des Merveilles de . . . Fontainebleau* (Paris: Cramoisy, 1642).

J. Evelyn, *Diary and Correspondence*, written 1641 to 1706 (London: Bell, 1857).

C. Saunier, *Les Conquêtes Artistiques de la Révolution et de l'Empire; reprises et abandons des alliés en 1815 et leurs conséquences sur les musées d'Europe* (Paris: Laurens, 1902). Compare an extract from Saunier in the Appendix, p. 249.

M. E. Müntz, "Les Annexions de collections d'art ou de Bibliotheques. Leur Rôle Dans les Relations Internationales, principalement pendant la Révolution Française" *Revue de l'Histoire Diplomatique*, vol. VIII(1894), pp. 481 – 497; vol. IX (1895), pp. 375 – 393; vol. X (1896), pp. 481 – 508.

La Commission du Musée et la Création du Musée du Louvre, 1792 – 1793, eds. A. Tuetey and J. Guiffrey (Paris: Schemit, 1909).

The origin of the word "Louvre" is undecided. It may derive from the Frankish word for "moat" (*Loever*), from a term used for an enclosure for animals or for a hunting lodge.

[2]Similar views were expressed by contemporary statesmen and authoritative speakers in other countries.

In Austria, in 1725, Kaunitz, minister of state under the Empress Maria Theresa drew up rules for the Academy of Vienna which were to serve "the recognition of arts, the promotion of commerce and the improvement of taste of artisans."

In Denmark, the minister-dictator Struensee wrote about the same time as follows: "L'Académie est utile à l'état et aux finances des Rois . . . elle forme des artists . . . qui seront moins chers que les Étrangers. . . ."

In England, Mr. B. West in his presidential address to the Royal Academy in 1792 declared: "The instruction acquired In this place has spread itself through the various manufactures of the country."

[3]Lafont de St.-Yenne, *L'Ombre du Grand Colbert*, Paris: "Vous vous souvenez sans doute, ô grand ministre, de l'immense et précieuse collection de tableaux que vous engageâtes Louis XIV a faire élever à l'Italie et aux pays étrangers avec des frais considérables, pour meubler dignement ses palais. Vous pensez (Qui ne le penserait comme vous?) que ces richesses sont exposées a l'admiration et a la joie des Français de posséder de si rares trésors, ou a la curiosité des étrangers, ou enfin a l'étude et a l'émulation de nôtre école? Sachez, ô grand Colbert, que ces beaux ouvrages, n' ont pas revu la lumière et qu'ils ont passé, des places honorables qu'ils occupaient dans les cabinets de leurs possesseurs, à une obscure prison de Versailles, ou ils perissent depuis plus de cinquante ans."

[4]Francis Henry Taylor, *The Taste of Angels* (Boston: Little, Brown and Co., An Atlantic Monthly Press Book, 1948).

[5]Saunier, *Les Conquêtes Artistiques.*

Müntz, "Les Annexions de collections d'art.

". . . Sauver de la fureur du vandalisme les monuments d'art, était assurement une chose louable . . . C'est sur le lieu même où un monument a été élévé, qu'il est beau, qu'il est beau, qu'il est utile de venir l'admirer. La Republique possède un complément auquel ne pourrait atteindre aucune nation . . . La nation francaise, après avoir terrassé ses ennemis, doit encore les enchaıner par l'admiration . . . de tributs volontaires . . . Les Musées de France, excepté celui qui est au Louvre, sont tous des établissements imaginés depuis la révolution; ils doivent leur existence aux spoliations des temples: . . . le vandalisme . . . sera dans tous les temps la honte de révolutionnaires . . ."

These extracts are taken from a pamphlet published in the years when the Museum in the Louvre was established on an unprecedented scale and furnished with objects taken from the countries occupied by Napoleon's armies and from Catholic churches in France where the revolutionaries were still a leading power. (*Opinion sur les Musées — où se trouvent retenus tous les objets d'art, qui sont la propriété des temples consacrés à la religion catholique, par un Membre de l'ancienne Académie de Peinture et Sculpture.*) The author who severely criticized the confiscation of Church property found pardonable similarly violent means of appropriation outside the Church and in foreign countries.

As in matters of politics, so in the lesser problems of the Musée du Louvre, Napoleon was anxious to gain British sympathy. It was considered a great success when Mr. West, the President of the Royal Academy in London, accepted an invitation to Paris, and a poetical panegyric, declaimed as an after-dinner speech at a meal in Mr. West's honor, was published in 1802 by Lavallé.

[6]Stampart and Prenner, *Prodromus* . . ., preliminary catalogue of the imperial collections in the Stallburg (Vienna, 1735).

[7]W. Wymetal, *Catalogue . . . du Belvedere* (Vienna, 1873).

E. v. Engerth, "Über die im kunsthistorischen Museum neu zur Aufstellung gelangenden Gemälde," *Jahrbuch der Kunsthistorischen Sammlungen des allerhöchsten Kaiserhauses*, vol. I (Vienna, 1883).

[8]L. Viardot, *Les Musées de l'Allemagne et de Russie* (Paris: Hachette, 1844).

[9]Von Rittershausen, *Betrachtungen über die K. K. Bildergalerie zu Wien* (Vienna: 1785).

[10]J. H. Schnitzler, *Notice sur les principaux tableaux du Musée Impérial de l'Ermitage à Saint-Petersbourg* (Paris, 1828).

L. Viardot, *Les Musées de l'Allemagne et de Russie* (Paris: Hachette, 1844).

P. P. Weiner, *Meisterwerke der Gemäldesammlung in der Eremitage zu Petrograd* (Munich: Hanfstängl, 1923).

L. Reau and G. Lukomski, *Catherine la Grande, Inspiratrice d'Art et Mécène* (Paris: Calume, 1930).

Maurice Tourneux, *Diderot et Catherine* (Paris: Lévy, 1899).

N. Holst, "Sammlertum und Kunstwanderung in Ostdeutschland und den benachbarten Ländern," *Jahrbuch der Preussischen Sammlungen* (1939). The article is of special interest because of its account of rules of admission.

N. F. Levinson-Lessing, *The Hermitage Museum* (London: Hamlyn; Prague: Artia, 1964).

[11]P. de Madrazo, *Catálogo de los cuadros del museo del Prado de Madrid* (Madrid, 1855).

M. Haverty, *Wanderings in Spain* (London, 1844), vol. II, pp. 138 – 145.

C. de Ris, *Le Musée Royal de Madrid* (Paris, 1859).

L. Gielly, *Le Prado* (Paris: Librairies des Arts Decoratifs, 1939).

Henriqueta Harris, *The Prado* (London: Studio, 1941).

Harry B. Wehle, *The Prado* (New York: Abrams, 1956).

[12]"A curious practice which prevails at this, and some other museums of Madrid, is that of compelling the visitors to uncover their heads on entering. . . . At my first visit . . . I had my hat unceremoniously removed by one of the keepers who accompanied the action with some muttered insults." Haverty, *Wanderings*, vol. II, p. 217.

[13]"Zur Geschichte der Königlichen Museen zu Berlin," *Festschrift zur Feier ihres fünfzigjährigen Bestehens* (Berlin, 1880).

W. Wätzold, "Entwicklung der Berliner Museen."

L. Stock, "Urkunden zur Vorgeschichte der Berliner Museen."

Both essays were published in the *Jahrbuch der Preussischen Kunstsammlungen*, (1930).

L. Kuhn-Busse, "Der erste Entwurf für einen Berliner Museumsbau," *Jahrbuch der Preussischen Kunstsammlungen* (1938).

[14]Among them was Dr. G. F. v. Waagen, whose visit to Britain resulted in his book *Treasures of Art in Great Britain* (London: Graves, 1854).

[15]For illustrations see *Jahrbuch* . . . (1930), quoted above.

[16]L. v. Ledebuhr, "Geschichte der Königlichen Kunstkammer in Berlin", *Allgemeines Archiv für Geschichtskunde des Preussischen Staates*, vol. VI (1831).

[17]G. Monti, *Descrizione di Roma Antica e Moderna* (Rome, 1755).

F. Schottmüller, "Entwicklung der Römischen Museen," *Museumskunde,* vol. IX, Berlin (1909).

[18]Pope Leo X, a son of Lorenzo the Magnificent of the famous Medici family, was an ardent scholar and art patron. He won a place in history, however, by challenging Martin Luther to active opposition, which led to the Reformation: being in need of funds for the rebuilding of St. Peter's Cathedral, he encouraged the preaching of indulgences.

In 1755 the German antiquarian Johann Winckelmann went to Rome, and the result of his studies awakened the German-speaking world to a new awareness of ancient art. The collection in the Belvedere fascinated Winckelmann. *"Die erste Arbeit an die ich mich in Rom machte, war, die Statuen im Belvedere als das Volkommenste der (bis auf uns gelangten) alten Bildhauerei zu beschreiben."* (The description of the statues in the Belvedere was the first work which I undertook in Rome; these statues are the most perfect ancient statuary, at least among the preserved objects.) J. Winckelmann, "Beschreibung des Torso im Belvedere zu Rom," *Collected Works* (Donaueschingen, 1825), vol. I, p. 226.

A. Michaelis, "Geschichte des Statuenhofes im Vatikanischen Belvedere," *Jahrbuch des Deutschen Archäologischen Institutes*, vol. V (1890).

[19]"Da die berühmten Statuen und das neue Museum Clementi nun jetzt unter einem Aufseher stehen, so trifft man ihn schwer an. Denn wer er einmal mit Fremden im Museum ist, so schliesst er sich ein, und man kann ein paar Stunden lauern, bis er herauskommt, oder man muss gar wieder fortgehen ohne etwas zu sehen. Überhaupt ist es gut, den Vatikan mit einem darum Bekannten zu besuchen, damit man alles Merkwürdige daselbst zu sehen bekommt." J. J. Volkmann, *Historisch-Kritische Nachrichten* (Leipzig, 1770), vol. II, p. 126.

[20]R. Van Luttervelt, *Dutch Museums* (London: Thames and Hudson, 1960).

F. J. Duparc, and D. F. Lunsingh Scheurleer, "Origin and Administration of Museums in the Netherlands," *Museum*, XV, 2 (Paris: 1962), p. 74.

L. J. F. Wijsenbeek, "Art Museums," *Museum*, XV, 2 (1962), p. 81.

[21]Each member of the Civic Guards had to pay for his picture in a group portrait, and the contribution varied according to a man's place on the canvas. The average fee paid by the men represented in Rembrandt's *Nightwatch* was 100 guilders.

[22]Mr. Van Slingelandt had a way of weeding out weaker parts of his collection. He voluntarily limited himself to a collection of forty paintings, and as soon as he acquired one more he sold a piece of lesser quality.

[23]The Netherlands was reputed for its art auctions which were attended by an international assembly of connoisseurs. Art dealers from other parts of Europe came to Amsterdam to study its auctioneering methods. Noted sales were held at the Herenlogement, a former Hotel for Gentlemen. One winter a famous military leader, Prince Eugene of Savoy, stopped in Amsterdam between two campaigns against France, and was among the buyers.

Great Britain (pp. 101 – 105)

[1]H. Walpole, *Aedes Walpolianae*, or a Description of the Collection of Pictures at Houghton Hall in Norfolk, the Seat of the Right Honorable Sir Robert Walpole, Earl of Oxford (London, 1752).

[2]R. A. M. Stevenson, *Peter Paul Rubens* (London: Selley, 1909), p. 37.

[3]P. Hentzner, *A Journey into England. In the year 1598*, published in 1757, as a part of the *Itinerarium Germaniae, Galliae, Angliae* . . ., trans. R. Bentley and ed. H. Walpole in 1765.

An inventory of Henry VIII's furniture, pictures, sculpture, plate, glass, clocks, musical instruments, etc., is deposited in the British Museum, as Num. 1419 Harleian Manuscripts collection.

A *Catalogue* of King Charles I's *Capital Collection of Pictures, Statues, Medals and other Curiosities*, supposedly by Mr. Vanderdoort, keeper of the King's cabinet, was first published in London in 1758 from a manuscript in the Ashmolean Museum, in Oxford, transcribed for the Press by the late Mr. Vertue, and later finished from his papers.

[4]Claude Phillips, *The Picture Gallery of Charles I* (London: Seeley; New York: Macmillan, 1896).

Ursula Hoff, *Charles I, Patron of Artists* (London: Collins, 1942).

Brian Reade, "William Frizell and the Royal Collections," *The Burlington Magazine*, vol. LXXXIX (1947), pp. 70 – 75. Concerning Charles's early acquisitions.

[5]John Pye, *Patronage of British Art* . . . an account of the Rise and Progress of art and artists in London from the beginning of the reign of George the Second . . . (London: Longman et al., 1845).

[6]W. Sandby, *The History of the Royal Academy of Arts*, from its foundation in 1768 to the present time (London: Longman, 1862).

W. R. M. Lamb, *The Royal Academy*, a short history of its foundation and development (London: MacLehose, 1935).

Alma S. Wittlin, "Captain Coram and the Foundling Hospital," *Antiques* (June 1953). With regard to events preceding the Royal Academy.

[7]"Minutes of Evidence" of the Select Committee, etc., of February 25, 1836.

[8]Quoted by D. Murray, *Museums, their History and their Use* (Glasgow: MacLehose, 1904) vol. I, p. 139.

"About this time (1753) an act of parliament was passed for the purchase of the Museum or collection of Sir Hans Sloane (who died the 11th of January, 1753) and of the Harleian collection of manuscripts, and for providing one general repository for the better reception and more convenient use of the said collections . . . trustees were made a body corporate . . . upon this special trust and confidence 'that a free access to the said general repository . . . shall be given to all studious and curious persons, at such times and in such manner . . . as by the said trustees . . . shall be limited . . .'" (H. Chamberlain, *History and Survey of London*, London, 1770), p. 341.

Compare an account of 1748 of the collections of Sir Hans Sloane, Appendix, p. 248.

[9]S. F. A. Wendeborn, *Der Zustand des Staats, der Religion, der Gelehrsamkeit und der Kunst in Grossbritannien gegen das Ende des achtzehnten Jahrhunderts* (Berlin, 1785), II, p. 149.

"Directions to such as apply for tickets to the British Museum" (London, 1761).

[10]*Acts and Votes of Parliament relating to the British Museum, Statutes and Rules, and Synopsis of the Contents* . . . (1808).

The Frenchman L. Simond, who visited the British Museum in 1810, wrote in his *Journal of a Tour and Residence in Great Britain* . . . (Edinburgh: Ramsey-Constable, 1815): "We had no time allowed to examine anything; our conductor pushed on without minding questions, or unable to answer them. . . ." (vol. I, pp. 83 – 84).

These conditions remind one of customs in the treasure chamber of the abbey of St. Denis in France in the eighteenth century which were described by Valentini in his *Museum Museorum*, vol. II, p. 6. According to this description the doors of the cases holding the exhibits were opened only after the doors leading to the room and out of it had been carefully closed.

[11]From *The Gentleman's Magazine,* No. CLXXXII (London, May 1814), p. 458. *Montague House* (British Museum), Great Russell Street, Bloomsbury. Built by John, first Duke of Montague, favorite of Charles II, twice Ambassador at the Court of Lewis XIV; in disgrace with James II, honoured by William and Anne. Surveyed in May 1814.

"It appears that the Duke expended the greater part of his income in erecting this pile after the French taste, in which were engaged French architects, painters, &c., to design and embellish the same. . . . This house has more aspect of a palace for the abode of a prince than that of a subject . . . the whole several arrangements in communication one with other, giving that *coup d' oeil* in perspective diminution, so characteristic of interiors of this date."

On the occasion of the opening in 1851 of several new rooms of the expanding new building of the British Museum, the commentator in *The Illustrated London News*, of June 7, 1851, stated that "Montague House (the old building), of which the last remnant had disappeared in 1845, is among the things that were . . . the very model of ugliness and gloom. . . ."

[12]*The General Contents of the British Museum* (London, 1762).

A. Thomson, *Letters on the British Museum* (London, 1767).

A Visit to the British Museum (London, 1838).

D. Masson, *The British Museum, historical and descriptive* (Edinburgh: Chambers, 1850).

The Microcosm of London (London: Ackermann, 1808) vol. I, pp. 101 – 106.

Londina Illustrata (London, Wilkinson: 1819).

E. Edwards, *Lives of the Founders of the British Museum* (London: Trübner, 1870).

F. G. Kenyon, *The Buildings of the British Museum* (London, 1914).

[13]B. F. Saint Fond, *Travels in England, Scotland and the Hebrides* . . . (London: 1799), vol. I, pp. 85 – 90.

The United States (pp. 106 – 117)

[1]Richard Rathbun, *The Columbian Institute for the Promotion of Arts and Sciences*

(Washington, D.C.: U.S. National Museum, Bulletin 101, 1917), pp. 13, 16.

[2]Rathbun, *The Columbian Institute*, pp. 15, 16.

[3]George Brown Goode, "The Genesis of the United States National Museum," Report ending June 30, 1891 (Washington, D.C.: Government Printing Office, 1892), Section III, p. 290; repeated p. 304.

[4]*The Story of the United States Patent Office* (Pharmaceutical Manufacturers Association jointly with the U.S. Department of Commerce, 1965).

In 1790, when the law concerning the foundation of the Patent Office was promulgated, the United States had to import from abroad most manufactured products. For its further development the emerging nation needed inventors and men who would market new products.

[5]The account was by Francis Markoe, Jr., the corresponding secretary of the Institute, in cooperation with J. J. Albert. It was written on the request of George P. Marsh, a member of the Library Committee of Congress, who had asked for information that would enable him to meet objections made by unfriendly persons. At that time the collections were housed at such diverse places as the Patent Office, the Treasury, the War and State Departments, and even the homes of officers. Goode, "Genesis of the United States National Museum," pp. 322–323.

[6]Goode, Genesis, p. 331.

[7]Henry T. Tuckerman, "The Inauguration," *The Southern Literary Messenger*, XV (Richmond: 1849); referred to by Goode, p. 140. It was written on the occasion of the inauguration of a new president of the Institute.

[8]Whitfield J. Bell, "The Cabinet of the American Philosophical Society," in *A Cabinet of Curiosities* (Five Episodes in the Evolution of American Museums), introduced by Walter Muir Whitehill (Charlottesville: The University Press of Virginia, 1967).

[9]Clifford K. Shipton, "The Museum of the American Antiquarian Society," in *A Cabinet of Curiosities*.

[10]Charles Coleman Sellers, *Charles Willson Peale* (Philadelphia: The American Philosophical Society, 1947).

Wilbur Harvey Hunter, *The Story of America's Oldest Museum Building* (Baltimore. The Peale Museum, 1964).

Richard P. Ellis, "The Founding, History, and Significance of Peale's Museum in Philadelphia, 1785–1841," *Curator*, IX, 3 (1966), pp. 235–266.

[11]Whitfield J. Bell, Jr., "A Box of Old Bones: A Note on the Identification of the Mastodon, 1776–1806," *American Philosophical Society, Proceedings*, XCIII (1949), pp. 169–177.

[12]John G. Evers, "William Clark's Indian Museum in St. Louis," in *A Cabinet of Curiosities*.

[13]Loyd Haberly, "The American Museum from Baker to Barnum," *New-York Historical Society Quarterly*, XLIII, 3 (1959), pp. 273–287.

M. R. Werner, *Barnum* (New York: Harcourt, Brace and Co, 1923), Chapter III, pp. 43–76, "Barnum's American Museum."

[14]Abel Bowen, *Picture of Boston* (Boston: Lily, Wait and Co, 1938).

King's Handbook of Boston (Cambridge: King, 1878).

[15]Eugène Ney, "Voyage sur le Mississippi," *Revue des Deux Mondes*, second series, vol. I (1833), p. 484. Mr. Ney was of the opinion that everybody in America wanted to have a museum and to participate in the common passion at a cheap price.

Edward Hingston, *The Genial Showman, Being Reminiscences of the Life of Artemus Ward* (London: Hotten, 1871).

Louis Leonard Tucker, "Ohio Show-Shop, The Western Museum of Cincinnati," in *A Cabinet of Curiosities*.

[16]The Signers of the Declaration of Independence and their associates saw in the diffusion of education a guarantee for the preservation of the newly won democratic institutions and the proper exercise of the right of suffrage. Albert Gallatin was concerned with the raising of the "mind of the laboring classes nearer to a level with those born under favorable circumstances," Henry Adams, *The Life of Albert Gallatin* (New York: Smith, 1943), p. 648.

Jefferson considered that the great interests of humanity were both economic and moral. He aspired to a "national system of internal improvement," Adams, *The Life*, p. 350.

[17]Geological and biological surveys conducted in the 1830s led to the establishment of state museums—in New York in 1843, in Vermont in 1845, in Alabama in 1848, and so on.

[18]Jules D. Prown, *John Singleton Copley*, The Ailsa Mellon Bruce Studies in American Art (Cambridge: Harvard University Press for the National Gallery, 1966); compare pp. 10, 11, 24.

[19]Douglas and Elizabeth Rigby, *Lock, Stock and Barrel* (Philadelphia: Lippincott, 1944).
[20]Victor W. von Hagen, "Mr. Catherwood's Panorama," *Magazine of Art*, vol. *40*, 4 (1947), pp. 143–146.
Idem, Frederick Catherwood (New York: Oxford University Press, 1950).
Frederick Catherwood did not limit himself to the painting and the promotion of panoramas. His lithographs of Mayan art were the first to draw attention to their beauty, as Robert T. Hatt wrote in the thirty-seventh Annual Report of the Carnegie Museum of Science.

Early Museums:
Summing Up (pp. 117–119)

[1]*Adrastea*, 4, 212. "Es schweiget rings um mich – In dieser Wüste erkenn ich Dich, verehrte Roma, wieder? – Und Ihr Gestalten, die ich liebend grüsste. . . . Hier seh ich einen Rumpf, dort eine Büste – Grausam zerstückte, schöne Götterglieder – Geflickt und hingestellt, und Angst und Jammer, in ein Museum – eine Rumpelkammer!"
[2]F. G. Kenyon, *Museums and National Life* (Oxford: The Clarendon Press, 1927), p. 10.
[3]In 1824 the Franklin Institute was founded in Philadelphia, and a cabinet of models and minerals was considered to be an important aid in promoting the "Mechanic Arts."
[4]L. Viardot, *Les Musées de l'Allemagne et de Russie* (Paris: Hachette, 1844), pp. 7–8, described the new building of the Pinakothek in Munich which had been finished in 1836. Although built for the purpose of housing a public collection, the building still retained features of a princely residence. There were ten large rooms instead of a single gallery, but their proportions were on such scale as to produce an imposing effect. M. Viardot wrote as follows: " . . . *cela unit à l'effet de l'ensemble, à la majesté du coup d'oeil général.*"

5. Efforts at Reform

First Period: Up to 1914 (pp. 121–144)

[1]In the United States the number of museums in existence before 1860 was assessed at 327; around 1914 the number is believed to have doubled. (*A Statistical Survey of Museums in the United States and Canada* (Washington, D.C., The American Association of Museums jointly with the Smithsonian Institution and the U.S. Office of Education: 1965), p. 14.
In Germany the number of museums rose from 15 early in the nineteenth century to 179 a century later.
In Great Britain 59 museums supposedly existed around 1850, with the number rising to 354 in 1914. Sir Henry Miers, *A Report on the Public Museums of the British Isles* (Edinburgh, 1928), p. 10: "The richest period of museum development was perhaps the forty years, 1880–1920. . . . The first Act of Parliament appertaining to museums was the Museums Act of 1845, which enabled town councils to found and maintain museums."
[2]*Picture Galleries of England, Scotland, and Wales*, eds. Anthony Blunt and Margaret Whinney (London: Chatto & Windus, 1950).
Philip Hendy, *The National Gallery* (London: Thames & Hudson, 1963).
[3]H. Balfour, "The Relationship of Museums to the Study of Anthropology," *The Journal of the Royal Anthropological Institute of Great Britain*, vol. XXXIV (1904), pp. 10–19.
[4]J. H. Hefner-Alteneck, *Entstehung, Zweck und Einrichtung des Bayerischen Nationalmuseums in München* (Bamberg, 1890).
K. K. Eberlein, "Vorgeschichte und Entstehung der Nationalgalerie," *Jahrbuch der Preussischen Kunstsammlungen* (1930).
[5]A. Garcia Gutierrez, *Noticia historico-descriptiva del Muséo Arqueologico Nacional* (Madrid, 1876).
The Royal Decree, published on March 21, 1867, and explaining the purpose of the new museum contained the following passage: ". . . testigos incorruptibles de las edades que fueron, y comprobantes irrecusables del estado de la industria, de la ciencia, de las costumbres, de las instituciones y de la cultura general del pais en las varias épocas de su historia."
[6]Frederick W. True, "An Account of the United States National Museum," in *The Smithsonian Institution, 1846–1896: The History of its First Half Century*, ed. George Brown Goode (Washington, 1897); reprinted in the *Report of the U. S. National Museum* for the year ending June 30, 1896 (Washington: Government Printing Office, 1898), pp. 289–324.
[7]Samuel Pierpont Langley, "James Smithson," in *The Smithsonian Institution*, ed. George Brown Goode, pp. 1–24. Among Secretary Langley's sources was a memoir "James

Smithson and his Bequest" by William J. Rhees who referred to a book on America in
Smithson's library, to Isaac Weld's *Travels through North America*, of 1706. Weld, the
Secretary of the Royal Society, described the city of Washington as a future intellectual
center; his prophecy may have influenced Smithson in his decision to direct the bequest
of his estate to the United States. Smithson had feelings of antagonism with regard to
England: he was the natural son of the Duke of Northumberland and was deprived of the
customary privileges of men of his station; furthermore, the papers he wrote in his later
years were supposedly not accepted by the Royal Society.

[8]George Brown Goode, "The Genesis of the National Museum," *Report of the National
Museum* for the year ending June 30, 1891 (Washington: Government Printing Office,
1892), Section III, pp. 273–380. With regard to the use of the term "national" see especially pp. 305, 306, 317.

The memory of this great man to this day remains alive in the minds of museum people.
". . . in 1965 Mr. G. Carroll Lindsay . . . of the New York State Museum and Science
Service in Albany, remarked in an essay on Goode: 'As an organizer of museum activity,
Goode had no peer. . . . He was the first American to begin to realize the role of the
museum in synthesizing the study of science, art, and history.'" Quoted by Geoffrey T.
Hellman, *The Smithsonian: Octopus on the Mall* (Philadelphia, Lippincott: 1967), p. 198.

[9]Congress was also unreceptive to a proposal, in 1891, to cover sixty-two acres of Washington, D. C., with full-size replicas of famous buildings of different countries, including
the Greek Parthenon twice its size. Whatever the artistic qualities of the plan may have
been, its international spirit is remarkable. F. W. Smith, *Design and Prospectus for a
National Gallery of History and of Art in Washington* (Washington: Gibson, 1891).

Europeans encouraged the establishment of the cement outdoor museum. Concern
was expressed that America's new steel kings, oil magnates, and Trust barons might
buy up "the whole art of Europe from the dawn of history to the present day, and therewith
lay the foundation for a civilization of their own." William Treue, *Art Plunder, The fate of
works of art in war, revolution and peace* (London: Methuen, 1960), p. 212.

[10]Pertinent statements made by Secretary Henry in several of his *Annual Reports*:

Referring to the collections of the Institution in his *Report* for 1856, p. 43; "However
valuable these collections may be in themselves, they are but the rough materials from
which science is to be evolved; and so long as the specimens remain undescribed, and
their places undetermined in the system of unorganized beings, though they may serve
to gratify an unenlightened curiosity, they are of no importance in the discovery of the
laws of life."

In his *Report* of 1876, only two years before his death, he restated his conviction that
the Smithsonian Institution had little to gain from growing permanent collections: "It is
the design of the Museum to continually increase its collection of material objects; of the
Institution, to extend the bounds of human knowledge."

As Wilcomb E. Washburn wrote, "The great achievement of the Smithsonian Institution
. . . was its ability to attract, aid and encourage the most original scientific thinkers of
mid-nineteenth-century America." The Influence of the Smithsonian Institution on
Intellectual Life in Mid-Nineteenth Century Washington, *Records of the Columbia Historical Society of Washington, D.C.* (1966).

A statement from Henry's *Annual Report* for 1875, p. 9, gives balance to the apperception of his attitude toward museums. He referred to the importance of a National Museum
in the country's capital "as exhibiting the natural resources of the country, as well as a
means of public education; . . ."

Wilcomb E. Washburn, "The Museum and Joseph Henry," *Curator*, VII, 1 (1965), pp.
35–54.

[11]E. T. Hamy, "Les Origines du Musée à Ethnographie, *Revue d'Ethnographie*, vol. VIII
(1899).

K. Bahnson, "Ethnographical Museums," *The Archaeological Review* (1889).

Edmé-François Jomard, *Lettre à M. Ph.-Fr. Siebold sur les collections ethnographiques*
(Paris: Bourgogne et Martinet, 1845).

Balfour, "The Relationship of Museums to the Study of Anthropology," *Journal of the
Royal Anthropological Institute*, vol. XXXIV (1904).

H. J. Braunholtz, "Ethnographical Museums and the Collector: Aims and Methods,"
The Journal of the Royal Anthropological Institute of Great Britain, vol. LXVIII (1938),
pp. 1–16.

[12]Walter Muir Whitehill, *The East India Marine Society and the Peabody Museum of
Salem, A Sesquicentennial History* (Salem: Peabody Museum, 1949).

[13]The literature concerning International Expositions and the Fairs preceding them is

too abundant to be quoted in this context. *The Encyclopedia of the Social Sciences* may be consulted for a summary; see also Merle Curti, "America at the World Fairs, 1851 – 1893, *American Historical Review*, vol. LV, no. 4 (1950), pp. 833 – 856, especially with regard to the problems encountered by American exhibitors. The assistance they received from the government in 1851, on the occasion of the first international exposition, in London, was limited to vessels for the transportation of their materials.

[14]Louise Hall Tharp, "Professor of the World's Wonder," *American Heritage*, XII, 2 (1961), pp. 56 ff.

Compare: Ralph W. Dexter, "Frederick Ward Putnam and the Development of Museums of Natural History and Anthropology in the United States," *Curator* IX, 2 (1966), pp. 151 – 155.

Alden Stevens, "The First Ninety Years: The American Museum Celebrates an Anniversary," *Natural History Magazine*, V (1959).

[15]With regard to the evolution of the habitat group, see A. E. Parr, "The Habitat Group," *Curator*, II, 2 (1959).

With regard to new developments in general see G. Brown Goode, "The Museums of the Future," in *A Memorial Volume of George Brown Goode*, together with a selection of his papers on museums, *Report of the U. S. National Museum* for the year 1897, vol. II, pp. 263 – 354.

[16]Winifred Howe, *A History of the Metropolitan Museum* (New York: Metropolitan Museum of Art, 1913 – 1946).

Lillian Beresnack Miller, *Patrons and Patriotism, The Encouragement of the Fine Arts in the United States*, 1790 – 1860 (Chicago: Chicago University Press, 1966).

[17]T. Greenwood, *Museums and Art Galleries* (London: Simpkin, Marshall & Co, 1888), p. 4.

[18]"Report on Museums," *Proceedings of the Society of Antiquaries of Scotland* (1888), p. 721.

[19]Julius Langbein, *Rembrandt als Erzieher* (Leipzig, 1890), p. 17. Compare Benjamin I. Gilman, *Museum Ideals* (Cambridge: Harvard University Press, 1923), XVII.

[20]G. Brown Goode, "Museums of the Future," *Annual Report* of the U.S. National Museum for 1897.

[21]Gilman commented on the traditional use of top light in museum buildings and on their connection with ancient Greek temples. Originally, the temple had been the abode of the gods and worshipers gathered outside the darkened room, but when the "temple" became a model for museum architecture light was needed, and the roof was taken off.

"The temple type hitherto accepted without question is about to be abandoned for a basilica type," wrote Gilman, who considered the Roman basilica with its high windows or clerestory around the central hall more desirable for the housing of collections. In ancient times the basilica had served as a roofed-in forum or public meeting place. Gilman, *Museum Ideals*, pp. 435 ff.

[22]K. Freyer, "Ein Wandermuseum," *Museumskunde* (1913).

[23]L. V. Coleman, *Historic House Museums* (Washington, D. C.: The American Association of Museums, 1933), p. 18.

[24]G. B. Alcorn, "The Role of Agricultural Extension in California," in *The New Challenge in Lifelong Learning*, Resolutions and Proceedings of a Conference on the future role of the University in relation to public service, presented by the Academic Senate Committee on University Extension, University of California (1965), p. 9.

[25]Sir Patric Geddes, "Civic Museums," *Sociological Papers*, vol. III (London: Sociological Society, 1905).

Second Period of Reform: Between the Two World Wars (pp. 144 – 163)

[1]B. Adler, "Das Museumwesen in Russland während der Revolution," *Museumskunde*, (1924).

[2]K. E. Grinevich, "The First All-Russian Congress of Museum Workers," V. O. K. S., II, 4 (1931), pp. 81 – 85.

S. A. Abramov, ed. *Museums and Collections of the Soviet Union.*

U. V. Sergievski, *Museum of Descriptive Art* (Moscow, 1930).

B. N. Ternovetz, *Museum of Modern Art* (Moscow, 1934).

Musées. Enquête Internationale, ed. G. Wildenstein (Paris, 1937). (Article on Russian Museums)

The Russian State Museum (Moscow and Leningrad: State Art Publishers, 1939).

[3]B. Legran, *La Reconstruction Socialiste de l'Ermitage,* trans. M. Meloup and H. Notgaft (Leningrad, 1934).

[4]In the Historical Museum in Moscow, the student-visitor is offered drawers with card

indexes on which every single specimen of the museum is described and shown in a photograph. In the manner customary in libraries, the visitor applies for certain specimens by naming them by their numbers registered on index cards, and the desired objects are brought to him on a tray, which is so constructed that it slides into a cabinet when the objects are kept in store. Only a small part of the specimens, selected in accordance with a special period or a type of exhibit, are on show. See W. M. Conway, *Art Treasures in Soviet Russia* (London: Arnold, 1925), p. 173.

Wilhelm Treue, *Art Plunder, The Fate of Works of Art in War. Revolution and Peace,* (New York: Day, 1961), p. 253, contains a quotation from the book of Mr. Conway, who visited Russia as an emissary of the British Parliament:

"Apparently the psychology of the Russian masses must be entirely different from that of the mob in the French Revolution. There were moments of the greatest danger, but all the museum staff and their employees down to the last charwoman were at one in the resolute defence of the public property committed to their charge . . . not a single theft took place. . . ."

In the Toy Museum in Moscow children are the chief visitors, and their cooperation is invited by the management. They are asked to give their views on models for new toys to be produced in the museum and to suggest ways of improving models. W. M. Conway, *Art Treasures*, p. 136.

C. M. Legge, on Russian Museums, *The Museums Journal* (April 1936 and October 1938).

[5]G. Q. Giglioli, *Museo dell' Impero Romano* (Rome: Colombo, 1938), p. X. "La risorta coscienza nazionale, lo spirito che il Fascismo ha infuso negli Italiani, hanno portato come naturale conseguenza, un ritorno entusiasta al culto della romanità . . . Su tutta l'Europa, l'Asia e l'Africa dove si svolse la civiltà antica, restano le tracce di Roma con monumenti di arte e piu ancora di sapienza civile."

[6]Giglioli, ibid.; p. XI. "Quando poi si porterà ordinare in degna sede il materiale que si sarà raccolto, non solo gli studiosi, ma il pubblico colto e especialmente i giovanetti e i fianciulli delle scuole, potranno, passando di sala in sala, ammirare riprodotto ció che i Romani fecéro in Gallia e in Spagna, in Britannia e in Oriente, in Asia e in Africa, e avere in un momento la visione e la conscienza di ció che l'Impero di Roma fu ed è ancora nella Storia dell' incivilimento umane."

[7]D. Mustilli, *Il Museo Mussolini* (Rome: La Libreria dello Stato, 1939).

[8]B. Negara, *Monumenti, Musei e Gallerie Pontificie* (Rome: Pontificcia Accademia Romana de Archeologia, 1936 – 1939).

A. Lipinsky, "Pinacotheca Vaticana," *Museumskunde* (1937).

[9]F. T. Schulz, "Die Notwendigkeit der Umgestaltung unserer Museen," *Museumskunde* (1933).

[10]W. Uhlemann, "Die historische Bedeutung der Heimatmuseen," *Museumskunde* (1931).

K. H. Jacob-Friesen, "Ein Preisausschreiben zur Beurteilung der Heimatmuseen," *Museumskunde* (1933).

H. Preuss, "Das Heimatmuseum im Dritten Reich," *Museumskunde* (1933).

H. Weigold, "Deutsche Heimatmuseen als Kulturzentren – ein Fernziel," *Mitteilungen des Museumverbandes für Niedersachsen* (1933).

[11]H. G. Presker, "Heimatmuseum und Schule," *Museumskunde* (1938).

O. Haase, "Der vorgeschichtliche Arbeitsraum im Schulmuseum der Stadt Hannover," *Museumskunde* (1938).

[12]"Eine Zeit wiedererstarkenden Wehrgeistes und Wehrwillens muss natürlich den Heeresmuseen, Hütern der kriegerischen Vergangenheit eines Volkes, erhöhte Aufmerksamkeit zuwenden."

"Die Aufgabe der Heeresmuseen ist . . . eine bestimmte geistigseelische Grundlage zu schaffen . . . durch Darstellung der Idee des Soldatentums . . . so die Erziehung des Volkes zur geistigen Wehrbereitschaft entscheidend zu fördern."

W. Hahlweg, "Das Deutsche Heeresmuseum," *Museumskunde* (1935), pp. 59, 61.

[13]The German National Museum of Folk Culture was opened in Berlin in 1935.

The requests of the Nazi authorities that museums of ethnology should be used for the propagation of "racial philosophy," emphasizing the superiority of the Germanic master race and the inferiority of "non-Aryan" peoples, and the consequences a curator had to face who did not comply with such orders, were described by a curator's wife, Mrs. Eva Lips, in a book entitled *What Hitler did to us*, trans. Caroline Newton (London: Joseph, 1939).

14The chapter on museums in the *Catalogue* of the Paris World Exhibition, 1937, contained the following passage:

". . . cependant dans certain pays modernes où l'action politique tend à devenir le point de convergence de toutes les forces de la nation, le Musée voit son rôle social et pédagogique l'emporter de plus en plus sur son rôle esthétique et sensible. . . . Dans l'équipement social pédagogique de ce Musée l'oeuvre d'art est considéré un facteur historique et complété par tout un matériel auxiliaire, composé de moulages, de copies, de statistiques, de cartes, de tableaux démonstratifs."

15W. Schöne, "Neuordnung der Nationalgalerie," *Museumskunde* (1936).

16Schlesisches Museum, Breslau.

17Francis H. Taylor, *Babel's Tower. The Dilemma of the Modern Museum* (New York: Columbia University Press, 1945), p. 21.

18In 1914 the estimated number of museums in the United States was 600; by 1938 the figure had risen to 2500. The investment in museum buildings had roughly doubled every ten years since 1880, except between 1910 and 1920. Attendance in 1944 was considered to have reached 50 million people.

19A. C. Parker, *A Manual for History Museum* (New York: Columbia University Press, 1935). p. 7.

20R. T. Adam, *The Civic Value of Museums* (New York: American Association of Adult Education, 1937), p. 9.

21T. L. Low, *The Museum as a Social Instrument* (New York: American Association of Museums, 1942), pp. 9, 21, 23.

Laurence Vail Coleman estimated the average expenditure for education to represent one third of available funds in American museums, with two thirds being spent on administration and on the preservation of materials.

22T. L. Low, *The Museum as a Social Instrument.*

23Grace Fisher Ramsey, *Educational Work in Museums of the United States* (New York: Wilson, 1938).

At the 1939 – 1940 New York World's Fair "visitors attended the Hall of Science in numbers 30 times as great as that of any concession on the Midway." The statement was made by Lenox R. Lohr, the fair's general manager, and was reported by Gilbert Millstein in an article in the *Times Magazine.*

24Benjamin I. Gilman, *Museum Ideals* (Cambridge: Harvard University Press, 1923), pp. 41, 51.

25John Walker, "The Genesis of the National Gallery of Art," *Art in America*, XXXII, 4 (1944).

26Ramsey, *Educational Work in Museums,* pp. 217, 218.

27Adam, *The Civic Value of Museums,* pp. 14 ff.

28Adam (1937), *ibid.,* especially p. 92, concerning the "Neighborhood Circulating Exhibitions" of the Metropolitan Museum of Art. Sets of 50 to 400 objects were lent for a period of 8 to 10 weeks to "organizations with established quarters, a program of educational work and a neighborhood following."

L. V. Coleman, *College and University Museums* (Washington, D. C.: The American Association of Museums, 1942), pp. 12, 13.

With regard to Museum School Services, see Ramsey, *Education Work in Museums,* pp. 56. 67, etc., and Appendix in this book, pp. 235 – 240.

29The Cloisters contain an outstanding collection of medieval sculpture and architectural material assembled by George Grey Barnard. In 1925 John D. Rockefeller financed the purchase of the collection by The Metropolitan Museum of Art and provided funds for its maintenance. The construction of a new building overlooking the Hudson River began in 1934. Entire medieval cloisters, Romanesque and Gothic Chapels, and statuary from France and Spain form a beautifully synchronized setting. Further objects were donated by the John Rockefellers and their friends. James J. Rorimer, *The Cloisters*, The Building and the Collections of Medieval Art in Fort Tryon Park (New York: The Metropolitan Museum of Art, 1939).

30L. V. Coleman, *Historic House Museums* (Washington, D. C.: American Association of Museums, 1933), pp. 102 ff.

31Edward P. Alexander, "Bringing History to Life . . .," *Curator,* IV, 1 (1961).

Raymond B. Fosdick, *John D. Rockefeller, Jr., A Portrait* (New York: Harper, 1956). Compare p. 143, what Eduard Fuchs said with regard to the lack of reality in museums — his statement has not lost much of its validity.

32William Adams Simonds, *Henry Ford and Greenfield Village* (New York: F. A. Stokes, 1938).

33Milton W. Brown, *The Story of the Armory Show* (New York: The Joseph H. Hirshhorn Foundation – Distribution by the New York Graphic Society, 1963).

Walter Pach, *The Art Museum in America* (New York: Pantheon, 1948).

A. Saarinen, *The Proud Possessors* (New York: Random House, 1958), especially with regard to the early crusaders for modern art in the United States, Katherine Sophie Dryer and Walter Arensberg, who organized traveling temporary exhibitions. Miss Dryer indefatigably lectured and took her message from the Colony Club on Park Avenue to the Workers Club on Union Square, from the Jewish Community Center in Brooklyn to the Finishing School, Washington, D.C., as she herself put it.

Peggy Guggenheim's creative efforts on behalf of abstract and surrealist art were described by Aline Saarinen, and later by Nicolas and Elena C. Calas, *The Peggy Guggenheim Collection of Modern Art* (New York: Abrams, 1966). In the Guggenheim "This Century Gallery" on Madison Avenue, Frederick J. Kiesler housed cubist paintings in a tentlike room and surrealistic ones within concave walls; paintings hanging in midair seemed to float; spotlighting and accompanying sounds came on and went off. With gravity and other forces that rule human existence on earth seemingly conquered, he provided "happenings" and "turned people on" a generation before such experiences were becoming a part of our culture.

34John Walker, *The National Gallery of Art* (New York: Abrams, 1956).

35E. S. Robinson, *The Behaviour of the Museum Visitor* (1920).

Marguerite Bloomberg, *An Experiment in Museum Instruction* (1929).

A. W. Melton, *Problems of Installation in Museums of Art* (1935).

A. W. Melton, Nita Goldberg Feldman, and C. W. Mason, *Experimental Studies of the Education of Children in a Museum of Science* (1936).

M. B. Porter, *Behavior of the Average Visitor in the Peabody Museum of Natural History* (1938).

All these studies were published by the American Association of Museums, Washington, D.C.

36Francis Henry Taylor, *Babel's Tower*, p. 6.

Compare the more optimistic views of William Valentiner, "The Museum of Tomorrow," in *New Architecture and City Planning*, edited by Paul Zucker (New York: Philosophical Library, 1944), pp. 656–674.

37England: 1919. The Commission on Adult Education, set up by the Ministry of Reconstruction, issued an *Interim Report on Libraries and Museums*.

1920. The British Association for the Advancement of Science published a Report, begun before the war, on museums in relation to education.

1928. Interim Report of the Royal Commission on National Museums and Galleries. The Report was completed in 1929.

1928 and 1938. *Reports on the Museums and Art Galleries of the British Isles* (other than the National Museums) made to the Carnegie United Kingdom Trustees, the first by Sir Henry Miers, the second by Mr. F. S. Markham.

Holland: After the termination of the First World War, the Dutch Archaeological Association published a memorandum entitled *Over Hervorming en Beheer onzer Musea* – on the reform and the management of museums. Owing to economic circumstances the immediate effects of the study were scarce, but it awakened the interest of the government in museums. A national Advisory Committee on Museums was established and was given the task of advising the Minister of Education, Arts and Sciences. See F. J. Duparc and D. F. L. Scheurleer, "Origin and Administration of Museums in the Netherlands," *Museum*, XV, 2 (1962), p. 75.

Rapport der Rijkscommissie van advies in zake reorganisatie van het museumwezen hier te lande ingesteld oij koninklik besluit. (Gravenhage, 1921).

Germany: W. R. Valentiner, *Umgestaltung der Museen in Sinne der neuen Zeit* (Berlin, 1919); *Kunst und Künstler* (Berlin, 1919), with articles by several contributors, O. Wulff, "Lehrsammlungen, eine Neuaufgabe der Deutschen Museen" *Museumskunde* (1920).

Austria: H. Tietze, *Die Zukunft der Wiener Museen* (Vienna, 1923).

Italy: F. Sapori, "Réorganisation des Galeries et Musees Nationaux," *Mouseion* (Paris, 1927).

Rumania: A. Tzigara-Samurcas, *Museografie Romaneasca* – with a summary in French – (Bucarest, 1936).

Compare for France and Spain note 39.

[38]The *Muséographie* was published in 1934, following an international conference in Madrid on the subject "The Architecture and the Management of Museums of Art."

The International Museum Office was affiliated with the Institut de Coopération Intellectuelle in Paris, an offspring of the League of Nations.

Another collective declaration of international museum experts appeared in the publication "Musées," in the series *Cahiers de Sciences, de Lettres et d'Arts* (Paris, 1937).

[39]"Le Plan d'extension et de regroupement méthodique des collections du Musée du Louvre," *Bulletin des Musées de France* (January 1934).

J. Alvarez de Sotomayor, "La transformation récente du Prado à Madrid," *Mouseion* (Paris, 1927).

[40]J. Rothenstein, *The Museums Journal*, London (October, 1937).

[41]The illustrations contained in the two volumes of the *Muséographie* (1934) give some evidence of the progress achieved in European museums roughly between the end of the nineteenth century and 1934. See, for example, vol. I, pp. 28 and 31, for solutions in adapting students' galleries to the use by the general public in the New Museum in The Hague and in the Far East Museum in Stockholm; compare the approach to the problem in the Musée de Guimet.

[42]F. S. Markham, *Reports on the Museums of the British Isles*, opening paragraph; further, p. 166, ". . . nearly 250 (smaller) museums (in Great Britain) (one in three) require drastic reorganisation."

[43]H. Read, "The Museum Scandal," *The London Mercury* (February, 1939).

[44]Considerable interest in Folk Museums was shown in England, where the York Castle Museum was opened in 1938. The collection of Yorkshire Bygones was housed in an old building that previously had served as a prison. In the fashion of Scandinavian open-air museums, old shops, a post office, and a coach station were reconstructed. In 1929 a Royal Commission had reported a plan for a national folk museum which was not put into realization.

[45]S. H. Daukes, *The Medical Museum*, based on a new system of visual teaching (London: The Wellcome Foundation, 1929).

S. H. Daukes, "The Historical Medical Museum — its Future and Possibilities," *The Museums Journal*, London (May 1944).

[46]O. Neurath, *The International Picture Language* (London: Paul, Trench, Trubner & Co., 1936).

O. Neurath, "Bildhafte Pädagogik im Gesellschafts- und Wirtschaftsmuseum," *Museumskunde*, New Series, vol. III.

[47]Tietze, *Die Zukunft der Wiener Museen*.

Arrangements in synthesis style in the Louvre were described in the *Bulletin des Musées de France* (Paris, June 1938). Objects of a variety of raw materials and styles were combined to reproduce a general impression of the character of a particular period of history.

[48]The exhibition was set up by *The International Foundation for Visual Education* and was shown in the department stores Bijenkorf in Amsterdam, Rotterdam, and The Hague. It was a continuation of the work done by O. Neurath and his collaborators in Vienna, who at the time lived in Holland.

Third Period of Reform: From 1945 to the Present (pp. 163 – 193)

[1]Germany inflicted considerable losses on museums in the countries it occupied and suffered losses itself. Even before the outbreak of the war there was "Plunder on the Home Front . . .," as Wilhelm Treue called it in *Art Plunder: The fate of works of art in war, revolution and peace* (London: Methuen, 1960), Chap. 19, pp. 232 ff. The art plunder in occupied countries proceeded according to a well-organized strategy.

On the home front, and before the outbreak of the Second World War, the Nazis confiscated modern paintings, including such masters as Kokoschka, Picasso, and even Gauguin, and took them out of circulation except for small selections which they sent around as traveling exhibitions with vilifying gibes as labels. Some pictures were sold on international markets, with the profits going to German armaments. When the warehouse used for storage was needed as a depository for grain, over 1000 oil paintings and close to 4000 watercolors and drawings were burned. See: Paul O. Rave, *Kunstdiktatur in Dritten Reich* (Hamburg: Mann, 1949).

When the war broke out, the cellars of the Kaiser-Friedrich Museum in Berlin served as the shelter of world-famous paintings by old masters, some of which remained uncrated for lack of lumber. As Allied bombing increased, the pictures were evacuated to an air-raid shelter and later to a Flak Tower, where about four hundred perished in explosions and fires; four hundred more were found by Russian troops on their entry into Berlin. Another batch of masterpieces survived a hazardous trip in open trucks to a salt mine near Erfurt, 2100 feet underground, where they were located by American troops.

Art treasures captured by the Allied armies were examined by experts and were given the necessary care. Museum pieces traveled thousands of miles over land and across the ocean to temporary storage places and back to the countries in which they had been kept before the war. On a single day a train of forty-five freight cars under American control in Germany returned works of art to France; according to estimates the Hermitage Museum alone at one time housed 500,000 objects belonging to Germany. Two hundred and two selected paintings, mostly from the Kaiser-Friedrich Museum in Berlin, were given shelter in the National Gallery in Washington, D.C., and were sent on a touring exhibition to several large museums in the United States before being returned to their owners.

John Walker, "Europe's Looted Art," *National Geographical Magazine*, vol. LXXXIX, 1 (1946), pp. 39–52.

Harry A. McBride, "Masterpieces on Tour," *National Geographical Magazine*, vol. XCIV, 6 (1948), pp. 717–750.

"Of the 395 museums which existed in Germany before the second world war, 108 were totally destroyed and 149 partially destroyed during the war. However, a large proportion of the art treasures were successfully preserved and are now relocated. . . ." Stephan F. Borhegyi, *Report of a Study Trip*, sponsored by The German Federal Government and InterNaciones, July 1967. Mimeographed copy obtained by the courtesy of the author.

In Russia measures were taken at the beginning of the hostilities to protect museums and monuments. Wax paper was used to protect objects against moisture. Some of the outdoor statues were dismantled and buried under sandbags, or were coated with industrial vaseline, and hidden in trenches. Evacuation was another means of seeking protection for valuable materials. Nevertheless destruction and pillaging by enemy troops occurred on a large scale. See *Museum*, IX, 4 (Paris: 1956), "The Protection of Cultural Monuments and Museum Treasures," and *Museum*, XIX, 3 (1966) "Museums in the Ukraine," with regard to the damage suffered by museums in a single Soviet Republic.

Italian museums suffered more from a dislocation of their contents than from their destruction, but some of the buildings were damaged: G. C. Argan, "Renovation of Museums in Italy," *Museum*, V, 3 (1952).

[2]In Germany 600 new and up-to-date museums existed in 1967 and others were at the stage of being built or planned. This represented an increase of over 50 percent in comparison with the number of prewar German museums. The Deutsches Museum (of Science and Industry) in Munich was visited in 1966 by 700,000 people. Borhegyi, *Report*.

The entire issue of the UNESCO quarterly *Museum*, XXI, 2 (1968), was devoted to museums in the German Federal Republic. Compare:

Hermann Jedding, *Keyser's Führer durch Museen und Sammlungen* (Munich: Keysersche Verlagsbuchhandlung, 1961).

Bibliotheken und Museen, ed. Paulgerd Jesberg (Stuttgart: Krämer, 1964).

Encyclopedia Britannica, 1967, "Museums."

With regard to new developments, see especially *Stiftung Preussischer Kulturbesitz*, ed. Ursula Meurin, published by the Foundation (Stiftung), undated, but printed in the later sixties. Further, Otto Harrassowitz, *Museum Insel, Berlin* (Munich, 1965).

An account of museums in Eastern Germany is given in *Handbuch der Museen und Wissenschaftlichen Sammlungen in der Deutschen Demokratischen Republik*, ed. I. A. Knorr (Halle an der Saale: Fachstelle für Heimatmuseen beim Ministerium für Kultur, 1963).

[3]Michael Brawne, *The New Museum Architecture and Display* (New York: Praeger, 1965), p. 273. A sketch of Cicero Dial's picture gallery and references to other techniques of moving exhibits in front of seated viewers are on p. 328.

Brawne is interested in museum architecture and offers ample illustrative material. Compare Roberto Aloi, *Musei, Architettura-Tecnica* (Milan: Hoepli, 1962). Both books have an international scope.

[4]Quoted in an article on "Museums and Temporary Exhibitions in Belgium," *Museum* XX, 4 (1967), p. 281. Compare in the same issue a description of educational services in Belgian Museums.

[5]*Museum*, XIV, 1 (1961) and *Museum* VII, 2 (1954).

[6]*Museum*, V, 4 (1952).

[7]*Museum*, XVII, 3 (1964) and *Museum* VII, 2 (1954), article on the Leonardo da Vinci

Museum of Science and Technology, Milan, which was established in an ancient cloister on the occasion of the fifth centenary of da Vinci's birth. It was expanded in the subsequent years; see *Museum* XII, 2 (1959).

[8]Compare *Museum*, IX, 1 (1953), XII, 3 (1959), XIV, 4 (1961).

[9]Jean Milliadis writing about the new Acropolis Museum in Athens, *Museum*, XII, 1 (1959), is a partisan of the aesthetic approach.

[10]Two entire issues of UNESCO's quarterly journal *Museum* were devoted to museums of science and technology in different countries, in and out of Europe. VII, 3 (1954) and XX, 3 (1967). Compare an account about the Science Museum in London: *The Science Museum, The First Hundred Years* (London, The Stationery Office: 1957).

[11]*Museum*, I, 1 (1948).

The Standing Commission on Museums and Galleries, *Report on the Area Museum Services* (London, The Stationery Office: 1967).

Gudmund Boesen, *Danish Museums* (Copenhagen, Committee for Danish Cultural Activities Abroad: 1966), p. 14. For local history museums in Denmark see *Museum*, XIII, 2 (1960).

[12]Borhegyi, *Report*, p. 5.

[13]Eivind Engelstad, *Norwegian Museums* (Oslo, Office of Cultural Relations, Ministry of Foreign Affairs: 1959). For a general survey of Swedish museums see *A Key to the Museums of Sweden*, ed. Gertrud Serner (Stockholm: The Swedish Institute, 1960).

With regard to local Dutch ethnographic museums and exhibitions see: *Museum*, XV, 2 (1962). The story of the Zuidersee is pictured in one of these museums, and there is an African Museum in Berg en Dal.

[14]The (British) Museum Association will no doubt continue their efforts in upgrading the profession by offering courses and holding examinations. The Association publishes a series of manuals dealing with various aspects of museology. Details can be obtained by writing to the Association, 87 Charlotte Street, London, W. 1.

[15]A. Zaks and A. Khanukov, "Soviet Museums are fifty years old," *Museum*, XX, 1 (1968), pp. 91 ff. This source was used for numerous statements in this chapter, especially with regard to quoted figures.

[16]T. Lazarova, "The Hermitage Today," transcripts of two lectures held in the Hermitage in February 1968; obtained by the courtesy of the U.S.S.R. Embassy in Washington, D. C.

Poland reported the destruction of two hundred of their six hundred History Museums.

[17]Among the publications of the Institute of Museology was a treatise, *Bases of Soviet Museography, Organization and Techniques of Museum Exhibitions*, by A. I. Mikhailova (1955), and *The History of Museology in the U.S.S.R.* This work was translated into Czech, Rumanian, and Chinese. Another study dealt with *The Increasing Role of Soviet Museums in the System of Public Education*. Compare *Beiträge zur Sowjetischen Museumskunde* (Auszüge aus "Grundlagen der Sowjetischen Museumskunde), eds. E. Ullman and H. Wolter (Halle an der Saale: Fachstelle für Heimatmuseen beim Ministerium für Kultur, 1960).

Articles on U.S.S.R. Museums were published in UNESCO's *Museum*, XVI, 1 (1963) and in the *Neue Museumskunde* 7, 4 (1964). The latter deals with the cooperation between museums and schools.

[18]David Douglas Duncan, *The Kremlin Treasures* (London: Studio, 1960).

Treasures in the Kremlin, ed. B. A. Rybakov (Prague: Artia, 1962; London: Nevill).

[19]S. Lorenz, "The Museums of Poland," *Museum* XIX, 3 (1966).

Stanisław Brzestowski, *Muzea w Polsce* (Warsaw: Wydawnictwo Zwodowe, 1968).

With regard to museums in Czechoslovakia see *Museum*, XI, 2 (1958).

With regard to museums in Bulgaria see *Museum*, XVI, 2 (1966).

Numerous references to museums in Eastern Europe are contained in many issues of this quarterly publication of UNESCO.

Museum und Schule in der Deutschen Demokratischen Republik ed. Erich Hobusch (Berlin: Zentrale Fachstelle fur Museen beim Ministerium für Kultur, with the aid of the UNESCO Commission for the Republik, 1966).

The book was issued jointly by the Ministries of Culture and of Education and deals with the cooperation between museums and schools. Museums are recommended as a medium serving the arousal of patriotism in young people and of their awareness of the contribution made by workers to the advancement of human rights. In terms of pedagogy, the author stresses the need for an adequate preparation of students for a museum visit and for their active cooperation in processes of learning.

[20]G. P. Kozlov, "The Polytechnical Museum, Moscow," *Museum*, XX, 4 (1967), pp. 195 ff. This museum is engaged on pioneering ways of adult education. Since 1947 it has been

a central institution of the all-union society *Znanye* with its motto "Knowledge for the
People." It acquaints laymen with the scientific bases of production, and has since 1959
conducted courses for specialists in a two-year program of its People's University. The
curriculum is adapted to current needs; during the first year of the project, courses were
offered in Automation of Production, in the Economy and Organization of Production,
and in the Technology of Railway Transportation. All instruction is done by volunteers
among whom are famous scientists and Academicians. Not only specialists but lay
visitors too have opportunities for active participation. Special events are staged during
International Youth Festivals. *Museum*, XI, 4 (1958).

Slovenia uses its Museum of Technology in Ljubljana as a popular technological university. C. Lugowsk, described the "Museum of Technology in Warsaw" (*Museum*: 1966),
which maintains branches in the provinces and participates actively in the scientific
and technological education offered by the schools. Poland has made plans for a considerable expansion of a greater number of science museums which will be specially devoted to matters related to agriculture, public health, and other topics of primary rele
vance to citizens. Special events are planned for the five-hundredth anniversary of the
birth of Copernicus. All these museums stress science and technology in the present in
distinction to the traditional science museum, which used to illustrate the historical
development of science and technology.

[21] The Republic of Sculptors was described by Irena Jarosinska in *Poland Magazine* of
May 1968.

[22] Among research projects was the archaeological work done by the Cherson Museum
in the Ukraine. I. A. Antonova, "Field Research by the Cherson Museum," *Museum*, XIX, 3
(1966), pp. 172 ff. The Museum of Industrial Art in Prague staged an exhibition on New
Archaeological Finds in Czechoslovakia, which dealt with developments since the termination of World War II. *Museum*, XX, 1 (1968), pp. 96 ff.

[23] Tomás Bernard, *Experiencias en Museografía Historica* (Buenos Aires: Ediciones Ana-
conda, 1957).

Heloisa A. Torres, *Museums of Brazil* (Rio de Janeiro: Ministry of Foreign Affairs, Publication Office of the Cultural Division, 1953).

F. dos Santos Triguiros, *Museus; sua importância na educação de povo* (Rio de Janeiro:
Pongetti, 1956).

Junio C. Tella and T. Mejia Xesspe, *Historia de les museos nacionales del Peru* (Lima:
Museo Nacional de Antropologia y Arqueologia de la Universidad Nacional de San
Marcos, 1967).

A list of Latin American museums, with unavoidably brief but relevant notations, can be
found in a paper "Museums of the World" prepared for *Collier's Encyclopedia* by Stephan
F. Borhegyi and Irene A. Hanson. The mimeographed copy sent to me by courtesy of the
senior author was undated.

[24] *A Statistical Survey of Museums in the United States and Canada* (American Association of Museums, Washington, D.C., 1965) pp. 15, 16.

[25] *Museum News*, 40, 1. Joseph Allen Patterson was the director of the Association and
made the statements referred to as well as the following one.

While preparing a report on museum facilities for the Subcommittee on Economic
Progress of the Joint Economic Committee, Congress of the United States, the Association's Documentation Center developed information on museum capital construction,
and the Association's director, Mr. J. A. Patterson, wrote as follows:

"Since World War II there have been two distinct periods of museum construction.
From 1950 to 1956 an average of 8 new buildings and 8 new units (wings or other
building additions) were completed each year, with an average annual capital outlay
of $7.5 million per year for construction purposes. The only significant variation in this
period occurred in 1952 with construction slowed down due to manpower and material
shortages stemming from the Korean War. This deficit was made up in the following
year.

"Beginning in 1957, a new period of capital construction was introduced, with more
than twice as many new buildings being completed each year (an average of 16.3 new
buildings per year, 1957 – 1965). New units continued to be completed at about the
same rate, averaging 9 per year during the period. The average annual capital outlay
tripled, amounting to $21.54 million per year during the nine-year period." (*Museum
News*, 44, 9 (1966), p. 9.

[26] A. E. Parr, "Museums and Realities of Human Existence," *Museum News*, 45, 4
(1966), p. 25.

Compare Wilcomb E. Washburn, "Are Museums Necessary?" *Museum News*, 47, (1968).

[27]David W. Scott, *National Collection of Fine Arts* (Washington, D.C.: U.S. Government Printing Office, 1967). Originally known as National Gallery, the name was changed to "collection" when the present National Gallery was opened in the early forties, in consequence of Andrew Mellon's generous gift to the nation. Yet in the cosmos of the Smithsonian Institution, the arts continued their role "at the bottom of the hierarchy of 'natural history and objects of foreign and curious research,'" as John Walker, the present director of the National Gallery, wrote in 1944. The National Collection is devoted to the cultivation of American Art.

In September 1968 an enlarged Portrait Gallery was added. Its main theme and title are "This New Man/A Discourse in Portraits" — and is borrowed from St. John de Crevecoeur's *Letters from an American Farmer* of 1782 who raised the question "What then is the American, this new man?" The subtitles of the newly installed Portrait Gallery indicate the width and variability of America; there are Immigrants and Emigrés, Citizen-Lawmakers and Imagemakers, Pioneers in Space, Iconoclasts and Outcasts, etc.

The new recognition of art can be seen from a publication of 1968 which lists on 160 pages "Federal Funds and Services for the Arts." It was prepared by the National Endowment for the Arts, a part of the National Foundation of the Arts and the Humanities, established in recent years.

[28]John Walker and Guy Emerson wrote the Preface and Charles Seymour, Jr., supplied the Commentary to *Art Treasures for America*, The Samuel H. H. Kress Collections (London: The Phaidon Press, 1961). Mr. Kress was among the American collectors who during the decade following the second world war acquired works of art sold in America by European collectors whose names alone were a warranty of quality. Among them were the Prince of Liechtenstein, the Barberini and Alphons de Rothschild.

[29]L. J. Rowinski, "Alaskan Museums and the Centennial Year," *Western Museums Quarterly*, IV, 3 (September 1967.)

M. Graham Netting, "As the Dream Unfolds," *Carnegie Magazine*, XXXV, 9 (November 1961), pp. 293–297. Mr. Netting, for many years the director of the Carnegie Museum in Pittsburgh, wrote this paper on the occasion of the five-year anniversary of the Powder Mill Nature Reserve,

[30]Ralph H. Lewis, "Site Museums and National Parks," *Curator* II, 2 (1959).

[31]A. E. Parr, "Museums and Realities," p. 29.

[32]The Botanical Garden in St. Louis, Missouri, has a remarkable ecological exhibit in its "Climatron Greenhouse" with its geodesic dome. In his paper presented to the section of botanical sciences of the American Association for the Advancement of Science at one of its recent annual meetings, Warren H. Wagner, Jr., of the University of Michigan Botanical Gardens, expressed the view that students were shifting their interests away from molecules and reductionist problems toward questions of whole organisms and populations; and that ecology would be in the forefront of interest in the coming years. Compare William G. Conway (general director of the New York Zoological Society), "Zoos: Their Changing Roles," *Science*, 163 (January 3, 1969), pp. 48–52.

[33]Hermann H. Frese, *Anthropology and the Public; The Role of Museums* (Leiden: Rijksmuseum voor Volkenkunde-Brill, 1960). See especially Introduction and pp. 63 and 69, where Frese refers to the influence of sociology on anthropology.

[34]Stephan F. Borhegyi, "A New Role for Anthropology in Natural History Museums," paper delivered at the annual conference of the American Association of Museums in Orleans, 1968. The quoted sentence appeared on p. 7 of the mimeographed copy.

[35]Bruno Gebhard, "The Development of the Health Museum," *Museum News*, 43, 6 (1965). Dallas, Texas, and Hinsdale, Illinois, have active Health Museums. The Lankenau Hospital near Philadelphia had a small Health Museum a few years ago. Some of the large Science Museums offer exhibits related to the human body in conditions of health and of disease. As Dr. Gebhard pointed out, World's Fairs in the thirties (Chicago, 1933; New York, 1939) encouraged the establishment of the first Health Museum in the United States, in Cleveland, in 1940.

[36]*Exhibits in the Museum of History and Technology*. Prepared by the curators of the museum (Washington, D.C.: Smithsonian Press; 1968).

[37]Francis J. Dallett, "Export Extraordinary: The American Museum in Britain," *Wisconsin Magazine of History*, XLVI (1963).

[38]William N. Richard, "The William Penn Memorial Museum and Archives Building," *Curator*, X, 3 (1967).

[39]*Museum News*, 40, 1 (September 1961), p. 3.

[40]Natural Science for Youth Foundation, 114 East 30th Street, New York 10016. John

Ripley Forbes is president. Their directory for 1968 – 1969 lists on sixty-one pages Natural Science Centers for Youth in the United States and Canada. With regard to attendance in children's museums see the *Statistical Survey* made by the Association of American Museums, p. 16.

[41]Richard Grove, "A Progress Report: Federal Legislation and Museums," *Museum News, 44,* 6, (1966), p. 33.

Richard Grove, "Some Problems in Museum Education," in *Museums and Education* ed. Eric Larrabee (Washington, D.C.: Smithsonian Press, 1968), pp. 4 ff. Mr. Grove was at the time Museum Education Specialist of the U.S. Office of Education.

Compare Elena C. Van Meter, "A Continuing Look: Federal Aid to Museums," *Museum News, 45,* 10 (1967).

[42]A. E. Parr, "Museums and Realities," p. 25.

[43]Wilcomb E. Washburn, "Grandmotherology and Museology," *Curator* X, 1 (1967).

[44]Duncan F. Cameron, "Reaction and over-action to the Museum's Expanding Role in Education," *Museum News, 46,* 6 (1968), pp. 28, 29.

With regard to the difficulties of evaluating the educational benefits derived by children on the occasion of museum visits, compare Scarvia B. Anderson, "Noseprints on the Glass – or how do we evaluate Museum Programs?" in *Museums and Education,* ed. Eric Larrabee (Washington: Smithsonian Press, 1968). With regard to procedures which appear to promote results, see Appendix, pp. 235 – 240.

Compare also Michael Kennedy, "An Empirical Imperative: Education Must Become Museum Lexicon," *Museum News, 46,* 6 (February 1968). At the time of writing this paper, Mr. Kennedy was a public relations officer of Hofstra University; his theme is illustrated by the question, "If not educational adjuncts, then what are museums?" (p. 32).

[45]The first six exhibits of the Anacostia Museum were: ". . . a Mercury space capsule, a walkthrough reproduction of an 1890 Anacostia store, a little theater with closed-circuit television, shoebox collections on many natural science subjects, skeletons that can be disassembled and assembled, and a small zoo." (*Smithsonian Torch,* May 1967). During a Negro History Week tribute was paid at the Museum to outstanding Negro Americans.

The *Smithsonian Torch* published numerous references to the activities on the mall. (See especially the issues of April, May, and June 1967).

[46]Bernard J. Grad (architect) and Lothar P. Witteborg (educational consultant), "The New State Museum of New Jersey: Design and Exhibit Philosophy," *Curator,* V, 2 (1962), pp. 371 – 386.

[47]The Museum of Man in San Diego prides itself on its bilingual labels, English and Spanish.

I have in recent years heard of several plans for museums representing Negro culture, but I have so far not seen any completed. America's heritage from Africa has for years been held up by The Old Slave Mart Museum in Charleston, South Carolina, founded in 1937 and operated by The Miriam B. Wilson Foundation.

Allen H. Eaton, *Beauty for the Sighted and the Blind* (London: St. Martin's Press, 1959); especially chap. 9, "Museums and their Possible Service to Blind Persons," pp. 142 – 151.

Charles W. Stanford, "A Museum Gallery for the Blind," *Museum News, 44,* 10 (1966), describes a gallery in North Carolina, with labels and other verbal information provided in Braille. The project was financed by a private Foundation and by the Division of Vocational Rehabilitation of the U.S. Office of Education.

James L. Hazeltine, "Please Touch," *Museum News, 45,* 2 (1966), also deals with museum resources for the blind.

[48]The following statement came from Colonial Williamsburg: "Public education has been such an important and vital function of the American museum that frequently its research functions have been neglected. In the historical field, also, scholars have usually favored written documents over objects. Yet, the student of history, especially social history, should study books, manuscripts, and objects. Our leading museums in all fields should work with colleges and universities to advance the research function and make known the results through publication."

If the New York Hall of Science, the Science Museum which New York City is expected to finance, is established, it will receive a $1.5 million atomarium as a gift from the Atomic Energy Commission. While New York college students will be conducting nuclear research, the public will be offered displays offering information on nuclear matters. *Science, 163* (March 7, 1969), p. 1042.

[49]"University natural history museums have rather special educational opportunities which should not be diluted because of emphasis of repository and service function. . ."

"The plans of the University of Kansas Museum of Natural History . . . include the following: . . . field research and graduate education . . . in Latin America. . . . collaboration with the Department of Anthropology . . . collaboration with the School of Education. . . ." (From a letter received from the director in answer to my questionnaire.)

Another few examples may open wider vistas on research done by museums: The Museum of the University of Arizona in Flagstaff has studies under way in geology, biology and anthropology; the Idaho State University Museum has been publishing papers on its field work in anthropology, archaeology, vertebrate paleontology and ethnomicology; the collections of the University of Alaska Museum have grown rapidly in consequence of an increasing interest in the new state's history extending thousands of years into the past, and owing to the research activities in the Department of Anthropology and the Cooperative Wildlife Unit added to the University after the second world war. In Honolulu, Hawaii, the Bishop Museum houses the Pacific Science Information Center; the University of Missouri and the Corning Museum, New York, are jointly conducting excavations in Israel and are studying ancient techniques in glassmaking.

Compare G. Carroll Lindway, "Museums and Research in History and Technology," *Curator*, V, 3 (1962).

[50]Hugo Rodeck director of the University of Colorado Museum, "Our Philosophical Framework," *Museum News, 46*, 5 (1968).

[51]Impressions gained in an interview with Dr. Herbert Friedman, director of the Los Angeles County Museum of Natural History, and from a mimeographed description of his plans I received through his courtesy.

[52]The collections of the American Museum of Natural History comprise 800,000 birds, more than one million shells, two million anthropological specimens, twelve million insects and arachnids, and some 100,000 fossil vertebrates.

James A. Oliver, "The American Museum of Natural History celebrates a Century," *Museum News, 47*, 9 (1969), pp. 28 – 30. Remarks made by Mr. Oliver, the director of the museum, at its Centennial Convocation.

Geoffrey Hellman, *Bankers, Bones and Beetles*. The First Century of the American Museum of Natural History (Garden City, New York: Doubleday-Natural History Press for the American Museum of Natural History, 1969).

[53]S. Dillon Ripley, Jr., "A Perspective of the Smithsonian Program in Ecology," address to the National Parks Association on the occasion of a conference on *Conservation Education*, mimeographed paper received from the News Bureau of the Smithsonian Institution and dated March 15, 1966.

[54]"Programmes and Methods of Display in Natural History Museums," an international survey written by Ned J. Burns, Roger Heim, George Mack, Pierre Revillard, and Cecil Tose, *Museum*, VI, 3 (1953), pp. 143 – 193.

André Léveillé, *L'Activité des Musées Scientifiques et Techniques et des Planetaria* (Paris: I. C. O. M., 1953).

[55]R. F. Inger, "Expeditions as a Research Function of Natural History Museums," *Museum News, 45*, 2 (1966). The author was a staff member of the Field Museum of Natural History, Chicago. The cultural infiltration in prehistoric times in the Southern Maya area was studied by the Milwaukee Public Museum.

[56]Percy Madeira, Jr., *Men in Search of Man*, The first seventy-five years of the Museum of the University of Pennsylvania (Philadelphia: University of Pennsylvania Press, 1964).

[57]Stephan F. Borhegyi, *Description of Museum Specimens: A Brief Guide for Cataloguing*, read in a mimeographed account provided by the courtesy of the author.

S. F. Borhegyi, "Curatorial Neglect of Collections," *Museum News, 43*, 5 (January 1965). The paper offers directives for an Accession Sheet and for a Field Manual preceding the cataloguing.

[58]Neal FitsSimons, "Emergency Measures and Museums," *Museum News, 43*, 5 (February 1965). The author was on the staff of the Office of Civil Defense, Office of the Secretary of the Army.

An Emergency Planning Research Center for the study of the loss and damage to works of art in the United States in the case of a nuclear attack was established in 1962 at the Stanford Research Institute.

[59]The first Act for the Preservation of American Antiquities, passed in 1906, represented the principle that all federal lands and resources are held in trust for the people by the national government. The Act indicated an awakening of interest in conservation and extended the concept of conservation from natural resources to works of man.

[60]*Exploration of the Ways, Means and Values of Museum Communication with the View-*

ing Public. Symposium at the Museum of the City of New York. Principal speakers: Marshall McLuhan, Harley Parker, and Jacques Barzun (New York: Museum of the City of New York, 1969).

[61]John E. Anglim, "Exhibits Laboratories for All," *Museum News,* 44, 9 (1966), p. 9.

[62]*Museum News,* 46, 5 (January 1968).

[63]The Senate Bill, S.1310, was introduced by Senator J. W. Fulbright and was cosponsored by Senators Clinton P. Anderson and Leverett Saltonstall. The three senators are Regents of the Smithsonian Institution. In the House of Representatives the Bill is designated as H.R. 7315.

[64]The President's letter was reproduced in its original appearance in *Museum News,* 46, 7 (March 1968), p. 25.

[65]*America's Museums: The Belmont Report,* ed. Michael W. Robbins (Washington, D.C.: The American Association of Museums, 1969). The report is named after the estate in Maryland where the conferences leading up to the final statement were held.

[66]Archie F. Key, *Canada's Museum Explosion,* The First Hundred Years. Reprint obtained by the courtesy of the Canadian Museums Association; it bears no date of publication but appears to be up to date. Mr. Key was the Association's field director in 1966.

[67]George MacBeath, "Canada's Centennial Centre of Science and Technology," *Museum News,* 44, 5 (1966), pp. 27–31.

Centennial Centre of Science and Technology, *Annual Report 1967.* From a description of the purpose of the Centre, p. 2 of the Report:

"The Centre is endeavoring to create an atmosphere in which imagination is nurtured, inquiry is invited, challenge is encouraged and understanding increases naturally for visitors of all ages and backgrounds.

"The challenge to the Centre is to help dispel public confusion and apprehension about what science and technology are doing today, and to build confidence in their future course."

Compare John J. Brown, "A Survey of Technology In Canadian Museums," *Technology and Culture,* VI, 1 (1965).

[68]Vancouver City College, a vocational training college, offers a two-semester technical training course in preparation for lower-echelon museum positions. Several Canadian museums offer in-service training.

[69]Pedro Ramirez Vásquez, "The new gallery of the National Museum of History, Mexico D.F.," *Museum,* XV, 1 (Paris: 1962). The same issue contains articles on the Folk Art Museum and the Museum of Pedagogics.

Alejandro Caso, "Proposal for a Museum of Natural History for the National University of Mexico," *Curator,* IV, 4 (1961), pp. 341–351. Since the publication of this proposal, the *Museo de Flora y Fauna Nacional* has become a reality and is housed in several interconnecting hemispheric domes.

Ignacio Bernal, "The National Museum of Anthropology," *Museum,* XIX, 1 (Paris: 1966).

Ignacio Bernal, "The National Museum of Anthropology of Mexico, *Curator,* IX, 1 (1966).

Mimeographed communication received in the summer, 1968, from the office of the director general of the Museum of Anthropology.

Compare a paper on Regional Museums in Mexico in *Museum,* XI, 3 (Paris: 1958).

The Area of New Expectations (pp. 193–201)

[1]"The problems of museums in countries undergoing rapid change," *UNESCO Reports and Papers on Museums,* I, prepared by the Swiss National Committee of ICOM (Berne-Paris, 1964).

[2]"Museums and Anthropological Research in the Service of Development," *Report on an International Seminar in Tanzania* (Berlin-Tegel: German Foundation for Developing Countries in collaboration with the International Council of Museums and the Museums Association of Tropical Africa, 1968). The seminar dealt exclusively with African problems. Conference speakers stressed the importance of museums in Africa where the oldest evidence of human culture was found dating back to prehistoric times, and side by side with still existing isolated groups of game hunters in Tanzania who live in the manner of prehistoric people. See G. Smolla, "Stone Age Africa and the Cultural History of Mankind" and Freda Kretschmar, "Anthropological Research and Museums." Dr Kretschmar, a former professor of anthropology at the University of Delhi, pointed out that some three thousand human cultures are believed to have vanished from earth without leaving a record.

With regard to African museums see also *Museum,* XIII, 2 (1960), XIV, 1 (1961), XVI, 3 (1963), XVIII, 2 (1965), XX, 2 (1967).

"The Place and Role of Museums in the Plan for the Economic and Social Development of Africa," *Abbia*, No. 7 (Cameroon: October 1964).

"The role of museums in contemporary Africa," *Sixth Regional Seminar, Final Report* (Paris: UNESCO, 1964).

[3]M. Messalam Hassan, "The Science Museum, Cairo," *Museum*, XX, 3 (1967).

[4]With regard to museums in Israel compare *Museum*, XIX, 1 (1966); the entire issue XX, 1 (1967) was devoted to museums in Israel.

Gustav Faber, "Israel baut Museum-Pavilions," *Museumskunde*, 3rd series, II, 1 (Berlin: 1961), pp. 51–57.

Museum Guide for Israel (Jerusalem, Government Printers: 1964).

The Jerusalem Post, special edition on museums, Independence Day, May 1965.

[5]From a mimeographed communication received by the courtesy of the Israel Museum.

[6]The Israel Museum represents an international venture. The government of Israel contributed the land, and the United States government assisted in the establishment of a museum of international significance with a grant of funds. Contributions amounting to millions of dollars came from the Bronfman family in Canada and the R. H. Gottesman family and Foundation in New York. The sculpture garden is a gift of the American performer Billy Rose and was designed by the Japanese-American Isamu Noguchi; Frederick Kiesler, an artist of Austrian extraction, designed the Shrine of the Book jointly with the American architect Armond P. Bartos. The Israel-America Cultural Foundation has given generous assistance to museums as well as to other cultural enterprises in Israel.

[7]Jitendra Nath Basu, *Indian Museum Movement* (Calcutta: Benson, 1965).

Mohan Lal Nigam, *Fundamentals of Museology*. Foreword by Grace McCann Morley (Hyderabad: Navahind Prakashann, 1966).

[8]*Museum*, XVII, 3 (1964).

[9]"Urgent Ethnology and coordinated development of museums and scientific research." *Museum News*. 46, 4 (1967). Account of a conference in Baghdad in 1967.

[10]A provision of basic science museums, or units, for the developing countries is under consideration. William T. O'Dea, director general of the new Science Center in Toronto, Canada, takes a leading part in the project.

Compare: Frank Greeneway, Althin Torsten, W. T. O'Dea, and W. Stephen Thomas, *Science Museums in the Developing Countries* (Paris: ICOM, 1962).

[11]A Report to ICOM about the Center was rendered by Paul Philippot, assistant director of the Center, in 1965. Under ICOM's aegis a meeting on conservation took place in Russia in 1964. Transfer work on loess wall paintings from Central Asia had been successfully conducted in the laboratories of the Hermitage Museum. They were desalted by electrodialysis, and synthetic resin was used as fixative. Another example of recent restorations of ancient works of art occurred when mural paintings at Faras, in Sudanese Nubia, were discovered by a Polish excavation team from the Warsaw National Museum in Poland. UNESCO had launched a worldwide appeal for safeguarding the monuments of Egypt and Sudanese Nubia with the help of archaeological missions from different countries. The paintings at Faras are believed to have been buried under sand for centuries and to originate from the sixth century A.D. See *Museum*, XIX, 3 (1966), pp. 198 ff.

[12]*Museum* XIX, 4 (1966).

[13]Following upon the UNESCO Museum Seminar in India in 1966, the magazine *Cultural Forum* filled numbers 1 and 2 of its volume VIII with papers on Museology.

[14]A. J. Rose, "Le Palais de la Découverte," *Museum*, XX, 3 (1967) pp. 206 ff.

[15]At the International Center for the Study of the Preservation and Restoration of Cultural Property in Rome, to which reference was made before, an international faculty conducts a training program for specialists who are in short supply.

[16]A. A. Moss, "The Application of X-Rays, Gamma-Rays, Ultra-Violet and Infra-Red Rays to the study of Antiquities," *Handbook for Museum Curators* (London: Museum Association, 1954).

Abstracts of the Technical Literature of Archeology and the Fine Arts, ed. R. J. Gettens (London: International Institute for the Conservation of Museum Objects, c/o The National Gallery, Trafalgar Square).

M. J. Aitken, *Physics and Anthropology* (New York: Interscience Publishers, 1961).

Archaeological Chemistry: A Symposium, ed. Martin Levy (Philadelphia: University of Pennsylvania Press, 1967).

Experiments related to the dating of works of art through their natural radioactivity were reported by the investigator Bernard Keisch, of the Mellon Institute in Pittsburgh, *Science*, 160 (April 26, 1968), pp. 413–415.

A growing literature exists on such and related topics, which leads beyond the framework of this book.

[17]The science laboratories attached to the Soviet Ministry of Culture were established in Moscow in 1958 and are divided into seven sections. They deal with chemical, physical, and biological processes; with paintings in tempera and oil; with sculpture and applied arts. The Ministry holds examinations for candidates for positions in the laboratories and confers on them the title of Restorers. See Ivan Gorvine, "The Restoration of Works of Art in the U.S.S.R.," *Museum*, XX, 2 (1967).

For a comparison of problems in preservation under different climatic conditions, compare P. Coremans, "Preservation of the Cultural Heritage in Tropical Africa," *Museum*, XVIII, 3 (1965).

Charles P. Parkhurst, director of the Allen Art Museum at Oberlin College, advocates a cooperative solution of problems of conservation in small museums. In 1961 the cost for basic laboratory equipment, salaries, and materials approached the sum of $20,000. Parkhurst suggests that the expense for conservation should not exceed 10 percent of the operational budget of an institution. See his paper "Museum Conservation: A Cooperative Solution," *Museum News*, 40, 5 (January 1962), pp. 34 ff.

[18]Freda Kretschmar, "Anthropological Research and Museums," *International Seminar in Tanzania*, October 1968 (Berlin-Tegel: German Foundation for Developing Countries, 1968), II, p. 3.

[19]Experiments on "Thermoluminescence" have been carried on at the Research Laboratory of the University of Oxford.

[20]A study is being conducted at the Mellon Institute in Pittsburgh; it is financed by the National Gallery and the Atomic Energy Commission.

[21]Kenze Toishi, "Characteristic Features of Eastern Bronze Buddhas as shown by Gamma Radiography," *Museum*, XI, 4 (1958).

[22]Michael Brawne, *The New Museum. Architecture and Display* (New York: Praeger, 1966). Brawne suggests that museums borrowed lighting styles from industry. He offers a good summary of lighting problems in museums.

Robert L. Feller, "Control of Deteriorating Effects of Light upon Museum Objects," *Museum*, XVII, 2 (1964).

Light activates atoms and molecules and stimulates chemical changes. The shorter the wavelength, the greater the energy. The fading and embrittlement of materials are slowed up with a decrease of oxygen in the air; evacuated chambers are used on occasion.

Although the ancient Greeks and collectors in the Middle Ages were unaware of these circumstances, they did provide some protection for works of art. Shutters were added to valuable paintings, which were shut at times. Pausanias wrote about pitch being used as a coating of votive shields in Athens to prevent corrosion from rust. In the Parthenon vats of oil were placed at the feet of the *Athena Parthenos* by Phidias to protect it against the dryness of the atmosphere. Germain Bazin, *The Museum Age* (New York: Universe Books, 1967), reported about a Conservation Center in Naples in the seventeenth century.

[23]"Museums Today," *Science*, 161 (August 9, 1969), pp. 548–551. The participants of the Symposium were Sidney R. Galler, assistant secretary (science) of the Smithsonian Institution, James A. Oliver, director of the American Museum of Natural History, New York, H. Radclyffe Roberts, director of the Academy of Natural Sciences of Philadelphia, Herbert Friedmann, director of the Los Angeles County Museum of Natural History, and Donald F. Squires, deputy director of the Museum of Natural History, Smithsonian Institution.

[24]Wilcomb E. Washburn, "Are Museums Necessary?" *Museum News*, 47 (1968), in the column "Opinion."

The *Smithsonian Torch* of May 1967 reported that the sixty million items of the Smithsonian Institution are to be catalogued by computers.

Compare *Museum News*, 46, 6 (1968), p. 6:

"Fifteen museums in New York City and one in Washington, D.C., have announced plans to set up the first central archive of our nation's principal art resources. To be known as the Museum Computer Network, the archive would be maintained in computerized form at a headquarters location from which stored information would be retrieved and distributed on request over a network of terminals placed in museums, libraries, and other educational institutions. The archive will at first record the public collections of the New York City and Washington, D.C. areas and eventually be extended to cover the entire country."

[25]Virginia Burton, "Computers Confront the Curator," *Metropolitan Bulletin of Art*, XXVI, 1 (1967). Carl Dauterman, associate curator of Western decorative arts at the Metropolitan Museum of Art, who uses an IBM System/360 Model 30, described his work on Sèvres

porcelain at a conference held at the museum jointly with the International Business Machines Corporation in April 1968.

[26]Institute for Communication Research, Stanford University. Representatives of the Institute distributed leaflets containing this information at the Smithsonian Conference on Museums, November 20–21, 1968.

Compare George W. Pierson's views, "The Case against the Computer in the Humanities" in *Computers for the Humanities*, a record of a Yale Conference (New Haven: Yale University Press, 1965). He recognizes the value of computers where quantification is needed; in recording iconographic details, and the geographical or chronological distribution of objects, but expresses himself against atomized information and a desensitizing of man by a lack of value systems.

6. A Twelve-Point Program For Museum Renewal (pp. 203–219)

[1]Dr Grace Morley, the first director of UNESCO's Division of Museums, at the time of the agency's founding, wrote about the need for a more philosophical consideration of the aims and tendencies in museums. "Museums Today and Tomorrow," *Museum*, X, 3 (1957), p. 240.

[1]"Museums Today," account of a symposium at the annual meeting of the American Association for the Advancement of Science, December 1967, *Science, 161* (August 9, 1968). See especially "The computer comes to the aid of museums," by Donald F. Squires, pp. 550–551.

Wilcomb E. Washburn, "Are Museums Necessary?" *Museum News, 47* (1968), in the column "Opinion."

[2]The visitor explosion in the National Parks equals if not surpasses that in museums. 300 million visits are expected by 1977. The administrators of the National Parks are beginning to change their policy and lay less emphasis on travel statistics than on the quality of the experience – on bringing man and his environment into harmony. See *Science, 162* (October 18, 1968), p. 307. Letter from Douglas W. Scott, Department of Forestry, University of Michigan, Ann Arbor.

[3]Fundamentally there appear to be two problem areas that await further exploration by neurophysiologists and psychologists specializing in visual perception and in processes of human learning:

(a) One problem area is related to the stimulation of the brain of a person exposed to objects, irrespective of their appearance and meaning, and as distinguished from disembodied, symbolic communication, mainly in the form of language. To become visible, objects have to be struck by light, and the electromagnetic energy of light waves projected on the retina of the eye appears to have a stimulating effect on the brain.

(b) The other problem area concerns the effects of a message expressed by a number of objects. In this context the physical properties of the objects represent only a part of the stimulus; the interpretation of the message by the brain provides additional stimulation. Are these two sources of stimulation related to one another? How are they related? Are there great differences in the reactions of different individuals? Are some people more "object-prone" than others?

Museums have no exclusive claim to exposing people to objects of a variety of physical properties as well as of relevance to the beholders. Our daily environments of domestic and professional character include objects and the bodies of organisms; there are nature areas and cityscapes, good, bad, or indifferent. Yet museums could make it their business to act as optimal visual stimulators. It is easier to rebuild an exhibit hall than a city block. In this manner museums could provide people with a gratifying experience comparable with that of music; they would offer relief in the visually monotonous or depressing environment in which so many of us live.

Compare:

Conrad G. Mueller, *Sensory Psychology* (Englewood Cliffs, N.J.: Prentice-Hall, 1965).

Duane P. Schultz, *Sensory Restriction, Effects on Behavior* (New York-London:Academic Press, 1965).

Progress in Physiological Psychology, eds. Eliot Stellar and James M. Sprague (New York-London: Academic Press, 1966), vol. I.

None of these books provides answers to the raised questions, but all of them stimulate thinking.

[4]Kenneth E. Boulding, "The Role of the Museum in the Propagation of Developed Images," *Technology and Culture, 7,* 1 (1966), pp. 64–66.

[5]G. G. Simpson, *The Meaning of Evolution* (New York: Mentor Books, 1949). G. G. Simpson, "Naturalistic Ethics and the Social Sciences," *American Psychologist, 21* (1966), pp. 26–36.

Bentley Glass, *Science and Ethical Values* (Chapel Hill: University of North Carolina Press, 1965).

[6]See, for example, Herman Kahn and Anthony J. Wiener, *The Year 2000* (New York: Macmillan, 1967).

[7]For many years André Malreaux conducted a crusade against Western man's ways of exhibiting works of art, without coherence of either content or style, and crowded together on walls with people walking by them. He contrasted our ways with those of the Orient, where a single work of art is shown in isolation from conflicting experiences. *The Voices of Silence*, translated by Stuart Gilbert (New York: Doubleday, 1953).

Compare a modern sociologist's views about the homelessness of the visual arts in our society, where they are neither a mass entertainment nor an enhancement of class or group pride. He wrote of the "uncreative curiosity" of many visitors of art museums. Rudolph E. Morris, "The Art Museum as a Community Center," *Museum News*, 43, 5 (January 1965), esp. pp. 28, 30.

[8]LaBarre Weston, *The Human Animal* (Chicago: Chicago University Press, 1954). Man has been facilitating his lot on earth by inventing devices magnifying his powers, contrary to other creatures, which very gradually undergo bodily changes. A microscope is a very advanced amplifier of the eye; an automobile tremendously amplifies the speed of human limbs. Other amplifiers are related to mental work.

[9]The role of the curator in maintaining standards of knowledge, which some administrators and educators tend to downgrade, was stressed by Wilcomb E. Washburn in his article "Grandmotherology and Museology," *Curator*, X, 1 (1967). On page 45 he wrote: "The emergence of a powerful new administrative element has led to a further confusion of aim and purpose in the museum world."

The multiplicity of tasks and roles of a curator, and the lack of criteria in selecting personnel, were discussed by Donald F. Squires, "Schizophrenia: The Plight of the Natural History Curator," *Museum News*, 48, 7 (1969), pp. 18 –21.

Organization men having to contend with problems on several fronts may draw comfort from the statement made by Joseph Henry, the first Secretary of the Smithsonian Institution, that votes ought to be weighed, not counted. Henry spoke up boldly against the control of science by amateurs and politicians. Wilcomb E. Washburn, "The Influence of the Smithsonian Institution on Intellectual Life in Mid-Nineteenth Century Washington," *Records of the Columbia Historical Society* (1966); see especially pp. 119 and 121.

[10]Warren G. Dennis, *Changing Organizations* (New York: McGraw-Hill, 1966).

[11]The low achievement standards of graduates of public schools in the United States became once again evident from results of The Armed Forces Qualifying Test. The estimated percent of illiteracy in the population over fourteen years old in 1960 was 2.9 for New York and stood at 5.3 in Louisiana. Average draftee failures in the notoriously easy army tests amounted in 1965 to 10.1 percent in the national levels.

According to an estimate of the U.S. Office of Education, published in the *New York Times*, October 11, 1969, p. H 35, twenty-four million Americans aged eighteen and older are functionally illiterate. One million people are participating in courses in basic skills.

[12]Dr. Hugo Rodeck, director of the University of Colorado Museum, wrote in a bulletin issued by the museum: "The presence of comprehensive and interpretive exhibits on an all-day, every-day basis on the campus offers the university student body the opportunity to gain some understanding of aspects of our world which might otherwise remain eternally opaque."

[13]*America's Museums: The Belmont Report*, ed. Michael W. Robbins (Washington, D.C.: The American Association of Museums, 1969), p. viii.

[14]The statement made by René Dubos was published as a "Letter to the Editor," *Science, 154* (November 4, 1966), p. 595.

Pleas for a professional critique of exhibits were made repeatedly. See Thomas W. Leavitt, "Toward a Standard of Excellence; the nature and purpose of Exhibit Reviews," *Technology and Culture*, 9, 1. (1968). The conflicting views of museum workers with regard to the reviewing of exhibits are illustrated by "Letters" to *Museum News* (December 8 and April 10, 1968).

[15]Training facilities are listed by William A. Burns, *Your Future in Museums* (New York: Rosen Press, 1967).

[16]Among my most gratifying experiences were sessions at The Henry Francis Winterthur Museum-The University of Delaware, arranged by Mr. Craig Gilborn, of the Education Division of the museum.

[17]". . . Unless the Builder also Grows . . .," *AAUW Journal* (Washington, D.C., January 1968), p. 52. Before assuming her position as president of Cedar Crest College, Allen-

town, Pennsylvania, Dr. Pauline Tompkins was general director of the Association of American University Women.

[18]THIS IS

   . . . a recreation center

   . . . a place to learn

   . . . a collector's paradise

   . . . a research laboratory

   . . . a craftsman's mecca

   . . . a "World's Fair" of art

THIS is YOUR family's PERSONAL Museum

of Fine Arts

Walter Muir Whitehill, *Independent Historic Societies: An enquiry into their research and public functions, and their financial future* (Boston: The Boston Athenaeum; distributed by the Harvard University Press, 1962), p. 539, quoting a publication of the Boston Museum of Fine Arts.

Appendix

The Term "Museum" and Some Other Terms of Similar Meaning

(pp. 221 – 225)

[1]Pauly's *Real-Encyclopädie der Classischen Altertumswissenschaft*, ed. G. Wissowa. Vol. XVI, pp. 797 ff., newly edited by Wilhelm Kroll (Stuttgart: Metzler, 1933).

Wilamowitz-Möllendorf "Antigonus von Karystos," *Philologische Untersuchungen*, vol. IV (Berlin: 1881).

The Muses of Greek mythology were the daughters of Zeus who by their dance and song helped men to forget sorrow and anxiety. Their birth was a memorial to the new order which their father, through his conquest of the Titans, had brought into the world. They were credited with creative imagination, with infinite memory, with which they could succor mortals, and with foresight. The remembrance of glorious events of the past, folk art, music, and poetry, gentle gaiety, and harmony were associated with the Muses. P. Decharme, *Mythologie de la Grèce Antique* (Paris: Garnier, 1886).

[2]The Museum at Alexandria was a foundation of the Ptolemies in the later part of the third century B.C. and existed up to the fourth century A.D.

Pauly-Wissowa, *Real-Encyclopädie*, pp. 801 – 821.

G. F. C. Parthey, *Das Alexandrinische Museum* (Berlin: Nicola, 1838).

T. Schreiber, "Alex. Toreutik," *Abhandlungen der Kgl. Sächsischen Gesellschaft der Wissenschaften* (1894).

Claire Preaux, "Alexandria under the Ptolemies," in *Cities of Destiny*, ed. by Arnold Toynbee (New York: McGraw-Hill, 1967).

Concerning the activities of the Attalids as collectors in general see E. V. Hansen, *The Attalids of Pergamon* (Ithaca: Cornell University Press, 1947).

[3]The brief list of these examples could no doubt be continued into even more recent years. The use of the term "museum" for a compilation of writings does not appear to be dated.

[4]The term "encyclopaedia" is believed to have been used in England for the first time in Sir Thomas Elyot's *Latin Dictionary* of 1531, where it is explained as the learning that comprehends all liberal sciences and studies. Chamber's *Enciclopaedia* goes back to 1728, and the French *Encyclopédie* connected with the famous "Encyclopédistes."

[5]The distinction between "Museum" and "Gallery" seems to be more customary in Great Britain than in other countries.

[6]In his account in *The New Atlantis* (London, 1660, pp. 61 – 71) of an imagined ideal community, F. Bacon described the monarch's palace, and the "Gallery" and "Closet" in that palace. According to this description there were in the long and large gallery "statues of all the prime inventors in many past ages (of paper, glass, gunpowder)," discoverers of lands and artists, physicists, mathematicians, and doctors. After having passed through the gallery, the visitor was told by his guide that now his fantasy would be entertained by being shown various rarities and was led into a little closet at the end of the gallery where he saw, among other things, precious magic stones, sympathetical powder, and purified ice.

Compare Appendix, pp. 245, 242: extracts from Ray's and Misson's descriptions of the Medici collection at Florence.

[7]With respect to the collection on Castle Ambras, Tyrol, the following reference was made ". . . und eine schöne lange galeria so zu beiden Seiten Fenster hat, hoch, und gar licht

ist." M. Zeiller, *Itinerarium Germaniae* (Reyssbuch durch Hoch- and Nider Teutschland . . . und benachbarte Lande) (Strassburg, 1632), p. 349.

[8]". . . per trattenersi a passeggio i personaggi nelle corti, le proportioni loro si cavano dalle Loggie; ma sòno alquanquanto meno aperte di esse . . . si sono introdotto nelle case di molti . . . Gentilhuomini, e persone virtuose Il far raccolte, e studij di . . . Marmi, e Bronzi, e Medaglie . . ." Scamozzi, *L'Idea della Architettura Universale* (Venice, 1615), vol. I, p. 305.

[9]Vitruvius, *De Architectura* (Lugd., 1586), pp. 14, 228, 236.

[10]Pliny, *Natural History*, XXXV. ii. 4, trans. E. Rackham (Cambridge: Harvard University Press; London: Heinemann, 1952) ("And in the midst of all this, people tapestry the walls of their picture-galleries with old pictures").

E. Bonnaffé, *Les Collectionneurs de l'Ancienne Rome* (Paris: Aubry, 1867), pp. 53 ff.

L. Julius, "Die Gemälde des Polygnot in der Pinakothek der Propyläen," *Mitteilungen des Archaeologischen Institutes* (Athens, 1887).

Compare on the subject of the "gallery" Frimmel's *Handbuch der* Gemäldekunde (Leipzig: Weber, 1904), pp. 271 ff.

[11]M. F. L. Hervey, *The Life, Correspondence and Collections of Thomas Howard, Earl of Arundel* (Cambridge: Cambridge University Press, 1921), p. 62.

[12]B. Facius, *De Viris illustribus*, ed. Mehus (Florence, 1745), pp. 46, 48.

[13]G. G. Leibnitz, *Protogaea, sive de Prima Facie Telluris et Antiquissimae Historiae Vestigiis . . . Dissertatio.* (Göttingen, 1749), para. XXXV, p. 63.

Compare Appendix, p. 243, extracts from Browne's account of the imperial collections in Vienna in the seventeenth century.

[14]"Guarda robba del Gran Duca piena di preziosi, e ricchi arnesi, di gran numero di tavole dipinte da' migliori maestri . . ." M. F. Bocchi, *Le Bellezze della citta di Firenze*, ed. M. G. Cinelli (Florence. 1677), p. 95 (first published in 1591).

Compare the inventory made after her death in 1593 of the personal property of Queen Elisabeth of France; published as No. 12154 in the *Jahrbuch der Sammlungen des . . . Kaiserhauses*, vol. XV (1855).

[15]Commentary to the *Praetorian Edict*, 31st Book, quoted by Pauly-Wissowa, *Real-Encyclopädie*, earlier in this chapter.

Compare Appendix, p. 244: an extract from Evelyn's seventeenth-century account of the Medici collection in Florence.

[17]L. Beger, *Thesaurus Brandenburgicus* (Colonlae Marchicae, 1696 –1701).

L. Beger, *Thesaurus ex Thesauro Palatino Selectus . . .* (Heidelberg, 1685).

[18]C. F. Neickelius, *Museographia*, ed. D. J. Tanold (Leipzig, 1727), p. 409.

Ways and Means of Acquiring Specimens (pp. 225 – 235)

[1]A letter from Philip II of Spain to Titan:

"Amado nuestro vuestra carta de vij de Março he recibido y visto por ella como tencis acabadas algunas pinturas que nos he mandado hazer de que he holgado mucho y os tengo en seruicio el cuydado y diligencia que en ello aueys usado. Bien quisiera que me huuierades scripto particularmente quales eran estas pinturas que teneis acabadas y pues el daño que recibio el Adonis se le hizo aqui quando lo descogieron para verle. Y agora las pinturas que me embiaredes estaran libres de correr este peligro yo os encargo mucho que luego en recibiendo esta embolnays muy bien las pinturas que tumieredes acabadas de manera que se puedan traer sin que reciban daño en el camino y las entregueys al Embaxador Francisco de Vargas a quien yo scriuo y mando que con el primer correo que viniere si ser pudiere, o por la mejor via y manera que le paresciere me las embie con la mayor breuedad que sea posible. Vos hareys de manera que por lo que se tumiere de hazer de vuestra parte no se difiera este que en ello me hareys mucho seruicio.

"De lo que toca a vuestras cosas me auisareys si se han complido porque a no hauesse hecho yn mandare scriuir al Duque Dalua de manera que se cumplan.

"De Brusselas a iiij° de Mayo de M.D.L.VJ.

"Yo El Rey."

The original letter is kept in the archives of Simanca and is filed as item Leg° 1498, f° 107, among the documents Sria de Estado. Published by J. A. Crowe and G. B. Cavalcaselle, *The Life and Times of Titian* (London: Murray, 1881), vol. II, p. 511.

[2]Carl Justi, *Miscellaneen aus Drei Jahrhunderten Spanischen Kunstlebens* (Berlin: Grote, 1908), vol. II, pp. 301 ff.

[3]*The Mirrour of true nobility and gentility, being the Life of Nicolaus Claudius Fabricius, Lord of Peiresc, called Peireskius*, englished by W. Rand (London, 1656).

[4]The son of the farmer who happened to dig up the *Laocoön* and who sold the statue to the Pope received "*militiam curialis officii lucrosam.*" A man from whom the Vatican acquired another valuable ancient statue, *Ariadne*, was granted exemption from tax payable for keeping sheep and goats for a period of four years, and derived from this privilege a benefit of about 700 gold skudi. J. Burckhardt, "Die Sammler," ed. H. Wölfflin, *Beiträge zur Kunstgeschichte, Collected Works* (Stuttgart: Deutsche Verlagsanstalt, 1930), vol. 12, p. 336.

The famous goldsmith Cellini as a young man stayed for some time in Rome, in the early sixteenth century. In his *Autobiography* he described how he used to spend his leisure time. Plague was rampant, and people died in great numbers. To overcome his fear of what was happening around him, the young artist sought relief in visiting the ancient buildings, copying them in wax and pencil, and shooting the pigeons housing in the ruins. "My gun was also the cause of my making acquaintance with certain hunters after curiosities, who followed in the track of those Lombard peasants who used to come to Rome to till the vineyards at the proper season. While digging the ground they frequently turned up antique medals, agates, chrysoprases, cornelians and cameos; also sometimes jewels. . . . The peasants used to sell things of this sort to the traders for a mere trifle; and I very often, when I met them, paid the latter several times as many golden crowns as they had given giulios for some object. Independently of the profit I made by this traffic, which was at least tenfold, it brought me also into agreeable relations with nearly all the cardinals of Rome." J. A. Symonds, *The Autobiography of Benvenuto Cellini*, The Harvard Classics (New York: Collier & Son, 1910), pp. 51, 52.

[5]J. Burckhardt's German text, in which he quoted a passage from Marin Sanudo's *Diari*, runs as follows: "Kardinal Domenico Grimani, als er 1505 in Rom die Gesandten seines Heimatstaates bewirtete, zeigte ihnen eine grosse Menge von Marmorfiguren und viele andere antike Sachen, welche alle in seiner Vigna unter der Erde gefunden worden waren, als man für den Bau seines Palastes die Fundamente grub." "Die Sammler," *Collected Works*, vol. 12, p. 335, footnote 4.

[6]G. Gronau, "Alfons d'Este und Tizian," *Jahrbuch der Kunsthistorischen Sammlungen in Wien*, New Series (1928).

M. Boschini, *La Carta del Navegar (in l'alto Mar de la Pitura)*, an imaginary dialogue between a Venetian senator and a professor of art (Venice, 1660), p. 169.

[7]L. Cust, "Notes on the Collections Formed by Thomas Howard, Earl of Arundel and Surrey," *The Burlington Magazine*, vol. XIX (1911), pp. 278 –286; vol. XX (1911), pp. 97 – 100; vol. XX (1912), pp. 233 –236 and 341 –343.

Mary F. S. Hervey, *The Life, Correspondence and Collections of Thomas Howard, Earl of Arundel* (Cambridge: Cambridge University Press, 1921), pp. 266 –279.

The dangers to personal safety which the traveler-collector sometimes had to face may be illustrated by the experiences of Mr. Petty, who acted as agent and buyer on behalf of the Earl of Arundel and the Duke of Buckingham. Returning from Samos, he narrowly escaped with his life in a great storm, but lost all his curios and was imprisoned for a spy. After obtaining his liberty, he pursued his researches.

Horace Walpole, *Anecdotes of Painting in England*, collected by George Vertue and edited by F. J. Dallaway (London, 1826).

[8]Lord Elgin's "marbles" aroused a controversy in England; some people criticized his manner of acquisition, and others questioned the authenticity of the sculptures. In the end Parliament voted in favor of purchasing the unique statuary for £ 35,000. Lord Elgin's costs had amounted to £ 51,000, without considering the interest on this sum that would have accrued.

Adolf Michaelis, *Ancient Marbles of Britain*, trans. C. A. M. Fennell (Cambridge: Cambridge University Press, 1882), pp. 133 ff.

A. H. Smith, "Lord Elgin and his Collection," *Journal of Hellenic Studies*, vol. 36, Second Part (1916), pp. 163 –372.

[9]Pausanias's *Description of Greece*, ed. J. G. Frazer (London: Macmillian, 1898), Book IX. xxxiii, 6; Book X. vii, 1; Book VIII. xlvi, 2.

Cicero, *The Verrine Orations*, trans. L. H. G. Greenwood, The Loeb Classical Library (Cambridge: Harvard University Press; London: Heinemann, 1953).

L. Völkel, *Die Wegführung von Kunstwerken aus eroberten Ländern nach Rom* (Leipzig, 1798).

F. K. L. Sickler, *Geschichte der Wegnahme und Abführung verzüglicher Kunstwerke aus den eroberten Ländern in die Länder der Sieger* (Gotha, 1803).

Wilhem Treue, *Art Plunder, The fate of works of art in war, revolution and peace*, trans. Basil Creighton (London: Methuen, 1960).

[10]F. Palermo, *Narrazioni e Documenti sulla storia del regno di Napoli* . . . (1522–1667), (Naples: Archivo Storico Italiano, 1842).

Boschini, *La Carta del Navegar* . . . , pp. 170–171.

Arte en España (October 1876).

Carl Justi, *Miscellaneen*, p. 194.

[11]C. Saunier, *Les Conquêtes Artistiques de la Révolution et de l'Empire; reprises et abandons des allies en 1815 et leurs conséquences sur les musées d'Europe* (Paris: Laurens, 1902). Passages from Saunier are in the Appendix, pp. 249, 250.

M. E. Müntz, "Les annexions de collections d'art . . . et leurs rôle dans les relations internationales, principalement pendant la Révolution Française," *Revue d'Histoire Diplomatique* (Paris, 1894–1896), vol. VIII, pp. 481–497; vol. IX, pp. 375–393; vol. X, pp. 481–508.

Dorothy McKay Quynn, "The Art Confiscations of the Napoleonic Wars," *American Historical Review*, vol. L, 3 (1945), pp. 437–460.

Frenchmen in positions of authority protested against Napoleon's plunder. The appeal of the Secretary of the Académie des Beaux-Arts to General Miranda was of little avail, but it represents a document of fine humanity. Quatremère de Quincy warned the general of the consequences of his actions. He pointed out that it would be more becoming to France to investigate in a scholarly fashion the ancient ruins on its own soil. Quatremère de Quincy, *Lettres au général Miranda sur le préjudice qu'occasionnerait aux arts et à la science le deplacement des monuments de l'art de l'Italie* (Paris, 1796).

[12]W. Buchanan, *Memoirs of Painting; with a chronological history of the importation of pictures by great masters into England since the French Revolution* (London: Ackermann, 1824).

[13]E. K. G. Wellington, *A description and historical catalogue of the collection of paintings and sculpture at Apsley House* (London, 1901).

The collection contains pictures which fell as booty to the Duke of Wellington in the course of a battle, at Vittoria, with Joseph Bonaparte on his retreat from Spain. After the Peninsular War the Duke wished to return to Spain the art treasures which by accident had come into his possession, but the King of Spain asked the Duke to keep the paintings in memory of the aid given to Spain by England. (In 1945 Apsley House together with its precious artistic contents was presented by the Wellington family to the English nation.)

[14]*Egerton MS.*, No. 1636 of the collection of manuscripts, British Museum.

G. F. Waagen, *Treasures of Art in Great Britain*, being an account of the chief collections of pictures, drawings, sculptures, etc. (London: Graves, 1854), p. 13.

[15]O. Granberg, *Collection de Tableaux de Christine de Suède* (Stockholm, 1897).

Ferdinand Boyer, "Les Antiques de Christine de Suède à Rome," *Revue Archéologique*, 35 (1932).

[16]The Flemish, Dutch, and German paintings owned by Orleans were also sold in London, in 1792. Compare *The Great Historic Galleries of England*, ed. Lord Ronald Gower (London: Sampson Low, 1880–1885).

[17]*Cultura Española* (Madrid, 1907), vol. V. Compare British Museum, "*A Guide to the Mediaeval Room*" (1907), p. 236, Fig. 171.

[18]L. Mehus, *Kyriaci Anconitani Itenerarium* (Florence, 1742).

[19]H. Florke, *Studien zur Niederlandischen Kunst- und Kulturgeschichte* (Leipzig 1908), p. 203.

Algernon Graves, *Art Sales, From Early in the XVIII Century to Early in the Twentieth Century* (London: Graves, 1918–1921).

Maurice Rheims, *Art on the Market*, Thirty-five centuries of collecting and collectors from Midas to Paul Getty, trans. David Pryce-Jones (London: Weidenfeld & Nicholson, 1961).

Germain Seligman, *Merchants of Art* (New York: Appleton-Crofts, 1961), based on the personal reminiscences of a member of a well-known family of art dealers, mainly with regard to recent decades.

The market value of objects of art varied not only from period to period but from one locality to another. "Drawings, paintings and sculpture . . . are twice as expensive in Warsaw as in France, Italy and Germany," wrote a traveler toward the end of the eighteenth century. (*Reise eines Livländers* (Berlin, 1795), vol. II, p. 108, quoted by Holst, "Sammlertum und Kunstwanderung in Ostdeutschland und den benachbarten Ländern bis 1800," *Jahrbuch der Preussischen Sammlungen* (1939).

[20]Carl Justi, "Rubens und der Cardinal Infante Ferdinand," in *Miscellaneen*, vol. II.

[21]Hervey, *Arundel*, p. 270.

[22]Alexander Pope, *Moral Essays*, Ep. Iv, quoted by D. Murray, *Museums; their History and their use* (Glasgow: MacLehose, 1904), vol. I, p. 137.

Compare with this chapter the account of the fate of European museums during the Second World War, pp. 163.

See also:

"Tentative list of Jewish Cultural Treasures in axis-occupied countries, ed. Commission on European Jewish Cultural Reconstruction," *Jewish Social Studies*, Supplement to vol. VIII, 1 (New York, 1946).

A. Noblecourt, *Protection of Cultural Property in the Event of Armed Conflict*, Museums and Monuments VIII (Paris: UNESCO, 1958).

Museums and Children, or Children's Museums (pp. 235 – 240)

[1]My first contacts with children occurred at the time of my apprenticeship at the State Museums in Berlin. In those years "educational work" was less highly regarded than scholarship in European museums and was delegated to apprentices. My failure in establishing communication with school groups stirred my interest in communication; I was unwilling to believe that there were no ways of communicating with laymen in the setting of an exhibition hall. Opportunities for testing theories came years later in England, while I worked at the Museum of Archaeology and Anthropology of the University of Cambridge in England. Although the museum was a part of the University's Department of Archaeology and Anthropology and served first of all students of the Department, the public was admitted. Without participating in my experimental work, the Museum allowed me to use their premises and collections for my studies.

Since schoolchildren are more easily available for group experiments than adults, and can be identified as homogeneous populations, I concentrated on working with them. Compare note 7 with regard to later experimental work.

[2]Alma S. Wittlin, "Junior Museums at the Crossroads: Forward to a New Era of Creativity or Backward to Obsoleteness," *Curator*, VI, 1 (1963).

For a comparison of different points of view see

Helen V. Fisher, "Children's Museums: A Definition and a Credo," *Curator*, III, 2 (1960).

A. E. Parr, "Why Children's Museums?" *Curator*, III, 3 (1960).

Molly Harrison, *Changing Museums: their Use and Misuse* (London: Longman, 1967).

Barbara R. Winstanley, *Children and Museums* (Oxford: Blackwell, 1967).

Helen V. Fisher is a leading American expert on Children's Museums so are Molly Harrison and Barbara R. Winstanley in England. Dr A. E. Parr is the former director of the American Museum of Natural History, New York; his interests are encyclopedic.

Museum School Service, prepared by The Group for Elementary Services in Museums and edited by Francis Cheetham (London: Museums Association, 1967).

E. E. Herff, *Museen im Dienst der Schule* (Bad Godesberg: Verlag Wissenschaftliches Archiv, 1967).

Ornul Vorren, *Museet og Skolen* (Tromso: Universitetsforlag, 1967).

[3]The Brooklyn Children's Museum, New York, has started on its second half century. The Children's Museum in Jamaica Plain in Boston, Massachusetts, is another veteran that in recent years began a new life-cycle.

[4]Compare Alma S. Wittlin, "Scientific Literacy Begins in the Elementary School," *Science Education, 47*, 4 (1963); especially p. 4 and Bibliography.

[5]Not too long ago I saw a crowd of preschoolers from a Head-Start Project in a Museum of Science and Industry where to my knowledge no special facilities existed for young children; a special talk by a staff member who is probably not too well acquainted with this segment of the population ought not to be mistaken for a special facility. A human being of any age may gain some knowledge from any kind of experience in the home or the street, but the use of a "learning environment" calls for a better "fit" between human minds and things to which they are exposed. Museums deriving most of their support from public funds are by necessity interested in showing high attendance figures and a variety of services they render; we seem to need an expert "Audit" for the benefits derived by human beings — an Audit for figures is not enough.

[6]Marguerite Bloomberg, *An Experiment in Museum Instruction* (Washington, D. C.: The American Association of Museums, 1929).

A. W. Melton, Nita Goldberg-Feldman, and C. W. Mason, *Experimental Studies of the Education of Children in a Museum of Science* (Washington, D.C.: The American Association of Museums, 1936).

[7]The experimental studies begun in Cambridge were continued on a much larger scale in London under the auspices of the National Foundation for Educational Research for

England and Wales, and with the cooperation of the Institute of Education of the University of London and the London County Council Schools. Thirteen hundred and fifty children from forty schools participated in these studies. Three museums in London provided rooms and materials: the Victoria and Albert Museum, the Science Museum, and the Horniman Museum of Anthropology.

[8]After the end of the Second World War I was asked by a Settlement House in Stepney in the East End of London to undertake a project in a city school in that rather unprivileged area. An entire class of girls had failed the "eleven plus" examination, which separated entrants into an academic type of higher school from others. The level of both knowledge and morale was low; many of the girls, aged eleven to fourteen, came from broken homes or had delinquency records.

Stepney having a tradition of vocational ties with textiles, which go back to the days of Protestant refugees from France in the seventeenth century, we decided to organize activities around an exhibition of clothing, from Eskimo fur coats to South Sea grass skirts, from samples of Renaissance textiles to contemporary work. Tools for spinning and weaving were among the specimens borrowed from several museums and from factories. Large wall mirrors were important parts of our equipment; the girls were not willing to listen to a talk or even to view things, but they were anxious to dress up and to see themselves in mirrors. Eventually they became interested in acquiring some information in order to communicate it to others. We ended up with the performance of a play, "What the Wool Industry Meant to Our Country," and the performers never tired of repeating it.

On this occasion static museum resources became the framework of a dynamic sociodrama, and a school project became a community event.

To avoid redundancy, the index was set up without references to individual museums. Only a few collectors are referred to; others appear in groups. Both the Contents and the List of Illustrations should assist the reader in locating individual personalities and institutions. One of my purposes in the selection of the index entries was to emphasize some of the intellectual ideas of the book.